John B. Gough

Sunlight And Shadow

John B. Gough

Sunlight And Shadow

ISBN/EAN: 9783744725637

Printed in Europe, USA, Canada, Australia, Japan

Cover: Foto ©Thomas Meinert / pixelio.de

More available books at **www.hansebooks.com**

SUNLIGHT AND SHADOW;

OR,

Gleanings from my Life-Work.

COMPRISING

PERSONAL EXPERIENCES AND OPINIONS, ANECDOTES, INCIDENTS, AND REMINISCENCES,

GATHERED FROM

THIRTY-SEVEN YEARS' EXPERIENCE

ON THE

PLATFORM AND AMONG THE PEOPLE

AT HOME AND ABROAD.

BY

JOHN B. GOUGH.

WITH FULL-PAGE ENGRAVINGS, AND STEEL-PLATE PORTRAIT OF THE AUTHOR.

London:
HODDER AND STOUGHTON,
27, PATERNOSTER ROW.
MDCCCLXXXI.

TO

MY WIFE,

*THE FAITHFUL FRIEND, LOVING HELPMEET,
AND JUDICIOUS ADVISER FOR
THIRTY-EIGHT YEARS;*

WITH UNABATED TRUST, AND EVER INCREASING
LOVE,

I Dedicate this Book.

PREFACE.

IN the preface to a work entitled "The Odious, Despicable, and Dreadful Condition of a Drunkard," by Junius Florilegus, published in London in 1649, the writer—not dreaming that an American would borrow it two hundred and thirty years after—says:

"Experience teaches that no one thing (be it the violet) will please every one. That nothing is more easier than to find a colour of exceptions. That men's censures are as various as their palates. That some are as deeply in love with vice as others with virtue. That crossed wickedness proves desperate, and instead of yielding seeks for revenge of its own sins upon others' uprightness. Shall I then make myself the subject of every opinion, wise and weak? Yes, I had rather hazard the censure of some than hinder the good of others. Again, if I do ill, no plea can warrant me; I cannot be discouraged with any censures; my desire is to satisfy all honest minds. Therefore, the medicine must be fitted to the disease; the wedge proportioned to the timber, for the harder and more knotty our hearts are, the harder and stronger must be the blows and wedges that rive them. .·. . There needs neither reasons to be given, nor excuses or apologies to be made, where the word is our warrant, and the benefit of our fellow-men our aim. Thus most humbly beseeching God to bless this effort, I leave its success to Him, and its use to the world."

So, borrowing the preface of Junius Florilegus, written in 1649, I send out my book, earnestly hoping it may be of benefit to some, and harmful to none.

JOHN B. GOUGH.

HILLSIDE,
Worcester, Mass., October, 1880.

CONTENTS.

CHAPTER I.

LOOKING BACK OVER LIFE.

Retrospection and Reflection—"The Chief End of Man"—The Secret of Happiness—Experience, a Teacher—The Guiding Hand—Trifling Incidents and Momentous Consequences—My Father in the English Army—Famine and Despair—Lying down to Die—Struggling back to Life—Looking for Work—The Office Boy—The Shop Boy—Power of Circumstances in shaping Character—Man, Arbiter of his own Fortune—Knotty Problems—Dr. Wm. M. Taylor's Advice—Unbelief no Refuge—Boast of Napoleon—Circumstances not Despotic—Influence of Early Training—My "First Shop"—Downward Road Easy—Turn in the Tide—"Man's Extremity, God's Opportunity"—Seven Years' Night—"Morning Light"—The Day—Striving upwards—Aim of this Volume, . . . Page 1

CHAPTER II.

OUR WELCOME TO ENGLAND—OLD AND NEW FRIENDS.

Revisiting England—The Welcome—Old Friends missed—Kindness of Dean Stanley—"Sermons in Stones"—Coronation Scenes—Downing Street—First Address in Metropolitan Tabernacle—An Overpowering Reception—Warm Heart and Open Purse—Early Dinners and Success—Mercantile Life—The Flowing Bowl in Business—"Brackley-Street Mission"—Costermongers' Homes—War Nurses—"The Gift of Giving"—Children taking the Pledge—Total Abstinence pays—Value of Half a Sovereign—"A Jolly Good Fellow"—Rebuking Evil in High Places—"Another Nail in my Coffin"—England's Lord High Chancellor—His Official Dignity—Amazing Progress—The Great Supper—Temperance in English Parlours—"Persistence a Cardinal Virtue," 8

CHAPTER III.
STREET LIFE AND SCENES IN THE WORLD'S METROPOLIS.

London—Life in the Metropolis—Great Contrasts—Unknown Depths—"The London Market"—Shops of London—Streets and Palaces—Distinctive Communities—A World in Miniature—Street People—Cab Experience—Gathering a Crowd—"Vot's hup, Cabby?"—Excitements of the Streets—Street Children—"It looks werry nice, Sir"—Street Boys' Histories—Awful Surroundings in Childhood—"Never had a Chance"—Barnabas or Barabbas?—After the Funeral—How the Boy became an Outcast—Vice and Crime—The Orphan's Lot—Sixteen Hundred Waifs—Sleeping in an Iron Roller and in the Boot of an Omnibus—"We must go to Business"—Money-Making—Diving in Sewers—"Mud-Larks"—"Wagabones and Hactors"—Street Arabs—"Peelers'" Difficulties—Street-Boys' Wit—"Penny" Merchants—Street Wares—Cheap Books—"Raising the Wind," 26

CHAPTER IV.
HIGH AND LOW LIFE IN LONDON—CABMEN AND COCKNEYS.

Cabmen of London: their Great Number—"Exact Fare"—"I shan't forget the Phiz"—A Dandy discomfited—Wealth of London—Men who have risen—"Cat's-Meat"—Where the Dead Horses go—Fortunes by Sharp Practice—Roguery reduced to a System—The Wine Business—Tricks of Trade—High Art—Auctioneers—Jockeyism and Horses—Bought his Own Horse—Londoner's Self-Esteem—"Connoisseurship in Wines"—Tricks of Professional Beggars—The Blind Man who could see—"Eddicatin' Dogs"—The Lord Mayor's Show—Hardships of the Lord Mayor's Office—"Who is He?"—Self-made Men—Baron Rothschild's Remark on "Selling Matches"—Schools of the Corporation—Disrespectful Children—"'Ow is yer 'Elth?"—Inconvenience of the Letter H—The Gentleman's Story—Meeting with an "Hawful Hend"—Dilemma of the Alderman's Daughter—The Omnibus Conductor's Vocabulary, ... 38

CHAPTER V.
JUSTICE AND INJUSTICE—SCENES IN THE CRIMINAL COURTS OF LONDON.

The Old Bailey—A Complete Establishment—"Tried in Drawing-Room; hanged in Back Kitchen"—A Criminal Trial, a Sensation Drama—Waiting for the Verdict—Atmosphere of the Dock—Crime shown in the Face—The Ragged Youth and his Counsel—Police Courts—Ludicrous Scenes—Women's Quarrels—"The Love-lorn Widder"—Supporting Nine Children—The Irishman's Family at the Bar—Disagreeing Evidence—Children hired out to Beggars—The Magistrate and the Chimney Sweep—Drunkenness the Path to the Police Court—"Taking in" People—Bird Fanciers cheated—Painted Sparrows—Uncertainty of the Law—The Thief and his Cherries—Barnacles—Expense of the Civil Service—Government Leeches—The Mysterious Warning—Premium on Idleness—"How not to do it" 48

CHAPTER. VI.

LIFE AMONG COSTERMONGERS, BEGGARS, AND THIEVES—SCENES AT VICTORIA THEATRE.

The Costermongers—" Picking up Crusts "—Street Fellowship—Religion and Respectability—Kindness appreciated—Children near Houndsditch—The Coster Boy—In Business for Himself—Chaffing a " Peeler "—Forgiveness a Rare Trait—The Coster Girl—Profound Ignorance—Forced to Cheat— " It's werry 'ard, isn't it, Sir ?—Shaming the Donkey—Costermonger's Education—Victoria Theatre—The Multitude of Boys and Girls—Excitements in the Gallery—" Pull hup that 'ere Vinder Blind "—" Light up the Moon "—Reception of a Tragedy—Whitechapel and Butcher's Row—Scene of a Saturday Night—Penny Gaff or Theatre—Dirt, Smoke, and Vulgarity—" 'Ere's yer Pannyrammar "—" Legitimit Dramay "—Ratcliffe Highway—Ballad Singers—Street Scenes—Catching Sailors—The Sailor's " Futtergruff "—Beer Houses and Gin Shops—Beggars and Thieves—Inside a Thieves' Lodging House—The Countryman's Adventure, ... 55

CHAPTER VII.

HAUNTS OF CRIME—THE CITY MISSIONARIES OF LONDON AND THEIR WORK.

London essentially Cosmopolitan—Byron's " Superb Menagerie "—Thackeray's " Vanity Fair "—Solitude in the Crowd—Munificent Charities—Cures for every Ill—The Aristocracy—Extremes of Character—The Middle Class —Homes of Virtue—" The Bray of Exeter Hall "—City Missionaries—Heroism in " Little Hell "—" Never rob a Parson "—Training-Schools for Thieves—" Practising at picking Pockets "—Perverse Judgments of Perverse Natures—At Enmity with the World—" The Gospel-Grinder " —Philosophy of a Boy-Thief—Selling " Hinguns "—A Rough-and-Ready Missionary—" No Genus in picking a Pocket "—" Fear makes Cowards of us "—Religion hurts the Business—A Publican spoiled—Real Courage—The Sermon of the Converted Sweep—Parable of the Ignorant Cabman—Rough Welcome to the Preacher, ... 67

CHAPTER VIII.

WAR WITH VICE—TEMPERANCE WORK AMONG THE DESTITUTE AND DEPRAVED.

Street-Preachers—Fitness for their Work—A Striking Scene—" Music with no Melody, Laughter with no Mirth "—" Murder, Murder, Police ! "—The Street-preacher and his Audience—Plain Preaching and its Power— " Reformatory and Refuge Union "—Thirty-four Benevolent Institutions under One Control—Good work of a Brewer's Son—Lambeth Baths—Hoxton Hall—A Converted Building—William Noble's Mission—The Blue-Ribbon Army—An Audience of Reformed Men—London *Times* on Gough in Hoxton Hall—Report of the *Record* on the same Meeting—Four Great Branches of the Temperance Work—United Kingdom Alliance—Temperance in Politics—"Medical Temperance Society"—"London Temperance Hospital"—Eight Thousand Patients in Six Years—Medicine without Alcohol—Results, ... 77

CHAPTER IX.

TRAGEDIES—THE SHADY SIDE OF LIFE.

Power of Kindness—The Scotch Minister and the "Brute"—"I'll kick you downstairs"—"The most God-forsaken Wretch on Earth"—Perseverance rewarded—"Clothed and in his right Mind"—The States-Prison Convict—"The Cold, Glittering Eye"—The Hard Heart melted—The Mother's Influence—Scene in Gray's-Inn Lane—The Excited Crowd—The Tattered Group, and Death among them—The Bullet-headed Man—"'Ere's a Swell vants to know vat's the Matter"—Alone with the Mob—Striking Experience with a London Crowd of the Worst Characters—An Easy Escape—Men beyond Sympathy—The Toad in the Stone—The Murderer in the Portland Prison—Celebrating his release by a Boose—Human Parasites—Trading on the Benevolence and Generosity of the Soft-hearted—Tramps—Soup-Kitchens—Getting Something for Nothing—Able-bodied "Sponges on the Generous"—"Loafing Gentry" and Shirks, ... 85

CHAPTER X.

AMONG THE POOR—THE TRAFFIC IN DRINK—SOCIETY'S CURSE.

Sunday-Morning Breakfast for Waifs—Homeless Multitudes—A Strange Audience—Economizing for a Drink—The Man who loved Beer—His heroic Self-Defence—A Pint every Two Hours—"Breakfast for Nothing"—Thirty Years lost—Drink, the Cause and Curse of Poverty—Soup-Kitchen in Glasgow—Free Sunday-Morning Breakfasts in Edinburgh—Seventeen Hundred Victims of Drink—"We get Hot Victuals at Home"—"Ducks and Green Peas"—"Good Times" turned to "Hard Times"—Extravagance of the Poor—Satire of "Punch"—The Irish Famine—Distilleries at Work—"Irish Distress, Irish Drinking"—Burton-on-Trent—Bass's Beer-Mills—Bass's Annual Beer-Profits £450,000—The Drink Bill—London Paper upon Mr. Bass, M.P., ... 93

CHAPTER XI.

LIFE AMONG THE LOWLY—HOMELESS HOMES—DARKNESS AND LIGHT.

Homes of the London Poor—Cellar Dwellings—Description of a Court in Gray's-Inn Lane—King Cholera—Horrible Filth—"Work in the Five Dials"—Dark Pictures of Life—Tour of Inspection with Hon. Maude Stanley—Visiting Low Localities—My Audience—A Motley Crowd—Coffee-Palace opened by Dean Stanley—The Bright Side—The Honest Girl in the Thieves' Court—The Newspaper-Vendor and the Pocket-Book—"A Real Case"—Artful Dodges—The Workman's Independence—

"Principled agin taking Money"—Trust and Patience of the Poor—Life among the Lowly—The Crippled Saint—Blue Skies reflected from Muddy Pools—The Story of Thomas Wright—A Devoted Son—Examples of Nobility in Humble Life—Demands for Human Sympathy, . . . 100

CHAPTER XII.
OPPOSITION TO PROGRESS—THE WORLD'S BENEFACTORS, AND WHAT THEY HAVE ENDURED.

Great Discoverers and Inventors—The Opposition they have met—Satire upon Dr. Jenner—An Amusing Picture—Employing the Assistance of the Devil—The "Swing-Swang"—Practice often against Theories—"Horses going to the dogs"—Liverpool and Manchester Railway—Railway Engines and Sheep's Wool—Alarming Predictions—The Old Coachman—Heroism for the Truth's Sake—Puritanic Strictness—The New-England Sabbath—"Straining at a Gnat"—Drunk on the Sabbath—Whistling for a Dog—Wife-Thrashing and Sabbath-Breaking—True Liberty and Sunday Trains—Testimonies to the Christian Sabbath: Macaulay, Blackstone, Adam Smith, Webster, Theodore Parker, etc.—Holiday not Holy Day—Jurists and the Sabbath—Physicians and the Sabbath—Statesmen and the Sabbath—The Old Book—Liberty under Law, ... 109

CHAPTER XIII.
MANLINESS AND MORAL PRINCIPLE—INDUSTRY VERSUS IDLENESS.

False Ideas of Manliness—Physical Strength no Test—Lord Bacon a Swindler—Fast Living, cowardly—Horse-Racing and Prize-fighting—Manliness is Godliness—False Opinions scorn Labour—"Only a Mechanic"—The Fashion of Useless People—"Only a Third-Class Carriage"—Story concerning Lady Charlotte Guest—The Cinder-hole—Labour and Etiquette—Idle Men mischievous—The Dandy—Consequences of a Useless Life—Career of Beau Brummell—The Fop in a Breach-of-Promise Suit—Influence of Society upon us—Example better than Precept—Value of a Noble Life—Ministers and the Half-price—Genius no Substitute for Moral Principle—Burn's Perverted Genius—The Painter Haydon . . 117

CHAPTER XIV.
HAPPINESS AND TRUE HEROISM—GOLD, WHAT IT DOES AND WHAT IT DOES NOT BRING.

Signing away Liberty—False Ideas of Happiness—Rothschild—John Jacob Astor—A Girl's Idea of Perfect Happiness—The Snow-blocked Train—Lord Chesterfield's Confession—Irishman's Complaint of the Moon—"If"—The Two Buckets—Sir John Sinclair and the Labourer—"A New Way to pay Old Debts"—The History of Misers—Experience of a Millionaire—"The Happiest Fellows in the World"—Anecdote of John Wilson—Happiness among the Poor—Lord Braco and the Farthing—The Celebrity and his Hat—The Burden of a Debt—The Clergyman and the Collection—Dodging Creditors—Indebtedness degrades—Extravagance—Church Debts—Sacrifice for Others—Moral Heroism—Victory over Self, . 124

CHAPTER XV.
KNOWLEDGE AND CURIOSITY—ABSURD BLUNDERS AND LAUGHABLE MISTAKES.

What is Knowledge?—Ignorance with a Library—Wisdom is applied Knowledge—George Cruikshank the Simon Pure—Blunders in Spelling—"Preshus Sole"—Laughable Mistakes—The Deacon who thought he could preach—Anecdote of Robert Hall—Self-knowledge and Physical Health—Knowing Others—"Brass" no Test of Character—Misjudging Others—Knowledge through History—Goodness—Mental Cultivation and Moral Corruption—Inquisitiveness—"Funnels of Conversation"—How a Man lost his Leg—Anecdote of John Randolph—Misapplied Labour—Dinner and Duel—How to collect a Crowd—Van Amburg's Lion—Feats of Legerdemain—Sir Charles Napier and the Indian Juggler—Ignorance and Superstition—Whimsical Vagaries—Senseless "Omens"—Sowing for the Harvest—Immortality revealed—De Quincey upon the Present—Faith a Necessity—The Story of Poor Joe, ... 136

CHAPTER XVI.
COMEDIES—THE HUMOROUS SIDE OF LIFE.

The Art of Putting Things—Illustrative Anecdotes—Macklin at the Theatre—The Smoker on a Coach—Mr. Parker's Preaching—Managing Others—The Scolding Schoolmaster—The Inhuman Teacher—Appeals to Honour better than Brutality—The Model Principal—The College President's Lecture on Spontaneous Combustion—The College President guarding his Hen-roost—The Midnight Ride—Acknowledgment of Errors—Bonnie Christie—Matter-of-fact People—"Sixpenny Caliker"—No Devils ever cast out of a Man—The Quaker's Answer—The Physician and the Stone-Mason—A Digression, but not an Argument—Henderson the Actor—Difference between Settling down and Settling up—Wit of Dr. Samuel Cox—The Conceited Count—Practical Jokes—My Sacramento Acquaintance, ... 155

CHAPTER XVII.
VICTIMS OF DRINK—SCENES FROM LIFE.

Beer as a Beverage—Beer Drunkenness among Women—Great Britain's Curse—"Doctored" Beer—The Inside of a London Gin-Palace—What is "All Sorts"?—Kinahan's L. L.—The Landlord—The Bar-Maid—The Customers—Life in the Bar-Room—Disgraceful Scenes—"Fair Play"—What the London *Times* says—A "Genteel" Gin-Palace—Rev. Wm. Arnot on the Liquor Traffic—The Fratricide—A Hardened Woman—The Gambler's Suicide—A Horrible Sight—Suicide of McConnell—The Blood-Stains on the Floor—The Meanest Man in the World—The Rum-seller's Bargain—Result of the Trade—Dr. Guthrie's Testimony—That of Canon Farrar—"Fruits of the Traffic"—A Ghastly Story of the Prisoner at Dartmouth—The Convict's Story—Rum and Murder—Remorse—Waiting for Death, ... 167

CHAPTER XVIII.

DESPAIR AND DEATH—STORIES OF RUINED HOMES AND BROKEN HEARTS.

The Prisoner's Testimony—How Prisons are filled—The Offspring of Drink—Appalling Statistics—The Inhuman Father—Selling a Child for Two Pairs of Stockings—Getting Drunk with the Proceeds—The Drunken Mother and her Dying Children—An Affecting Story—Sufferings in the Best Circles—A Terrible Story—The Brutal Husband and his Dead Wife—Horrible Brutality—Truth stranger than Fiction—The Clergyman's Suicide—The Lawyer's Despair and Death—Rum unmakes the Gentleman—A Dreadful Domestic Scene—The Beaten and Disfigured Wife—Destruction of Property—The Mountaineer's Home—Rum-Madness—Driven from Home—The Night on the Mountain—Terrible Destitution and Sufferings—The Desolate Home—Enticed to a Grog-Shop—A Drunken Sot—The Winter's Night—Eaten by Swine, ... 179

CHAPTER XIX.

FOOTPRINTS OF RUM—STORIES OF RUINED HOMES AND BROKEN HEARTS (CONTINUED).

A Cry from Connecticut—Drunkenness worse than Death—Five Days with Delirium Tremens—Hope deferred—The Drunkard's Adopted Child—The Murdered Babe—The Wife shielding the Murderer, only to be murdered Herself—The Murderer's Suicide—Last Scenes in the Domestic Tragedy—The Drunkard and his Dead Wife—The Drunken Clergyman preaching Old Sermons—Stealing Postage-Stamps to buy Rum—Another Clergyman ruined by Drink—An Unfeeling Father—Stealing his Little Boy's Shoes to buy Drink—The Drunkard's Cry—Pity for the Victims—A Blasted Life—The Drunkard's "Ode to the Departing Year"—"What of the Ship?"—The Redeemed Man's Narrative—Evils of Social Drinking—Bitter Recollections—Maddening Desire for Drink—What is to be done?—The Dram-Shops of Birmingham—Sunday Drinking—Terrible Results, ... 190

CHAPTER XX.

"SECRETS" AND "TRICKS" OF THE LIQUOR TRADE—A GLANCE BEHIND THE SCENES.

Rum is Rum the World over—Drunken Mohammedan is said to have "gone to Jesus"—Speech of Canon Farrar—Ludicrous Side of the Question—The Connoisseurs of Liquors—Wine-Drinkers humbugged—The Secret of Success in the Manufacture of Liquors—Ingredients—How "Imported Cognac Brandy" is made—How Schiedam Schnapps and Common Gin are made—Champagne Receipt—" Native Catawba Wines " made without Grapes—" Fine Old Port "—Receipts for making Porter—" Ale " good to sleep on ; how made—To the Uninitiated—How to Bottle neatly—Sugar of Lead as a Sweetener—Filthiness no Hindrance to the Drinker—The Effect of these Revelations—The Slaves of Fashion, ... 202

xvi   CONTENTS.

CHAPTER XXI.

SOME OF MY EXPERIENCES WITH BRAZEN-FACED PEOPLE.

The Life of a Public Man—Peculiar Annoyances—Kind Treatment of the Press—"Interviewing"—An Unfortunate Little Notice—"John B. Gough lying dangerously ill"—Mistakes in reporting Lectures—Amusing Specimen—Applications for Help—Begging Letter-Writers—Tramps preferable to these—Extracts from Begging-Letters—Young Man's Strange Request for Fifteen Hundred Dollars—Request for One Thousand Dollars—What the Lord is reported to have said—One Thousand Dollars wanted to educate two Nieces—"I am taken in"—Notes and Promises to Pay—A New Method—A Curious Plan of Professionals—Begging "Mediums"—Letter purporting to come from my Mother—An Incident in Scotland, ... 212

CHAPTER XXII.

AMUSING EXPERIENCES WITH LETTER-WRITERS, BEGGARS, AND ASPIRANTS FOR FAME.

Letter-Writers and their Wants—A Lady "wishes to get married;" full Particulars—Specimen of a Class of Oddities—What "the Simple Son of a Carpenter" desires—An Unappreciated Benefactor of his Country—A "Big Thing" to be accomplished—Applications for Old Lectures—The Ambitious Young Man with a "Hobby"—An Aspirant for Fame—Newspaper Man wishes two "Worn-out" Lectures—Request for a "Moddle" Lecture—Receipt for a "Moddle" Lecture—A Few Hints to the Ambitious—Requests for Autographs—Levying Black-mail—Take Warning—Dr. Chalmers on Autographs—Demand for Photographs—"Very like a Bore"—Not limited to Friends—Comical Arrangements of these Pictures—Side by Side with the Gorilla, ... 221

CHAPTER XXIII.

UNENDURABLE BORES—MY EXPERIENCES WITH THEM—AFFECTATION AND "STYLE."

A Class of Bores—An Aggravating Case—Its Sequel—Incident of a Lecture—Two Hingham Callers—The Brilliant Young Man in a Joking Mood—The Conundrum, "Canaan"—"Old Dog Tray"—President Woolsey and the Joking Boy—Cultivation of Affectation—Indifference—Imitating Enthusiasm—Affectation turning into a "Lithp"—Unstylish Persons in Style—Tarts "Fourpence a-Piece, Ma'am"—Late-Comers in Church and Lecture—"Who art Thou?"—An Officer of Her Majesty's Service—Making Puns—Dealing with the Superlative in Conversation—Common Mistakes—Petty Expressions—"Lor', how cunning!"—Exaggerations in Speech—Trivial Faults mar the Enjoyments of Life. . 232

CHAPTER XXIV.

THE SPEAKER AND HIS AUDIENCE—ANECDOTES AND INCIDENTS.

Dread of an Audience—Personal Physical Suffering—Mutual Sympathy required—Incident in the Church of Dr. Joseph Parker—Efforts at Reading a Hymn—Experience with President Finney at Aberdeen—The Minister's "Supplication"—Involuntary Selection of Persons in every Audience—My Feelings on the Platform—Vivid Recollections—My Stolid Hearer—Method of Preparing Lectures—Five Thousand Temperance Addresses in Seventeen Years—Interview with the Actor Macready—His Method—My Early Experience with Books—"Rollins' Ancient History," and "Putnam's Library"—My Earlier Addresses—Gathering and Using Incident at Rhinebeck—Illustration from Niagara Falls—Taking an Awful Risk before an Audience—Taking down the Scaffolding from my Temple—An interesting Experience—"Gough is a Story-teller"—A Silly Charge—The Wonderful Story—"Gough a Retailer of Anecdotes"—My Sense of the Ridiculous—Value of Incidents, ... 242

CHAPTER XXV.

WHAT OPPOSITION WE MEET—FALSE CHARGES AND MIS-REPRESENTATIONS.

"Gough not a Thinker"—Unexplainable Knowledge—Plagiarism and its Meaning—Satire on Plagiarism of "The Little Busy Bee"—Gough's Apostrophe to Water, and that by Paul Denton—History of its Inception —Reply to a Shameless Attack—Increased Consumption of Beer—Our Pullman Cars and Liquor-Drinking—Increase of Intemperance in Thirty Years—Worcester as an Example—1843 and 1880—Washingtonianism— Drinking among Ministers—Drinking among Women—Murder as excited by Beer—Hereditary Effects of Beer-drinking—Paper circulated by Life Insurance Men—Reported Interview with the Oxford Students—The True Story and the Scene—The Happy Conclusion, ... 254

CHAPTER XXVI.

ON THE PLATFORM—PERSONAL EXPERIENCES AS A PUBLIC SPEAKER.

The Judge's Speech—Power of his Example—"Give it to him, Old Man"— Self-Possession necessary under Embarrassments—Man in Faneuil Hall, and Story for his Benefit—Woman and her Crying Child—"Did he lose his Eggs?"—One Handkerchief for Two—Power of Audience over the Speaker—The Man with the Newspaper—How the whispering Young Ladies were stopped—Cultivation of the Voice—Power of Sarcasm—The Donkey at Snowdon—Sarcasm of O'Connell on Benjamin Disraeli—John Randolph and the "Vacant" Seat—Tom Marshall's "Demijohn" all but the Straw—Personal Experience under Trying Circumstances—"Here's one of your Cigars, Mr. Gough"—Quotations from Locke and Walter Scott which were not quotations, ... 265

CHAPTER XXVII.
MEN I HAVE KNOWN—PULPIT AND OTHER ORATORS OF GREAT BRITAIN.

Public Speakers—Lectures I have heard—Personal Experience as to Public Occasions—Ministerial and other Acquaintances—Thomas Guthrie, D.D. —The Audience—Guthrie's Philanthropy—His Appearance in the Pulpit— Not a "Weeping Preacher"—My first Impressions—Power of his Utterance — William Arnot, D.D. — Appearance and Manner—"Figs of Thistles"—Newman Hall, D.D.—Lincoln Tower of Christ Church—Mr. Martin of Westminster Chapel—Strange Texts—"Man of One Book"— Cowper's Model Preacher—Some of my Chairmen—Lord Shaftesbury— John Bright—Bright's Speech at Henry Darby's Feast—Sir Fitzroy Kelly: his Style and Manner—Joseph Parker, D.D.—Immense Power —Pulpit Apologetic Manners out of Place—Dr. Parker at Home and as a Preacher—First Impressions of the Preacher—Vividness of Description— "God's Testimony against Sin"—Sins of Presumption—Where do Texts come from?. 276

CHAPTER XXVIII.
MEN I HAVE KNOWN (CONTINUED)—SPURGEON—AMERICAN CLERGYMEN.

C. H. Spurgeon: Early History—His First Sermon—"Who is this Spurgeon?" Park Chapel and Exeter Hall—The Metropolitan Tabernacle—Publication of Fifteen Hundred Sermons—The Man a Miracle—Public Institutions for Missions and Benevolence—The Beautiful Work of Mrs. Spurgeon —Pedigree of Pulpit Story—Ministers must be "Thick-Skinned"—Anecdotes—Spurgeon a Total-Abstainer—Boy's Orphanage at Stockwell— Reception of Mr. Spurgeon—The Little Consumptive—True Greatness— Sources of Power as a Preacher—The Book of Books—Comments on Proverbs—Tale-bearers and Dissemblers—Mr. Spurgeon and the Dog— Edward Norris Kirk, D.D.—Oratory and Elocution—Our Last Interview —Elocution sometimes a Hindrance—George H. Gould, D.D.—Rev. David O. Mears—William M. Taylor, D.D.—Power of the Scriptures— Helpful Themes—Theodore L. Cuyler, D.D.—Preacher and Correspondent, ... 289

CHAPTER XXIX.
OLD-TIME AND MODERN PREACHERS—WORDS WITH AND WITHOUT SENSE.

Sheridan Knowles—Varied Pulpit Ministrations—Old-time Discourses—Quaint old Books—Travesty on the Little Busy Bee—The Plagiarized Sermon— Sermon on the Slothful Man—"Awake, Pesaltery-tree and Harp"— Who were the Patriarchs?"—Grandiloquent Oratory—Exordium upon Intemperance—"Wrecked on the Tempestuous Sea"—The baneful Upas-Tree—The Drunkard's Career on the Broad Road—Peroration—The Nobleman's Speech and Observations—Speech of an Agitator—"Bruce the King of England"—"Battles of Greasy and Potters"—"Pass round the Hat," 304

CHAPTER XXX.

CHURCH SERVICES—IRREVERENCE, BUFFOONERY, AND CANT.

Ridiculous Side of Negro Preaching—Absurd Mistakes—The Plantation Preacher—"Glad Tidings and Hallelujah"—The Dirty Boy—Church Services—Singing in Mr. Spurgeon's Tabernacle; and in Dr. Parker's Church—The D.D.'s Stratagem—The Scotchman's Experience—"Don't sing, Sir"—Hymns of my Boyhood—Mutilated Hymns—Irreverence of Hymnology—Revivalists' Buffoonery—The Name above every Name—Christian Irreverence—Pious Cant—More Puritanism needed—The Christian Ideal and its Opposite—Possible Future Pulpit Notices . . 313

CHAPTER XXXI.

MY VIEWS ON THE TEMPERANCE QUESTION.

Drunkenness a Sin and a Disease—Is Moderate Drinking a Sin?—My First Intoxication—Rum and Water in a Temperance Meeting—"Gentlemanly Inebriation"—The Intoxicated Boy—Pathology of Drunkenness—Testimony of Dr. Richardson—Destructive Effects of Alcohol on the Mind—Statement of Joseph Cook—Legend of the Triple Choice—The Sin is in the Cause, and not the Effect—Statements of Wm. Arnot, D.D.—Two Ways of keeping a Nation sober—Total Abstinence as an Unfailing Remedy—Prevention better than Cure—The Giant's Hand—Drunkenness unnatural—Testimony of Distinguished Physicians—Case of the Hon. E. C. Hannegan—His former Useful Life—The Terrible Fall and Dissipation—The Murder 324

CHAPTER XXXII.

TEMPERANCE AND "THE GRACE OF GOD"—MY OWN EXPERIENCE AND THAT OF OTHERS.

Is Reform possible without Religion?—Grounds of Appeal—Total Abstinence does not renew Nature—My First Pledge without "the Help of God"—The Memory of the Garret Bedroom—My Second Pledge under the Grace of God—Does the Grace of God take away the Appetite?—Poison kills the Christian and the Hottentot—The Grace of God includes Voluntary Total Abstinence—Is the Drunkard's Appetite left?—My Disgust at the Drink no Proof that Appetite is gone—Communion Wine; its Effect—Wines in Cooking—Religion removes the Desire, but not the Appetite—Self-Deception on this Point—Thrilling Letter of a Clergyman—The Converted Rum-seller's Experience—The Fallen Minister—The only Safety is in Total Abstinence—"The Pledge and the Cross," . . . 33

CHAPTER XXXIII.

MODERATE DRINKING AND TOTAL ABSTINENCE.

The Moderate Drinker—The Moderate Drinker of Stockholm—Gough and his Moderate-drinking Friend—Dr. B. W. Richardson on Moderate

Drinking—Alcohol not included in the Scheme of Life—The Most Helpless Period passed without it—The Four Stages of Life—Voice of Science—Stimulation Harmful to Health—Foods and Alcohol—"The Alcoholic Stages"—"The Devil and the Peacock"—Wine and Civilization—Wine-drinking Nations—Wine only Dirty Water—Total Abstinence for the Sake of Others—Abusing the "Moderate Drinker"—A Dinner without Wine—The Right, the Wrong, the Doubtful—A Touching Story—The Idolized Son—Wine at New Year's Calls—Misnamed Friends . . . 345

CHAPTER XXXIV.

TEMPERANCE AND THE BIBLE—MY VIEWS ON THE SCRIPTURE QUESTION—INCIDENTS.

Assistance demanded from all Sides—Charity—The Truth our Weapon—Scamp's Tavern—"'The Seven Last Plagues' for Sale here"—Specimen of Liquor-Sellers' Work—The Wine of Scripture and of Commerce—Conflicting Authorities—One of the "Doubtful Disputations"—Dr. Norman Ker's Statement—The Hieroglyphical Argument—Assumed Biblical Commands against Strong Drink—Dr. Samuel H. Cox and J. Fenimore Cooper upon Bible Miracles—Absalom's Hair—What Fish swallowed Jonah—Good Men who endeavour to sanction Drinking—How to answer these Men—Advice to the Reformed Man—Let Arguments alone—The Outcast's Conversion—Many Churches unsafe for the Reformed Drunkard, ... 355

CHAPTER XXXV.

WAR WITH DRINK—TEMPERANCE ORGANIZATIONS—WOMAN'S WORK AND INFLUENCE.

The National Temperance Society—Women's Christian Temperance Union—The Blue and Red Ribbon Armies—American Temperance Society—Growth of the Work—Washingtonian Movement—Growing Unpopularity of Washingtonianism—Favourite Epithets—"We don't want any Religion in the Movement"—Poor Tom Marshall—Danger to Reform Clubs—Sympathy demanded for the Lost—Give the Reformed Man Work—The Temperance Hall a Place of Safety—The Dirt and Discomforts of some so-called Temperance Hotels—Personal Experience—The "Model" and "Central" Coffee-Houses of Philadelphia—The Medical Question—Rum by the Keg—Physician giving Poison for Health—Heroism and Fanaticism —"Stand to your Principle," 365

CHAPTER XXXVI.

STRIKING EXPERIENCES.

Compensations of Old Age—This Young Man—The Old Warrior—Amusing Peculiarities of Public Life—The Liverpool Barber—"'Enery, sweep up this 'Air"—Great Changes—Reforms—Improvements—Children are

Forces—An Important Question—Casket and Jewel—Testimonial presented—Boys' Work Twenty-five Years ago—The Results—Drunkard's Child—"My Little Testament"—Testament sold for Whiskey—"God be merciful!"—"Evil Habits"—Custom and Habit—No Man lost on a Straight Road—A Good Resolution—Hugh Miller, ... 377

CHAPTER XXXVII.
LAST GLEANINGS.

My First Visit to the Theatre—Booth and Hamblin—"Apostate," and "Review"—The Old Bowery—My Passion for the Stage—Interview with a Manager—Comic Song at the Chatham—Persevering Efforts to be an Actor—The Summit of Ambition—The Old Lion of Boston—Charles Thorn—Charles Eaton—"Roll him in and tap him"—Tinsel and Sham—My Disenchantment—Thanks that my Way was blocked—Power to overcome—Coleridge—A Good Impulse—"Art thee crazy, Lad?"—The First Sermon—Paying Debts like a Christian—The Last Race—Retrospection—Contrasts—Lessons learned—Encouragements—Last Words, . . 390

LIST OF ILLUSTRATIONS.

1. PORTRAIT OF THE AUTHOR, ON STEEL . . . . *Frontispiece*
   From a photograph taken expressly for this work, by *Fredericks*, New York, in August, 1880, and Engraved on Steel by *J. J. Cade*, New York.

ENGRAVINGS ON WOOD.

No.	Title	Artist	Engraver	Page
2.	TRAINING SCHOOL FOR THIEVES.—INTERIOR OF A KEN OR LODGING HOUSE.	S. G. McCutcheon.	J. P. Davis.	To face 65
3.	A STREET PREACHER AND HIS AUDIENCE	Geo. G. White.	John Karst.	" 73
4.	ONE OF DEATH'S VICTIMS.—THE WIDOW AND THE FATHERLESS	Fred'ck Dielman.	Charles Speigle.	" 60
5.	THE BLOOD ON THE CEILING	F. O. C. Darley.	John Foster.	" 174
6.	A CELLAR SCENE.—THE BRUTE AND THE LAMB	Fred'ck Dielman.	J. P. Davis.	" 181
7.	DRIVEN FROM HOME.—THE REFUGE ON THE MOUNTAIN SIDE	Geo. G. White.	John Karst.	" 188
8.	A HOMELESS HOME.—DESTITUTION AND DESPAIR	F. O. C. Darley.	Charles Speigle.	" 194
9.	RUM'S FOOTPRINT.—DEATH AND DRINK.	F. O. C. Darley.	N. Orr & Co.	" 204
10.	MEMORIES OF THE GARRET BEDROOM	F. O. C. Darley.	N. Orr & Co.	" 335
11.	A FATHER STEALING A TESTAMENT FROM HIS DYING CHILD	S. G. McCutcheon.	Charles Speigle.	" 380
12.	LOOKING FOR FATHER.—AN INCIDENT THAT LED TO THE REFORM OF A RUMSELLER	F. O. C. Darley.	J. P. Davis.	" 396

CHAPTER I.

LOOKING BACK OVER LIFE.

Retrospection and Reflection—" The Chief End of Man "—The Secret of Happiness—Experience, a Teacher—The Guiding Hand—Trifling Incidents and Momentous Consequences—My Father in the English Army—Famine and Despair—Lying down to Die—Struggling back to Life—Looking for Work—The Office Boy—The Shop Boy—Power of Circumstances in shaping Character—Man, Arbiter of his own Fortune—Knotty Problems—Dr. Wm. M. Taylor's Advice—Unbelief no Refuge—Boast of Napoleon—Circumstances not Despotic—Influence of Early Training—My " First Shop "—Downward Road Easy—Turn in the Tide—" Man's Extremity, God's Opportunity "—Seven Years' Night—" Morning Light "—The Day—Striving Upwards—Aim of this Volume.

WHEN the noon of life is passed, and the shadows begin to lengthen, as the bustle and worry and excitement are less active, we look back and ask the question, "Have we lived the threescore years?" It is worth while to remember, as years increase, that our lives are not measured by the years we have existed, but by the years we have lived. The time that has been misapplied, devoted to mere self-indulgence, to the gratification of unworthy appetites, is lost, and time lost is not lived; so that the question comes, How much have I lived? not, How many years have I existed? Fuller says, "He lives long that lives well." Seneca says, "To live well is a greater benefit than life itself."

There is a right ring in the good old question and answer in the Catechism—"What is the chief end of man? To glorify God and to enjoy Him forever." If we could comprehend at our starting-point more fully all that is involved in "glorifying God," that it is to be in entire harmony not only with eternal wisdom and beneficent law, but especially with their Source and

Author, surely our lives might be filled to the brim with happy usefulness, and move on with no more friction or jar than do the processions of the seasons.

With the conviction that often the experience of years may be helpful to the young, and hoping that the reflections and recollections of a life that has been for many years so fully among men may be profitable to those who have all of life before them, I venture to gather the incidents and experiences of these years, and, without apology, present them to those who may choose to accept them. A writer has said, "There are few minds but might furnish some instruction and entertainment out of their scraps, their odds and ends of thought. They who cannot weave a uniform web may at least produce a piece of patchwork which may be useful, and not without a charm of its own." So I venture on my patchwork by jotting down observations, thoughts, and conclusions, gathered from wayside opportunities and sources in the course of a long experience.

Shakespeare asserts: "There is a divinity that shapes our ends, rough-hew them as we will." Canon Farrar says: "The overruling providence of God is so clearly marked in the progress of human events that the Christian hardly needs any further proof that there is a hand that guides." More incisive yet are the wisest man's words: "A man's heart deviseth his way, but the Lord directeth his steps." All our personal experiences reveal to us the fact of an overruling Providence; that we are not the creatures of chance. A very trifling incident may change the whole course of our lives.

During a retreat of the English army, when closely pursued by Marshal Soult, about the year 1809, my father, then about thirty years of age, was a soldier in the Fifty-second Light Infantry. He had been slightly wounded in the chest, and though his wound was not considered fatal, it was painful and irritating. The army had suffered fearfully from exposure, famine, and the heavy fatigues of an active campaign. I well remember my father saying to me, "John, you will never know what hunger is till you feel the two sides of your stomach grinding together." In that campaign, men mad with hunger fought like wolves over the half-decayed hoof of a bullock; and often when one of these poor animals, overcome with weakness and starvation, was staggering as if about to fall, the ready knife was applied to the throat, and the fainting soldiers, eagerly catching the blood in their hands, and hardly waiting for it to congeal, made it take the place of food. In this retreat, the Fifty-second Regiment became—to use the American term—demoralized; and while they staggered on, my father threw himself out of the ranks, under the shadow of a large rock, to die: he could go no farther. Lying there, he took from his inner pocket a hymn-book (which I have to-day, with all the marks of its seventy years upon it), and began to read the hymn in which is the verse—

> " When in the solemn hour of death
> I own Thy just decree,
> Be this the prayer of my last breath:
> O Lord, remember me."

He must die—it seemed inevitable—though far from home, in a strange land. He was a Christian, and endeavoured to prepare himself for the change. Suddenly a large bird of prey, with a red neck growing out of a ruffle of feathers, came swooping along, almost brushing my father's body with its wings; then circling up, he alighted on the point of rock, and turned his blood-red eye on his intended victim.

As my father saw that horrible thing watching, and waiting to tear him in pieces even before life was extinct, it so filled him with horror and disgust that he cried, " I cannot endure this: it is too terrible. When I am unable to drive that fearful thing away, it will be tearing my flesh. I cannot endure it!" He rose to his feet and fell, then crawled and struggled away, till at length he crept into a poor hut, found safety, and soon after joined his regiment. Though he was very, very ill after that frightful episode, he recovered, and died in 1871, at the remarkable age of ninety-four years.

I enjoy tracing some of these experiences in my own life. When a boy doing errands for a family about to emigrate to

America, the lady, who was in a very good humour, said, "John, how would you like to go to America with us?" It was said jestingly, yet that playful word grew into the decision that made me an American citizen.

In 1832 or 1833, two boys sought employment at the same establishment, in the same week. One was duly engaged as errand-boy in the office, the other as errand-boy in the book-bindery. The first was thrown into good society, among refined, Christian people, and brought under restraining influences. The other was surrounded by an entirely different atmosphere —nothing elevating, very little that was "pure, lovely, or of good report." The office-boy, encouraged by good advisers, grew in the right direction, obtained an education, became a minister, a professor in a college, a celebrated Greek scholar, and died, leaving behind him a splendid reputation. The shop-boy, with no restraining influences, naturally impulsive and yielding, went sadly astray, until he became as near an outcast as a young man could well become, with only a limited education, while all the natural powers God had given him were running to waste. For years he groped in darkness and almost despair. One of these became the Rev. Dr. McClintock; the other is writing these lines to-day.

It is true, as the prophet records—and we would not have it otherwise—that "the way of man is not in himself;" yet it is undoubtedly a fact that a man is in a great degree the arbiter of his own fortune. I know I have a will to do, or not to do. Locke says, "We were born with powers and faculties capable of almost anything, but it is the exercise of these powers and faculties that gives us ability and skill in anything." We are conscious of possessing a will that can consent or refuse to exercise these faculties.

I know that here we trench on a great mystery, God's plan and man's will—a mystery we have neither skill nor ability to unravel. I remember once, when confronting some of these knotty problems,—such as the origin of evil, and the eternity of sin,—I went to my dear friend Dr. Wm. M. Taylor, of New York, and asked him to give me some light. Putting his hand on my shoulder, he said, "John, lay these things on the shelf. We shall see light by and by, when He shall reveal to us the deep things of His wisdom." So I have come to the conclusion that my great aim must be to bring my will into submission to His, in perfect harmony; believing that all I do not know now I shall know in His right time, who knows the end from the beginning. I therefore seek to put away all that childish rubbish that hedges up a belief in what I cannot understand; inasmuch as the insoluble perplexities of unbelief are far greater than any that hover about faith and trust in God.

Napoleon Bonaparte, when intoxicated with success and at the height of his power, is reported to have said, "I make circumstances." Let Moscow, Elba, Waterloo, and St. Helena, that rocky isle where he was caged until he fretted his life away, testify to his utter helplessness in his humiliating downfall.

We cannot create circumstances, but we can make the best of them when they come. Their power is not despotic, and, by God's help and our own endeavour, we may make them our servants. How much of the success or failure in life depends on the manner in which we are able to deal with the circumstances of our early life! Cowper has written that "The colour of our whole life is generally such as the first three or four years in which we are our own masters, make it." The results of early training, reading, study, self-control or indulgence, are rarely overcome. In very early life, Little's poems were Lord Byron's favourite study. ."Heigho!" he exclaimed, in a letter dated 1820, "I believe all the mischief I have ever done or sung, has been owing to that confounded book." As I look back to the early years of my life, when at the age of fourteen I was my own master,—so far as the control of my leisure was involved,—I attribute much of the influence leading me in the wrong direction to the surroundings of that first shop into which I entered. Mark, I do not wish to excuse or palliate any wrong into which I drifted, but simply to state the fact that a boy, coming fresh from the country and the restraints of home, untainted, ignorant of the world, and "green," I was brought into daily companionship with men acquainted with, and many of them adepts in the vices of a large city. There I saw the mystery of wickedness; there I learned to like the drink; there I became soiled; there I took the wrong direction,—and thus seeds were sown that brought a bitter fruit and a wretched harvesting. I will not linger on this page, only to say that I began the drifting into darkness, hopelessness, and the sunless gloom of moral night; but "there is a tide in the affairs of men which, taken at the flood, leads on to fortune," and a kind Providence was bringing me unconsciously to it. "Man's extremity is God's opportunity;" and in the darkest hour of my life,—no light, no sun, no stars, not a gleam of hope, no expectation of a change, only a dreary and restless waiting for the end,—the miracle of morning came to me, beginning with the dawn.

When the night has reached its limits, and its visions are broken, how great is the change made by the first line of morning light! Most things are more clearly defined by the light; but in the experience of many the welcome and unwelcome visitations of night have only vanishing outlines, and lose shape as morning grows into day.

Thirty-eight years ago ushered in the dawn of such a morning to me. The night had been one of seven years' length, and filled with murky conditions; but though clouds were not absent from my horizon, the break of a new day had certainly come, and a total change in the direction of my life's journey must be taken. Henceforth, though the path promised to be steep, I resolved to reach higher levels, and get away from the poisoned air and treacherous ooze of that deep morass into which the seven years' night had led me. After this, to feel the ground firm under foot; to see the sunlight touching the summits of the hills of life; to have consciousness of growing purpose to reach these safe distances in the strength of the Mighty Hand reached down to help,—is best comparable to the opening morning of a new day.

Thus for all these years, though I have seen storms and sometimes cloudy skies, in difficulty and danger, in changes various and experiences manifold, it has never been dark: in the gloomiest hour there has been a consciousness of sunlight beyond the cloud. Though sorely tried, I have never despaired. In weakness I have experienced the truth that "He giveth strength to the feeble;" and I have the consciousness of having been enabled to help some to a better life, to encourage some desponding hearts, and to lift up some that were sinking. For this I am most devoutly thankful, and put forth these experiences, observations, and opinions, hoping that the cause of truth and right may thereby be advanced.

I pretend to no literary ability, and am aware that I am more at home on the platform than with the pen. Thus I pay little regard to the "unities," or the chronology. My book will be somewhat desultory, one thing leading on to another. My aim is to interest, perhaps amuse, and, above all, to help.

CHAPTER II.

OUR WELCOME TO ENGLAND—OLD AND NEW FRIENDS.

Revisiting England—The Welcome—Old Friends Missed—Kindness of Dean Stanley—"Sermons in Stones"—Coronation Scenes—Downing Street—First Address in Metropolitan Tabernacle—An Overpowering Reception—Warm Heart and Open Purse—Early Dinners and Success—Mercantile Life—The Flowing Bowl in Business—"Brackley Street Mission"—Costermongers' Homes—War Nurses—"The Gift of Giving"—Children taking the Pledge—Total Abstinence Pays—Value of Half a Sovereign—"A Jolly Good Fellow"—Rebuking Evil in High Places—"Another Nail in my Coffin"—England's Lord High Chancellor—His Official Dignity—Amazing Progress—The Great Supper—Temperance in English Parlours—"Persistence a Cardinal Virtue."

FEELING the necessity of rest, after thirty-six years of almost unbroken hard work, I determined to revisit England, see my old and valued friends, accept the numerous offers of hospitality, and spend perhaps two years in Europe. In answer to repeated and urgent requests, I proposed giving thirty lectures while in England, and to pass some months on the Continent. So on the 10th July, 1878, Mrs. Gough and myself sailed from New York for Liverpool, two of our nieces accompanying us.

On our landing, we were met by a committee of the "National Temperance League," of the "United Kingdom Band of Hope Union," of the "Good Templars," who presented me with a beautifully engrossed address of welcome; and a deputation from the "Liverpool Temperance Union," and from the "Liverpool Popular Central Association." My dear, good friend William Logan, who went home to heaven on the last day I spent in Glasgow, came from Scotland to greet us, and John M. Cook, Esq., rendered us valuable assistance.

It had been pleasantly arranged that there should be a social gathering of the friends to meet me, before commencing my public work. By the kind permission of the Dean and Chapter, a garden party was given in the College Gardens of Westminster Abbey. It was a peculiarly gratifying occasion, especially considering the high social position of those who gave me their greeting. The American minister, Hon. Mr. Welch, was present; also several dignitaries of the Church, some members of Parliament, and a splendid representation from the different temperance organizations.

Tea and coffee were served in a *marquee*, and during refreshments the band of the Royal Greenwich Hospital performed a selection of music. It was a most enjoyable affair. Many of our dear old friends, and many new ones, were there; yet we missed several familiar faces that our hearts yearned again to greet. But I will not dwell on this very pleasant episode, and only say that after speeches by Samuel Bowly, Esq., his Excellency the American minister, Canon Duckworth, Dr. Richardson, Canon Ellison, Samuel Morley, Esq., M.P., Dean Stanley spoke a few words of welcome, and offered to conduct us through the Abbey, which he did to our great delight. That beautiful garden, the smooth lawn, the surroundings—on one side the gray towers of the venerable Abbey, and on the other the clock-tower and Victoria tower of the Parliament houses—the whole scene so charming, will never fade from my memory.

Any attempt to describe Westminster Abbey would be presumptuous, following the many who have so eloquently succeeded. If it is true that there are "sermons in stones,"— and that there are, we have the authority of Shakespeare,— where shall we go for a better sermon than to Westminster Abbey? standing, as it does, grey and hoary and majestic, rich with the memories of the past, and consecrated with the bones and ashes and reputations of the great! All that Britain contained, or contains of the illustrious or good, of genius or culture, have trodden its aisles, have come hither to worship, to admire, to mourn, or, it may be, after life's fitful fever, to sleep. Here majesty, amidst pomp and splendour, has assumed the crown, and amidst equal pomp and circumstance, has laid it down; here the nation has mourned the bard whose verse is as immortal as her tongue : and here she has wept over her greatest statesmen—dead.

In the neighbourhood of the Abbey we are in the centre of English civilization, and near the brain of government—that Downing Street from which England, Scotland, Ireland, ay, and lands far remote, peopled by alien races, professing alien creeds, speaking alien tongues, are ruled. Royalty resides in close proximity; and in ermined gown and solemn wig and official pomp the proud peers of Britain assemble to legislate, not a stone's throw from this sacred shrine.

It was arranged to commence my public work at the Metropolitan Tabernacle (Rev. Mr. Spurgeon's) on Tuesday, September 22nd. After spending a week with our dear friends Mr. and Mrs. George Brown, of Houghton, Hunts, we started for the Continent; but after four weeks of almost incessant wet weather, we returned to London, and took lodgings at 185, Piccadilly, resting till the important evening should arrive. What an audience, and what a greeting! It was overpowering. The papers stated that seven thousand were present. It was a happy beginning of our allotted work. The chairman on that occasion was Sir Charles Reed, honoured as chairman of the London School Board, formerly M.P. for the borough of Hackney,* a leading man in every good word and work. He is the second son of the celebrated philanthropist, the late Dr. Andrew Reed, who was sent as a deputation to America by the English Congregationalists as far back as 1833. Sir Charles is a typefounder in Aldersgate Street, and was intimately associated with our illustrious Peabody, of whose estate he was the executor. He is also one of the leading men in connection with the Sunday School Union. He is a prompt man of business, always managing to come at the right time, say and do the right thing, and then be off to another meeting or committee elsewhere. He is a brother-in-law of Hon. Edward Baines, the proprietor of that influential journal, the *Leeds Mercury*. Sir Charles has been a successful man through

* Elected in 1880 as a member for St. Ives.

life, and for years has been more or less a public man, especially in connection with the city of London : and I believe he might have been Lord Mayor had his ambition led him in that direction, but as he refrained from coming forward as an alderman, of course he cannot rise to that dignity. His hair is white, his form erect, and there is a hearty glow on his benevolent face, which shows that his work agrees with him. He has an easy and natural way of speaking. What he says seems to come to him naturally and with little effort. He is very popular, and is generally hailed on his public appearances with hearty applause.

The chairmen of my other meetings have impressed upon me the conviction that never before has the Temperance cause been more thoroughly allied to the highest culture. Vividly do I recall Samuel Morley, M.P. for the city of Bristol, one of those merchant-princes who are the glory and pride of London, and of England. He is a tall, well-made man, with rather a serious, but extremely intelligent and attractive face, with a warm heart and a smile for every earnest worker in the cause of humanity. Nor is this all. His purse is as big as his heart, and he rarely refuses a handsome donation in every case of real distress. To him many have been indebted for the building of a chapel, Wesleyan, Baptist, or Congregationalist, and the erection of mission halls or coffee palaces ; to the establishment of school and college, or to special efforts made by the Bible and tract societies, and the "Sunday School Union." I think he is almost seventy years old, and he seems to have an immense power of work in him yet, looking much younger than his years. I am told that of his income, which is set down at £70,000 a year, half of it is spent in charity. In politics he is one of the Liberal leaders in the city. He is a Dissenter and a Congregationalist. As a man of business he has few equals. His factory is at Nottingham ; his warehouse in Wood Street, Cheapside ; and he has a superb residence some way from town, in one of the most beautiful districts of the county of Kent. He does not make long speeches, but what he says is always to the point, and comes from the heart.

In spite of his great wealth he always dines in the middle of the day, as his young men, of whom there are some seven or eight hundred, dine at that time. Such a habit gives him ample opportunity to devote his evenings to useful, philanthropic, and religious work. This dinner-hour was recommended to him, when quite a young man, by his uncle, who said to him, " Now, Samuel, never give in to the fashion of late dinners; if you do, you will never be able to do any good in the world." And Mr. Morley has ever since avoided late dinners, and thus devotes the time he has gained to the promotion of the welfare of his fellow-man and to the glory of God. A more sincere Christian man I know not.

In the city he is an earnest supporter of the Temperance movement. He was also one of the first members of the London School Board. There is a great deal of drinking in London mercantile life. The great houses have their buyers, and these buyers are exposed to great temptations. The agents of the manufacturers invite them to heavy lunches, or grand dinners, where the wine circulates freely, and business is transacted over the flowing bowl. Against this custom Mr. Morley ever utters a conscientious protest, and he will not sanction it in any way, as he has seen so much of the mischief, and the mental, bodily, and spiritual ruin it creates. He is President of the " Band of Hope Union," and often stands side by side with the noble Earl of Shaftesbury in the cause of ragged schools.

One sees Mr. Morley driving about in a fine mail phaeton, as if he were some thirty or forty years younger than he really is. I can quite understand his desire to take things a little easier, but it seems that people will not let him; for instance, he wishes to retire from Parliament, but the Bristol people insist on retaining him as their M.P.

In one thing he is especially interested, and that is in the Brackley Street Mission. You must know that though they are pulling down all the old houses, and all the unhealthy, fever-breeding tenements in London, as fast as they can, many of them are still left. One of these is in Brackley Street, a very low part of the city, where a great number of the costermongers live, not very far from the grand warehouses in Cheapside and

Gresham Street. In this street Mr. Morley's employés have established a mission church, where a city missionary preaches every Sunday. A flourishing Sunday-school has also been established, where all the agencies connected with such places are worked by Mr. Morley's young men. At Christmas time a grand dinner of roast-beef and plum-pudding is provided for the poor people connected with the mission hall, and presents are given to the children; and Mr. Morley is sure to be present on such occasions.

There is another institution in the suburbs of London, almost entirely supported by Mr. Morley and his brother, viz., the Protestant Deaconess' Institute, at Tottenham, just opposite the spot where dear old Isaac Walton, the angler—as he tells us in his book—loved to refresh himself when he went fishing in the direction of the river Lea. There Dr. Losereau, a medical man, has found a nice old-fashioned house, which he has converted into a hospital, and in which he appoints a certain number of respectable, religious young women of the middle class, whom he trains to nurse the sick, and at the same time to minister to the mind diseased, and to solace and strengthen it with the consolations religion imparts. In all parts of the country these nurses have been employed. They have also been useful in the East, and in the war between France and Germany; and whatever power they have been for good has been chiefly due to the constant and liberal support of such a man as Mr. Morley. Yet with all this, Mr. Morley is a perfectly unostentatious man.

Often if *A* gives a hundred pounds to some charity, *B* gives another to prove himself as good a man as *A*. In a fashionable comedy, a city merchant is represented as telling his private secretary to send so many hundred pounds to all the charities which published the names of the donors, and to put it down under the head of advertisements. Mr. Morley is not a man of that class. Nor is he like a wealthy brother of whom I heard the other day. He belonged, it seems, to the Baptist denomination; and, upon an intimation to the church of his desire to be set apart for ministerial training, a deputation was appointed to confer with him on the subject. After due and anxious deliberation they returned with their report. It was to the effect that the young man in question had one great talent which might be usefully employed for the good of the community, for the service of the church, and for the honour of God; and that was the gift of giving. Mr. Morley has that talent in perfection, and he makes a noble use of it; but he has other and greater and better gifts as well.

Another chairman was Canon Farrar, the author of the most successful "Life of Christ" that has appeared in our day. He is the son of a clergyman, and with his delicately chiselled face and fair complexion, looks every inch a gentleman. Originally he devoted more time to teaching than to preaching. He was one of the masters at that beautiful Harrow school, where Lord Byron and Sir Robert Peel were trained. Mr. Farrar was appointed head master; he is now, however, one of the canons of Westminster, and one of the most attractive and fascinating orators in the English Church. He has a calm and gentle, and yet very telling way of speaking, and when he preaches at Westminster, the grand old Abbey is crowded in every part. He is quite in the prime of life—indeed he looks very young, considering the work he has done, and the reputation he has gained. His books have a great sale, and so have his single sermons. He has also written some good stories for boys.

He presided twice in Exeter Hall at my lectures. I heard him speak only for a few minutes, but there was a magnetism about him making us long to hear more. His utterances for temperance are not uncertain: he is thoroughly in earnest, and speaks powerfully and very eloquently. He has spoken in the Sheldonian Theatre, Oxford; and at Cambridge, Edinburgh, Glasgow, and Aberdeen universities, and is doing a very important work. He told me that all his children had signed the total abstinence pledge. He is a most valuable acquisition to the temperance cause in England, and his influence through his published speeches is extensively acknowledged in this country.

Another chairman was the Lord Bishop of Exeter, a great contrast to his predecessor, the renowned Tory, Bishop Philpots. Dr. Temple was at one time master of Rugby Grammar School, the successor of Dr. Arnold, whose life was admirably written by Dean Stanley while a professor in Oxford, and who raised the reputation of that school to the very pinnacle,—Rugby made so familiar to us by Thomas Hughes in his "Tom Brown's Schooldays." Bishop Temple reminds you not a little of Dr. Cummings, of the Scotch Church, in his best days. He is dark in complexion and hair; he has an ecclesiastic, scholastic, and high-bred appearance. There was what I have heard called a "tremendous row," when he was made Bishop of Exeter, as he was one of the seven who wrote the "Essays," which some years ago made so much talk, and were the theme of so much discussion in England, on the Continent, and in America. The doctor has outlived the *odium theologicum*, perhaps one of the most virulent forms of human animosity, and is universally esteemed and respected. His speech on temperance was very attractive and decisive; he impressed me as a man with profound convictions, who knew what he was talking about, and uttered every sentence with a decision that impressed you with his sense of the importance of his own utterances. His language was perfection. He was received by the audience at Plymouth with great enthusiasm.

Another, who presided at my lecture at Croydon, was the Lord Bishop of Rochester, who has one of the sweetest faces I ever looked upon. He is small in person, but great in effort, dignified, but not stiff, exceedingly courteous and genial, and the perfect gentleman. A short time since, he was a hard-working English clergyman; now he is an evangelical bishop in one of the busiest of English dioceses. His speech is grave but forcible, and to the point. He said emphatically: "I deserve neither praise nor pity for being a total abstainer. I do not deserve praise, because I never did a better thing for myself in all my life; nor do I deserve pity, for it has doubled my working power." He is held in high esteem, and is universally respected and beloved. He spoke to me of the great delight which he has always experienced in his repeated visits to the United States.

The Bishop of Bangor presided at my lecture at Carnarvon,

but, owing to his late arrival, I saw but little of him beyond the personal formalities of the immediate occasion.

The Bishop of Bedford presided at my lecture in Oswestry. He preached the Temperance sermon in Westminster Abbey for the League, in March last. Canon Ellison presided for me at Oxford; Canon Wilberforce at Southampton; Canon Connor, at Newport, Isle of Wight; the Dean of York, at York; the Dean of Durham, at Newcastle; the Lord Lieutenant and father of the House of Commons, Hon. Mr. Talbot, at Swansea; the Lord Mayor of Dublin, at Dublin. What a change in public sentiment in twenty years! when it was rare to obtain the service of a clergyman to preside.

Another chairman was Benjamin Whitworth, a man who has made his own way in the world, and who is now, or was till lately, one of the largest employers of labour in England. He is a man of middle height, gray hair, pleasant in aspect, calm and convincing in speech. Said a friend of mine to one who knew him well some years ago, "How did Mr. Whitworth make all his money?" "Why, by borrowing half a sovereign," was the reply. My friend said to me, "I'm afraid that cannot be the secret of his success, as I went at once and borrowed a sovereign, and yet I am far from having made a fortune. It requires financial genius to make a fortune out of half a sovereign; but that genius Mr. Whitworth has in an eminent degree, and it has made him a Member of Parliament, and a man of mark." He commenced his speech of introduction with a few very pithy remarks, announcing himself as the oldest total-abstainer perhaps in the world, as he was sixty-two years of age, and had never tasted intoxicating drink in his life. With such a record, he carries a great deal of power; and, though rich and of commanding influence, he is very simple in his manners, thoroughly the gentleman without any superciliousness. I was very much attracted to him, and enjoyed meeting him exceedingly.

I had the pleasure and privilege of meeting Sir Wilfred Lawson, the president of the United Kingdom Alliance, who was the chairman at my third lecture in Mr. Spurgeon's taber nacle. He is one of the wittiest men in the House of Commons. I am told that his income from land alone is £100,000 per annum. If he were not a teetotaler, he would be a "jolly good fellow," perhaps, in the bacchanalian sense of the term; as it is, he is a "jolly good fellow" in a higher and nobler sense. It is impossible to converse with him for five minutes without being affected by his goodness and humour. He overflows with what Lord Beaconsfield terms "gay wisdom," and is even more witty in private than in public life. His wit seems to be hereditary. Many years ago, when Henry Brougham canvassed Cumberland, Sir Wilfred's grandfather was his vigorous supporter. On one occasion, observing that the Conservative side of the hustings was crowded with clergymen, the old gentleman stretched out his hand towards them, exclaiming, "The Lord gave the word, and great was the company of the preachers,"— an allusion that was extremely well relished in the hustings. Sir Wilfred takes the world easily. He is good-tempered, and makes you good-tempered as well. He has a fine, manly presence, and looks as if he might do good service to the cause of temperance and righteousness for many years to come. As a speaker, he is very fascinating, and at once puts his audience *en rapport* with himself. Whenever you see a speech of his reported, you find constantly the notice "roars of laughter;" not that he is flippant, by any means; but he introduces side hits that are irresistibly funny, and seems to do so sometimes with an utter unconsciousness that he has said anything ludicrous; and his half-inquiring, half-surprised look at the convulsed audience only adds to their merriment. He exhibits in his speeches sound common-sense, unanswerable argument, logic without a flaw, and what in other men would be a break or digression, with him is only reaching out for and employing some outside implement to drive home the truth. His good-nature is unshaken by opposition; and when sometimes he utters an unpalatable truth,—for he is fearless in his expressions of belief,—there may be a storm of hissing, he is perfectly imperturbable, and will quietly introduce a story or illustration so pat, so apt, as to throw the laugh upon his opponents. This he does so gracefully that the objectors are to be seen laughing as heartily as the others at their own discomfiture, reminding you of Charles Lamb when he hooted and hissed as loud as any of the audience who condemned the farce on which he had built such hopes of emolument.

I heard him twice: once at a meeting of the United Kingdom Alliance, and again when he presided at Mr. Spurgeon's tabernacle. I was very anxious that he should speak at length, and accordingly asked him to occupy as much time as possible. I thoroughly enjoyed his speech. As a specimen of his style, though his manner is unapproachable and indescribable, I give a few sentences from one of his speeches on the liquor traffic. He said: "The publicans, if you read their speeches at their dinners, generally tell you that they are licensed by the law as the guardians of public morality; and we all know that the police are the guardians of the public peace. Therefore we may say, with regard to this licensing question, and this conjunction of publicans and police, that righteousness and peace have kissed each other."

He is a strong Liberal, and often introduces a hit, very keen, but very smooth, at the Opposition. One of the mottoes of the Conservative party in reference to the mission to Berlin, is, "Peace with honour;" so in speaking of the publicans, he said: "If you read their speeches as I have done, you would say that the whole tone of them is, that they are great public benefactors, unappreciated by a hard-hearted world, who would retire and take refuge in some less philanthropic and arduous business, where they might find 'Peace with honour,'"—here he was interrupted by cheers, laughter, and hisses, when he finished with—"if it were not for their burning desire to minister to their own comfort, and promote the happiness and well-being of the people." Take him for all in all, he is one of the most effective speakers for the legislative temperance question in England. He has pungent sarcasm without bitterness, meets opposition with unfailing good-humour; his wit is sharp, but never causes a rankling wound. He is immensely popular, and the very announcement of his name creates enthusiasm. I met him at the dinner of the Medical Temperance Society, at Langham Hotel, and was charmed by his easy and gentlemanly courtesy.

I venture to give a short extract or two from his speech at the Tabernacle, believing it will be interesting to many:

"Ladies and Gentlemen: I was at a large meeting last night. I took up the *Echo* newspaper just before I came here this evening, and I saw a paragraph in which it stated that Sir Wilfred Lawson made a 'tolerably long speech.' I am afraid there was a little misprint, and that the writer meant an *intolerably* long speech. [Laughter.] I shall take warning, and not make you an intolerably long speech to-night; but Mr. Gough kindly wishes me to say a few words before I have the pleasure of introducing him to this magnificent meeting, [loud cheers,] for it is the grandest meeting which ever I had the pleasure of addressing. [Renewed cheers.] I thank those gentlemen who have promoted this meeting for having done me the honour of asking me to preside over it. I feel that it is an honour, and more than that, it is a luxury; for I am more in the habit, at these meetings, of speaking than of listening. To-night I shall have the treat—which will be all the greater because it will be shared by the many thousands whom I see around me—of hearing. . . . . . And another reason why I feel it pleasant to come to this meeting, is because I am in the habit of about five times a week attending another meeting, [laughter,] which is held at St. Stephen's, and I assure you I do not attend it with much pleasure, for the business which we are engaged in, in that great assembly, is one which is enough to wound the heart of any man of feeling. ["Hear, hear."] There we are, day by day, and night by night, devising means for the torture and the slaughter of our fellow-men." [Uproar.]

In speaking of the results of drink, he said:

"Take lunacy. Lord Shaftesbury, himself a lunacy commissioner, has told us that drink is one of the principal causes of madness in this country. By-the-bye, while I am talking about lunacy, there comes into my mind a remark which was made in this very borough, I think, or near it, by a very great friend of your member's, who sits by my side. That good friend was Mr. Morgan Howard, who, making a speech at a political meeting not long since, assured his audience that during the time when Mr. Gladstone was in office there were more lunatics in the asylums of this country than at any other period. [Laughter.] I state that to show you the enormity of the evil, because I am quite sure you will agree with me that, since the present government came in, the lunatics have got loose!"

And in conclusion he said:

"I don't need to tell you to *hear* him; what I do tell you, is to *heed* him, to take to heart the counsels which he will give you, and to send him back, when in a short time he goes across the Atlantic, to the Republic of the West, with a message that we intend to live henceforth in unity and peace with them, [loud cheers], and that the only strife between us shall be the generous rivalry as to which country first shall overthrow that foul and degraded system, based on prejudice, on tyrannous custom, and on unjust laws, which at present is the greatest hindrance in all the paths of virtue and holiness and of true glory, which yet blocks the way of the two greatest nations of the world." [Applause.]

One of the men upon whom the friends of temperance in England rely very much for medical testimony against alcoholic drinks is Dr. Richardson, and I believe the cause has received through his advocacy a most powerful impetus, not only in Great Britain, but all over the world where the English language is spoken; moreover, his works have been translated into several foreign languages. He hails from the county of Leicester, and was born in the year 1828. His education was chiefly in Scotland. In 1855 he originated the first sanitary English journal, the *Journal of Public Health and Sanitary Review*, which he edited for several years. In 1856 he gained the Astley Cooper prize of three hundred guineas for an essay on the coagulation of the blood, and he became a member of the Royal College of Physicians. As a lecturer and writer on the diseases of modern life, on the influence of alcohol and other matters of similar character, no one is more popular or more successful than Dr. Richardson; and he speaks with the more authority and effect, because at one time he believed in and used wine, and recommended its use. His numerous works speak for him. His style is very attractive. I heard him lecture once in Exeter Hall, and was fascinated from the first utterances to the closing words; and so intense was the interest which he awakened, that at his conclusion, when the spell was lifted, there was left the regret that I could not hear it all again. To those (and there are many in this country) who have read his works, I need not say how charming as well as vigorous is his style.

He is not very tall, rather stout, but well formed, and with a face of remarkable intelligence and geniality. He was one of the first to greet me on my arrival in England, and I found him a sincere friend and cordial ally. The last evening I spent in London was at a farewell reception in his house, where I met a delightful company; among them the venerable S. C. Hall, known for two generations as an authority on matters of art, the editor for years of the *Art Journal*, and a good worker for temperance; his wife, Mrs. Anna Maria Hall, who has written very eloquently on social reform, was detained by ill-health.

Another medical man claimed by the total abstainers (I was not so fortunate as to meet him), and received as an authority by those who are engaged in the temperance work, is Sir Henry Thompson. He was born at Framlingham, in Suffolk, the son of a grocer and draper, and became in course of time, when a young man, a partner in his father's business; but he soon left it, and entered himself as a student at University College, London, with an aim to study medicine. He passed successfully through all his classes, and then went to Paris to study the French language and surgery. He returned to London, married Kate Loder, the celebrated pianist, set up in practice in Wimpole Street, in the fashionable quarter of the town. Here his essay won the Jacksonian prize for the year, and he at once became a man of mark. He was brought under the notice of the King of the Belgians, on whom he performed a successful operation, where surgeons in Paris and London had failed. The result was that he rose at once to the first rank in his profession. The King of the Belgians gave him, so I have heard, £3,000. The Queen of England made him a knight, and nobles and great men consulted him; and it is said that his practice is worth £20,000 per year. His letter to the Archbishop of Canterbury, on the evils of moderate drinking, begging his Grace to use his influence to stop it, created an immense sensation, and did much to open men's eyes, and convince them of the evils of the moderate use of alcohol. Sir Henry has great talents as an artist, and has been a frequent exhibitor in the Royal Academy. His Thursday dinners, at which the artists and wits assemble, are among the most celebrated in London. He is tall, thin, gentlemanly, with a gray, thick moustache, a dark eye that looks you through and through, and a clear, emphatic manner, which make the patient feel that he is safe in his hands. Calm, imperturbable as he is, Sir Henry feels much. It is said that at the end of a very difficult operation he has exclaimed, "There's another nail in my coffin."

I was brought into contact with these men by my connection with them as chairmen at special efforts in the Temperance cause. My list would be incomplete without mentioning one of the noblest men of England. I refer to the then Lord High Chancellor, Lord Cairns ; the man who stands next to the throne in official circles ; the chairman of that august assembly, the House of Lords ; a man who would not bind himself to any cause that was not a noble one ; who has all a lawyer's caution ; who has in his bearing that hardness which constitutes a man of the world, before whom sophistry and sentimentalism plead in vain. It was a beautiful sight to see him, in the height of the London season—when time was with him most valuable, when his mind was most strained with important state affairs—devote one afternoon to preside at a lecture of mine in Exeter Hall; and, with chastened eloquence and matured wisdom, earnestly commending the cause of which I was the advocate, and with which I have been identified so many years. In his gown and wig, on the woolsack in the House of Lords, with his gold mace before him, the Lord High Chancellor is a very formidable personage. Even as a plain man in the streets, you would notice Lord Cairns by his stateliness and calmness, indicative of a temperament and resolve of iron, which has lifted him up, the son of a clergyman, to the very topmost pinnacle of the London world. When such a man is delighted to lend the weight of his name and influence and presence and speech to such efforts, how great has been the progress of temperance principles in the highest circles of the old country! And what a personal triumph, to be thus honoured for my work's sake in the land where I was born to so low a lot !

Truly the progress in twenty-five years has been amazing

and remarkable. At Rochdale, where I spoke, the Mayor of the city was in the chair, the Mayor of Bury supporting him on one side, the Mayor of Oldham on the other, giving their countenance, in their official capacity, (for they wore the massive gold chains and insignia of office,) to the temperance cause. In Glasgow the Lord Provost Collins presided, and entertained us at his residence. He is thoroughly devoted to the reform, gives liberally, and is always ready to give his whole influence most heartily to the work. On January 1, 1879, he entertained eight thousand of the unemployed at a substantial meal. Several of the largest halls in Glasgow were engaged for the occasion, and appropriate speeches were made by ministers of the Gospel and by others. In many ways he has manifested his deep interest in, and sympathy for, the poor people, especially the deserving working class.

The Duke of Westminster had engaged to preside at my meeting at Chester, but a severe attack of bronchitis prevented. He is the wealthiest man in England; a small, thin, dark-complexioned man, not celebrated as an orator, but a nobleman who manifests a deep interest in the temperance cause, and who exerts a powerful influence. He has been the means of reducing the number of public-houses on his large estates. He is a personal abstainer. Though occupying so high a position, he is very unassuming, as all truly great men are. A friend of mine, who was a stranger to his Grace, was one day at a musical *soirée* in the great reception-rooms of Grosvenor House, and as he was standing with some others in the doorway, a gentleman asked them to take a seat in the next room, "where," he said, "you can hear just as well." "Oh," said my friend, "I don't care where I sit, so long as I can hear what the Duke has to say for himself." "Oh," observed the stranger, "I will let you know when I am going to speak." My friend was talking to the great Duke himself.

I was delighted to meet again my dear and honoured friend, Samuel Bowly, whose tall, erect, and manly presence shows how well teetotalers can bear the heat and burden of the day, and who has for many years constantly and liberally devoted his time and means to the promotion of every good work. In his advanced age he is as useful and powerful, and I believe more influential, than ever. With his high social position, he has done a great work for the temperance cause among those who could not otherwise have been reached, by his very successful parlour-meetings at the houses and in the drawing-rooms of the wealthy and educated, introducing teetotalism into many a circle where it was once a thing to be scoffed at. As a deputation for the National Temperance League, of which he is the honoured president, he has presented the cause all over the country by his excellent and persuasive platform speeches, and by his agency the principles are honoured and revered where they were once held in contempt. I know of no man more universally beloved than dear Samuel Bowly, of Gloucester.

Robert Rae, Secretary of the National Temperance League, is one of the noble self-sacrificing workers that inspire with new courage those who are ready to faint; always hopeful, ever striving for an object, constantly organizing for some new effort, he is invaluable to the association. One of the most patient yet persistent men I ever knew; holding his own, when convinced he is right, against all opponents without flinching, yet with wonderful equanimity; never dictatorial, but always firm; a reliable friend, and a generous enemy; bold in denouncing sin, yet tender to the sinner, with a stern rebuke for the persistent transgressor, but with deep sympathy for the unfortunate; never compromising wrong, yet very gentle to the wronged. He is one whom all respect and many love.

A grand worker and representative Scotchman was Thomas Knox, of Edinburgh, whose sudden death last December was felt as a national loss, and most keenly mourned by the temperance friends, who had known him for so many years as a firm adherent to our principles. He once said to me, "I believe persistence to be one of the cardinal virtues;" and most thoroughly did he exhibit that virtue. When I was in Scotland, as early as 1853, he was writing powerful articles in the secular papers on education, and proposed the introduction of temperance lesson-books. He was strongly opposed by one section of the community, and barely tolerated by another, while many of the friends of temperance looked coldly on his scheme. But he persevered, and for twenty years worked for this object, with small encouragement from any source, and lived to see his plan becoming popular,—lived to see temperance literature introduced into many of the schools of his beloved Scotland, and to know that his scheme is extensively advocated and adopted, not only on the continent of Europe, but in the United States. He was a genial man, one for whom I have a strong affection. He has encouraged me when desponding, cheered me when sad, comforted me when suffering, helped me when I needed it. He was my firm, true, tried, and trusted friend, and I shall always thank God that I ever knew Thomas Knox.

As I pen these recollections of good men, I see them coming in troops before me, and I must forbear, or I should fill my book with the outpouring of my heart towards the dear, true friends of my life.

CHAPTER III.

STREET LIFE AND SCENES IN THE WORLD'S METROPOLIS.

London—Life in the Metropolis—Great Contrasts—Unknown Depths—"The London Market"—Shops of London—Streets and Palaces—Distinctive Communities—A World in Miniature—Street People—Cab Experience—Gathering a Crowd—"Vot's hup, Cabby?"—Excitements of the Streets—Street Children—"It looks werry nice, Sir"—Street Boys' Histories—Awful Surroundings in Childhood—"Never had a Chance"—Barnabas or Barabbas?—After the Funeral—How the Boy became an Outcast—Vice and Crime—The Orphan's Lot—Sixteen Hundred Waifs—Sleeping in an Iron Roller and in the Boot of an Omnibus—"We must go to Business"—Money-Making—Diving in Sewers —"Mud-Larks"—"Wagabones and Hactors"—Street Arabs—"Peelers'" Difficulties—Street-Boys' Wit—"Penny" Merchants—Street Wares—Cheap Books—"Raising the Wind."

AS this book is intended for, and will be read principally by, Americans, I venture to introduce many of my experiences and jottings in London and England.

London is a fruitful theme; every year a fresh crop of material springs up. I do not say that he who has seen London has seen the world, but I do say, that to all of Anglo-Saxon origin on the face of the wide world, there is no city fuller of interest and excitement than London. The traditions and archives of our race are treasured there. To us, when we cross the Atlantic, London holds out a friendly hand; and I say of London, as Cowper said of England,—for I have tasted its hospitality, partaken of its generosity, and been familiar with its people,—

"London, with all thy faults, I love thee still."

Yes; London, the great metropolis, whose street scenes so fascinated me; London, with its contrasts, its squalid poverty and its enormous wealth. I explored London with great interest, becoming more attracted with a closer acquaintance. How few know London! Though I spent days and nights in my explorations, I know but very little of the great metropolis. Out of America, I had rather live in London than in any city in the world. You cannot know it by merely spending a few weeks in a lodging-house or hotel, and "doing the sights:" you must explore. By simply skimming the surface, you know nothing, comparatively. It is a place that grows in interest on acquaintance. At first, it seems darker, duller, noisier, and more bustling than any ordinary town or city. Few like London on a first visit; no one who has long lived there but leaves it with regret. The fairest of England's daughters, the manliest of England's sons, all press to London as the fitting arena of enterprise, conquest, or display. London drains the country, and from it the country is supplied. Go to the Land's End, or the Scilly Isles, and see field after field grown with vegetables; inquire, and you are told "they are for the London market." In the most remote parts of Scotland, ask the sportsman shooting grouse the destination of those waggon-loads of game, and you are told "they are for the London market." Cross to Ireland, that butter and those pigs on the quays of Dublin and Cork are for the London market. Sail up the remotest bays and fiords of old Norway, and ask whither they are sending those lobsters, crabs, and salmon; plant yourself in some picturesque part of Normandy, and ask why they are filling these vessels with potatoes and eggs, the answer is still the same,—"for the London market."

In the shops of London, the finest and rarest productions of the world are to be found. In Covent Garden you may buy green peas, ripe strawberries, and exquisite flowers the year round; and, as I said, it is from London that the country is supplied. Perhaps you are dining with a gentleman two or three hundred miles from town, by the seaside; you ask where he obtained so fine a fish, he tells you it was brought by train from London. I was at one time engaged to speak near Loch Leven. The gentleman who entertained me said, "I shall give you a rare treat for supper to-night,—Loch Leven trout." "Not very rare to you," I replied, "for you must have them in abundance during the season." "Indeed," said he, "we do not; we who live here cannot obtain them for love or money, except on special occasions, and this is one. The tacksman sent me a fine dish of them, that you might eat trout on the borders of Loch Leven, which we very seldom do." In reply to my inquiry, he told me that all the fish were contracted for in London at a certain rate, on condition that none should be sold under any circumstances; and that the disposal of a single trout for money would break the contract; and said he, "if we want Loch Leven trout, we must obtain them from London."

London is a very fascinating place to most who have resided there long, in spite of its smoke, dirt, and fog. Charles Lamb, in a letter to Manning, in reference to a journey in the country, thus speaks of London : "Streets, streets, streets, markets, theatres, churches; Covent Gardens ; shops sparkling with pretty faces of industrious milliners, neat seamstresses, ladies cheapening, gentlemen behind counters lying ; authors in the streets with spectacles; lamps lit at night; if you happen to wake at midnight, cries of fire ! and stop thief ! inns of court, with their learned air, and halls, and butteries, old book-stalls, Jeremy Taylors, Burtons on Melancholy, and Religio Medicis at every stall ;—these are thy pleasures, O London ! and for these may Keswick and her giant brood go hang ! "

Dr. Johnson could live nowhere else but in London with comfort. London is several cities rolled into one. If you walk along Regent Street, it is a city of gorgeous shops; if you turn to the west, of parks and palaces ; if you travel St. Giles, of gin and dirt; in Belgravia, it is rich and grand ; in Pimlico, it is poor and pretentious; in Russell Square it is well-to-do,—successful professional men abiding in what Mr. Wilson Croker called its unexplored regions. You will find between each neighbourhood a regular line of demarcation. "When I consider this great city," wrote Addison,—and the language is applicable now,—"in its several quarters and divisions, I look upon it as an aggregate of various nations, distinguished from each other by their respective customs, manners, and interests. The courts of two countries do not so much differ from one another as the court and city of London, in their peculiar ways of life and conversation. In short," he says, "the inhabitants of St. James, notwithstanding they live under the same laws, and speak the same language, are a distinct people from those of Cheapside, by several climates and degrees, in their way of thinking as well as conversing."

Fashion migrates to the west; actors and musicians live about Brompton; the medical students take possession of whole streets in the vicinity of their respective hospitals; the inns of court are chiefly inhabited by barristers; France, Italy, Hungary, Poland, you will find represented by the cafés and cigar-shops, billiard-rooms and restaurants of Leicester Square; Wapping, Rotherhithe, and the Commercial Road abound with sailors of every nation under the sun; Quakers live about Edmonton and Stoke-Newington; Jews congregate in Houndsditch. In short, the swells in the parks, the millers in Mark Lane, the graziers in the new Cattle Market, the prim, pale lads in the city, the silk-weavers of Spitalfields, or the sugar-bakers of Whitechapel, really form distinct communities, and seem absolutely localized in their ideas.

The late Dr. Arnott, one of the greatest sanitary reformers of the age, used to say, that though London was not a place where the rate of mortality was very high, yet it was a place where no one enjoyed very good health. There is more and more danger every year of its health being diminished, by want of fresh air. People live out of town, rents are too high in the city, and, in consequence of its rapid extension, the great and growing evil is the want of fresh air. It is stated, in confirmation of this fact, that every year the hospital surgeons in London find it more difficult to cure wounds and injuries to the human body, on account of the growing impurity of the London air. A few years ago there was such a fog in London, not only in the city, but at the Agricultural Hall at Islington, that fat cattle worth hundreds of pounds—cattle that had won prizes at various fairs—were actually suffocated. Long ago, that famous man, Count Rumford, used to estimate the amount of coal suspended in the London air as some millions of chaldrons. It is a curious fact that Sir Rutherford Alcock, when he visited the great wall in China, brought back with him a couple of bricks; one of these bricks he put outside a London balcony. In two years it had gone entirely to pieces, being disintegrated by the action of the atmosphere. This materially affects out-of-door monuments in particular, and street architecture in general. They have been compelled to cover the Obelisk on the Embankment with a preparation, to preserve it, as it began to crumble.

The people in the London streets, by day or night, are fascinating to me; and I never weary of strolling about and watching them. It is very easy to gather a crowd: a horse falls down, and in a few minutes it requires a policeman to clear the street. One evening I started in a cab from the Midland Railway Station for Piccadilly, accompanied by a lady. We had passed the Five Dials, and were in Gerrard Street, when the horse staggered and fell. At once a crowd of men, women, boys, and girls gathered round us. "Vot's hup, cabby?" "Vy, don't yer see vot's hup? My 'orse is down; that's vot's hup." "Yah, he's got the staggers, blest if he 'asn't." "'Old 'ard, hold feller;" to the horse, who was struggling. "Now, then, stupid, do you vant your blessed legs broke vith them 'ere 'eels?" "Vot are ye vipping him for?" "Vun of ye sit on 'is 'ed, and vee'l get 'im out of the shafts in a jiffy." Such a din! boys laughing, women screaming at every fresh struggle of the wretched horse, or pitying him with, "poor thing!" "vot a shame!" The poor, beer-soaked cabman was perfectly bewildered, the crowd and confusion increasing, some one cried out, "'ere's the perlice," and by his direction we transferred our luggage to another cab; and paying half-a-crown in fees, beside the cabby's fare, we got away, leaving the poor horse on the ground, and the crowd undiminished. You hail a cab, or hansom, where there is a stream of passers-by, and immediately a group of persons will stop to see you get in. Stand stock-still, and stare in one direction, and a dense crowd will soon be formed; ask a man, "What is the matter; what are the people standing like that for?" He doesn't know, he says, and yet he is staring as earnestly as any.

The street folks are easily excited. In some parts of the city, in the evening, you see an organ-grinder at work, and young girls dancing with as keen an enjoyment as the fashionable lady at the stylish ball. These street boys and girls are uncontrollable. I found them, after twenty years, just the same,—keen, sharp, impudent. Coming through the Strand, a flake of soot fell on my moustache. I began to run my fingers through the hair, when a ragged, little bit of a boy looked up at me and said, with a perfectly sober face, "It looks wery nice, sir."

It is to be hoped that the compulsory education by the school boards will be effectual in repressing them in some degree; but it is wonderful the numbers who evade the provisions of the School Act, and every day the "Bobbies," as they term the policemen, are commissioned to arrest a truant. It is vastly amusing when a policeman undertakes to capture one or more of these wild boys or girls, as they rush about, followed by the panting "Bobby," out of breath, and altogether too heavy to cope with such small fry. The little one has the game in his own hands, and he knows it. Policeman has no chance in a fair race; at a long distance the odds might be in his favour. He has long legs; he has, perhaps, more than an average amount of bone and muscle; but he is not fairly matched: he can't dodge under horses; he can't crawl between the wheels of a street car, or an omnibus; he can't hide his portly form behind a pillar box; and his pursuit is like a buffalo chasing a butterfly, which generally ends in failure, and perhaps the last act of the farce is the little rascal taking a sight at him.

Occasionally one is caught; and now let us question the poor little fellow. You find he is shrewd, quick, sensitive, yet thoroughly wicked,—a waif of the streets. Read his history before you pass judgment. His home is a cellar; his mother a shameless beggar; his father a drunkard; his sisters, with livid, withered, sad faces, ply their dreadful trade. His family are vagabonds and outcasts. He dwells amid uncleanness and cruelty, catching the contagion of sin, and sympathy with polluted humanity in every form. His history? It is one of darkness, without one ray of light; a history which, if traced in tears and written in blood, none of us would have nerve enough to read. Born and brought up in the midst of such horrible surroundings, he is what he is. How can he grow God-like, while all the influences of his life tend to make and keep him morally hideous? Take one of your own dear ones, and give him the education that boy has had, with all his woful experience of life, and he would be as he is—no better, no worse. Would you be what you are if your infancy and childhood had been passed among all the horrible influences that have surrounded him? Think of this, and look at him as he is; and do not sweep him away with the pitiful leavings of the street, but help him, give him knowledge, teach him the Lord's Prayer, tell him of Jesus. That boy may be made a Barnabas instead of a Barabbas. As we know more of such neglected ones, the less critical and the more loving we shall be. He who knew the hearts of all was the most gentle in dealing with ignorance. He, the undefiled, endeavoured to win the hearts of the guilty, because He loved them; and surely we may be patient—ay, even believing and hoping—in all our efforts to lift up the unfortunate, and thus do Christ's work on earth. Solomon says, that "Foolishness is bound up in the heart of a child;" and what is to be expected of these boys born and bred in the streets? I have seen the children from a Christian home go astray. Some of the sons of the wealthy and refined have become poor and coarse; but these children of the drunkard and the thief never had a chance.

A poor working-man in Lambeth, when returning one Sabbath afternoon from a ragged school, found a little boy sitting in a very destitute condition on a door-step, took him home, and asked his history. The lad was about ten years of age; his mother had died when he was a baby, so that he had no recollection of her; his father had been dead about twelve months—partly from the effects of drink. The furniture of his room was sold the day of the funeral to pay the expenses. When the lad returned from the grave, he found a man busy removing the poor sticks and rags from the wretched apartment, making it more desolate in its emptiness. The boy left that room an outcast. The first night he slept in a court; then he found refuge in a railway arch; then in the boot of an omnibus. Such was his story. Is it wonderful, when we think of these things, that there should be vice and crime in London? Sixteen hundred of these poor little waifs were gathered from the streets, and, on examination, one hundred and sixty-two confessed that they had been in prison — not merely once or twice, but several of them many times; one hundred and sixteen had run away from their homes; one hundred and seventy slept in the lodging houses; two hundred and fifty-three had lived together by begging; two hundred and sixteen had neither shoes nor stockings; two hundred and eighty had no cap or covering for the head; one hundred and one had no linen; two hundred and forty-nine had never slept in a bed; sixty-eight were the children of convicts. How did they live? Why, as they could: by sweeping crossings, turning somersaults for the amusement of passers-by, selling lucifer matches, oranges, tapes, or ballads. One boy, during the inclement winter, passed the greater part of his nights in the large iron roller in Regent's Park. As an illustration of the low rate of morality, I would mention what passed at a ragged school, to which some fourteen or fifteen boys were admitted. One Sunday evening, when the clock struck eight, they all arose. The master took one little fellow by the arm as he was leaving, and said, "You must remain, the lesson is not over." The reply was, "We must go to business." The master inquired what business; the answer was, that they must be off to "catch the people as they came out of churches and chapels." In short, they were pickpockets.

Lord Ingestre says, in his "Meliora," that he visited some low dancing-saloons. In one, a man was pointed out, respectably dressed, who gained his living by drawing pictures of a ship or steam-engine on the pavement. These pictures were sold to boys at one shilling each. The man made several of these drawings in various localities before people were about, and thus did very well.

In London there is an immense variety of methods for making money. A lady was one day driving along one of the green lanes that are still to be met with in the vicinity of London, and saw a poor woman gathering some chestnut-leaves. She stopped and asked for what purpose; the reply was, that the leaves were sold to the fruiterers in Covent Garden, to put in their baskets of fruit. On another occasion it came out that women and children tore down the placards in the streets at night, and thus made a trifle by selling them as waste paper. One man dives in the sewers for what may be washed away. A capitalist buys up all the dust and ashes of the city, and they are sifted by women so black and grimy, that you could scarcely tell them to be women at all.

There is no waste in London; everything is picked up and turned to account. One man buys old bones; another, old rags; another buys cigar-ends for snuff,—in short, there is nothing so mean or filthy but is made merchandise by the poor of London. One man advertises for old postage-stamps that have been used, on the pretence that some crusty old parent will not let his daughter marry till she has collected a million. The pretence is a hoax; the old stamps are pasted together, and in some of the obscure parts of the town are offered you at a reduced price. The post-office authorities have issued a new pattern of stamp, because nearly one-third received had been cancelled and renewed. There are five or six hundred boys and girls called "mud-larks," who live by searching the mud of the Thames for bones, coals, and other articles. You often see men who may be called "Jack-of-all-trades," who run "herrands," "'old yer 'oss,"—reminding you of Billy Downey, in the "Unfinished Gentleman," who sold clothes-props and pins. Then in the literary line, carrying round newspapers, spreading knowledge and information. Then in the "wagabone" line, a "hactor," performing the "'ind legs of the helephant fifty-three successful nights," till the chap "vot done the forelegs" and he happened to get into a fight "while they vos hin the helephant;" and the "consekens vos, they hupset the 'ole concern," and of course he got the bag from the theatre; and now he "'olds 'osses, runs herrands, blacks boots," and makes himself generally useful.

Some of these little arabs are too restless and irritable to be easily reclaimed; the monotony of decent life is almost insupportable. If you reclaim them, many of them will contrive to get away again.

Not long since some children were poisoned by drinking some belladonna. It appears they had stolen it out of a case in the street off Covent Garden, had put it in a bottle with water, and sold it to other children at a pin for a spoonful, thinking the belladonna was Spanish liquorice; and in this way had carried on an active business.

A gentleman by the name of Driver, who had been for years engaged in endeavouring to reclaim these little urchins, says that on one occasion he met some of them, all dirt and rags, near the Nelson Monument. Said he: "I addressed myself principally to one boy, whom some time before I had pulled from underneath a tarpaulin in Covent Garden Market in the middle of a winter's night. He had been twice under my care for short periods, but gave the preference to a street life. I said, 'Well, Jim, are you not tired of this sort of life?' 'No,' he answered with a grin, 'not yet; and when I am, sir, I will come to you.' 'Very well,' I replied; 'I suppose you will have your game out first.' 'Now, sir, I'll tell you the real truth. I'd come to you to-morrow, if you'd give me an ounce of 'bacca a week, some ha'pence in my pocket to spend, and an hour's holiday every day; it would not be worth my while to do it under that—it would not, indeed, sir!'"

All these ragged urchins have an object—and, I fear, but one object—of terror, and that is a policeman. They will teach their dogs to bark furiously at the word "Bobby" or "Peeler." They will tease them in all possible ways. A policeman brought a boy before a magistrate on a charge of insulting him. "What did he say to you?" "Oh, he said nothing *to* me." "What did he do?" "Well, he pointed at me, and asked another boy if he ever see a rabbit-pie made out of mutton." "Oh, I cannot entertain such a charge as that." At every accident to a policeman their delight is uncontrollable. "Jem, hi! Look 'ere! come 'ere! sitch a lark! Hooray! Oh my! 'ere's a perleeceman fell down on a slide! Hooray!!"

To a flashily dressed snob they are very provoking. "Oh my! hi! there goes eightpence out of a shilling!" If on horseback so much the worse. "Hi there! you'll tumble off the shop board!" If he is a timid rider, "Billy, see, 'ere's a swell; let's frighten 'is 'oss!"

As witty a thing as I ever heard, was a remark made by one boy to another, as a showily dressed person passed, evidently vain of his appearance: "Hi! 'ow does that 'ere chap's hat stay up, without nothing hunder it?" Ask this ragged little wretch, "Can you read?" "No; but I can stand on my 'ed and drink a glass of gin." A judicious old lady said, when a boy accosted her with "Stand on my 'ed, ma'am, for a penny," "No, little boy; there's a penny for keeping right side upwards." Another boy,—"Now, my little man, what would you say if I should give you a penny?" "Vy, that you vas a jolly old brick." *Punch* gives some very graphic descriptions of this class of boys.

A stroll through the streets amazes you at the variety of methods for "turning a penny." Everything is a penny,—cigar lights, pencils, sham jewellery, ingenious puzzles, and very questionable publications, which yield enormous profits, one of them realizing for the ignoble owner many thousands a year. At one time it is the *Devil* that is put for sale at the price of one penny; at another, *London Life, London Gossip,* or *Town Talk.* There is also always a great sale of prints and photographs, all at one penny. The run on the evening papers —particularly when there has been a sensational murder, or a divorce case with spicy details—is immense; and as edition after edition is worked off, the streets are filled with men and women, lads and girls, offering them for sale. In this way a good deal of money is made, especially by the vendors who manage to get first in the neighbourhood of the Exchange and the Mansion House, and thus reach a class of customers who are not particular in the matter of change. Unprotected females, as they walk down Cheapside, are exceedingly annoyed by the impertinence of some of these fellows, who thrust the *Matrimonial News* before them, as they bawl in stentorian tones, "Want an 'usband, marm? Lot's of 'usbands to be had. Only a penny!"

One thing to be noted is the temporary character of these penny saleable articles. Some are to be met with all the year round, such as studs, cigar-lights, pocket-books, diaries, almanacs, beetles (which, attached to an india-rubber string, dance about as if they were alive), india-rubber balls, specimens of geology, steel pens, note-paper, German toys, refreshment drinks, bird-whistles, etc. Others are dependent on the season, and you get wonderful flowers,—camellias made of turnips,—apples, pears, oranges, walnuts, and slices of pineapple; and the costermongers who thus cater for the million are indeed a blessing, as they supply the poor of the metropolis with cheap fruit. In the summer you have the retailer of sherbet and the penny ice and shell-fish; in the winter the same man deals in roasted chestnuts or baked potatoes, or keeps a coffee-stall. All the year round some enterprising individuals supply the public, who need to have their blood purified, with penny sarsaparilla drinks.

When Lord Beaconsfield came back from the Berlin Congress, there was a card hawked about called the "European Mystery," and the puzzle was to find Lord Beaconsfield in the picture.

One of the most curious efforts I heard of in London for "raising the wind" was the "Continental Advertising Refreshment Plate Company," the aim of which was to distribute neatly designed advertisements on the rims of refreshment plates, dishes, saucers, etc., made of porcelain, china, earthenware, or other material, among the different hotels and cafés and restaurants in the various cities and towns of France and Belgium. It was reckoned this was to be the cheapest way of advertising ever known; and to carry it out only £5,000 were asked, which the promoters, however, probably failed to obtain, as the company was never started.

CHAPTER IV.

HIGH AND LOW LIFE IN LONDON.—CARMEN AND COCKNEYS.

Cabmen of London: their Great Number—"Exact Fare"—"I shan't forget the Phiz"—A Dandy discomfited—Wealth of London—Men who have risen—"Cats'-Meat"—Where the Dead Horses go—Fortunes by Sharp Practice—Roguery reduced to a System—The Wine Business—Tricks of Trade—High Art—Auctioneers—Jockeyism and Horses—Bought his Own Horse—Londoner's Self-Esteem—"Connoisseurship in Wines"—Tricks of Professional Beggars—The Blind Man who could see—"Eddicatin' Dogs"—The Lord Mayor's Show—Hardships of the Lord Mayor's Office—"Who is He?"—Self-made Men—Baron Rothschild's Remark on "Selling Matches"—Schools of the Corporation—Disrespectful Children—"'Ow is yer 'Elth?"—Inconvenience of the Letter H—The Gentleman's Story—Meeting with an "Hawful Hend"—Dilemma of the Alderman's Daughter—The Omnibus Conductor's Vocabulary.

THERE is no class of men less understood than the cabmen of London. The general verdict is, "Oh, they'll overcharge and bully you whenever they get a chance." Not more than the hackmen of New York. It is to be expected that, among twelve thousand or more men, with few advantages and constant exposure, meeting and dealing with all shades of character, there will be some hard cases, and a good many. But in my experience, with only a few exceptions, I have found them civil, and nearly always grateful for liberal treatment. To the screw who will pay them the "exact fare"—and there are many who pride themselves on always paying the "exact fare" of one shilling with two persons for a two-miles' ride—they sometimes give a little chaffing. One of this class, who had paid the "exact fare," was asked, "Beg pardon, but are you all pretty much alike in your family, sir?" "Well, yes, a little so." "Oh, all right; I shan't forget the phiz, and blowed if any of you will ride in my cab again." On one occasion two ladies had paid the shilling for the two miles, with one fourpenny-bit, two threepenny-pieces, one penny, and two halfpence; cabby looked at the coins, and turning them over in his hand, said very insinuatingly, "Well, how long might you have been saving up for this little treat?" They can discover the weak points in any they choose to chaff; as, when an exquisite dandy had handed two ladies into a cab, and drawled out, "Dwivah, dwive these ladies to 44, Manchester Square,—just two miles,— and here's the shilling," cabby said, "All right; but, I say, mister, you ain't sent them oats round to our place yet, that we ordered;" which took him down most essentially. *Punch* gives some capital hits at, and illustrations of, the peculiarities of the cabmen.

The wealth of London is enormous, and the fortunes accumulated are in their extent bewildering; yet many of the wealthy men in London have risen from obscurity. A certain late Lord Mayor, when a boy, swept the office of which he became the head. There was a member of Parliament, and a man of wealth, who once cleaned the shoes of one of his constituents. As you walk along Cheapside, you see warehouses of vast extent, filled with the costliest productions; the owners of many of these places live in magnificent villas, yet some of them came penniless to London. It is stated that Lindsay, the well-known shipowner, was a wretched, half-starved boy in Liverpool. Johnson Fox, who became the member for Oldham, was a Norwich weaver-boy. The late chairman of the Oriental Steam Navigation Company was a poor Highland laddie. I have heard John Cassell, the publisher, say that he came to London with three halfpence in his pocket; and he died leaving a splendid business. I suppose, from the days of Whittington, such cases have been frequent.

In America we know that very many of our rich men rose from obscurity and poverty; but the opportunities and advantages for such a rise are a hundredfold greater here than in England. Princely fortunes are made by trifles in London, as well as in New York. Out of the profits of his Vegetable Pills,

Morrison purchased a splendid estate; Holloway, of the world-renowned Ointment, drove in one of the handsomest "turn-outs" you will meet in the Strand. I was once riding in the suburbs, when one of the prettiest country houses I ever saw was pointed out to me; the grounds were laid out, and the very rails of the iron fence were gilt. I was told that the proprietor was actually a dealer in "cats' meat." He bought up old, sick, or dead horses, and I assure you he made the most of them. I was informed that he cut up the flesh for "cats' meat;" that, besides the hair and hide and bones,—the uses of which we can all understand,—the nostrils and hoofs were used for gelatine, and the blood was employed in the manufacture of ketchup, to which it is supposed to impart a delicious flavour; the livers were burned, to be mixed with coffee. So we see a great deal can be made of a dead horse.

There, as here, fortunes are sometimes made by sharp practice. An intelligent lawyer once said that he did not believe there was such a thing as commercial morality at all—altogether a too sweeping assertion; but there is an enormous amount of unfair dealing, in adulteration and various other methods of dishonesty. The Bankruptcy Court has developed an immense amount of villainy. The number of those who live by rascality is very great, and astounding disclosures are made of the almost perfect system by which their roguery is accomplished. There are no limits to the tricks and deceptions of trade. In one shop there is a sale going on at an enormous sacrifice,—but the purchaser, not the seller, makes it; in another, new goods are sold as second-hand. This is a favourite and very successful trick with the pawnbrokers. But of the wines, the pictures, I can hardly trust myself to speak. The wine, when it is brought into England, and before it is taken to the wine-merchant's cellar and pays duty, is kept in the docks. It undergoes a wonderful transformation. In one case, some wine deposited as very superior sherry was found to have been transmogrified into very fine old port. In another case, some wine that had been in the dock a few years, in spite of leakage and what had been subtracted for samples, had in a most remarkable manner increased bulk. I saw an account of an action in which it came out that a man had contracted to turn a certain quantity of British wine into genuine sherry.

As to pictures, the mock-auction in which paintings—not by the old masters—are sold, is generally held in some leading thoroughfare. The auctioneer is well dressed, facetious, fluent, and well up in the slang of art; he can talk of the tone of this picture, and the colouring of the other, of the chiar-oscuro, etc. The verdant provincial steps in, and sees what he believes to be a genuine picture worth hundreds going for as many pounds; he bids, and immediately there is a furious competition. Around him are confederates, whom he imagines to be strangers like himself: they bid against him; he becomes excited, and finds himself the possessor of a copy worth but little.

It is the same with other auctions; where the stranger sees the bidders quarrel, and the auctioneer refuses to interfere, he thinks the sale must be genuine, and buys—his belief to the contrary—at a costly rate.

The deceptions in the horse-trade are still bolder and more ingenious. Very often a man does not know his own horse when he gets it into the dealer's hands. I have heard of cases in which a man has unknowingly bought back a horse, at a high figure, which he had previously disposed of as almost worthless. You read in the *Times* (and whenever a Londoner wants to know where to buy anything, he is sure to look in the advertising columns of the *Times*) that a horse, quiet to ride and drive, the property of a gentleman who has no further use for him, is to be parted with; you are referred to a certain livery stable; you see the animal, as strong and showy a beast as you can possibly desire; indeed, it is vamped and doctored in a wonderful manner; if slow, it is made to run fast, if lame, to walk; the horse strikes you as like Barry Cornwall's Gamana—

> " Strong, black, and of the desert breed,
> Full of fire and full of bone,
> All his line of fathers known;
> Fine his nose, his nostrils thin,
> But blown abroad by the pride within;

> His mane a stormy river flowing,
> And his eyes like embers glowing
> In the darkness of the night;
> And his pace as swift as light."

While you are admiring this creature of man's ingenuity, a groom in livery comes into the yard for some well-known nobleman, or public character anxious to secure this horse at any price; but the dealer has offered him to you, and he won't deviate from his word. You buy the animal, and, when you get him home, you find out your mistake. Sometimes the confederate is a commercial traveller: he happens to come into the yard just as you are examining the horse; he seems so respectable a man, and so fond of his horse, and so reluctant to part with it, that you are completely thrown off your guard.

The Londoner of a certain class, however, is never deprived of his self-esteem; he is a judge of everything; especially he prides himself on being a judge of wine, spirits, and porter. I give you a fact. Three gentlemen were dining together at the house of one of them, and after dinner a bottle of claret was produced. The connoisseurs turned up their noses, and declared it would not do. Their host was very sorry; apologized; said he would give them a bottle of a better sort: he stepped down into his cellar, and, without their knowledge, gave them a bottle of the same kind. "Ah!" said the connoisseurs, "that is beautiful; that has the real bouquet; that is the real thing!" So much for connoisseurship in wine. Every London tavern-keeper could tell scores of similar tales. A great judge of wine, a nobleman, had placed before him a bottle of champagne and a bottle of gooseberry wine. The noble lord was requested to judge which was the genuine article. He, after much consideration, gave the preference to the gooseberry wine. In England, at dinner time, when wine is served at table, the custom was for one gentleman to say to another, or to a lady, "Sir, (or madam,) may I have the pleasure of taking a glass of wine with you?" "With pleasure." The glasses are then filled, and, as they drink, they look at each other and bow. Theodore Hook was once observed, during a dinner at Hatfield House, nodding like a Chinese mandarin in a tea-shop. On being asked the reason, he said, " When no one asks me, I take sherry with the epergne, and bow to the flowers."

As I am speaking of drinking, I would here refer to the celebrated " whitebait,"—a sound very musical to Cockney ears. To the large taverns at Blackwall and Greenwich gourmands flock to eat " whitebait,"—a delicious little fish caught in the reach of the Thames, and directly netted out of the river into the frying-pan. They appear about the end of March, or early in April, and are taken every flood-tide till September. The fashion of eating them is sanctioned by the highest authority, from the Court of St. James in the west, to the Court of the Lord Mayor in the east. The Cabinet winds up the parliamentary session with an annual whitebait dinner, to which they go in an ordnance barge or government steamer. Whitebait are eaten with lemon and brown bread and butter. I believe that, after all, there is not much in them, but that gentlemen make a whitebait dinner an excuse for a run out of town, a little bit of holiday, and for drinking champagne and iced punch.

London is not a cheap place to live in; yet an economical man, I believe, may live as cheaply there as in any city in the world. He may read all the newspapers and magazines for a penny; he may pass the day in exhibitions and museums without spending a farthing; he may find a decent bedroom for five shillings a week, and may dine comfortably for a shilling. Mr. Wellesley Pole used to say it was impossible to live in England under £4,000 a year. Mr. Brummel told a lady of rank, who asked him how much she ought to allow her son for dress, that it might be done for £800 a year, with strict economy. Mr. Senior, in an article in the " Encyclopædia Metropolitana," stated that a carriage for a woman of fashion must be regarded as one of the necessaries of life; and every young swell must have his brougham, his man, and his own establishment. But a great deal is done on credit. " What a clever man my son is !" said an English gentleman, speaking of the well-known Tom Duncombe. " I allow him £300 a year, and he spends £3,000 !"

The tricks of the professional beggars are almost inconceivable.

They will simulate every disease under the sun. Sometimes they are thrown off their guard. A man was standing with a board in front of him, with the inscription, "I am blind," when a gentleman threw a shilling on the ground : the blind man instantly picked it up. The gentleman said, "Why, I thought you were blind." The fellow, after a moment's hesitation, looked at his board, and then said, "I'm blessed if they haven't made a mistake, and put a wrong board on me this morning! I'm deaf and dumb!" A man, being led by a dog, was accosted by a policeman : "You're not blind." "Vell, vot if I ain't?" "What are you going through the streets for with that dog?" "Vy, Lor' bless ye, I eddicate dogs for blind men."

I must say a word or two about the Lord Mayor, and the Lord Mayor's Show, which I saw during my recent visit, and which seemed to me more popular than ever, and about as silly. For the day, business is almost suspended. At an early hour the leading streets are closed to traffic; the shop-windows are filled with young people and their papas and mammas and older relatives. The streets are crowded with spectators all the way from the city to Westminster Hall, where the Lord Mayor is officially introduced to the judges, and invites them to dinner. I suppose a million of people come to see the Lord Mayor's Show, which returns by the Thames Embankment—a famous place for a crowd, and where generally, in spite of the police, there is a good deal of horse-play on such occasions, as it is there the riffraff of the metropolis love to meet. The Lord Mayor of London, for the time being, is the first man in the city; and by the city I mean the busy hive of industry devoted entirely to business, in which few people live, situated between what was known as Aldgate Pump, in the east, and Temple Bar, in the west. He has usually a hard life of it, as for the year of office he is chairman of almost everything that goes on in the city; even his Sundays he cannot call his own, as on that day he is generally expected to attend, in state, some city church on the occasion of a charity sermon. He has the Mansion House to live in, and has some twelve thousand pounds allowed him to spend, which he generally spends, and often a good deal more.

I have been informed that he gives a bond of £4,000 for the plate. He is much thought of in foreign parts—more than in London, where it is the fashion of the great city merchants to look down upon the corporation, and where the city is, as regards size and population, such a small section of the great metropolis itself; but to the eyes of foreigners, the Lord Mayor of London is a mighty personage indeed.

Earl Russell told Lord Albemarle that when, as a young man, the late Lord Romilly visited Paris, at a time when he was giving promise of making a figure at the English bar, some French friend said to him, "To what dignities may you not aspire? You may become Lord Chancellor; who knows? even," he added, "Lord Mayor of London!" Twice the Lord Mayor has paid the French metropolis a visit, and on each time great was the sensation he produced. On the first occasion,—that is, after the Exhibition of 1851, the *Journal des Debats* observed that his "physiognomy implied deference and respect." Another spoke of his appearance as indicating the possession of good and loyal sentiments. As the municipal procession made its way through the streets, the "gamins" in the crowd shouted, "*A bas l'aristocrat.*" There was one person, however, whom all conspired to honour, and that was the Lord Mayor's coachman, in his state livery, all gold and silver, silk and velvet. I suppose he is more ornamental than useful, as the grand grooms on each side of the six horses take care that they shall go right; but he is a sight, with his gold cap and grand bouquet of costly flowers, his silk stockings, and his shoes with silver buckles, his scarlet face,—for he is generally what is called a good liver, though his own liver may be ever so bad. "Who is he?" anxiously asked the French, as he passed along. The reply of one, who appeared to be—or pretended to be—better informed than the rest, was, that he was the Lord Mayor's chief *chasseur*, who attended his lordship on all his hunting expeditions! I can assure you the Lord Mayor of London finds very little time to go a-hunting, even if he had the inclination and the means. Many of the Lord Mayors are self-made men, and began the world quite low in the social scale. In all England, as everywhere else, "it is the hand of the diligent that maketh rich;" and the people who begin the world with half-a-crown in their pockets, and so make a fortune, are almost as plentiful in London as they are in America, or anywhere else, and deserve as much credit, if obtained honestly.

One day a lady who was seated next to the great Rothschild at a dinner party, kept tormenting him by asking what business she should put her son to, in order to make a fortune. "Madam," was the reply, "selling matches is a good business if you sell enough of them." And so it is. Only a year or two ago, there died in the city of London, a Jew who was worth a million at the time of his decease. He began with lucifer matches, thence he went on to pencils, and so on till he got into the wool trade, and died rich, as I have said. It is from such men as these that the ranks of the Lord Mayors of London are recruited.

There are many schools in and about London, belonging to the great city companies, under the patronage of the Lord Mayor and Aldermen, who visit them on the occasion of the distribution of prizes. I have been told that it is occasionally quite amusing, after the Lord Mayor and his friends have left, when the ceremony is over, to find the scholars—especially the girls—taking off the defects of their illustrious visitors, saying to one another, "'Ow is yer 'elth?" "Give us yer 'and." I am told that such is a fact often taking place, and will be, till the corporation of London is reformed, and Lord Mayors are elected by a wider mass of citizens, and not as now by a mere handful.

It is really comical the work the cockneys make with the letter *h*; not only the cockneys, but many in other parts of the province. I was once at a gentleman's house, surrounded with all that wealth could procure,—pictures, plate, an elegant residence,—and the gentleman said to me, "He met with an hawful hend; he was riding near the railway, and 'is 'orse threw 'im hover 'is 'ed, and the hengine run hover 'im, and mashed 'im to hattoms."

I was told that not long since a London alderman gave a

grand garden party at his beautiful seat in the picturesque village of Highgate, where Coleridge lived, and where Lady Burdett-Coutts now lives. The Alderman had a handsome daughter, who, when taken out to lunch by a West End swell, quite perplexed him by innocently asking him, "Do you think I get pretty?" She was thinking of "Highgate," and not of herself.

I heard of an omnibus conductor that was calling out,—

"'Ere ye are, 'ighgate, 'ighgate; hall for 'ighgate."

Some one said,—

"You've dropped something."

"Vot 'ave I dropped?"

"Only some H's."

"Oh! that's nothing; I'll pick 'em up ven I gets to *H*is-lington."

Two costers were looking at a railway time-table.

"Say, Jem," said one of them, "vot's P. M. mean?"

"Vy, penny a mile, to be sure."

"Vell, vot's A. M.?"

"'A'-penny a mile, to be sure!"

CHAPTER V.

JUSTICE AND INJUSTICE.—SCENES IN THE CRIMINAL COURTS OF LONDON.

The Old Bailey—A Complete Establishment—"Tried in Drawing-Room; hanged in Back Kitchen"—A Criminal Trial, a Sensation Drama—Waiting for the Verdict—Atmosphere of the Dock—Crime shown in the Face—The Ragged Youth and his Counsel—Police Courts—Ludicrous Scenes—Women's Quarrels—"The Love-lorn Widder"—Supporting Nine Children—The Irishman's Family at the Bar—Disagreeing Evidence—Children hired out to Beggars—The Magistrate and the Chimney Sweep—Drunkenness the Path to the Police Court—"Taking in" People—Bird Fanciers cheated—Painted Sparrows—Uncertainty of the Law—The Thief and his Cherries—Barnacles—Expense of the Civil Service—Government Leeches—The Mysterious Warning—Premium on Idleness—"How not to do it."

THE Old Bailey is one of the institutions of London, associated with greasy squalor, and crime of every description; a cold, bleak-looking prison, with an awful little iron door, three feet or so from the ground. The Central Criminal Court is "*par excellence*" the criminal court of the country. It is said that more innocent men are charged with crime, and more guilty men escape, at the Old Bailey, than at any other court in the kingdom. It is said that the Old Bailey barrister is loud of voice and insolent in manner. The Old Bailey is very compact. You can be detained there between the time of your committal and your trial; you can be tried there, sentenced there, and comfortably hanged and buried there. Since there are no more public executions, there is no occasion to go outside the four walls; as some one has said, "You are tried in the drawing-room, confined in the scullery, and hanged in the back kitchen."

A criminal trial is a fearfully interesting sight,—a real sensation drama; as the case draws to a close, it grows more exciting:

the charge to the jury; the waiting for the verdict; the sharp, anxious look the prisoner casts around him as they render the verdict; see the compressed lips and contracted brow, and listen to the great, deep sigh as he learns the worst! Then the sentence! The silence is awful,—broken, perhaps, by a woman's shriek; and all is over, as far as the spectator is concerned. It is said that the atmosphere of the dock invests the very countenance of one who may happen to be in it. A well-known counsel who was defending a singularly ill-favoured prisoner said to the jury, " Gentlemen, you must not allow yourselves to be carried away by any effect which the prisoner's appearance may have upon you. Remember he is in the dock; and I will undertake to say, that if my lord were to be taken from the bench and placed where the prisoner is now standing, you would find, even in his lordship's face, indications of crime which you would look for in vain in any other situation."

There is a curious tale of a youth whose ragged head was frequently to be seen in the dock of the Old Bailey. It turns upon the affection of the criminal for his pet counsel, and his utter dislike to be defended by any one else. The youth had appeared in the dock after having been at large only a short time, and immediately objected to the case being proceeded with, as he was not properly represented by counsel. The judge pointed out to him that that must not be allowed to delay the trial. The pupil of Fagin replied, "That won't do, my lord; my counsel is Mr. ——, (naming a well-known barrister), and I cannot be tried without him." The judge postponed the case till the next day, when the same little scene was enacted, and the young rogue maintained that he had paid for his counsel, and that he would be defended by *him*, and by no one else. At length, after several similar delays, the case was adjourned until the next session, when the barrister whom the "young gentleman" had paid for appeared, and succeeded in obtaining an acquittal.

In the many police-courts of London are to be witnessed some queer scenes, and some phases of humanity that can be seen nowhere else. Go to Bow Street, or Worship Street; and there, as has been said, sits an educated gentleman, receiving £1,200 per year, settling petty squabbles between quarrelsome women, as part of the duties of his office. The most ludicrous scenes take place during the testimony. Take the following as recorded. A woman appears as a complainant for an assault: the defendant is placed in the bar.

His Worship: "Well."

Woman: "Please, yer 'onor, this woman at the bar, if she can call herself such——"

"Now, no reflection on the defendant, if you please."

"Well, sir, ever since last Tuesday week, come last Christmas——"

"Never mind about Christmas; tell us what happened."

"Please, yer worship, she told Mr. Waters——"

"Don't bother us with what she said to Mr. Waters; tell us what she said to *you*."

"Well, sir, Mrs. Finch told me——"

"Never mind what Mrs. Finch told you."

"Please, yer worship, I'm a lone, 'lorn widder, without an 'usband to pertect my character, and I lives by working 'ard at the tub for the support of nine children, four living and five dead, and ever since that female," etc.

The magistrate was compelled to let her tell her story her own way.

Take another reported case. A forlorn-looking Irishman, accompanied by his wife and two children, is found begging, contrary to law. When brought before the magistrate, they are examined separately, the wife first, the others being out of the court.

"Now, my good woman, that's your husband, is it?"

"Yes, please yer 'onor; and a honest, hard-working——"

"Never mind that. When were you married to him?"

"When, yer 'onor? Well, about twelve years ago, and I——"

"Where did the marriage take place?"

"Did ye say where? Yes, sir, I think it was in Tipperary, and hard work it was——"

"What is your husband's name?"

"His name, yer 'onor? Macarty, yer 'onor."
"What was your name before you were married to him?"
"Cromartie, yer 'onor."
"Are these your only children in twelve years?"
"Well, yer 'onor, they are the only darlings left to us; or there would have been five, but for the three that were taken from us by the typhus; and a trouble it was to raise the money——"
"Call in the man."
"What's your name?"
"Kelly, yer 'onor."
"Oh, I thought it was Macarty."
"So it is, yer 'onor; I didn't know it was my other name ye were axing for."
"And so this woman is your wife, is she?"
"Yes, yer 'onor; and a hard-working——"
"Wait a bit. What was her name before you were married?"
"Well, yer 'onor, I hardly remember, for it was a long time ago."
"A long time ago?"
"Not exactly that; I meant about seven years ago, and it's a long time to remember a name that you have no further use for."
"Oh, then you've been married seven years?"
"About that; but if ye'll ax my wife——"
"Where were you married?"
"I'm not sure, yer 'onor; I've a bad memory; but if ye'll ax my wife—"
"Surely you remember *where* you were married?"
"Well, then, I think it was Dublin, to the best of my belief."
"Then if your wife said Cork——"
"Oh, certainly; yes, Cork it was."
"How many children have you?"
"There is the two darlings in court to-day, yer 'onor."
"Oh, but haven't you lost some children?"

The woman, who has remained in court, slyly holds up there fingers.

"Please yer 'onor, I did not think of the three that died with the measles."

"But how many have you had?"

The woman holds up five fingers; the man mistakes her meaning.

"Well, I never thought to mention the five we have in service."

"How many children do you make of it altogether?"

"Please yer 'onor, I'm no hand at calculations; but if ye'll ax—"

"I think I can help you. Two here to-day, three dead, five in service,—that makes ten,—ten children in seven years! Can you explain that?"

"Well, yer 'onor, I'm no scholar; but if ye'll ax my wife ——"

"Stand down; put the boy in the box."

"Now, boy, look at me; where's your father and mother?"

"Please sir, my father's in jail, and my mother sells oranges in the street."

And so it turns out that these children are rented at sixpence a day to these street beggars, and they are committed as rogues and vagabonds.

One can always see or hear something amusing in a police court. When I was in the city, the following dialogue took place between a sweep, who was as black as an African, and the presiding magistrate. Said the latter, "My good man, how often do you wash yourself?"

"Once a week, regular, whether I wants it or not."

"Well, you might wash yourself more often, I think."

"I cleans myself of a Sunday, sir."

The sweep was evidently a strict disciplinarian; there was no shrinking from the weekly tub, no namby-pamby thoughts that perhaps it might be as well to postpone the painful operation till a warmer day. No, the sweep was above all that. And you can see some heart-rending cases of brutality, especially to women. Drunkenness brings nine-tenths of the cases to the police-court. A few weeks ago, a clergyman of the Church of England was brought up and fined five shillings for drunkenness.

The next case was a physician, fined the same sum and costs for the same offence; and in another court that day, one, who called himself a gentleman, and refused to give his name, was committed for drunkenness. Ah! if I should go on, I could fill page after page with the records of the doings of drink.

Some people are easily taken in. In horse trades, all tricks seem to be lawful. It is just the same in London with the birds. The latest example of this kind of swindling was exposed lately in a London police-court. The swindler was charged with obtaining a watch from a pot-man, by palming off on him a painted sparrow for a piping bullfinch. When the next morning came, the imposition was detected. There was a further charge against the same person of obtaining a diamond ring, value £10, from a medical student, by pretending that a common starling was a rare American bird. Of course the prisoner was convicted; but doubtless he had taken many people in, in a similar manner.

The glorious uncertainty of the law was illustrated about the same time, in the case of a William Smith, charged with walking off from Covent Garden with a basket of cherries without the owner's consent. In mitigation, he pleaded that the porter ought to have stopped him sooner, and not to have allowed him to go so far. The vindication apparently satisfied the court, and he was discharged, when he said, "Vould yer lordship give me a few coppers, as I have only twopence-halfpenny in the world." Actually, the judge and jury and counsel took up a collection for his benefit. There is another tale told in which the case did not end quite so happily for the defendant, who had stolen a piece of bacon, and was asked how far he had carried it. "O, only a hundred yards or so, yer lordship," was the man's reply. "Ah, well," said the judge meditatively, "then I am afraid you have carried the joke a little too far. Three months' imprisonment."

It was Dickens who gave the name of Barnacle to the officials and employes in the public offices; and I believe that many are still making John Bull bleed pretty freely, by giving him as little work as they possibly can for their money. In

1857—58, the sum required for the civil service was £14,300,000. In 1877—78, the estimates were £23,400,000, being an increase of £9,000,000 during a period of what was termed reorganization and retrenchment. A little while ago, a new writer was appointed to work with the Barnacles in the custom-house. He says that when he took to his work in the way he was accustomed to do it in the city warehouses, every eye was turned upon him, with an expression of the deepest pity and amazement. Suddenly, a bit of paper fell upon his book; the writing on it ran thus,—"A nod's as good as a wink to a blind horse." The new hand says he went on with his work harder than ever. Then came another bit of paper,—"Why work so desperately hard? Nobody works hard here." Regardless of the advice, he kept on writing as if he were in a commercial warehouse in the city.

In a few minutes, an angry voice sounded in his ear: "For God's sake, man, don't look like that; you'll have the whole office against you, and you won't do yourself a bit of good."

"Indeed!" was the reply.

"Yes, it is a fact. Nobble's got to give you the next book when you've done, and he won't be ready for you before next Saturday."

Now the natural query of the new employe was, how he should kill the remaining time.

"Why," said the older Barnacle, "look about you, read the papers, do a bit, then stop and rest. If you don't all the fellows in the Barnacle office will be dead against you." It was there the man tells us, that he first learned his lesson in "how not to do it." He began to look about him, and to dawdle over his work. Somehow he discovered, as he confessed, that to look about him and to daily grumble, are the chief occupations of her Majesty's Barnacles.

CHAPTER VI.

LIFE AMONG COSTERMONGERS, BEGGARS, AND THIEVES—SCENE AT VICTORIA THEATRE.

The Costermongers—"Picking up Crusts"—Street Fellowship—Religion and Respectability—Kindness Appreciated—Children near Houndsditch—The Coster Boy—In Business for Himself—Chaffing a "Peeler"—Forgiveness a Rare Trait—The Coster Girl—Profound Ignorance—Forced to Cheat—"It's werry 'ard, isn't it, Sir?"—Shaming the Donkey—Costermonger's Education—Victoria Theatre—The Multitude of Boys and Girls—Excitements in the Gallery—"Pull 'up that 'ere Vinder Blind "—" Light up the Moon"—Reception of a Tragedy—Whitechapel and Butchers' Row—Scene of a Saturday Night—Penny Gaff or Theatre—Dirt, Smoke, and Vulgarity —" Ere's yer Pannyrammar "—" Legitimit Dramay "—Ratcliffe Highway —Ballad Singers—Street Scenes—Catching Sailors—The Sailor's " Futtergruff"—Beer Houses and Gin Shops—Beggars and Thieves—Inside a Thieves' Lodging House—The Countryman's Adventure.

COSTERMONGERS deserve a passing notice. They are a large and varied class, numbering some sixty thousand, seen nowhere else but in London or some of the larger towns of England. They pick up their living in the street, selling anything by which they may, as their saying is, "Pick up a crust."

Charles Knight, in his "London," says: "The costermonger was originally an apple-seller; a particular kind of apple, called a costard, gave them their name."

The working life of a coster is spent in the streets, and his leisure very much devoted to the beer-shop, the dancing-room, and the theatre; yet there are exceptions, some of them being very sober, orderly, God-fearing people. Home has few attractions to a man whose life is a street-life. They have their own beer-shops, theatres, and other places of amusement. They are rather exclusive, and like to be let alone. They are true to each other. If a coster falls ill, and gets into the hospital, he is visited by scores of his fellows.

Religion is rather a puzzle to the costermongers. They see people coming out of church, and, as they are mostly well-dressed, they somehow mix up being religious with being respectable, and have a queer sort of feeling about it. They will listen to the street preacher; but I think the most unimpressible of all with whom I have been brought into contact, on purely moral and religious subjects, are the London costermongers. They do not understand how it is possible that you can feel any interest in their spiritual welfare; but if you relieve the necessities of anyone in distress, you are at once popular.

Once near Houndsditch I saw some poor, pinched little creatures playing in the gutter. I said to one, "Do you want an orange?" The child looked up, half timid, half scared, and said nothing. I stepped up to the stand and took an orange, and offered it to the child; it was at once taken; and then they flocked around me, and I must have given twenty or thirty oranges away, when I saw a group of costers looking on. As I left the crowd, the men gave a hurrah, and said, "That's a gentleman;" whereas if I had offered them a tract, I might have had some chaffing. But the city missionaries, of whom I shall speak in another chapter, are doing great good among them.

The life of a coster-boy is a hard one from morning till night: at first hallooing for his father, then in business for himself with a barrow; next he looks out for a girl to keep house for him. Very many are not married to the women with whom they live, yet they are very jealous, and sometimes behave very badly to the girl. One fellow about sixteen said to Mr. Mayhew, "If I seed my gal a-talking to another chap, I'd fetch her sich a punch of the 'ed as 'ud precious soon settle that matter."

These boys are very keen; as an old coster said, "These young 'uns are as sharp as terriers, and learns the business in half no time. I know vun, hate years old, that'll chaff a peeler monstrous sewere."

As I said, they have strange ideas about religion. In the

"London Labour and London Poor" there are very many interesting details in reference to this class, and several conversations between Mr. Mayhew and the street-folk are reported. One of them said, " I 'ave heerd about Christianity; but if a cove vos to fetch me a lick of the 'ed, I'd give it to 'im again, vether he was a little vun or a big 'un." The idea of forgiving injuries and loving enemies seems to them absurd. One said, "I'd precious soon see a henemy of mine shot afore I'd forgive 'im." Said another, "I've heerd of this 'ere creation you speaks about. In coorse God Almighty made the world, but the bricklayers made the 'ouses ; that's *my* opinion. I heerd a little about the Saviour: they mean to say He vos a goodish sort of a man ; but if He says that a cove is to forgive a feller as 'its 'im, I should say that He knows nothing about it." Another said, "I know they says in the Lord's Prayer, 'Forgive us our trespasses as we forgive them ;' but no coster can't do it."

The coster-girl's life is very sad : her time, from her earliest years, is fully occupied in doing or getting something. "Education? vy, that von't earn a gal a living!" Mind, heart, soul, all absorbed in the struggle to live! One of the coster-girls said, in reply to some questions, "Father told me that God made the world, and the first man and woman ; but that must have been more than a hundred years ago. Father told us that the Saviour gin poor people a penny loaf and a bit of fish vonce ; which shows He was a werry kind gentleman. He made the ten commandments and the miracles." When questioned on the principle of forgiveness, she said, "I don't think I could forgive a henemy. I don't know vy, excep' I'm poor and never learned." Said another girl, "It seems to me vonderful that this 'ere vorld vos made in six days. I should have thought that London vould have took up double that time. If ve cheats, ve shan't go to 'even ; but it's werry 'ard on us, 'cos customers vants happles for less than they cost us, so ve're forced to shove in bad 'uns with the good 'uns ; and if we've to be shut out of 'even for that, it's werry 'ard, isn't it, sir?"

There are grades among the costermongers, some of them

more intelligent than this; sometimes they keep donkeys, and are occasionally very kind to them. Driving up Holborn Hill, one of these donkeys, in spite of all coaxing, refused to go farther; so the man took the animal out of the shafts, and began pulling the cart up the hill. Some one asked why he did that. "Oh, I'm trying to shame 'im into it." Some drive a barrow, and many carry their loads on their heads. They are a peculiar folk, and we mourn over the ignorance and immorality of this large class; but we shall be less surprised at it if we visit their places of amusement, or what may be called their "educational institutions."

Victoria Theatre is the great place of amusement for a costermonger. By a little management, we get a seat in the side or sixpenny gallery. On an attractive night, the rush to the threepenny gallery of the "Vic" (as it is called) is awful. We have a good view of them. It is the largest gallery in London; it will hold 1,500 to 2,000 persons. The majority of visitors are lads from twelve to fifteen years of age, and young girls are very plentiful. When the theatre is well packed, it is usual to see crowds of boys on each other's shoulders at the back of the gallery. As you look up the vast slanting mass of heads, each one appears on the move. The huge heap dotted with faces, spotted with white shirt sleeves, almost pains the eye; and when they clap their hands, the twinkling nearly blinds you. The men take off their coats, and the bonnets of the women are hung over the iron railing in front; and one of the amusements of the lads is to pitch orange peel and nutshells into them—a good aim being rewarded with shouts of laughter. When the orchestra begins, you cannot hear the music. It is laughable to see the puffed cheeks of the trumpeters, the quick sawing of the fiddlers, the rise and fall of the drum-sticks, and to hear no music. But we have not come for music or performance, but to see this wonderful audience,—to be seen nowhere else than in the galleries of the "Victoria." Hear them! "Bill, Holloa!" "What's hup?" "Where's Sal?" "Ha, ha, ha, Bob!" "Holloa!" Look! see that boy coming actually over the heads of the mass; he must roll over into the pit below! No, they catch him! See the confusion! There's a fight; every man rises from his seat; a dozen pair of arms fall to; and the whole gallery moves about like eels, with shouts, and screams of "Bravo!"

In the midst of all this uproar, the curtain rises, when there are cries of "Order;" "Silence;" "Down in front;" "Hats hoff." They fall into their places as merry as if nothing had happened. If the curtain is not high enough to suit them, they will sing out, "Pull hup that 'ere vinder-blind;" "Higher the blue;" "Light up the moon." To the orchestra, the minute the curtain is down, "Now, then, catgut-scrapers, give us a pennyworth of liveliness." The "Vic" gallery is not moved by sentiment; a hornpipe or a terrific combat is sure to be encored. A grand banquet on the stage is certain to call forth, "Here, give us a bit of that 'ere?" All affecting situations are interrupted with, "Blow that," or else the vociferous cry of "O-r-d-a-r-e." The heroine begging for her father's life is told to "Speak hup, hold gal!" But if the heroine should turn up her cuffs, and seize on one or two soldiers and shake them by the collar, the enthusiasm would know no bounds, and "Go it, my tulip," would resound from every throat. Comic songs and dances are popular; and during a highland fling, the stamping of feet, beating time, and the whistling drown the music. But the great hit of the evening is when a song is to be sung in which all can join in the chorus. While the solo is rendered, all is still. If any one should break in before the time, the cry is "O-r-d-a-a-r," and at the proper time the noise is almost deafening. Sometimes the singer on the stage will give the cue, "Now, then, gentlemen, the Hexeter 'all touch, if you please," beating time with his hand, to their uncontrollable delight, and there is sure to be an encore to that. Occasionally, a heavy tragedy is tolerated, and sometimes in parts listened to; but a terrific combat must be introduced in something of this style, with accompaniments.

Actor. "Ha! sayest thou?"
Audience. (*Get over on t'other side.*)
Actor. "Aye! by the mass."

Audience. (*Cut away, hold feller.*)
Actor. "Have at thee, then."
Audience. (*Go it, tights.*)
Actor. "Thy life or mine."
Audience. (*Play hup, fusic.*)
Actor. "Blood shall wipe out blood."

And at it they go, striking one another's swords: the more fire they strike out, the better. One, two, three; keeping time, advancing and retreating; one makes a blow at the other's feet, who, jumping a yard high, comes down with his hands on his knees, crying out, "No, ye don't," to the rapturous applause of the audience, after a sword exercise, reminding you of "Crummles" in "Nicholas Nickleby." One falls; the other, about to dispatch him, is prevented by some heroine; they separate with—

"We shall meet again, Sir Count."

Then, if the tragedy is very heavy, they will hear it, especially if the actor mouths and rants. This is a favourite style:

"Ha-ha-ha-ha, what have I—ha-ha—to do—ha-ha-ha—with—ha-ha—happiness?"

Sometimes they will join in a running accompaniment, and woe to the actor who shall lose his temper. The great object seems to be to make the tragedian laugh. Some poor luckless wight perhaps is cast for Richard III., and the performance commences something like this:

"Now is the winter of our discontent—"

("*Louder! Louder! 'old hup yer 'ed.*")

"Made glorious summer by this sun of York."

("*Hooray! Brayvo, old feller!*")

"And all the clouds that lowered above our house."

("*Meauw; Bow-wow; Hooray!*")

"In the deep bosom of the ocean buried."

("*Blow that 'ere; hoff, hoff, hooray! did yer go to the funeral?*") and so on, whenever this poor victim makes his appearance. Sometimes these actors are mere sticks. I heard of one who rendered the passage—

> "Instead of mounting barbed steeds,
> To fright the souls of fearful adversaries," etc.,

thus—

> " Instead of mounting *bare bedsteads*,
> To fright," etc.

Let us take a run down to Whitechapel, past St. Paul's, through Cheapside, strike up Cornhill, cross Gracechurch Street! Oh, how fascinating to me is a night ride or stroll in London streets! We cross the Minories, and we are in Butchers' Row,* Whitechapel. The gas glares from primitive tubes on a long vista of meat, meat, meat everywhere—legs, loins, shoulders, ribs, hearts, livers, kidneys—buy, buy, buy. Along the whole line are every description of butchers crying out "buy, buy." Women are here by scores, pretty, ugly, old, young—all chaffering, higgling, beating down, and joking. On the opposite side of the pavement are the interminable lines of trucks, barrows, baskets, boards on trestles laden with oysters, vegetables, fruit, combs, ballads, cakes, fried fish, artificial flowers, chairs, brooms, soap, candles, crockery-ware, iron-ware, cheese, walking-sticks, looking-glasses, frying-pans, Bibles, toys, firewood, and so on. Here's a woman fiercely beating down the price of carrots, while that newly-married artisan's wife, who has just begun life as a housekeeper, looks on bewildered and timid. Here's a blackguard boy, with a painted face, tumbling head over heels in the mud for a halfpenny. Oh, the noise of Butchers' Row, Whitechapel, especially on a Saturday night! Yelling, screeching, howling, swearing, fighting, laughing. It's a combination of commerce, fun, frolic, cheating, begging, thieving, devilry, short pipes, thick sticks, mouldy umbrellas, dirty faces, and ragged coats. Here are gin palaces in profusion. The company such as you see nowhere else, yet, as I said before, the sameness is sickening. In some of them it is hardly safe to venture without a policeman ; very few barmaids—men, strong, stout, fighting-men dispense the liquor.

Let us step into this penny gaff or theatre. We are now past Butchers' Row and out in High Street, Whitechapel. " Vun penny, if you please, unless you takes a stall, and them's tuppence." We take a stall ; the place is horribly dirty. A

* Part of this description I have borrowed from *Household Words*.

low stage at one end, and the body filled with the company. Oh, what a company! Some light their pipes at the foot-lights —for two-thirds are smoking. The curtain rises, a man and woman sing a comic duet; they quarrel, they fight, they make up again; but towards the close—ugh! it's too vile, let us come away. We leave just as a young lady, in a cotton velvet spencer, short white calico skirt, bare arms and neck, is received with screams of applause. "Here's your pannyrammer," says a man with a blackened face, at the door of a dirty den,—"honly a penny;" and we enter. We sit for a few minutes, but we can make neither head nor tail to the matter; but we are here to see the company, and it is the same as at the gaff.

Cross over the street—there's another. Hear the doorkeeper —that little stunted, pockmarked man, with small keen eyes,— "'Ere's the legitimit dramay; threepence for the stalls if you please." There's a fellow on the stage, evidently doing a heavy business. Hear him rant to the awe-struck audience

"May yon blew Evin a
Pour a down rew-ing a
Hon the tarator's 'ed."

That'll do. We come out, and before we turn down to Ratcliffe Highway, take another look at Whitechapel, shops, gaffs, thieves, and beggars.

Ratcliffe Highway lies contiguous to the port of London, and always has a strong offensive, sickening odour of fish fried in oil. As we pass down the street, you notice the shops, and the character of the wares: enormous boots, oil-skin caps, coats and trowsers, rough woollen shirts, compasses and charts, huge silver watches and glaring jewellery, fried fish, second-hand clothes. Everything has a nautical adaptation. The ballad-singers deal in nautical songs. See that poor, half-naked man, with an old tarpaulin on his head. Round him gather a crowd of men, women and children. He sings with more energy than harmony, and bawls more fact than poetry. Hear him.

"Come all good Keristians
And give attenshin

THE HANDSOME "FUTTERGRUFF."

> Unto these lines I will unfold
> With heartfelt feelinks
>   To you I'll menshin.
> I'm sure that it will make
> Your werry hearts'-blood run cold.
>
> The good ship Mariar, she
>   Sailed from the Humber
>   On the twenty-fourth of October,
>   Eighten hundred and forty-three.
> Her crew was seven men and a boy in number
> Which was all swallowed up by the raging sea."

Hartley Coleridge said, "There is certainly nothing so lugubrious as the cracked voice of a ballad-singer in a dull, ill-lighted back street, on a rainy night in November."

Up and down Ratcliffe Highway, the sailors of every country stroll. Negroes, Lascars, Britons, Italians, Yankees, Danes, men who worship a hundred gods and men who worship none. Now let us walk carefully, taking no notice of any remarks as we explore. Here is where poor Jack is "taken in and done for." Whatever Jack may be at sea, on shore he is often the weakest and simplest of men, and there is but little need to cover the hook with bait to catch him. When ashore, he seems to have but one idea, that is to spend as much money in as short a time as possible. A photographer in Plymouth told me that a shock-headed, jolly-looking, but by no means handsome sailor, came in one day,—"Here, shipmate, I want a futtergruff, as 'andsome as hever you can make it." The "futtergruff" was taken. "That me? That's too blessed hugly; I want it for my mother and sister, and I shan't send such a looking chap as that ere down, as me. Take another." Another and another was taken, but none was satisfactory, and by his wonderful efforts to look handsome, the pictures were anything but flattering. At last, looking at the pictures on the wall, he said, "Why don't you make as 'andsum one as that 'ere?" pointing out the most genteel among them all. "Come, shipmate, sell me vun of them;" and he actually bought and paid for one—frame and all, and went away happy to think he had got a "futtergruff" that would do him credit at home.

Every few yards we come to a beer-house, or gin-shop, doorways temptingly open; from the upper rooms come the tramp of feet and the sound of the violin. Attached to many of the houses is a crew of infamous women to tempt Jack in to treat them. His drink is drugged, and against their villainy he has no chance. It is said that many so-called respectable people have made fortunes there. Grog and dancing meet us at every turn. Women—wild-eyed, boisterous, cheeks red with rouge, flabby with intemperance, decked with ribbons of gayest hue, all coarse, insolent, unlovely—dancing in the beer-shop, drinking at the bar, all bent on victimizing the poor sailor.

Let us take a peep into this music hall. See how crowded it is with sailors and women seated with pots of porter before them; every tar, and some of the women, with pipes, listening to songs; and witnessing performances of a very questionable moral character, and not very artistic. Some of these places of amusement are of too low a character to be described, yet licensed by Act of Parliament. By-and-bye the grog will do its work. Then unruly tongues are loosed; there are quarrels and blows; heads broken; cries of "police!" victims for the hospital, station-house, or lunatic asylum; and perhaps some poor wretch, maddened by drink and shame, plunges into the muddy waters of the nearest neighbouring dock, seeking vainly the oblivion never found in the dancing, drinking-houses of Ratcliffe Highway.

I made some explorations among the beggars and thieves of London; sometimes with police officers, at other times with city missionaries in the thieves' district. You get more information in company with a missionary than with a policeman; for while the latter knows almost every thief in the city, the thief knows every policeman, whether in uniform or not, and they are generally reticent while in their presence.

Come with me, and I will show you where the lowest class live; come down this narrow street, as we advance, picking our way through kennels, stumbling over heaps of rubbish and oyster-shells. All the repulsive and hideous features of the place are disclosed before us. Every human being seems brutalized

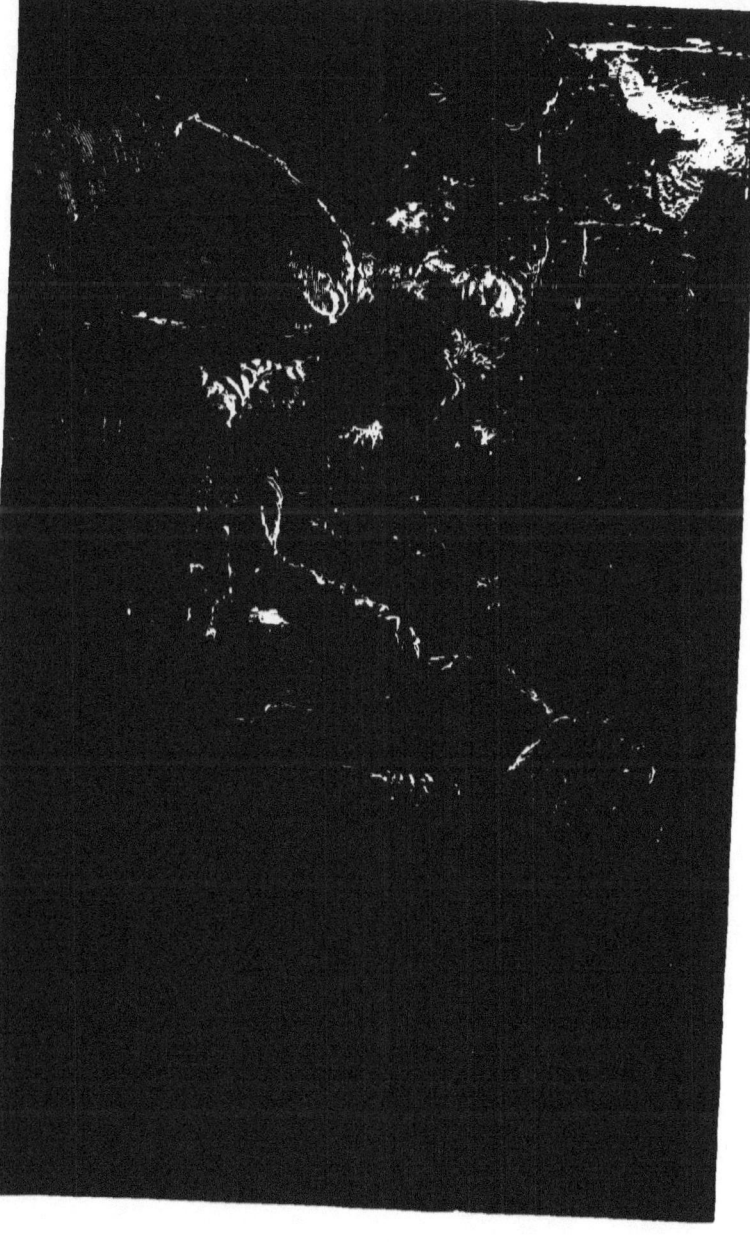

TRAINING SCHOOL FOR THIEVES.—INTERIOR OF A KEN OR LODGING HOUSE.

and degraded. We go down this dark and noisome alley; as the detective lifts the latch of the door, we enter a sort of kitchen, —this is a thieves' ken or lodging-house. On one side there is a long table, at which sit a number of men of sinister aspect. The principal light is afforded by a candle stuck against the wall. In one corner, with his head resting on a heap of coals, lies a boy as black as a chimney-sweeper,—that is the waiter. "Here's some company come to see you, lads! Here, you, stand up and take off your cap." You see the thief cowers before the representative of law, lawless as he is. Let the officer simply say, " My lad, I want you," he would probably turn to the others and say, " Good-bye, coves," and march off without another word. As we turn to leave them, we see by the expression of their faces that we are not wanted.

They have but very little mercy on their victims.

I was told that a countryman was leaning on the parapet of one of the bridges in London, when he was accosted by a thief.

" Nice river."

" Ees, I'se been looking at it awhile; wot lots of ships!"

" Lord love ye, them ain't ships, they are boats; vos you never in London before?"

" No, I never was."

" You'll have to look out sharp."

" Why, what for?"

" For the thieves; the pickpockets will get all your money."

" No, they won't. I aren't afeard of a pickpocket."

" Perhaps you ain't got no money."

" Oh, ees I have. I got a sovereign."

" Vere do you keep it?"

" Ah, that's telling."

" Oh, I know; you keep it in yer handkerchief back of yer neck."

" No, I don't."

" Then you keeps it in yer stocking."

" No, I don't. I don't mind telling where I do keep it; ha! ha! I've got it in my mouth, right agin my cheek, away back; and no thief will get that, I know."

"You're a deep one, you are. Good day."

In a short time, a boy runs up against the countryman, and drops a handful of coppers, with one or two pieces of silver,—"Oh, dear! oh, dear! my money,"—and commences to pick it up, assisted by the countryman and others, who gather as a crowd will gather at a moment's notice in London. Still, when all the pieces had been returned to the boy, he cried, "Oh, my money! my money!" Some one said, "Have you not got your money?" "Oh, no; I 'ad a sovereign! I 'ad a sovereign!"

Up steps the thief, who had come, mingling with the crowd. "You've lost a sovereign, 'ave ye?"

"Yes, sir. Oh, dear! oh, dear!"

"Vy, I see that chap there," pointing to the countryman, "pick up something, and put it in his mouth."

At this the countryman stands bewildered, till some one cries out, "Find out whether he's got it;" another catches him by the throat, and squeezing him till nearly choking, to save himself from strangulation he ejects the sovereign, which is given to the boy, with a great deal of sympathy. The poor countryman is hustled by the crowd, and may consider himself lucky if he escapes a ducking in the river.

CHAPTER VII.

HAUNTS OF CRIME—THE CITY MISSIONARIES OF LONDON AND
THEIR WORK.

London essentially Cosmopolitan—Byron's "Superb Menagerie"—Thackeray's "Vanity Fair"—Solitude in the Crowd—Munificent Charities—Cures for every Ill—The Aristocracy—Extremes of Character—The Middle Class—Homes of Virtue—"The Bray of Exeter Hall"—City Missionaries—Heroism in "Little Hell"—"Never rob a Parson"—Training-Schools for Thieves—"Practising at picking Pockets"—Perverse Judgments of Perverse Natures—At Enmity with the World—"The Gospel-Grinder"—Philosophy of a Boy-Thief—Selling "Hinguns"—A Rough-and-Ready Missionary—"No Genius in picking a Pocket"—"Fear makes Cowards of us"—Religion hurts the Business—A Publican spoiled—Real Courage—The Sermon of the Converted Sweep—Parable of the Ignorant Cabman—Rough Welcome to the Preacher.

LONDON and its people are an inexhaustible theme. The different opinions of different people about London would fill volumes. Dr. Johnson says: "I have often amused myself with thinking how different a place London is to different people. A politician thinks of it merely as the seat of government; a grazier, as a great mart for cattle; a man of pleasure, as an assemblage of taverns and theatres; a mercantile man, as a place where a prodigious amount of business is done upon 'Change; but the intellectual man is struck with it as comprehending the whole of human life in all its variety, the contemplation of which is inexhaustible." The same great authority declared that Fleet Street contained "the most sublime and picturesque combinations of objects within the periphery of our terraqueous ball." On another occasion the sage exclaims: "Sir, no man that is at all intellectual will leave London. No, sir. When he has exhausted London, he has exhausted life; for there is in London all that life can afford." "The literature of England, of Europe, of the world, at any place or any time," wrote the author of "Modern Babylon," "contains not a page, a volume, or a book so mighty in import, so magnificent in explanation, as the single word London." Byron called London "one superb menagerie;" Cobbett called it "a great wen;" Thackeray called it "Vanity Fair." Charles Lamb, Horace Smith, and other wits, could live nowhere but in London. As these men loved London for its society, so other men love it for its quiet. "A man of letters," writes the elder D'Israeli, "more intent on the acquisitions of literature than on the intrigues of politicians or the speculations of commerce, may find a deeper solitude in the populous metropolis than in the seclusion of the country." Gibbon in the same spirit tells us: "While coaches were rattling through Bond Street, I have passed many a solitary evening in my lodgings with my books. I withdrew without reluctance from the noisy and extensive scene, of crowds without company, and dissipation without pleasure."

The philanthropist may contemplate with delightful astonishment the amazing charities of London. All thoughtful foreign visitors are struck with the munificence and charities of London. What a noble array of charities for the sick body, the suddenly disabled by accident, the means of cure for blinded eyes, for deafened ears, for the cough of the consumptive, and the tearing fingers of cancer! In short there is a refuge in London for almost every bodily ill, where all that science, skill, and experience can do is freely given to the poorest. How these streams are kept in a perennial flow you see by the words carved high on all these noble institutions: "Supported by voluntary contribution."

I have dwelt long on the darker shades of London life, on some saddening parts of it. I have given you my experiences, the results of observation and investigation; described to you scenes I have looked on, and shown you pictures of a certain phase of life in the great metropolis; I have brought before you what are termed the "lower classes," between whom and the higher classes, the aristocracy and nobility, there is a "great gulf fixed," across which I have never attempted to pass, and should probably have been foiled if I had. I can tell you nothing of the habits, manners, or customs of that class, and will only say that among them there are some of the noblest and some of the meanest of mankind, the most liberal and the most conservative, the most sympathetic and the most heartless. We know this from their work, not by contact with them, except on occasions when their benevolence and desire to advance the interests of the people have brought us together for a brief space.

But between the two extremes of society we find most of the active benevolence, the saving influences; and it is delightful to know that in London, with all its crime and poverty and degradation, there are so many thousand rills of loving and holy effort to heal the moral sicknesses. We can only faintly picture the household fires gleaming warm and bright on groups where cultivated parents so train and guard the children as to see them walk the path of life with unspotted garments. Space would fail to record the pure pleasures, the lovely social gatherings; the quiet plans of employers to make those who serve them wise concerning the good, and simple concerning the evil; the scores of meetings every night pulsating with hearty effort to dry up the fountain of sin and suffering, and to get help from above in a work that, in the aggregate, is enough to appal the most courageous benevolence. I could tell you of Exeter Hall, now purchased by the Young Men's Christian Association, the name having been for years the synonym for benevolent and reformatory effort. This Exeter Hall influence on religion and reformatory progress was unwillingly avowed when, in a moment of vexation at its blocking his path in some degree, a great man called it, in his place before the people, "the bray of Exeter Hall." We will show you some of the modes of operation outside the direct teaching and influence of the churches.

The City Missionaries are indeed a self-denying class of men, living on a bare pittance, and often sharing their poor crust with the destitute. They are not "Stigginses," nor "Chadbands," nor "red-nosed shepherds." From my heart I pity those who can find no better representatives of these Christian workers.

Read the following, from the "Romance of the Streets," relating to a missionary: "During fifteen years he worked in one of the worst districts of the metropolis, in the rear of Lisson Grove. In one street, known by the name of 'Little Hell,' he attended eighty-five cases of typhus fever. As a common visitor among divers diseases, he has never personally suffered, but his children have more than once been prostrated by infection carried home. In this infamous rookery he walked safely at all hours among the haunts of the most vicious of our race, so completely were the respect and confidence of the inhabitants gained. There was not a ruffian in the entire length of the street who would not have defended the 'parson' by word and hand, had occasion arisen."

One may ask what possible good can a religious teacher do among this class. Frequently one of these missionaries seems to be qualified in a remarkable degree for this work. It is not by his soft speech nor his polished eloquence, but often in a blunt, rough-and-ready way; he will lose no chance of warning the younger ones of the evil of their ways. All these are wonderful men, going about their business in a cheerful, hopeful way, humming snatches of hymns. Sometimes the missionary will rescue a wife out of the cruel hands of her brutal husband, when policemen are loth to interfere. One of them told me that he had never lost anything but once, though he had worked amongst them sixteen years, and then a boy brought his handkerchief back to him the next day, apologising that it was a new boy that took it, "vot didn't know the missionary."

Rev. Charles Stovel said, in a speech at Exeter Hall: "Passing down Rosemary Lane, one night, a handkerchief was extracted from my pocket by a lad, who ran away with it. Soon afterwards, however, he returned, and said, 'Please, sir, is this yours?' 'Yes, it is,' I replied. 'Take it,' said he, and then added, 'Please, sir, give me something for bringing it back.' 'No, my boy,' I said, 'I must not do that; but I will leave a little book for you with my friend here.' The boy came the next day to the house of my friend, and said, 'Please, sir, was not that a minister?' 'Yes,' was the answer. 'Ah, well,' said the boy, 'I will never rob a parson, for God's sake.'"

It is pitiful to know that so many are trained as thieves. A city missionary has described how they are schooled. He says: "I found a room in my district in which children of both sexes were instructed on the doll. The image of a lady or a gentleman was dressed and suspended from the ceiling. A purse containing sixpence was placed in the pockets; a bell was hung on a spring in the inside of the figure; the youth who could extract the purse without ringing the bell, got the sixpence."

One man who pursued his mission among them said, that what renders their case almost hopeless is the fact that they have no faith in the sincerity, honesty, or goodness of human nature; they believe other people are no better than themselves, and will do a wrong thing when it suits their purpose as readily as they will. Only those who have tried the experiment can tell how difficult it is to make a thief believe you are disinterested and mean him well. They have an ingrained conviction that you are wrong—not they. You are wrong in appropriating the good things, leaving none for them, but such as they can steal. They are taught that the clergy are hypocrites, the magistrates tyrants, the policeman their natural foe, and all honest people their bitter enemies.

With the city missionary, you may obtain information from them. For although they call him the "Gospel-grinder," they are often quite free in their communications to him and before him. Once, exploring with a gentleman who had been very successful, he said, "These boys you see pitching pennies are thieves. I will call one of them, and ask him some questions. 'Jem!' 'Vell?' 'Come here.' 'All right.' 'I want you to give this gentleman some information.' 'All right ye are again, sir.' 'What makes boys thieves?' 'Vell, sir, because they von't let a boy get an 'onest living.' 'How's that?' 'Vell, I'll tell yer. Suppose my father, he says, "Jem, you go out and 'oller them inguns; you bring me back so much money or enough inguns to make your accounts square, or I'll vallop ye;" and boys don't like valloping, it 'urts. So I goes hout and 'ollers the inguns. I gets tired. I've been at it all day, and don't sell none. I sees a voman a-standing at her gate. I think she's fly, so I says, "Please, ma'am, do you vant to buy any inguns of a poor boy?" "How d'ye sell 'em?" she says. "Threepence ha'penny a bunch, ma'am." "I'll give ye threepence." "Couldn't let ye 'ave 'em for threepence." "Then I don't vont 'em." Now, vot vould a ha'penny be to her? Nothing; but it's a good deal to me; so I goes on a-'ollering. Another voman, she says, "'Ow do ye sell hinguns?" "Threepence ha'penny a bunch, ma'am." "I'll give ye threepence ha'penny, if you throw a couple of inguns in." Vell, I 'aven't sold any. I'm tired, and I thinks perhaps I'll make it up off somebody else; so I lets 'er 'ave 'em, and I'm ha'penny short; and so it goes on; everybody thinking I'm making a fortin selling inguns, and everybody beating on yer down. So I goes home short, and my father vallops me, and sends me to bed without nothing to eat, and ve precious soon finds out it's easier to prig than it is to get an 'onest living, ven everybody's beating on yer down.'"

One boy not twenty said to me, "There ain't no genius in picking a pocket; that's only sleight of 'and, anybody could do that. I'll tell ye vere the genius is. Ven you've got a gent's vipe out of his pocket, and he turns round and says, 'Somebody's picked my pocket,' and you look 'im right in the face and says, ''As there, sir? that's werry 'ard on you, sir,' that's cheek; that's genius." Another said, "The best lay we 'as is where they stick up, 'Beware of pickpockets!' Venever you see that advertisement, there you'll find the pickpockets;—in the post-office, round the bank, or the railway station. You see, sir, some cove 'as been to draw 'is dividends, or get money in the Corn Exchange. Arter he gets 'is money, he goes into the post-office or railway station, and ven he sees that 'ere advertisement, he says to hisself, 'Beware of pickpockets, so I must;' and then he puts 'is 'and vere 'is money is, and ve sees 'im, and finds out that he's got something, and vere he keeps it; and them 'ere two pints gained, the result is werry hobvious."

To return from the digression. We ask what good can be accomplished by Christian workers? One point to gain is to make them dissatisfied with present circumstances. Then you create a desire for something better. A youthful thief said of the mission work: "This 'ere has done me a deal of harm. I'll tell you why. Me and some of my pals here get our living how we can; cause why? we've got no characters, and nobody won't employ us. Ve can't starve, don't you know, and vot's a cove to do? Well, they're always preaching about God seeing you, and the like of that. It makes a cove afeard,—it takes all the pluck out of *me*, I know. I never thieve now, unless I'm forced to do it from hunger. If I go arter a handkerchief, when the pinch comes, I begin to think about God Almighty; for as they say, you know, fear makes cowards of us."

There are missionaries who visit the public-houses; read a description of one. A writer says: "Instead of a shabby-genteel, white-neckerchiefed creature of the preacher type, as I expected to find, he was a thick-set, determined-looking being, who, with the Bible in one pocket and a bundle of tracts in the other, went forth to work among the dens in a very matter-of-fact fashion." He is prepared for opposition, and argument or objection; but he is imperturbably good-tempered, and possesses an amazing amount of courage and tact, often receiving a rebuff, and then again a word in reply revealing a degree of interest, and some conscience. A poor drunkard, a young man, haggard, squalid, and ragged, received a tract, when the missionary laid his hand on his shoulder, and said in a whisper, "We must all give an account of ourselves to God." "A pretty account mine will be," was the answer, and so the way was open for a talk. A missionary offered a tract to a young medical student, as he was chatting with some of his friends. He took it, and when he discovered what it was, he said, "Please take it back; I have just passed my examination, and I am out for a spree. I am not in a fit state to have it; I am afraid I shall turn it into ridicule."

Sometimes the good influence extends to the landlords. Some roughs were evidently in a bad humour; something had ruffled them. "He won't serve you now, if you're only a bit tight; and if you let slip a word, he says, 'Now, then, that won't do in this house.'" "Well, he wasn't always so," said another; "he used to be as good a chap as any, and could swear a bit. I've heard him." "Ah," said a third, "he's not fit to be a publican now. What made him do so, do you know?" "Know! yes, to be sure I do. Why, them missionary fellows walk bang into the beer-shops now; and one's been in there, taking his religion and his tracts with him, and he's so worked on the landlord's mind that he's quite turned it, and now he treats his customers in this way."

Sometimes the surprise of onlookers at these operations is singularly expressed. One said, "My stars! a public-house is a rum crib for spouting in. Forty years I have been in and out of these cribs, and never heard a spouter before. What next, I wonder, after this?" One of the London newspapers remarks: "When we first heard of missionaries visiting public-houses, it struck us forcibly as casting pearls before swine, and exposing men to unnecessary insult and certain failure, but we were soon convinced to the contrary. In these dens of iniquity the agents seek out the very refuse,—the dregs of humanity,—and with the good old Book in hand, carry to them the news of a divine hope, even for the vilest of mankind. It may seem almost beyond belief, but such is the tact, the courage, and efficiency of the agents employed in this particular work, that when they become known to the habitual frequenters of any house, insult or attempted injury would be instantly hooted down by the company; and, more strange still, the publicans themselves often welcome the Society's agents to their doors, and do all that lies in their power to obtain a quiet hearing for them. He is a bold, good man, who, in the excitement of battle, with the eyes of the world upon him, and with the hope of the Victoria Cross before him, rushes into the ranks of the enemy to rescue a comrade from death; but he is a bolder and nobler man who, without excitement, and with no human rewards provided for him, can appear amid the reeking orgies of a low London tap-room, and speak, not only of wasted health, scattered wages, and deserted homes, but of souls lost, and to be redeemed by the most costly offering that Bounty could bestow for their salvation."

In some of the localities inhabited by costermongers and the very poor, the missionaries'. work has been productive of great good. It is really delightful to visit the renovated homes of some of these people. Here in a poor apartment, with but very little comfort, we find a man unable to earn a living, sorely afflicted, and a cripple, with his Bible, and cheerful in the prospect of a better inheritance. A woman who, after paying her rent, has two shillings left for the week, and a little bread and tea twice a day being her customary fare, says she is "thankful for that." From the often despised city missionary she has received something better than earth's riches or prosperity. Here in another room we find a costermonger and his family practising cleanliness and sobriety; and he is only a type of many others brought under the influence of the Gospel by the missionary, which has produced in him self-respect, so that he is striving after an honest independence, and often under difficulties. One of the costers said, "Can't be religious nohow; can't let the barrer be lazy on Sundays." But when they accept the Gospel you hear them exclaim, "Don't work on Sundays now, sir. A good day for trade I know, sir; but I likes to trade with heaven on Sundays, and learn a little about my soul there." One will say, "I ain't a eddicated person, but I knows wot's wot, and I know God never meant the likes of us to be religious. Vy, don't yer see it couldn't be done!" Yet when such are reclaimed, their Christian profession becomes very sincere, and their life a zealous service. "I allus felt ashamed of myself," confessed a converted sweep, "when I seed the people comin' out of church, and I'd been a cussin' and swearin'. Now, mates, you want to get to Heaven. I'll tell you how to get there. Trust in Jesus Christ; He'll never forsake yer. I, a poor sweep, am glad to wash my face when my day's work is done; but how much better to have Christ to wash your black soul!" "How do yer know you're going to Heaven?" asked one of his old mates. "Well," said he, "how do you know whether you've got sugar in your tea?"

The missionary must understand the method of approaching those he would help, and adapt his discourse to the condition of his hearers. Approaching a company of cabmen who were gathered round a public-house, one of them said, "Here's the parson, men, vot goes round to make people religious." The missionary said, "I want to tell you rather a queer tale about a young chap that thought he could be a cabman before he knew about the city," and then he quite humorously described the poor fellow's perplexity when he tried to find the Great Western Railway, and hunted for it down Shoreditch, and then at the Bank, and then at Whitechapel Church, and so on.

The men were very much delighted with the graphic description of the young man's blunders, and unanimously voted him a fool for driving round, when he only had to ask, and almost anybody would have set him right. When he had got them to this point, he cried out, "Now you're all driving wrong, and you should be civil to any one who knows the road, and would set you right. Here is God's road-book," opening the Bible. "Let me tell you how sinners may drive straight to Heaven." This was within the compass of their intellect, and they thanked him, and voted him to be a good sort of a fellow. One of these self-denying and useful men relates that on one occasion, when he called at a house where a large number of rough men were gathered, one cried out, "I say, mates, here's the gemman vot talks to poor people about summut better;" then to one who was six feet tall, he said, "Now, Buster, my hinfant, I vants you to 'ear the old buffer, 'cos you knows a thing or two; it's regular stunning, and vot's more, it's sometimes cutting. Come, mister, give these 'ere gents a stave; let's 'ear summut about that young rascal vot bolted away from his poor old father; that is a regular good thing, that is. Buster, my hinfant, come hand over the cushion; and, mister, you don't object to our taking a smoke;" and the missionary read the Parable of the Prodigal Son, with comments; and after half an hour he asked if they were tired, and all cried out, "Go on! go on!"

CHAPTER VIII.

WAR WITH VICE—TEMPERANCE WORK AMONG THE DESTITUTE AND DEPRAVED.

Street-Preachers—Fitness for their Work—A Striking Scene—"Music with no Melody, Laughter with no Mirth"—"Murder, Murder, Police!!"—The Street-Preacher and his Audience—Plain Preaching and its Power—"Reformatory and Refuge Union"—Thirty-four Benevolent Institutions under One Control—Good Work of a Brewer's Son—Lambeth Baths—Hoxton Hall—A Converted Building—William Noble's Mission—The Blue-Ribbon Army—An Audience of Reformed Men—London *Times* on Gough in Hoxton Hall—Report of the *Record* on the same Meeting—Four Great Branches of the Temperance Work—United Kingdom Alliance—Temperance in Politics—"Medical Temperance Society"—"London Temperance Hospital"—Eight Thousand Patients in Six Years—Medicine without Alcohol—Results.

WHILE the missionaries' work is exceedingly interesting and fascinating, I pass on to speak of the street preachers, for the missionary proper does not preach so much as visit and make personal appeals. The street preacher may not be suited to a fastidious audience. He may understand no rules of rhetoric, but he talks from his experience, and uses language easily comprehended by the audiences that listen to him.

A discourse should always be adapted to the character of the hearers, and no one can listen to one of these street preachers, at the "Seven Dials," or "Golden Lane," or "Ratcliffe Highway," and note the earnest attention of the ragged audience, without feeling that the speaker understands his audience, and that they understand him. What if they do mispronounce their words? What if they do drop their "h's" when they are needed, and take them up when not wanted? What if they do sometimes construct a sentence contrary to the rules of syntax?

Their influence is none the less powerful on those who listen to them. I think I never saw a more striking effect produced on an audience than I witnessed once in the streets. I stood with a detective and two gentlemen at the junction of three streets, listening to the din and confusion of that very bad neighbourhood. The detective had said, "Now, gentlemen, you stand here by me: do not answer any question that may be put to you, nor make any reply to any remark, but stand by me. Take care of your valuables, and listen." The raw night breeze brought to our ears the wailing cry of neglected children, the hoarse voice of blasphemy and cursing, the shuffling of feet, music with no melody, laughter with no mirth; when suddenly we heard a cry of "Murder, murder, police!" and a half naked woman dashed past us, her hair dishevelled, her face streaming with blood. "Stand still," said the detective, "this is an occurrence of every half hour. It is a fearful place this. I have brought missionaries from Africa here, and they tell me there is no heathenism in Africa equal to this in Christian London."

Soon we heard a clear, distinct voice, all out of place in the din, and the detective said, "Follow me, and I will show you something worth looking at." We went down the dim street, and soon came up to a group, evidently composed of some of the worst class of thieves and beggars, surrounding a plain-looking man in a fustian jacket, who stood with his back against a lamp-post; at his feet sat seven bleared, bloated, gin-soaked women on the curbstone. While we stood there he preached. Holding a pocket Testament in his hand, he said, " I've come down here to bring yer good news. It may seem strange that I should come to a place like this 'ere, to tell you good news, but the book what I hold in my hand says it's glad tidings of great joy: which is to all people, and that means us."

Then he went on to tell of one that was "King in Heaven, who had all that heart could wish; the very angels bowed down afore Him, and covered their faces when they spoke to Him: and He looked down on this 'ere world, and He heard the people a-crying, and He seen 'em suffering, and He came down to help 'em; but they wouldn't have nothing to do with Him. They

A STREET PREACHER AND HIS AUDIENCE.

slapped Him in the face, they spit on Him, and then hung Him up between two thieves." Then he said, "Why, my friends, He might have sent for twelve regiments of His Father's soldiers, and swept His enemies off the face of the earth, but He didn't. Oh no, He suffered for just such poor creatures as you and me. Now I want to tell ye more about Him. He never turned His back on a beggar; nobody ever came to Him, that He told 'em to go away. There ain't a thief that He wouldn't welcome, if he'd coom to Him. There ain't one of these poor women with her face blackened by the last night's fight, but His heart is full of sympathy for just such as she is. Why, my friends, they brought a woman to Him, what had been doing wrong, and they were going to stone her to death according to their law. What did He say to her? Why, He didn't say nothing till everybody was gone, 'cos He didn't want to shame the poor creature. And when they was all gone, He spoke to her just as He would to His own mother; 'Woman, where's them what's accusing of yer?' And she said, 'There ain't none.' And He said, 'No more don't I, my poor child. You go away, and don't do so any more.' That's what He said to her." One woman lifted up her hands, and said, "Oh, my God!" another swayed herself to and fro; another covered her face with her apron; one man dashed his hand across his eyes—it was too much for him. That was a sermon, powerful in its application to the class who heard it. Many of these street preachers are mechanics and working-men, who have been saved themselves, and now, in the true spirit of the Gospel, are striving to save others.

Space will not permit me to enumerate all the benevolent institutions that are relieving so much distress. I give you some statistics of one association, published some time since. This is the "Reformatory and Refuge Union." There were thirty-four institutions connected with and controlled by it, such as refuges for destitute boys and girls, for criminals, for the neglected, for the homeless, for vagrants, for young girls exposed to temptation and out of employment, for children of vicious or criminal parents, for deserted children, for poor servants out of employment, for destitute working-men, for those discharged from hospitals, for crippled and destitute girls, for women discharged from prison, for degraded outcast boys, for orphan street-boys, etc., etc. Then there are "Dr. Barnardo's East-End Juvenile Mission," "Home for Boys" at Stepney, and the "Girl's Home" at Ilford. The "Midnight Meeting Movement," "Friendless and Fallen Refuge," the "Boy's Home," Deptford, "Poor Cabman's Society," "Dock-Labourers' Mission," "Destitute Children's Dinners," "London Medical Mission," "Cow Cross Mission," "Sick Children's Dinners," "Sermon Lane Free Breakfasts," "Woman's Mission to Women," etc. In short, the benevolent and Christian enterprises are amazing in their extent.

Then there is Charrington's Mission. Mr. Charrington was the son of a brewer, and gave up a fortune for conscience' sake, and now supports a nightly meeting, and is doing a great work. Then the Central Hall meetings every evening, to provide for the people rational amusement and instruction without the appendage of drink, under the direction of Mr. Ling. Then the meetings at the "Edinburgh Castle," once a very immoral music-hall, now, under the superintendence of Dr. Barnardo, a place for Christian instruction. Then the Lambeth Baths, where the Rev. G. Murphy has the charge, and provides two thousand people, principally of the working classes, valuable instruction, both secular and religious, every evening from November till May (the rent of the Baths paid by Samuel Morley, Esq.) Then there are scores of temperance and other meetings constantly held in various parts of London, all of which it is impossible to describe, but intensely interesting to visit.

I must not pass over Hoxton Hall. On March 29th, 1878, Hoxton Music Hall—which had been a nuisance to the neighbourhood, and the ruin of many people, old and young, of both sexes—having become a music-hall of the lowest type, and lost its license through the abominations practised there, was hired by Mr. William Noble and a committee for three months, as an experiment. The object was to convert a place famous for its vileness into a place for instruction in righteousness, by holding continuous gospel temperance meetings. The plan was so eminently successful that it was deemed advisable to take the hall for a further period of twelve months.

At the expiration of that time those engaged in the good work must either purchase the hall or give up possession, when a friend who had taken great interest in the work came forward, and by his generosity the freehold was purchased and vested in five trustees, thus giving a permanent centre to the good work so successfully inaugurated. The hall is now being improved and repaired, soon to be opened and devoted to the same great purpose. Under the auspices of the "Blue Ribbon Army" (the name given to the temperance society grown out of the work) there have been held 1,335 meetings, with an aggregate attendance of 813,830 persons. This is an entirely unsectarian movement, and has been the means of rescuing thousands from the grasp of the destroyer, Strong Drink, and many who were apparently lost have been, by the influence of these gospel temperance efforts, brought to the saving knowledge of the truth.

I visited Hoxton Hall several times. Perhaps I can give a better idea of the work, if I venture to insert the following notice of my last visit there, from the London *Times* of October 6th, 1879 :—

"On Saturday Mr. Gough, the temperance lecturer, addressed an audience at the Hoxton Temperance Music Hall, Hoxton Street, composed mainly of 'reformed men and women.' The hall was thronged an hour before the time announced for the lecture. The audience was composed, with very few exceptions, of working-men and women, and when the Rev. J. Johnstone, in the prayer prefacing the address, begged for the Divine guidance of those who had fled from the temptations of drink, a fervid 'Amen' was murmured from many lips. Sacred songs, under the leadership of Mr. William Noble, the honorary director of the gospel temperance movement, were sung very heartily by the people, and Mr. Noble then asked all those who had signed the pledge in that hall to stand up. Nearly the whole of the audience rose, and he proceeded to say that among those were many reformed drunkards, as well as reformed men and women who had been moderate drinkers. He asked them to repeat their vow, and they, upstanding, solemnly said, 'I promise, by God's help, to abstain from all intoxicating liquors, and to discountenance their use in others. The Lord help me to keep this vow for Christ's sake. Amen.' Mr. Noble went on to say that Mr. Gough had given upwards of thirty addresses to the working classes of London without fee or reward, and in these the Hoxton people had largely shared.

"Mr. Gough had told the committee of the Blue Ribbon Army, that if they cared to take a large hall and make a charge for admission, his address should be in aid of the fund to carry on that mission, and if they had done so there would have been ten thousand people to hear him; but the committee had decided to have a meeting whereat the people who had been benefitted by Mr. Gough's labours could assemble to bid him farewell. Mr. James Rae, late of the Royal Artillery, Mr. Morgan, and Mr. Robert Rae, the secretary of the National Temperance League, then spoke, and acknowledged the services of Mr. Gough to the Temperance cause.

"On behalf of the mission, Mr. John Smith, a French polisher, presented Mr. Gough with an album containing portraits of those who had firmly enlisted themselves in the Blue Ribbon Army. When Mr. Gough stood forward to receive the gift, a poor woman pressed to the front and presented Mrs. Gough with a bouquet of autumnal flowers. Mr. Gough, who was received with repeated cheers, said he was unequal to the task of making a speech that night, for he was quite exhausted. Touching, however, upon the fact of finding devoted gentlemen acting as doorkeepers to that hall, he said he would rather be in that position himself than have all the profits of the largest Burton ale brewery for fifty years. He would rather have the lowest menial position in a work like that of the Blue Ribbon Army, than hold the highest position in a work coupled with any action which would do harm to a single soul. He proceeded to address his audience upon the pledge which they had repeated ; and after remarking that it was thirty-seven years since he had signed a similar pledge, he added that though he could not excuse drunkenness, yet it must be allowed that the circumstances under which drunkards were made were different. The appetite for drink, once obtained, never wholly forsook men. It would come to them with maddening force, and they must pray, not to be kept from drunkenness, but from the appetite for drink. Mr. Gough resumed his seat amid loud cheers ; and Mr. T. H. Ellis detailed the steps which were being taken to enlarge the hall, to carry on the mission week-days and Sundays."

I give a short extract from the *Record* relating to the same meeting :—

"We may state incidentally that the hall has now been opened for more than five hundred and eighty consecutive nights. The freehold of the building has been purchased, and shortly the place will undergo repairs, which are estimated to cost £1,000, of which money, the Hon. Sec. stated, the friends now stand in need. Indeed, Hoxton Hall fell into the hands of its present occupiers in a very dilapidated condition, and with the odour of its former *habitués* strong about it. It was once a so-called place of entertainment. Some years ago we remember to have seen in a newspaper an account of how it was opened as a 'family theatre,' and then it was stated that the proprietors intended to conduct it in a manner that should secure the support of the well-to-do working classes. Whether this intention was honestly adhered to or not we are unable to say; but when we next heard of the 'Hoxton Theatre of Varieties' it was as a music-hall of the lowest character. However, in spite of the drink, in spite of the gewgaw of the stage, and the obscenity of the 'comic' songs, and the profits which this combination is usually thought to bring, the place fell into difficulties, and in a happy moment it was secured for the gospel temperance work which Mr. Noble has since carried on.

"It was to this place that Mr. Gough repaired on Saturday night, and was received with a heartiness which showed that his intense sympathy with the struggling classes is not misplaced and is not unappreciated. Some of the proceedings were a little singular. For example, we do not remember ever to have heard a lady open a meeting with prayer, and yet this was the case here. Neither do we remember such hearty singing, or the impressive occurrence of a number of men rising in the body of the meeting and repeating the text of Scripture uppermost in their minds, —perhaps from the very fact that they were those which had brought the most comfort to their own souls. Some of these texts were suggestive. 'Hitherto hath the Lord helped me,' said one; 'God be merciful to me, a sinner,' said another; 'Do thyself no harm,' said a third; 'He that cometh to me I will in nowise cast out,' said a fourth; 'Bless the Lord, O my soul,' said a fifth; 'Keep thy heart with all diligence, for out of it are the issues of life,' said a sixth; and the whole of this exercise was closed with the Doxology."

I would state that on Sundays three meetings are held, one of them a Sunday-school; that women's meetings and Bible-classes are also held; so that there are many gatherings in the course of the week.

There are four great branches of the Temperance work to which I will barely allude before I close this section of my book: The National Temperance League, Samuel Bowly president, Robert Rae secretary; the United Kingdom Alliance, Sir Wilfred Lawson president, Thomas Barker secretary; the United Kingdom Band of Hope Union, Samuel Morley, Esq., president; and the Scottish Temperance League for Scotland, Hon. Wm. Collins (at present the Lord Provost of Glasgow) president, and Wm. Johnston secretary. All these are in full and active operation.

The United Kingdom Alliance, under the indefatigable

labours of its secretary and executive board, are constantly agitating the political question. The Band of Hope Union principally among the children, and the two Leagues for the promotion of total abstinence principles and prohibition of the liquor traffic. Then the Good Templars are rendering efficient service. The enterprises formed as auxiliaries to the great work are very numerous.

There is the "Medical Temperance Society;" and nearly every town and religious denomination in the kingdom has its efficient society. Then the "London Temperance Hospital" has been in operation about six years, and during that time about eight thousand patients have passed under treatment, eight hundred of whom have required continual nursing and clinical treatment. Alcohol has been excluded from all these eight thousand cases, with one exception, and in that one case the result was unfavourable. So that while intemperance abounds, there are earnest, self-denying, noble efforts to dry up this fearful ulcer, this moral pollution, which, if unhealed, must constantly and powerfully increase the corruption and hasten the decay of the nation.

As we rejoice in these efforts, and in so much of success as has crowned them, let us remember that other eyes than ours have been watching these efforts to save. Even the eye of Christian faith sees but dimly the "joy among the angels over one sinner that repenteth." But as we remember this, there come these blessed companion-words of Holy Writ: "He that converted the sinner from the error of his way shall save a soul from death and shall hide a multitude of sins;" and remembering also that "prevention is better than cure," we will thank God and take courage, believing that in His own good time He will crown every good work with His approval; and then, though we may have sown in tears, we shall reap in joy, and as we go home laden with sheaves we shall be welcomed as co-labourers with Him in preventing sin and saving men.

CHAPTER IX.

TRAGEDIES—THE SHADY SIDE OF LIFE.

Power of Kindness—The Scotch Minister and the "Brute"—"I'll kick you down-stairs"—"The most God-forsaken Wretch on Earth"—Perseverance rewarded—"Clothed and in his Right Mind"—The States Prison Convict—"The Cold, Glittering Eye"—The Hard Heart melted—The Mother's Influence—Scene in Gray's-Inn Lane—The Excited Crowd—The Tattered Group, and Death among them—The "Bullet-headed Man"—"'Ere's a Swell vants to know vat's the Matter"—Alone with the Mob—An Easy Escape—Men beyond Sympathy—The Toad in the Stone—The Murderer in the Portland Prison—Celebrating his Release by a Boose—Human Parasites—Tramps—Soup-Kitchens—Getting Something for Nothing—Able-bodied "Sponges on the Generous."

THERE are but few instances in which kindness has been fairly exercised where it has not subdued the enmity opposed to it. Its first effort will not probably succeed, any more than one shower of rain will reclaim the burning desert; but shed the dew of its holy influence repeatedly on the revengeful soul, and it may become beautiful with the flowers of tenderness. Let any person put the question to his soul whether under any circumstances he can deliberately resist continued kindness. Good is omnipotent in overcoming evil. I know there are hard cases,—men who will resist and resent every approach; but, from my experience and observation, I believe there are few so hardened but persevering, judicious kindness will touch some spot in the heart; for they are human.

A minister of the gospel—a parish minister in Scotland—told me that when he first went to Glasgow he determined that he would call on every individual in his parish,—every one. But there was one man of whom he was afraid. His friends said,

"Do not call on him; he may do you a mischief; it will do him no good; he is a brute." "Well," the minister said, "though I felt ashamed of my cowardice, yet day after day and week after week passed, and, while I visited every one else, I did not call on this man. One morning, feeling exceedingly well,—the sky was bright, the sun shining, the trees lovely in their foliage, just the morning when a man feels the warm blood healthily coursing through his veins,—I said, 'I will see that man to-day; I am in just the right trim for it.'" He went, up three or four pairs of stairs, knocking at the door. No answer. He knocked again,—no answer; yet again,—no answer. He opened the door and went in. As he saw the poor creature crouching by the empty fireplace, he became somewhat alarmed, and wished himself away. The man's hair was tangled, his clothing in rags, his person filthy, a four-weeks' beard on his face, his cheeks sunken and cadaverous. As he turned towards him, there was a wild glare in his fierce eyes that fairly made his flesh creep. The first words the poor wretch uttered were:

"Who are you?"

"I am the minister."

"Minister! What do you want?"

"I have called to see you."

The man rose upon his feet. "And then," said the minister, "I expected a struggle, and began to think where I should take him, for I was determined not to give him up." The man, coming closer, stretched out his hand and said:

"You've come to see me, have you? Then see me! Do you like the looks of me? I'm not much to see, am I? Come to see me!"

Then he came a step or two nearer, and the hot breath steamed into the minister's face as he said,

"Now I'll kick you down-stairs."

"Stop, stop! Don't kick me down the stairs now, for I have a call to make above, and if you kick me down now, I shall be obliged to come all the way up again, don't you see? Now, if it will be any gratification to you to kick the minister down-stairs, who has come to you out of pure kindness and good-will, let me go and make my visit, and then I will place myself at your disposal. That's fair!"

"Well, you are a rum one!" and he shuffled back to his seat.

The minister made his call, and upon returning, opened the door and said:

"Now, my man, here I am. I told you I would call again. If it will be any gratification to you to kick me down-stairs, I am at your disposal."

"Did you come to see me?"

"Yes, I did."

"Sit down;" and he began to talk with him, not as if he were a brute, but as a man and a brother. Soon the poor creature cried out, while the tears ran down his face, "Oh, sir, I am the most God-forsaken wretch on earth!" Then he told of a wife and children, of sorrow, sin, degradation, and despair. The minister poured the oil of sympathy into his broken heart. Many other interviews followed; and now, restored to wife, children, and society, he has been for some years a constant attendant on the ministrations of the man who by persevering kindness had touched the fountain of feeling in the heart so long hard. It pays to persevere.

In my own experience, I have found among those who seemed the most reckless and hardened some spot in the heart that was vulnerable, some chord that can be touched. Once while speaking to the convicts in one of the State prisons, a man sat before me with a face almost demoniac in its expression: it was a face that repelled and yet attracted me; it was what some one has called the "attraction of repulsion." As he fixed his eye on me, cold and steely, with the cynical curl of the lips and a sneer, he almost fascinated me, and I thought of Coleridge's lines in the "Ancient Mariner,"—

"He held him with his glittering eye."

My wonder was, Who can he be? Evidently a man of large brain, of more than average intelligence; and while he fascinated, he embarrassed me. The thoughts that flashed through my mind while I was speaking were, "I cannot move this man; my words fall on him like soft snow on a rock. I wish he would not look on me." I became almost confused, and saw a smile pass over his face,—a half-contemptuous smile,—as if he were conscious of the power he possessed. Seemingly, by concentrating all his powers of will, he had almost gained control of me. I turned from him with an effort, and said, "There may be some before me who think they are hardened, are past feeling; God only knows whether they are or not; but often we cultivate that hardness, when the world turns against us. There may be some here who had a good mother; and even here, when alone in your cell, in the silence of the night, you remember that mother, and the little prayer she taught you as you knelt at her side, and her gentle, loving hand rested on your head. You almost hear the words whispered in your ear; and no human eye seeing you, the tears come, and you are melted into tenderness; but in the morning you harden yourself again into recklessness." I said something like this, steadily keeping my face turned from the man, when I was interrupted by so bitter a cry,—"Oh, my God!"—that I turned, and the man, who had risen to utter the exclamation, had sunk in his seat and was audibly sobbing. I was told by one of the officers of the prison that he was one of the hardest cases, the most repelling, the most oblivious to kindness of any man that had ever come under his supervision. The remembrance of a mother whose heart he may have broken melted the strong man, and he became as a little child.

Sometimes, even among those whom society throws out as things unworthy of love or pity, a kind word may produce a wonderful effect: among those who prey on society, thieves or worse, an expression of sympathy, or an act of kindness, will touch the one vulnerable spot in their hearts, and the social tiger becomes human.

On one occasion, some years ago, I was strolling on a tour of observation up Holborn Hill,—this was before the splendid Holborn Viaduct was engineered,—and I turned into Gray's-Inn

ONE OF DEATH'S VICTIMS.—THE WIDOW AND THE FATHERLESS.

Lane. On the opposite side of the street, around the entrance to a court, in a very bad locality, I saw a group of tatterdemalions, men, women, and children, some fluttering in rags, the very refuse of the slums, evidently in a state of great excitement; something out of the common order had occurred.

As I was curious to know, for I often learn some lessons from the street folk, and get some ideas of strange phases of human nature in a crowd, I crossed over. Expecting to hear some foul language, somewhat in character with the appearance of the crowd I was approaching, I soon heard expressions like these : " Ah, God bless me, deary, deary me, poor thing ; well, well, ah well, poor thing." These were words of sympathy from human hearts for human sorrow. A man had fallen from a scaffold in a neighbouring street, and was being brought home dead ; and all this commotion was sympathy for the newly-made widow and her children. On the outskirts stood a very bad-looking man, with the closely cropped bullet-head, the bull-neck, the tiger-jaw, the small light-blue eye, a sinister-looking animal, one you would not care to meet alone in a dark street at night. He had a cat-skin cap, a belcher handkerchief tied loosely round his neck, and he evidently belonged to what are termed the criminal classes. I said to him :

"What's the matter here, sir?"

He turned his eye full on me for a moment, and then said to the crowd :

"Stand out of the vay, vill ye! 'ere's a swell vants to know vat's the matter."

I was not much of a swell, but I did want to know what the matter was.

A woman told me the facts of the case, and pointing to a miserable-looking faded creature, with three or four ragged children clinging to her skirts, said :

"That's the woman that's lost her husband."

I was startled by this time to find that the crowd had closed in upon me, and I must confess I was frightened; my knees grew weak, and I felt a dryness of my lips and throat from apprehension. Quickly it flashed through my mind—quicker than I can write it,—"Here I am in the midst of a crowd of the worst characters in London. I am shut out of all help; no policeman near should they see fit to assault me. I have a gold watch in my pocket, gold and silver in my purse. Some of these men and boys are thieves by profession; I do not like it. They might strike me a blow, drag me down this court, and no one would be the wiser. I should be missing," etc., etc. All this was very foolish, perhaps. The bullet-headed man was close to me, and I did not like that; my sensations were not agreeable.

Summoning up courage, I turned to this man, and pointing to the woman, I said:

"Is this woman very poor, sir?"

He replied savagely:

"Vat do you mean by that, hey? Poor? God Almighty help the woman! Look at her, vill ye?"

I did look: all the womanhood apparently crushed out of her. So I boldly pulled out my purse, as I said:

"Well, she looks as if she needed help; poor thing, I am willing to help her. I'll give her a half sovereign, if it will do her any good. Shall I give it to you, sir, or to some of these women, or shall I give it to the poor woman herself?"

"God bless you, sir," said one of the women; "give it to 'er, she needs it bad."

"Thank you, sir," said another.

One with a blackened eye said, holding up a child:

"Here's one of the children, sir." I turned to go away. A passage was opened for me; and though I am convinced there were men there who would have garrotted me for a shilling, or brained me with a life-preserver for half-a-crown, yet every man, as I passed out of the crowd, touched his rag of a cap, and said, "Thank ye, sir;" and even my friend with the belcher, and the cat-skin cap fitting close to his cropped head, looked more like a human being than an animal.

Yet I am compelled to the conviction that there are men and women thoroughly hardened—we might almost say, heartless. No kindness can move them, no sympathy touch them; who glory in their hardness, and seem proud that they are "past feeling."

The author of the "Mock Doctor" says: "Some men have hearts so thoroughly bad as to remind us of the phenomena often mentioned in natural history, namely, a mass of solid stone, only to be opened by force, and when divided, you discover a toad in the centre, lively, and with the reputation of being venomous." There are those that seem to become stolid, obtuse, or case-hardened by a continual course of recklessness, when the moral sense becomes stultified.

I give a fact as an illustration. A man in the Portland prison, England, was convicted of manslaughter (it should have been murder), and sentenced for five years. In a public-house brawl he had killed a man. He said he had no animosity against the man, and that if he had been sober he would never have hurt him; and yet this man, who knew that drink had made him a murderer, was so callous and degraded, that as his term of imprisonment drew to a close, he boasted that the gratification he promised himself after his release, was a drunken boose at the very tavern which had been the scene of the murder. Let us hope such cases are very rare. Yet we know there are men, and women too, who trade on the benevolence and generosity of the soft-hearted, in whose breasts there is no response to the kind word; in whom all appreciation of kindness is dead. Such become the parasites of the body politic in civilized communities; and every bit of benevolent effort towards them only hardens them, till they sink into the mean begging letter-writers, or the not less mean sponges on the generous.

Of this class are many of the tramps that have been like an incubus on the industrious and prudent. These persons are ever to be found at the soup-kitchens, free breakfasts, mingling with the deserving poor, and often obtaining the lion's share of the charity,—able-bodied men who will not work, whose sole business it is to get something for nothing; so that the system, sustained by the benevolent as a charity, tends to pauperize, rather than to stimulate to effort and industry.

I have more than once offered able-bodied men work, and they have given some frivolous excuse. I have induced some to work, and with the first result of honest labour in money, they have, on some pretext, left for the town, only to indulge in a heavy drink.

A year or two since, at a free breakfast given to four or five hundred of these men out of employment, Sir Alderman Carden offered to give work at three shillings per day to any really desirous of earning a living. A number of hands were held up, and some sixty or seventy finally resolved to accept the offer. Not one of them continued to work for a year, and most of them gave out long before the expiration of that time. The soup-kitchen, the casual ward, the chances of what they can pick up in the streets, are preferred by such men to honest labour.

A friend of mine met one of these loafing gentry begging.

"What do you want?"

"A job, if you please."

"Well, what will you come and work in my garden for?"

"Half-a-crown a day."

"Well, you come to-morrow, and I will give you three shillings."

The man went away apparently delighted at the thought of earning three shillings a day; but he never came near the place again. One of the surest ways to get rid of such leeches is to set them to work. Real helpless, deserving poverty often hides its rags, and shudders at publicity; but the idle "ne'er do well," without a blush go straight to the poor-box or the soup-kitchen.

CHAPTER X.

AMONG THE POOR—THE TRAFFIC IN DRINK—SOCIETY'S CURSE.

Sunday-Morning Breakfasts for Waifs—Homeless Multitudes—A Strange Audience—Economizing for a Drink—The Man who Loved Beer—His Heroic Self-Defence—A Pint every Two Hours—"Breakfast for Nothing"—Thirty Years Lost—Drink, the Cause and Curse of Poverty—Soup-Kitchen in Glasgow—Free Sunday-Morning Breakfasts in Edinburgh—Seventeen Hundred Victims of Drink—"We get Hot Victuals at Home"—"Ducks and Green Peas"—"Good Times" turned to "Hard Times"—Extravagance of the Poor—Satire of *Punch*—The Irish Famine—Distilleries at Work—"Irish Distress, Irish Drinking"—Burton-on-Trent—Bass's Beer-Mills—Bass's Annual Beer Profits £450,000—The Drink Bill—London Paper upon Mr. Bass, M.P.

IT has been the custom for years to provide a breakfast of bread and cocoa on Sunday mornings at the Field Lane Institution in London for the waifs who, sleeping in the casual wards of the workhouse, are literally without house or home; and the large room, capable of seating seven or eight hundred persons, is generally crowded. They are admitted about ten o'clock. A simple religious exercise lasting an hour is closed soon after twelve. Then a meal is served, sufficiently substantial to appease the pangs of hunger, but not appetizing enough to tempt those who are not absolutely in need of it.

The Field Lane Institution is truly a Christian work for the benefit of the poor, and has been extensively useful in educating thousands of children who would probably have grown up in ignorance, and perhaps crime. It has provided shelter and food for multitudes of homeless wanderers who seemed "ready to perish;" while boys in large numbers have been apprenticed to trades, and hundreds of girls have received suitable training for domestic service. Many illustrations can be given by the officers of the institution of the great good their agencies have been the means of accomplishing.

One Sunday morning I went by invitation to speak to the poor creatures who came in for the free breakfast. A lady who was present that morning wrote a letter in the evening to a friend, in which she says: "All day long I have seen the faces of that audience before me,—the hopeless, the careless, the weak in purpose, the improvident, those just plunged in the hungry gulf, some with the inherited stains, and all together such a mass!" It was a painful sight, and when I rose to address them I felt —as I always do before such an audience—a strange embarrassment. I felt for them a deep sympathy, and yet there were some to whom the scanty charity was not "a means of grace," who were the more hardened by the benevolence, and who simply endured the singing, praying, and speaking for an hour that they might get the cocoa and bread without spending the money they needed for the drink. At the close of my short speech a lady said to me, "There's a man who wishes to speak to you." I went to the corner of the room where he was seated, and I noticed that three or four men who sat near him had a strange look of expectancy, and the man had an assured look of confidence,—such a look as one might have on the eve of a victory; he had evidently sent for me to chaff me, and the other men were confident that their mate would let the "temperance bloke" down a few pegs.

The man began in quite an impudent style, "Did I understand you to say that you would take away the poor man's beer?" and without waiting for any reply, he continued, "Do you suppose I am going to give up my beer? No, sir, no! I couldn't think of such a thing,—oh, no, sir, couldn't possibly think of such a thing! ha, ha! No, sir! Give up my beer?" and with that voluble chaff tickling his mates, who wore a broad grin on their faces. "Let me see: I shall have work next week, and then I'll have a pint of beer every two hours,— a pint in all every two hours,—a half-pint every hour all next week! Would you take that away from me? Only think, a pint every two hours! I can get a pint for twopence : a half-pint is three halfpence; so I get more for the money by taking a pint every two hours;" and so he went on awhile.

I stood mute till he rested; then I said, "Do not suppose, my man, that I shall interfere with your beer-drinking; it is nothing to me, personally, what or how much you drink. Drink a quart every hour, if you can get it; but don't you think it is shockingly mean, and miserably contemptible, to brag about how much you will drink next week, and sneak in here to get a breakfast for nothing,—to boast of a pint every two hours for twopence a pint, while you hold in your hands the bread and cocoa provided by charity for the hungry and destitute? Had you not better save one or two of the two-pences to buy a breakfast for yourself next Sunday morning, than to sit with the deserving, honest recipient of this charity?"

The man's face was white, and as I turned to go away, one of the men said, "Well, Jem, you got it hot this time!"

The great difficulty in dispensing these charities is to keep out those that are undeserving, and who make capital of, and trade on, the benevolence of these institutions. At the close of the service, and after breakfast, a man wished to sign the pledge. As he took the pen, he said, "I wish I had done this Friday," as he had spent twelve shillings in drink on Saturday night, and had nothing left to pay for bed or breakfast. Another man came up and said he had heard me thirty years ago in New York, and he wished from the bottom of his heart he had taken the advice then. In all, thirty-nine names were registered on the pledge. This reveals the cause of the terrible degradation and suffering to be seen in our great cities, and the constant call for help.

Sir Wilfred Lawson said in Exeter Hall last year, "Pauperism, that great sore of the body politic! why, you all know that drink is almost the only cause. I do not wish to overstate the fact of pauperism in this country." The same may be said with truth in America. A late editor in Philadelphia said, "Close all the grog-shops in the United States, and all the poverty could be relieved by the present existing private charities, and in this republic there need not be an almshouse." In the winter of

1878—79 an immense soup-kitchen was established in Glasgow; the Lord Provost took charge of it. Thousands and thousands of people went through his hands, he giving them relief. He took the trouble of inquiring into the cases individually, and he found that there was not one teetotaller who came to ask for soup.

John Butters, Esq., in a letter to the Lord Bishop of Peterborough, says that "in Edinburgh there is an average attendance of twelve hundred every Sunday morning at the free breakfast, who are, with the exception of a mere fraction, victims of drink. On New Year's Eve there were assembled in the Drill-hall of Edinburgh seventeen hundred and fifty of these people, old and young : with fewer than fifty exceptions, they were all drunkards, or the suffering offspring of drunkards."

A little fellow was asked by a lady, "Why do you not come for cold victuals any more?" and replied, "Father's signed the pledge, and we get hot victuals at home."

I need not multiply evidence: the people know that drunkenness and consequent improvidence is the cause of seven-eighths of the poverty here and in Great Britain. I have it on good authority that during the "good times," as they were termed in England, three or four years ago, men who earned from five to six pounds per week had nothing by Thursday or Friday. One man bought a whole suit of expensive sealskin, and was found in the gutter drunk, and the sealskin soaked with the refuse of the streets.

Men who were earning large wages—five, six, or seven pounds a week—were, many of them, the first to apply for charity when the hard times came. They had lived extravagantly: as a lady said to me, they would have ducks and green peas before their employers thought they could afford them; they would drink champagne, and spend in treating on their pay-night two or three pounds. Some would keep dogs for the purpose of fighting, and many, even when receiving charity, retained the dog, and fed that while the children were suffering. The improvidence of a certain class of working-men is frightfully reckless. That satire in *Punch* had truth in it, in which a lady complains to the greengrocer that pineapples are too expensive for her. "Why, seven shillings for a pineapple? I must wait till they are cheaper." A miner came by in his rough clothes, and cried, "Give it to me; I'll give ye ten shillings for it, if ye'll tell me how to cook him."

There is, and has been for some time, great distress among the unemployed in England; and in Ireland it seems to have culminated in a famine, and calls are made for help, to which the people of this country have gradually responded. God forbid that I should say one word to check the flow of charity, or to depreciate the suffering that calls it forth; but will there be one gallon less whisky distilled for the scarcity of food? Will one fire of a distillery or brewery be extinguished? Not all the tears of starving thousands can stop that business. In the last famine, of 1848, it was stated that many million quarters of grain were destroyed in Ireland for whisky. When children were found dead with the sea-weed they had been sucking for nourishment between their teeth; when, as I was told in Brandon by the rector, they dreaded to go out at night for fear of stumbling over a dead body; when he fed at his gate three hundred of the poor creatures every day, and was compelled to sprinkle the stones on which they sat with chloride of lime, for fear of infection from the famine fever which was raging;—at that very time the smoke of the distilleries was darkening the air and intensifying the horror of the famine.

A nobleman has made some sensible suggestions that universal abstinence from whisky is a remedy for the Irish distress. Lord Longford says, "If all classes or individuals, without waiting for others, would spend on relieving the wants of their poorer neighbours, to their own credit, what they now spend on whisky, to their own destruction, it would be less necessary to make frantic appeals to the government, to the landlords, or to private charity. Temperance is its own government, its own landlords, its own Board of Works."

The *Irish Ecclesiastical Gazette* says: "Every one who lives in Ireland knows pretty well that the causes of its chronic distress really are (1) over-population, (2) over-drinking. In every town from which the cry of distress comes, the public-houses and their owners prosper." The present trouble arises, as we all know, from the failure of the crops for the past five years; yet the drinking habits of so many intensifies the evil. But that should not hinder our charities. I would feed a hungry man or woman, even though I knew their poverty was directly caused by drink. I only speak of the drink as one of the causes, and as an aggravation of the suffering we deplore and are ready to relieve. The *Gazette* concludes a long article with these words: "Those who discourage emigration, temperance, and honest industry, and foster in the Irish people the insane earth-hunger, the waste, the improvidence, the love of political excitement, rather than patient, plodding industry,—the sin, the misery, the nation's degradation, lie at their doors. They are the cause of the Irish distress." I merely quote these words for what they are worth.

I have before me an appeal to the Irish people, dated "Cork, Feb. 19th, 1880," entitled, "Irish Distress, Irish Drinking." After alluding to the dark cloud of poverty hanging over so many homes, the unfavourable harvest, the great loss in the entire failure of so much of the expected crop, it states that "drink is pauperizing the people to a far greater extent than the failure of the crops," and then asks the question, "Why talk of poverty, when £5,000 every week are spent in Cork alone in drink? It's all nonsense." These are not my words, but the words of a committee in Cork who have issued this appeal. In England there is great distress, but we do not hear so much of it: whether the English have greater powers of endurance, I know not. But spite of distress, the business of brewing and manufacturing strong drink is active and lucrative.

Burton-on-Trent is almost wholly given up to the manufacture of beer. The place is nothing more than a huge brewery, or nest of breweries. Beside the lesser ones, here are the beer-factories of Allsopp, Ind and Coope, Worthington, Nunnely, Robinson, representing millions of barrels of beer. Then there is Bass—his extensive beer-mills covering a hundred acres of land, and using two or three hundred quarters of malt every day, requiring the barley grown on sixty thousand acres of good English land, besides the hops grown on two thousand acres——yearly rolls into the groggeries of London and other great towns in England something like a million barrels of beer. He owns five miles of private railway in Burton, and pays £2,000 every week in wages. He is a Member of Parliament, and the profits of the firm in 1878 were £450,000.

In 1878, the people spent £160,000,000 for drink, half of which came out of the pockets of the poor. In one city, the amount sold across the counters of the public-houses was £20,000 per week; while at that very time £10,000 were raised to care for the poverty-stricken. Paupers who received out-door relief of half-a-crown per week, in several instances have been known to spend it all in one evening, and live by begging till the next day for their relief came round.

I quote from a London paper:—

"Of all the sickening announcements we ever read, the announcement that Mr. Bass, M.P., will find employment for men who have lost their work through bad trade is the most revolting. Mr. Bass is the most noted brewer, and that fact explains our revulsion. Trade is bad, but drink must be made; commerce is depressed, but beer is still demanded; profits have disappeared, but fuddling is well to the front! This is the horrible revelation which is made by Mr. Bass. It discourages us. It shows that, so far as our social economy is concerned, the last enemy that shall be destroyed is drink. The festive Chancellor of the Exchequer has been dining with the licensed victuallers at Exeter, and talking vinous nonsense to the beery horde. He has abused their traffic and patronized it in the same breath. He has told the victuallers how much better they are than their trade, and then that their trade must be watched and chained, and have a cordon of restrictions around its whole scope. Instead of damning it with the ardour of a patriot, he pets it and humours it like a receiver of taxes. He talks against revolutionary measures, and warns the country inferentially against the Permissive Bill, forgetting that a revolution is better than destruction, and that to be without drink is better than to be without character. The Licensed Victuallers' Benevolent Association! What cruel irony! What pitiless and bitter mockery to many hearts!"

CHAPTER XI.

LIFE AMONG THE LOWLY—HOMELESS HOMES—DARKNESS AND LIGHT.

Homes of the London Poor—Cellar Dwellings—Description of a Court in Gray's-Inn Lane—King Cholera—Horrible Filth—"Work in the Five Dials"—Dark Pictures of Life—Tour of Inspection with Hon. Maude Stanley—Visiting Low Localities—My Audience—A Motley Crowd—Coffee-Palace opened by Dean Stanley—The Bright Side—The Honest Girl in the Thieves' Court—The Newspaper-Vendor and the Pocket-Book—"A Real Case"—Artful Dodges—The Workman's Independence—"Principled agin taking Money"—Trust and Patience of the Poor—Life among the Lowly—The Crippled Saint—Blue Skies reflected from Muddy Pools—The Story of Thomas Wright—A Devoted Son—Examples of Nobility in Humble Life—Demands for Human Sympathy.

WE are often told that the excuse for drinking among the poor is their wretched homes, the want of air and ventilation. I grant it is almost an impossibility to give more than a faint idea of the homes of the London poor. Hundreds of people live under the surface of the streets, in rooms to which apertures not nine inches above the footpath, and not more than six or seven inches from the front of the building, afford the only means of light and ventilation. In addition to the want of light and air, these places are in most instances intolerably damp, and the back kitchen is generally used by the numerous tenants of the house for washing. In eight cases out of ten, the badly-formed drains allow gases to escape and quietly poison the inmates.

Some time ago, a Court in Gray's-Inn Lane was cleaned up and made meet for human habitation by Lord Shaftesbury's excellent Society for improving the condition of the working classes. Take the following literal description of what it was before it was reformed. The shutters and doors were broken;

from most of the windows projected a well-known drying apparatus for the day's wash; the pavement was irregular, retaining decomposing matter to contaminate the air; while the basement story of all the houses was filled with fetid refuse, of which it had been the receptacle for years. In some of the houses it seemed scarcely possible that human beings could live: the floors were in holes, the stairs broken down, the plastering had fallen; nevertheless they were densely populated, and as much rent paid for the rooms as ought to have obtained for the tenants decent accommodations. In one the roof had fallen in; it was driven in by a tipsy woman one night, who had sought to escape over the tiles from her husband. The foul effluvia in this court actually rendered it impossible for the workmen to proceed for some time after the surface had been broken up, and many of them were taken ill. It was in this court, which still bears his name, that Tyndal, "the true servant and martyr of God," as Fox called him, "translated the Bible; there, where Stowe wrote:

"And men and maids went Maying in the glad spring time."

In the London hospitals, from ten hundred to eleven hundred cubic feet of space are allowed to each person. In some of the houses of the poor, the cubic space afforded is less than a hundred and fifty feet per head. In the east of London, houses are several feet below the level of the Thames. Even the rich and refined pay a terrible penalty for the neglect of proper sanitary regulations. They speak correctly who make King Cholera sing:

> "What is my court? These cellars piled
>   With filth of many a year;
> These rooms with rotting damps defiled,
> These alleys where the sun ne'er smiled,
>   Darkling and drear.
> These streets along the river's bank,
>   Below the rise of tide;
> These hovels set in stifling rank,
> Sapped by the earth, damp, green, and dank;
>   These cesspools wide;

> These yards where heaps of dust and bone
>   Breathe poison all around;
> These styes where swinish tenants grown
>   Half human with their masters, own
>   A common ground."

The Hon. Maude Stanley published a book entitled "Work in the Five Dials," in which she says :

"Such is the scarcity of rooms, that once the working-man has got one, he gladly keeps it; and I have known women to be months and sometimes years trying to get into better quarters. In a house I knew well, for years the drinking water was drawn from an old beer-barrel without a lid, which stood between an unglazed window and an open door in the basement, and under a butcher's shop. Through the window, which was on a level with the street, every breath of wind would blow in the refuse, the germs of animal disease and animal life, so that in summer the water was alive with animalculæ visible to the naked eye. Can we wonder that the father should go to the public-house, preferring beer there to foul water at home?

"In another case, the death of a most excellent woman was caused by the condition of the water and the drains. Her husband had been in a wholesale business in the city, and she had lived in a good house of her own. Her husband lost everything by failure in the city, and died. Her sons were taken care of by friends, and her daughter served in a baker's shop. The mother had taken a poor little place, trying to earn a scanty living by selling a few groceries. Last summer she felt languid and ill from the bad odour outside the house, which came in through the open door. In vain she applied to the landlord. Nothing was done. At last she wrote to the Sanitary Inspector. The tank, which was under an oil and tallow chandler's shop, was emptied. At the bottom was found two inches of mud, the decomposing bodies of fourteen rats, a bar of soap, candles, and many dead beetles; and from this tank the poor woman had to get all the water she used. Soon the poor woman was taken to the hospital, where she died. Might not such hardships make them more drunken and immoral?"

I am well aware that to the poor denizens of these miserable tenements, the public-house, warm, well-lighted and cosy, offers a strong temptation; and I have the deepest sympathy with these poor unfortunates, whether brought to such straits by their own act or their parents' neglect. Still the fact stares us in the face, that you may search through London in its worst localities, street after street, court after court, alley after alley, and you will find but an almost infinitesimal portion of the inhabitants of these stifling dens are total abstainers from drink. Almost the first idea that takes hold of a man or woman when determined to be free from the drink, is to get out of the slums; the tendency at once in most cases is to cleanliness, and the struggle commences to get clear of their surroundings. I have seen, and so have all who have visited these localities, the poor attempts at comfort and personal cleanliness, with some little attempts at ornament, perhaps a poor flower in the window, or a cheap picture on the wall. I have spent many hours in company with city missionaries in visiting low localities.

The Hon. Maude Stanley sent me her book called "Work in the Five Dials," which led to an interview with her, and under her guidance I made a tour of observation in Princes' Row, Grafton Street, Porter Street, and several alleys and courts in the vicinity of Five and Seven Dials. She has done, and is doing, a noble work in efforts to ameliorate the condition of the people. I spoke to an audience of four hundred gathered together from the different streets in the neighbourhood; and after the address, a temperance society was formed. It was a motley crowd, an audience of great contrasts: there was the Right Honourable and the costermonger, the Countess and the unfortunate, the nobleman and the beggar, the refined and the degraded, the gentleman and the thief, the rich and the poor meeting together, and the Lord the maker of them all.

The temperance society is flourishing, and a few weeks ago I received a letter from Miss Stanley giving very gratifying accounts of the success, and the opening of a coffee-palace, called the Stanley Arms, by Dean Stanley and other gentlemen interested in the work. Wherever this work has been carried on, an evident improvement has been manifest in the habits of these people; many have become Christians, and the drink maniacs have been found clothed and in their right mind, sitting at the feet of Jesus. Notwithstanding the fact admitted by all total abstainers or otherwise that drunkenness is the chief cause of the misery of the poor, there are many—too many, for the credit of the Christian Church—of God's own saints hiding their sufferings and their privation, and bearing and enduring enough to appal the stoutest heart.

Why should we be ever hearing of one side, and that the worst, of the poor ones who perforce are compelled to dwell in the horrible surroundings of some of the slums? Just take the following well-authenticated fact.

One day, a little girl, living with her father in a court of ill-repute, picked up a pocket-book containing bank-notes of the value of forty-five pounds. The other contents of the packet included the address-card of the owner; and consequently a day or two after, a very poor-looking old man called at the gentleman's office, left his address, and requested Mr. —— to pay him a visit, if he had lost anything.

On receipt of this welcome news, the owner of the property hastened to the court designated—a place which was seemingly a rendezvous of thieves and loose women. The intruder found himself interrogated by an apparent descendant of "Bill Sikes," who in peremptory tones desired to know his business; but mentioning the name of the man wanted, he soon appeared on the scene, and the two made their way into one of the dens of an upper story, where a brief, whispered conversation ensued.

"Are you the gentleman I called on this morning?"

"Yes."

"Have you lost anything?"

"Yes; I have lost my pocket-book."

"What was in it?"

"Forty-five pounds."

"Oh, that's all right," the man went on. "Well, I've got it upstairs, under my bed. You go and walk up Holborn, and I'll follow you. Don't say nothing about it to nobody; they're all thieves. Be off as quick as you can, and don't look as if you thought I should follow you, but walk right away."

Obeying these injunctions to the letter, the gentleman was soon overtaken by the old man, who handed him his property from a bundle of rags. "There, there it is," he said. "My little girl found it, and brought it to me; and as I found your card in it, I came straight off to you about it. You'll find the money all right, and all the rest of the things just as she picked it up. But don't say nothing about it; 'cos if them fellows knowed I'd done this, they'd make the place too 'ot to 'old me. They are all thieves, and I was afraid that they might smell a rat if you stopped there."

When he received five pounds reward, and five shillings for his daughter, the old man was, if possible, as much dazzled at the liberality of "Verax," as the latter was surprised at so uncommon an example of honesty. As regards the finder of the book, no words can express her consternation at the sudden turning up of so grand a personage as the city merchant. She sobbed as though her heart would break, supposing she was about to be imprisoned for the crime of finding so much treasure. The father even offered an explanation by way of apology: "She so often hears of her companions being quodded, that she thought it had come to *her* turn." This is a highly gratifying but by no means solitary example of heroic honesty among the very poor.

On another occasion, three hundred and fifty pounds were picked up by a newspaper seller, and were faithfully restored to the owner.

Passing down Bishopsgate Street, one Saturday evening, I saw a group collected around a poor woman, who lay on a door-step, apparently very ill. I asked what the matter was, as the poor creature was groaning. How sad that, drunkenness being so common, my first thought should be, "She's drunk." As no one answered my question, I stooped over her to ascertain, but I detected no smell of drink; and after paying for a cab to convey her home, I turned to go away, when a man apparently of the poorest said, "That's a real case, sir; some is sham. Ah, I know a good deal about it, sir." I said, "What do you mean by sham?" "Vell, sir, I s'pose you know there's a wariety of dodges to get a little. Vell, poor things, I don't blame 'em; they 'as 'ard lines—vot with 'ard times and the drink, and von thing and another, ve all of us 'as 'ard times. Now, sir, you'd 'ardly think that I 'aven't put a drop of liquor to my lips for twelve years, and yet I'm werry often 'ungry; it's so 'ard to get work." I said, "I'll give you a couple of shillings to help you on." He said, "No, sir, I thank you, sir; I don't need it to-night. I had a job of work this week, and I'm going to get my money, eight shillings, and I expect another job next Thursday, and I'll get on werry well till then. I shouldn't find it so 'ard, but I'm keeping my old mother."

At this I urged him to take the money, or more if he needed. He said, "Vell, sir, you may think it hodd, but I have a principle never to take money unless I'm hawful 'ard hup, and can't get along novays without it. Now, sir, you give that money to somebody vat's vorse off than me. You'll find 'em. I can get along, and I'm principled agin taking money if I can get along without. I don't think it's right." And though I pressed the money on him, he refused, and said with a smile, as I left him, "Thank ye all the same, sir; it isn't a vim, it's principle. Good night." I said, "You'll shake hands with me?" and I gave him a hearty grip of the hand, and left him a gentleman of principle.

A gentleman—a clergyman—said to me: "I have visited at the houses of the rich, and stood by the bedside of the wealthy. But never have I been so lifted up above myself, and stimulated to a better life; never have I seen such grand examples of patience, trust, and endurance; never have I seen such cheerful submission to that which, when witnessed, amazes us that any poor human being can exist under its severity, than by the side of the bedridden, the crippled, and the suffering, who are in the midst of poverty, not knowing what would befall them on the morrow, living actually by faith, yet rejoicing and thankful in the midst of privation and suffering."

Come with me; turn under this low doorway; climb these narrow, creaking stairs; knock at the door. A pleasant voice bids you enter. You see a woman sixty-four years of age, her hands folded and contracted, her whole body crippled and curled together, as cholera cramped and rheumatism fixed it twenty-eight years ago. For sixteen years she has not moved from her bed, nor looked out of the window; and she has been in constant pain, while she cannot move a limb. Listen!—she is thankful.

For what? For the use of one thumb; with a two-pronged fork, fastened to a stick, she can turn over the leaves of an old-fashioned Bible, when placed within her reach. Hear her: "I'm content to lie here as long as it shall please Him, and to go when He shall call me."

Miss Maude Stanley, in her book, says:

"As in looking into a small pool of water remaining in the gutter of the dirtiest court, after a heavy shower of rain, we may see reflected the clear blue sky and the fleecy cloud, so may we see amongst the poorest and the most suffering, the reflection of Divine love and of Divine endurance. These sights may be hidden from the eyes of some; if so, let them cultivate their minds by literature and art, and they will lighten their own work and bring brightness to the homes they visit.

" And will my readers think with me that there is poetry in the story of Thomas Wright? They would find him in a low-roofed room of a London house; the walls are covered with dirty paper, the ceiling seems never to have been whitewashed. On the bed has lain for seven years a poor woman so disfigured that none will look on her willingly for the second time. And why is she here? Because she has an old husband and a strong son, who love her tenderly. Often has the relieving officer offered to take her into the infirmary; but no, the young man, who is past thirty, says he will never tire of working for his mother. For her sake he has never married. He and his father sit all day together at their bench, sewing and stitching away at the boots which bring them daily food and the few comforts they can get for the sick woman.

"For her sake, the son cultivates a few plants outside the window, so that the breeze may be scented as it comes to her lying on her poor bed. The father is past seventy, so that he earns but little; the son works early and late, for he wants all he can get to keep himself, his father and his mother. His rent is four and sixpence a week, and he pays a neighbour to come in every day to make his mother's bed. The bed is as nice and clean as it is possible for them to keep it. The neighbours tell me that Thomas will work hard till ten, and then he will go out and walk up and down the street smoking the pipe which he has denied himself before. If you speak to him of his mother, he says simply that he will work and work for her, for he could not bear to think of her being in the workhouse away from him. To me this seems a long enduring devotion that few sons in comfortable houses equal or surpass."

I give you one other description from her book. She says:

"Let us go up a dark and winding staircase, and there, high up, overlooking the roof, you will see a tailor sitting all day at his window cross-legged on his bench. He is always stitching at his work; and often you will see beside him the little child asleep; it has crept up to be near the father it loves so passionately. He is a Cumberland man, and in all the weary toil of his London life he will often turn his thoughts to those bluebells and those breezy moors which he has left for ever. In another room, smaller and more crowded, you may hear of the little boy who gets up of a cold winter's morning, long before his brothers and sisters are awake, to light the fire, so that father shall have a warm cup of tea in bed. The father is good and loving to his children; he works at home with his eldest son of nineteen at bootmaking. In this same room lives his wife, a girl of fourteen, and three small boys. The room is small, the walls have dirty paper, but within it there is a wealth of love, springing from that little Christopher to his ailing father."

Truly there are heroes in humble life. Poverty has its heroes not a few—its victims many. Sometimes victim and hero are blended in one poor, sinning, suffering, sacrificing, lovable soul. Oh, the stint that comes from the want of a penny! waste of life through want of food; death made gall and bitterness by the thought of dear ones left destitute! And yet poverty sometimes evolves the noblest heroism, touching bruised hearts with tenderest emotions, quickening poor souls with hope, evoking self-devotion, and exercising the magnanimity that doeth all it can, and giveth all it hath. Oh, ye whom God has enriched with many blessings, remember it is His will that pure hearts shall sympathize with His lowly, though erring ones; and that ready hands be stretched forth to succour and to save.

CHAPTER XII.

OPPOSITION TO PROGRESS—THE WORLD'S BENEFACTORS.

Great Discoverers and Inventors—The Opposition they have met—Satire upon Dr. Jenner—An Amusing Picture—Employing the Assistance of the Devil—The "Swing-Swang"—Practice often against Theories—"Horses going to the Dogs"—Liverpool and Manchester Railway—Railway Engines and Sheep's Wool—Alarming Predictions—The Old Coachman—Heroism for the Truth's Sake—Puritanic Strictness—The New England Sabbath—"Straining at a Gnat"—Drunk on the Sabbath—Whistling for a Dog—Wife-thrashing and Sabbath-breaking—True Liberty and Sunday Trains—Testimonies to the Christian Sabbath: Macaulay, Blackstone, Adam Smith, Webster, Theodore Parker, etc.—Holiday not Holy Day—Jurists and the Sabbath—Physicians and the Sabbath—Statesmen and the Sabbath—The Old Book—Liberty under Law.

PUBLIC opinion does not always determine what is right. Let any man venture to act an unusual part, and the world, or public opinion, will frown on his course. The history of discoveries and inventions will illustrate the fact. Because Roger Bacon understood "perspective," he was charged with being possessed of a devil, and was imprisoned for ten years. Galileo, for asserting that the earth moves, was condemned to imprisonment and to abjure his doctrine on his knees. Report has it that as he rose from his knees he said, "It does move, notwithstanding." Sir Isaac Newton's discoveries were ignored by his own university more than thirty years after they were published. Columbus discovered the New World, and met with opposition and persecution. Dr. Harvey discovered the circulation of the blood, and was attacked on all sides with every weapon that ignorance, prejudice, spleen and envy could frame against him.

The discoverer of vaccination, Dr. Jenner, was opposed by the medical profession and the public. I have a curious caricature by Cruikshank, dated 1812, entitled "The Cow-Pox Tragedy, Scene the Last," and dedicated to the "Associated Jennerian Cow-poxers of Gloster." It is described as a satire on Dr. Jenner and his discovery, and on the anticipated downfall of the Royal Jennerian College. A procession at the bottom of the picture is attending the funeral of Vaccination, aged twelve years. Above is a monument, inscribed "To the Memory of Vaccina, who died April the first." The mourners carry placards: "National Vaccine Institution for genuine Cow-Pox, by Act of Parliament; L——, undertaker," "Surrey Dispensary, etc." In the centre is a sun sending forth rays of light, inscribed "Common Sense," "Candid Investigation," "Reason," "Religion," "Truth." On a curtain near the top of the picture is written, "'Tis Conscience that makes Cowherds of us all." On one side is a cornucopia pouring out skulls and cross-bones, with labels, "Scald Heads," "Jennerian Scrofula," "Cow Itch," "Cow-pox Mange," "Tumid Glands," "Vaccine Eruptions," "Blindness." On the other side is a cornucopia pouring forth roses, with the names of the pamphlets issued in favour of Jenner, with ridiculous comments.

I might enumerate other discoverers. John Faust, the inventor of printing, was charged with employing the assistance of the devil in the manufacture of books. The inventor of the ribbon-loom, the stocking-loom, the spinning-jenny, were persecuted. The pendulum was ridiculed by the name of the "swing-swang." The inventor of the steam-engine was called a madman. The introduction of gas was ridiculed by the literary and learned, including such men even as Sir Walter Scott. Fulton was met by incredulous smiles, rude jokes, and contemptuous ridicule.

In every department of science and art inventors and discoverers have been opposed, even to our own day. Dr. Lardner proved by mathematical demonstration that a steamer could not cross the Atlantic, at the very time that the "Great Western" *did* cross it. The early history of railroads is a history of opposition, at which we smile to-day. The race of horses was to be extinguished. In my collection of caricatures I found one entitled "The Horses going to the Dogs." A steam-coach, called the "Wonder," is passing on the road, crowded within and without with passengers, some of whom are taking a sight at a group of horses which are standing in an inclosure, looking startled at the phenomenon. One blind horse says, "A coach without any horses! Nonsense! Come, come, Master Dobbin, you are a trotter, but you must not think to humbug me because I am blind." Another exclaims, "Well, dash my wig! if this is not the rummest go I ever saw." Two dogs are sitting in the foreground; one asks the question, "I say, Wagtail, what do you think of this new invention?" The other dog replies, "Why, I think we shall have meat enough soon." The cows would cease to give milk all along the line, vegetables would cease to grow, the cultivation of corn would be prevented, and all the springs would be dried up by the extensive excavations.

The Liverpool and Manchester Railway was opened on the 15th of September, 1830. Never was any scheme assailed with stronger invective or ridicule than the railway scheme in England. In 1825 the "Quarterly Review" says, "We should as soon expect people to suffer themselves to be fired off upon one of the Congreve ricochet rockets, as to trust themselves to the mercy of a machine going eighteen or twenty miles an hour." A member of Parliament declared his opinion "that a railway could not compete with a canal, for even with the best locomotive engine the average rate would be but three and a half miles an hour."

Among the reasons for preventing the London and North-Western Railway coming to Northampton, it was urged that the smoke of the trains would seriously discolour the wool on the sheep, and the passing so repeatedly through their meadows of such a rumbling, hissing, fiery serpent would so alarm, fret, and distract their cattle that they could not fat them; therefore the road was turned away from Northampton.

The innkeepers, coach-proprietors, hostlers, and coachmen made common cause against the rail. "Ah," said one of the last stage-coachmen, in giving a history of his opposition and final surrender, "Ah, sir, I did my hutmost to oppose 'um. I was von of the last to give in. I kep' a-losing day arter day. I drove a coach the last day vith an old voman and a carpet-bag hinside and some hempty trunks on the top. I was determined to 'ave some passengers, so I took my vife and children, 'cos nobody else vouldn't go. Ve vas game to the last, but ve guv in. The landlord of this 'ere 'ouse vas an austerious man. He use' to hobserve that he honly vished a railway committee vould dine hat 'is 'ouse,—he'd pizen 'em all; and he vould too, sir! Lor, sir, see vat ve've comed to, all along of the rail! Vy, sir, I've been werry popular, I have. I've been drownded in 'thank yers' from ladies for never letting nobody step through their bandboxes. Vy, sir, the chambermaids use' to smile hat me, the dogs vagged their blessed tails and barked ven I come. But it's all hover now, sir; and the gemmen that kep' this 'ere 'ouse takes tickets at a station, poor fellow! and the chambermaids makes scalding hot tea behind a mahogany counter for people as 'as no time to drink it in. Ah, vell, vell, sir, 'ow ve do run behind in this vorld, surely!"

In all the world's history, when men have touched a prejudice, or affected an interest, or interfered with some vested rights, or struck a blow at some old established wrong, they have borne the scorn, contempt, ridicule, persecution and opposition of public opinion, all the way to the victory. How often a really true and brave man has been hindered in a course of usefulness, by the slavish fear of incurring the censure of the world! I do not say that public opinion is *never* right. On abstract questions it is generally right; for instance, truth, righteousness, and justice are good, but in the application of these principles, public opinion is often at fault.

The great error with many of us is, that we do not try our conduct by the standard of eternal right, but by "What will others say?" "What will others think?" "How far will public opinion sustain me?" The world will never be the better for us, if we trim our sails to the breeze of public opinion. It is our duty to settle the matter—"Am I right?"—and then resist, as a rock resists the dashing wave. Let me

"Go forth among men, not mailed in scorn,
But in the armour of a pure intent.
Great duties are before me and great aims;
And whether crowned or crownless, when I fall,
It matters not, so that God's work is done."

Oh, it is grand to see a man confronting the crowd for their own good,—seizing a truth, standing by it, and, if need be, dying for it; becoming a pioneer of humanity in some new rough path; at his own risk and cost, building a pathway on which another generation shall march to higher degrees of wisdom, virtue, and freedom!

I know, too, it is becoming the fashion to rail at the Puritans and ridicule the strictness of our fathers, in moral and religious things,—a very easy thing to do. It always has been easy to ridicule any effort to be better, or do better; probably it always will be. The very imperfections of our earliest efforts in any direction leave many an open place for assault and ridicule. There have been very spicy things said and written about the dolefulness of the early New England Sabbath.

It is not to be denied, that in this age we are terribly afraid of being too good, of obeying God's law too strictly. "Being righteous over-much" is constantly quoted against those who plead for the stricter observance of the Sabbath, and protest against its violation. Any law or custom that interferes with our real, or supposed comfort, or the largest personal liberty, we are apt to resist as an injustice. I admit there is such a thing as "straining at a gnat and swallowing a camel." A lady in Edinburgh was walking in the street, one Sunday morning, with her pet dog, when the animal strayed from her. Seeing a man, who happened to be very drunk, she asked him if he would be kind enough to whistle her dog back to her. "Madam, I'm ashamed of ye, to ask a decent body like me to violate the holy Sabbath day by whistling."

A gentleman in Scotland hired a carriage to take him to church. He asked the driver what the fare was. "Our regular fare is one shilling, but we charge two shillings Sunday to discourage Sabbath-breaking."

In an old church register in New England is found recorded the fact that a certain man thrashed his wife one Sunday. The church dealt with him for Sabbath-breaking only, probably because thrashing his wife was either a work of necessity or mercy. To many it is very inconvenient to have such intangible things as scruples of law and conscience come up to bar the way against going where they please, when they please, and in what fashion they please. All the distortions of obedience to the biblical Sabbath requirements do not alter one hair's line the beneficent effect of obedience to them, or any other of God's laws. We are finding out, the medical faculty are finding out, the lunatic asylums are showing, the statistics are proving, and all thoughtful experience is testifying,—that the Sabbath, and the Bible way of keeping it, holds in its hands the life, health, sanity, wisdom, private and public virtue, well-considered statesmanship—everything outside of what is called religion that civilization values, and all of the true law of liberty in religion also.

There is no true liberty but in steadfast obedience to righteous law. That brotherhood of locomotive engineers that met some years since in St. Louis, had felt their way along the path of experience, when they adopted two things: one, a rule expelling an engineer addicted to the use of intoxicating drinks, and the other a resolution favouring the abolition of Sunday trains.

Is it reasonable to suppose that we can drop a corner beam out of our building in family or state, and not expect the whole structure to be unsafe? The very rate at which we are travelling, in our path of advance, should make us look well to every bolt and fastening. Lord Macaulay said, "If Sunday had not been observed as a day of rest, during the last three centuries, we should have been at this moment a poorer and less civilized people than we are." Blackstone adds his testimony: "A corruption of morals usually follows a profanation of the Sabbath." Says Adam Smith, "The Sabbath, as a political institution, is of inestimable value, independently of its claim to divine authority." Justice McLean declares, "Where there is no Christian Sabbath, there is no Christian morality; and without this, free institutions cannot long be sustained." Daniel Webster said: "The longer

I live, the more highly do I estimate the Christian Sabbath, and the more grateful do I feel toward those who impress its importance on the community." Theodore Parker (though he did not believe in the Sabbath as a divine institution, yet did believe in the day as a political necessity) said: "I should be sorry to see the Sunday devoted to common work; sorry to hear the clatter of a mill, or the rattle of the wheels of business on that day. I look with pain on men engaged needlessly in work on that day; not with the pain of wounded superstition, but a deeper regret." When Mr. Parker was travelling on the continent of Europe, he expressed the decided opinion that the New England method of keeping Sunday was far better than the European method: "For on the continent of Europe the Sunday is apt to be a mere holiday, while in New England it is a thoughtful holy-day." (Vol. iii. 89.)

After John Quincy Adams had been President of the United States, he presided at a large national convention for promoting the better observance of the Sabbath. He signed the appeal which the convention made to the country. Our greatest judge, Theophilus Parsons, would never give legal advice on the Sabbath-day, because he agreed with Sir Matthew Hale in thinking that the rest of one day in seven is a duty for all men, keeping the mind and body healthy.

The celebrated physician, Dr. Farre, declared that the keeping of the Sunday is necessary for the public health; and our own physician, Dr. J. C. Warren, fully endorsed the testimony of Dr. Farre. William Wilberforce said, "I can truly declare that, to me, the Sabbath has been invaluable." When Sir Samuel Romilly, Solicitor-General of England during Fox's administration, committed suicide (Nov. 2, 1818), Mr. Wilberforce said, "If he had suffered his mind to enjoy such occasional remission, it is highly probable that the strings of life would never have snapped from over tension." The celebrated Castlereagh, who was Foreign Secretary in 1812, committed suicide in 1822; Wilberforce said, "Poor fellow, he was certainly deranged,— the effect, probably, of continued wear of the mind and the non-observance of the Sabbath. It is curious to hear the newspapers speaking of incessant application to business; forgetting that by the weekly admission of a day of rest, which our Maker has enjoined, our faculties would be preserved from the effects of this constant strain."

We shall find, the more fairly we examine it, if we really desire to find, the way to give liberty and rights to all, if we wish to rule and make safe all dangerous classes, insure the largest culture, the happiness with least alloy, the safety in our progress, the most brilliant and steady light on the page of our future history,—we shall find the easiest, the least costly, and the surest way to do this contained in the leaves of an old Book that all the power of human research, all the pride of human opinion, or all the subtlety of mortal reasoning, can never put out of the world. God be thanked, so clear it is, and so simple, that a wayfaring man or a fool need not err in finding his right way by it. The Hebrew boy, Samuel, found it so, thousands of years ago, even though examples of moral weakness and wickedness poisoned nearly all the atmosphere about him. He never whined about its being hard to obey these laws, never considered himself abused that he could not follow a multitude to do evil, and be able at the same time to clutch the reward of obedience. He grew to make and unmake kings for his nation, and was *de facto* king in the sense of ruling; and his ruling in that fashion will live when Bismarcks and Beaconsfields have been obliterated from earthly history.

As in mathematics, everything possible in our mount to the farthest bound of the universe, and by which we measure, assign, and weigh all things, is wrapped in a few simple laws; even so all the possibilities of our personal future, all the hopes of a true and glorious national future, all that will yet glorify human life, find their only certainty in the steadfast obedience to and the practice of the few laws of that grand old Book to whose requirements we shall be compelled to submit in one fashion or another. Benjamin Franklin advised Thomas Paine not to print the "Age of Reason," "For," said he, "if men are so bad with the Bible, what would they be without it?"

CHAPTER XIII.

MANLINESS AND MORAL PRINCIPLE—INDUSTRY VERSUS IDLENESS.

False Ideas of Manliness—Physical Strength no Test—Lord Bacon a Swindler—Fast Living, cowardly—Horse-Racing and Prize-Fighting—Manliness is Godliness—False Opinions scorn Labour—" Only a Mechanic "—The Fashion of Useless People—" Only a Third-class Carriage "—Story concerning Lady Charlotte Guest—The Cinder-hole—Labour and Etiquette—Idle Men mischievous—The Dandy—Consequences of a Useless Life—Career of Beau Brummell—The Fop in a Breach-of-Promise Suit—Influence of Society upon us—Example better than Precept—Value of a Noble Life—Ministers and the Half-price—Genius no Substitute for Moral Principle—Burns's Perverted Genius—The Painter Haydon.

EVERY young man considers it high praise to be called a "manly fellow;" and yet how many false ideas there are of manliness! Physical strength is not the test. Samson was endowed with tremendous bodily powers. He was a grand specimen of humanity. See him rending the lion as he would a kid, or carrying away the gates of Gaza! But he was a weak creature after all, unable to resist the wiles of an artful woman.

Great intellect is not the test of true manhood. Some of the most intellectual men who have ever lived were not manly. Francis, Lord Bacon, was a prodigy of intellect,—the Sciences sat at his feet extolling him as their benefactor; yet we see him led down Tower Hill a prisoner for swindling! Was he manly when as Lord Chancellor he took with one hand £300, and with the other £400 from the opposing suitor, and then gave judgment in favour of the £400? See him enter his prison, convicted of bribery, fraud, and deceit! Was he, with his great intellect, manly?

Fast living is not manliness. Some men think that to strut,

and to swagger, and puff, and swear, and become an adept in vice, is to be manly. To some, the essentials of manliness are to "toss off their glass like a man," "spend money freely like a man," "stand up in a fight like a man," "smoke like a man," 'drive a fast horse like a man;" forgetting that virtue is true manliness. Temperance, chastity, truthfulness, fortitude, benevolence, are characteristics and essentials of manliness.

There is no manliness in sin of any kind. Vice is essentially unmanly. Just so far as evil habits are connected with what are called manly sports, degradation follows.

There may be manliness in a rowing-match, a foot-race, games of cricket or ball, pitching quoits, skating if disconnected with gambling; but prize-fighting, dog-fighting, cock-fighting, are not manly sports. I express my own opinion in saying that I do not consider horse-racing a manly amusement. Of the two, I think prize-fighting the more honourable. If two men choose to train themselves to endurance, patience, and skill, and then meet of their own free will to batter themselves to pieces, I consider it is more manly than to drive a horse, with whip and spur, till his reeking sides are covered with foam and dripping with blood and sweat; his nostrils distended and bleeding, his whole frame quivering with pain and exhaustion, for the sake of sport, and transferring cash from the pocket of one man to that of another without an equivalent.

To be manly is to be honest, generous, brave, noble, and pure in speech and life. The highest form of manliness is godliness. Some one has said, "An honest man is the noblest work of God." If we mean honesty in the common acceptation of the word, it is not true; a merely honest man is not the noblest work of God, but the man who is honest toward God and toward his fellow-man,—in short, a Christian man is the noblest work of God.

There is a class of men and women who despise labour, who avoid all intimacy or contact with those who work for a living. "Oh, he's only a mechanic!" "Oh, she lives out!" Some young ladies would be shocked at the idea of marrying a mere mechanic. In fact it is the fashion among the most useless of all God's creatures to despise those who are the most useful, and by whom they obtain all that makes them what they are. They revel in the wealth obtained by labour while they heartily despise it.

A gentleman was travelling in a train in England when a collision took place. He was greatly alarmed for his horses, and cried out, "Oh, my horses! my horses!" but, putting his head out of the window, he exclaimed, "Ah, thank God! it's only a third-class carriage!"

A story is told of Lady Charlotte Guest, the principal proprietor of the Dowlais Iron Works. Her aristocratic friends, while they enjoyed her princely hospitality, had often sneered at her extensive iron works, which they called her "cinder-hole." As soon as the balance-sheet of the works was completed, a copy was always dispatched to her wherever she might be. On one occasion she gave a grand party at her London residence, and when the festivity was at its height, a courier arrived from Dowlais with a tin box, containing the expected document. Lady Charlotte ordered it to be brought to her in the brilliantly-lighted saloon, where she was surrounded by a circle of her aristocratic friends and relatives, who probably occasionally enjoyed a sneer at the "cinder-hole."

"What's that, Lady Charlotte?"

All crowded round the tin box.

"'Tis our balance-sheet."

"Balance-sheet!" exclaimed the fair aristocrats. "What's a balance-sheet?"

"It's an account made up and showing the profits down at the works for the last twelve months."

The company laughed, for they thought of the "cinder-hole." "And so that's a balance-sheet!" crowding round the paper with the double entries, and the red lines, looking on it as a phenomenon. "Why, I never saw one before! But what are the profits?"

Lady Charlotte, not seeming to heed them, said as though she spoke to herself:

"Three hundred thousand pounds! a very fair year," and she recommitted the balance-sheet to its tin case, while peeresses looked almost petrified.

"Three hundred thousand pounds profits! What, you don't mean that in one year?"

"In one year," was the reply, as though there was nothing at all remarkable about the matter.

"I'd be a Cinderella myself!" said a Border countess, "to a husband with such a business. Three hundred thousand pounds, and all from that nasty cold iron, it beats the glass slipper!"

"Labour is the great law of the universe; labour is the law of humanity; labour is essential to the healthy development of our physical, intellectual, and moral life." Think of a man doing nothing! What weariness! What an intolerable life! Why, the most dreadful punishment is solitary confinement with nothing to do. Men have committed suicide, weary of living to eat, drink, and sleep. Idle men are generally mischievous, arising from the fact that a man *must do* something, and those who despise honourable labour verify the truth of Dr. Watts's lines:

"Satan finds some mischief still for idle hands to do."

They could sympathise with the boy who sings:

"I wish I was the President of these United States;
I never would do nothing, but swing on all the gates!"

and well would it be for society if they did nothing worse; but what miseries, what mental dyspepsia afflicts the wretch who has nothing to do!

Ezekiel says, "Behold this was the iniquity of thy sister Sodom; pride, fulness of bread, and abundance of idleness was in her!"

Milton puts this sentiment into the lips of Adam, "God hath set labour and rest as day and night to men successive." Man must labour. We must all earn our bread by the sweat of the brow, or of the brain, either with the hands, or feet, or head, on the bench, at the bar, in the pulpit, in the press, on the deck, or in the trenches, behind the counter or in the counting-house.

It is the great ambition of a class to be genteel; as Mrs. Richley says, "Let us be genteel or die!" We must do the genteel thing. Better tell a lie than break the rules of gentility! By gentility I do not mean good breeding, or politeness. It is bad manners to push a knife into your mouth while eating— very bad! but not so bad as to forget your true friends and follow after those of a higher degree. It is bad manners not to distinguish a fork from a toothpick, but it is not so mean as to be ashamed of honest poverty, or blush for an honourable calling. The gentility I mean is a "diabolical invention which kills natural kindness and honest friendship." The most genteel people are often the most heartless.

One of the most useless of all human animals is the dandy. He is a creation of the tailor. You measure his worth by the yard. You are puzzled to know whether he is a female gentleman, or a male lady; he will exhibit himself to the admiration, as he supposes, of every lady who is so fortunate as to cross his path. He does nothing for himself, or anybody else; his occupation is to dress, and perfume himself, and carry a dainty little cane, doing himself up as if he were a shirt.

There can hardly be a better lesson taught of the consequences of a useless life than that presented by the brilliant yet melancholy career of Beau Brummell, the refined, the fastidious Beau Brummell, the "glass of fashion and the mould of form," "the observed of all observers," the companion and pet of royalty and the nobility. At the last of his life he could not be kept clean. The poor, "dandled, deserted, doomed, demented dandy, died wretchedly on a straw mattress, in such a disgusting state as cannot be described."

Yet after all, some of these fops estimate themselves at about a fair price, as in a suit for damages in a breach-of-promise case, one of this class was offered two hundred dollars to settle it. "Two hundred dollars! Two hundred dollars for ruined hopes, for blighted affections, for a wretched existence! Two hundred dollars for a blasted life! Two hundred dollars for all this! No, never! never! Make it three hundred dollars, and it's a bargain!"

Almost every man is sensible of the influence of society on his own mind. We are often conscious of the influence for evil or good of a single mind with which we are brought in close contact. "A doubter will awaken in us a spirit of doubt; the caviller, a captious spirit; the cold-natured chills our own feelings; the man of low aims or small energy often leaves us listless, hopeless, or inoperative; the man of life, spirit, determination, and energy seems to quicken and inspire our own nature." The exhibition of what is noble, the embodiment of what is right, beautiful, and heroic in a life, produces a far greater effect on the human heart than precept or exhortation. "Example is better than precept."

When Lord Peterborough lodged for a season with Fenelon, he said at parting, "I shall become a Christian in spite of myself."

A young man, about to be ordained, stated that at one period of his life he had been nearly betrayed into the principles of infidelity; "But," said he, "there was one argument in favour of Christianity I could never refute, and that was the consistent conduct of my own father."

How many professed Christians fail in exerting an influence by inconsistency, their precepts differing from their practice.

A story is told of a minister, who, wishing to take advantage of the custom of charging ministers out West half price, said to the landlord of an hotel where he had put up, "I am a minister." "What! you a minister! I should never have guessed it; you asked no blessing at your meals. I went with you to your room, and took away the light, and you did not say your prayers. You ate like a heathen, drank like a heathen, slept like a heathen, and I guess you had better pay like a heathen."

All the talent, intellect, or genius that men ever possessed will not compensate for the want of fixed, moral principle. In the world's history, how many sad instances appear of men of genius dwarfed like wilted weeds, for the lack of moral principle, for the want of moral courage, shrinking ever from asserting what their own conscience dictates as right, if it shocks the prejudices of others; some are even like a very celebrated poet, with a warm heart, generous disposition, brave, and at times with high impulses, as when he penned the "Cotter's Saturday

Night;" but who for the lack of firm, moral, and religious principles, left behind him monuments of his perverted genius, in the shape of unpublished poems, songs, and letters, at which humanity must blush, and at which angels themselves might weep. Had he foreseen all the evil effects that some of his writings were to produce in that dear old Scotland he loved so warmly, he would have burned them and his pen too. A little before his death, he bitterly deplored the existence of the unworthy progeny of his genius, and declined with horror the proposal of some wretch of a bookseller to publish them in full.*

I might speak of many others, who by their perverted genius have "fanned the polluted fires of debauchery; have shed a rainbow lustre around mere animalism; taught blasphemers a more pithy profanity; insulted religion through its forms and its professors; treated sacred things with levity; and produced immeasurable mischief" among the young of both sexes.

The painter Haydon said: "Wilkie's system was Wellington's, —principle and prudence the groundwork of risk. Mine," said he, "was Napoleon's,—audacity, with a defiance of principle, if principle is in the way. I get into prison" (and, poor fellow! he killed himself soon after); "Napoleon died at St. Helena; Wellington is living, and honoured; Wilkie has secured a competency; while I am poor and necessitous as ever."

Let no man use evil as a means for the success of any scheme, however grand. "Permission of evil that good may come" may be the prerogative of Deity, and should never be ventured on by mortals.

Poor Haydon said once, "There are three things I long to see before I die: the Americans thrashed at sea, my own debts paid, and historical painting encouraged by the government." Poor Haydon! he died deeply in debt, neglected by the government, and the Americans unthrashed at sea.

* Byron said of Burns: "What an antithetical mind,—tenderness, roughness; delicacy, coarseness; sentiment, sensuality; soaring and grovelling; dirt and Deity;—all mixed up in that compound of inspired clay!"

CHAPTER XIV.

HAPPINESS AND TRUE HEROISM—GOLD, WHAT IT DOES AND WHAT IT DOES NOT BRING.

Signing away Liberty—False Ideas of Happiness—Rothschild—John Jacob Astor—A Girl's Idea of Perfect Happiness—The Snow-blocked Train—Lord Chesterfield's Confession—Irishman's Complaint of the Moon—"If"—The Two Buckets—Sir John Sinclair and the Labourer—"A New Way to Pay Old Debts"—The History of Misers—Experience of a Millionaire—"The Happiest Fellows in the World"—Anecdote of John Wilson—Happiness among the Poor—Lord Braco and the Farthing—The Celebrity and his Hat—The Burden of a Debt—The Clergyman and the Collection—Dodging Creditors—Indebtedness Degrades—Extravagance—Church Debts—Sacrifice for Others—Moral Heroism—Victory over Self.

WHAT false ideas many entertain of freedom! Every man desires to be free. God has implanted the desire in every human heart. What is freedom? A man once told me he would not sign the pledge, because that would be the signing away of his liberty! "What liberty?" "Why, to do as I please." To do as you please? Is that liberty? There is no liberty without law; it is licentiousness. To do as you please, independent of the law of God, is to be a slave. He only is a free man who renders strict and steadfast obedience to righteous law. True liberty consists as much in exemption from the slavery within, as the slavery without.

Remember, young man, whatever elevates man's nature, whatever lifts him above the trammels of earth and raises him nearer heaven, brings him nearer the standard of true freedom; and every passion indulged is a fetter placed on his intellect; every loitering in the mazes of unwholesome pleasure, if at all redeemed, must one day be redeemed at too dear a price. No man ever excelled without the exercise of self-denial. Beneath the allurements of passion there lurks a worse than Egyptian bondage.

Very few people in this world are contented—thoroughly contented. A man once put up a board on his land, with this notice: "I will give this field to any one who is really contented." An applicant came. "Are you really contented?" "Yes." "Then what do you want my field for?"

We have false ideas of happiness. What will make me happy—contented? "Oh, if I were rich, I should be happy!" A gentleman who was enjoying the hospitalities of the great millionaire and king of finance, Rothschild, as he looked at the superb appointments of the mansion, said to his host, "You must be a happy man." "Happy?" said he, "happy! I happy—happy! Ay, happy! Let us change the subject."

John Jacob Astor was told that he must be a very happy man, being so rich. "Why," said he, "would you take care of my property for your board and clothes? That's all I get for it."

I remember some years ago being very much amused at the idea of perfect happiness expressed by a young girl. On a very stormy night, the train between Syracuse and Utica was blocked by snow, and we were compelled to remain in the cars all night on the track. Of course, we were hungry, and the welcome news was brought to the patient passengers that tea, bread and butter, ham and eggs, could be obtained at a house but a few rods distant from the cars. Off I started, in the driving snow, stumbling along as best I could, and found the house. The room, almost the only one in it, was crowded with eager seekers after food. I waited some time to get a chance, when I accosted a young girl—plump, rosy, and apparently very good-natured—as she was rushing around, all excitement. I said, "Will you please give me some bread and butter and tea to take to a lady in the cars?"

"Oh, yes," said she, very volubly; "bread and butter! certainly. I'll give you some bread and butter. How much do you want; two or three slices? thick or thin? much butter or little? Certainly you shall have some bread and butter."

"And tea," I said.

"Ah, yes; tea. What have you got to put it in? You can't carry a cup and saucer and a handful of bread and butter through the snow. You'll fall down and spill the tea. I'll tell you what I'll do. I've got a mug—it's a pretty mug. I'll lend it to you; but you must not break it, and you must bring it back."

When she brought the refreshments, she said:

"Now I'll fix you. Hold the bread and butter in one hand; now put your finger through the handle of the mug. There, you are all right; but bring back the mug!"

"You have a great number of visitors at your house to-night?"

"Yes," she replied; "more than I ever saw in this house in all my life."

"You look very happy."

"Yes," she said, her face beaming with brightness; "it's perfectly delightful. I like company; it's splendid. I'm just as happy as ever I can be. Why, do you know it's almost as good as having a beau?"

I hope the young lady by this time knows by experience what it is to realize something more than perfect happiness. We sometimes hear the remark:

"Oh! if I could be elegant and accomplished and conspicuous, I should be happy." Few men have ever possessed greater advantages for the attainment and enjoyment of worldly pleasures, and no man drank deeper of the draught, than Lord Chesterfield. Hear him, at the last: "I have seen the silly rounds of business and of pleasure, and have done with them all. I have enjoyed all the pleasures of the world, and do not regret their loss. I appraise them at their real value, which is in truth very low. I have been behind the scenes. I have seen all the coarse pulleys and dirty ropes which exhibit and move the gaudy machines; and I have seen and smelt the tallow candles which illuminated the whole decoration to the astonishment of the ignorant audience. When I reflect on what I have seen, what I have heard, and what I have done, I can hardly persuade myself that all that frivolous hurry of bustle and pleasure of the world had any reality; but I look upon all that is past as one of those romantic dreams which opium commonly occasions, and I do by no means desire to repeat the nauseous dose for the sake of the fugitive dream. I think of nothing but killing time the best way I can, now that he has become my enemy." Yes, this killing of time is the most laborious of all work.

Much of the happiness or misery of our lives depends on ourselves. I have known persons who would not permit themselves to be happy, who always look on the shadows of life. There is more light than shade; yet some see gloom even in the sunshine —anticipating trouble, looking out for disaster—prophets of evil, they perceive the cloud in the brightest skies.

Observe such an one; he would throw a damper on a funeral. The face set in such a forlorn and doleful expression, you would imagine that no smile could ripple the hard surface, or relax the muscles, so rigid is the cast of utter misery. If the sun shines on a bright morning: "Ah, it won't last long! there's a mackerel sky." They are almost vexed at the moon in its beauty, "Because," as the Irishman complained, "it only shines on bright nights when we don't want it; if it would but give light when it is needed, it would be worth while." They make themselves miserable by the most absurd anticipations of what *may* come; like the servant-girl, who had never even received an offer of marriage, sitting on the curb of the cistern, crying bitterly.

"What is the matter?"

"Oh, dear! I was thinking that *if* I was married, and my baby should fall in the cistern and be drowned, how dreadfully I should feel."

Yes, and such persons do feel dreadfully in anticipation of what they should feel *if*—thus borrowing trouble. Why, man, wake up! Come out of the dreary atmosphere of *ifs*. Look about you. Have you no blessings? As the poor slave did, "reckon up your marcies." Are you in pain? No. Are you pinched and poor? No. Have your enemies triumphed over you? No. Then what is the matter? Rouse yourself from this chronic state of self-imposed misery—it does not pay. You are cheating yourself; you are drawing poison, like the spider, from the very flowers. Cheer up, man! and, like the bee, suck honey.

"How dismal you look!" said a bucket to his companion, as they were going to the well.

"Ah!" replied the other, "I was reflecting on the uselessness of our being filled, for let us go away ever so full, we always come back empty."

"Dear me! how strange to look at it in that way," said the bucket. "Now I enjoy the thought that however *empty* we come, we always go away *full*. Only look at it in that light, and you will be as cheerful as I am."

An old coloured woman, over a hundred years of age, said in answer to the inquiry, "Are you thankful for your pains?" "Yes, missus, I'se thankful for ebery ting as it comes I'se obleeged to ye."

Sir John Sinclair once alighted from his chariot near a singularly abject-looking hovel, and entered into conversation with an old labourer who lived there alone. On leaving, he asked if he could serve him in any way.

"Sir," said the old man, with a look of honest contentment, "there is not in this world a thing that I want."

Sir John often said that poor abode was the only home in which he had found perfect happiness, and requested his daughter to draw him a picture of that one-windowed hut where lived a man who had not a wish ungratified. When Sir John wished the great Lord Melville on his birthday many happy years, the minister of state replied, "They must be happier than the last, for I have not had one happy day in it."

When blessings come like "birds to the windows of your soul, singing their joyous notes and seeking a responsive melody in your own heart, why put shutters on the windows, why draw down the blinds and miss the sweet warbling and the comfort through your own perverseness? Tear down the blinds, let the flood of sunshine pour into your heart; throw wide open the shutters; let the music float in;" take a cheerful view of life; come out of the gloom of your morbid apprehensions—it will pay, and you will look from the heights into the dreary cell of your miserable fancies, as men look into the dark dungeon from which they have escaped.

Many men destroy the happiness of their lives by the absorbing passion for money-getting. It is not an unworthy ambition to get rich, to accumulate property; but the real gain depends on *how* you get it, and *how* you *use* it. While money may be a blessing to the possessor, and through him a blessing to the world, it may be and often is a curse to the owner, and through him a curse to the world. Ask the man who has stooped to mercantile dishonour and baseness, and who by successful villainy and swindling has realized an envied fortune, " What have you gained? "

" I have been shrewd, long-headed, smart. I am prosperous and a man of capital."

Is that all? A philosopher has said, " Though a man without money is poor, a man with nothing but money is poorer." What has such a man but money? Every piece of plate on his sumptuous table may reflect the pinched face of a hungry creditor, and the music in his gorgeous entertainments be discordant with the cry of a defrauded orphan. When Sir Giles Overreach in Massinger's play of *A New Way to Pay Old Debts* attempts to draw his sword, he is driven to bay, and says:

> " Ha! I am feeble. Some undone widow sits upon my arm,
> And takes away the use of it; and my sword,
> Glued to my scabbard with wronged orphans' tears,
> Will not be drawn. Ha! What? Are these hangmen
> That come to bind my hands and then to drag me
> Before the judgment-seat? Now they are new shapes,
> And do appear like furies with steel whips
> To scourge my ulcerous soul."

" Yes, he is a man of capital; he owns houses, lands, stocks, and shares." Capital! What is capital? Character is capital; honour is capital. What capital has a man when integrity and honour are gone, bartered for a miserable mess of pottage? Capital! when everything noble is stranded as an outcast thing on the sands of dishonour. He must be judged by what he *is*, not by what he *has*. What *has* he? By heartless villainy he has capital. What *is* he? Wretchedly poor in all that constitutes true and noble manliness. Perish gold and estate, stocks and shares; but give me integrity and honour, and when I die let me leave the record of an upright life.

Gold is a good thing in charitable fingers, but not when it becomes a golden calf for men's worship; then it does not pay. Paulding said, " Money has become our god, or rather our demon, and the belief seems to be fast gaining ground that to win a fortune and lose a soul is playing for a stake worthy of rational and immortal beings."

The madness for money is among the strongest and lowest of the passions. How pitiful to see a man willing to work, fight, beg, starve, lie, cheat, shave and steal for money, only to hoard it, gloat over it, count it, and handle it! Miserable is the man, with all his glorious faculties, whose sole ambition is to get and hold money, and then worship it,—commune with it, think about it, plan to get more of it, content never to part with it, when it becomes the sovereign good, yes, the heaven of a human spirit! Such a man might almost travesty the language of devotion, and, making gold his god, say of it what the Psalmist said, in his lofty aspirations after the highest good, " Whom have I in heaven but thee? and there is none on earth I desire above thee,"—to prize it, not for its uses, but for itself;—such a man, with untold wealth, is poor indeed.

A miser has been known to die in the dark, to save the expense of a candle. One poor wretch consoled himself, on his deathbed, at a crafty bargain he had made concerning his funeral, with an undertaker who had married his only child. The history of misers is but a record of wretched creatures who have submitted to inflictions, sufferings, and life toils, to hoard and worship money.

Rightly used, money is a great blessing. It is the procurer of comforts and luxuries, as well as the necessaries of life; gives us admission to many of the pleasant places of God's earth, to much that is rare, curious, and enchanting in nature and art;

and to lack money is a misfortune. Yet the heaviest ills that befall us money cannot cure: it cannot minister to a mind diseased; it cannot purchase health, or hinder the progress of decay; it cannot restore youth, or buy back fair fame to the dishonoured; it cannot restore to the bereaved the loved ones that are gone, nor cure the many ills so fatal to a man's welfare. Gold may buy a wife, but cannot purchase love; it may gain civility, but not respect; it may introduce to society, but cannot procure friendship; it may obtain servility, but not esteem; it may buy position and sumptuous living, but cannot purchase happiness,—*that* is a home-made article; it no more consists in the accumulation of wealth than in snuffing up the east wind.

A millionaire, upon being asked what was the happiest period of his life, promptly said, "When I was working on a farm at twelve dollars a month."

Some men have queer ideas of happiness. A captain of a man-of-war said, "I have left my ship's company the happiest fellows in the world: I've just flogged one half of them, and they are glad it's over, and the others are glad they did not get it."

John Wilson, after fishing in a loch in Selkirkshire, nearly all day, without a nibble, watched all the time by a shepherd and his dog, was turning despondently away, when the shepherd said:

"Ye'll no hae killed mony trout?"

"No; I've had no sport at all,—not a nibble."

"I dare say no; for it's weel kent there was never a trout in that loch since the beginning of creation."

A man who seeks happiness in mere money is fishing where there has been no fish since the creation of the world.

A poor man laughs oftener than a rich man. There is more merriment in the homes of the poor than is generally found in those of the rich; for with the deep-seated and rankling anxiety, the wearying solicitude that often accompanies wealth, pressing on his inmost soul, a man cannot be happy. The griping screw, whose god is Mammon, fattens on the misery of others, as the vulture on carrion; stalks up and down like a commercial buzzard, tearing away the substance of his victim. Can he be happy? Why, the workings of his mercenary soul tell on his very features; his extortion and usury harden his heart, stain his soul, and diminish his happiness by lowering the standard of self-respect. How mean men grow by this love of money!

"I've been a member of this church twenty years, and it has only cost me twenty-five cents!" said a man in a social meeting; when the minister said:

"The Lord have mercy on your poor little stingy soul!"

I heard of one very noisy in prayer-meetings, and who on one occasion, by his shouting "Amen!" and the like, disturbed the meeting so much that the leader requested a brother to try and stop that noise. In a moment the exclamations ceased.

"How did you succeed so quickly?"

"Oh, I just asked him for a dollar for foreign missions, and that stopped him."

Poor Lord Braco, rich in gold and silver, but poor in all that constitutes true manliness, once picked up a farthing. A beggar passing, asked his lordship to give it to him, as it was so small a coin. The possessor of thousands of pounds sterling said, as he carefully buttoned up his pocket, "Find a farthing for yourself, you poor body!"

A story is related of a certain celebrity, who inquiring the price of hats, the storekeeper presented him with a valuable beaver, and asked his acceptance of it.

"Ah, thank you,—thank you very much. How much should you ask for this hat?"

"Eight dollars."

"And you give it to *me*? Almost too good for me to wear. What's the price of this one?"

"Oh, that's not a good hat. Only three dollars."

"And you say you give me *this*?"

"Yes, if you will accept it."

"Well now, suppose I take the three-dollar hat, and you give me the five dollars, if it will be all the same to you,"—which was actually done!

A gentleman once asked why a certain person did not pull out the beam from his own eye. Foote replied, "So he would, if he could sell the timber."

There are very few things in this world that will destroy or mar a man's happiness more than the consciousness of debt; very few things are heavier than its burden. What an awful incubus is the dread of duns; to be afraid, in walking the streets, of meeting a creditor; to avoid one store after another, till nearly all are closed to you; to dread the arrival of the mail, fearing a reminder of debt; to sneak about, with furtive glances on either side! How the blood will tingle at the curt question, "When will it be convenient for you to settle that little bill?" It is always a *little* bill, though it might take all you are worth to pay it. Oh, the misery of being dunned! Men have been driven almost mad by it,—I speak of sensitive men,—and most men are ashamed of it.

An eccentric clergyman obtained an enormous collection by requesting that no one should contribute or put anything on the plate who was in debt; so every one contributed. But there is hardly any course that will toughen a man in meanness more than the persistent running in debt. Some men are constantly planning to deceive a creditor; they will lie unblushingly; make promises with no intention of performing. No genius can redeem a man from the unutterable meanness of reckless debt. While we may be amused at the wit in dodging a creditor, we are shocked at the heartlessness of the swindler. If one steals a penny, he is a thief; but is he not a thief who will "*do*" a creditor, shirk payment of an honest bill, or act the part of a mean trickster? "There goes a sculptor." "What do you mean?" "Only that he chisels tailors, bootmakers, and all who trust him."

How can a man strut about in unpaid-for garments, and ride in unpaid-for carriages, and gather his friends to admire unpaid-for furniture, or eat and drink at another's expense, without an inward sense of personal degradation? It *does* degrade a man, so that you can almost detect a shirking debtor.

In these days a labourer on two dollars a day must dress like the mechanic on four or five. The mechanic must dress like the tradesman with an income of $5,000 a year. The tradesman must live like the merchant with his $20,000; and the merchant must outstrip his richer neighbour in equipages, furniture, and entertainments; thus is the demon of debt invoked, and so it goes on. Churches become ambitious of rivalling or excelling their neighbours in superb architecture and gorgeous decorations, till, involved in debt, their energies are paralyzed, the minister crippled by the heavy outside load, the benevolences curtailed, and the strength and power which exercised for God and humanity might and would advance the best interests of the Church, and the salvation of men, are expended in devising ways and raising means to lift the indebtedness incurred in mere display. Only under certain circumstances does it pay for individuals, societies, churches, communities, or nations to incur the heavy load of debt.

The noblest work in which a human being can be engaged is for others; for all true heroism is the sacrifice of self for the good of others. It has nothing to do with mere abilities. We do not speak of heroic talent, heroic genius, heroic intellectuality; but heroic daring, heroic sacrifice, heroic endurance.

There is a daring that is far from heroic. Blondin was daring, but no hero; Sam Patch was daring, but died like a fool, and was no hero. If, capable of great deeds, a man lives for himself, all he leaves is a spectacle to wonder at, and not a benefit to enjoy. Some of the greatest instances of moral heroism in which the soul of man has asserted its Divine origin, may never be known on earth. The influence has been felt in the defeat of some legion of Satan's army, some array of deadly vices or phalanx of wild passions; but the brave hearts which wrought the victory may never be known till they are called forward to receive their crowns. How many real heroes pass by unnoticed—modest, quiet, unattractive, and unassuming; the gay avoid them, and pass them by with a sneer. Only those who know them fully, honour and love them. They would not particularly grace a drawing-room; the thoughtless throng heeds them not; to them they seem stained, marred. Why, my fine gentleman, these marks and stains are honourable scars, obtained in many a well-fought battle. They have entered the conflict of life with brave, true hearts, and will be at last ranked among those who "have overcome."

There are no victories more glorious than those which are gained over self, those in which a struggling soul becomes purified and ennobled by sacrifice and suffering for the good of others. Ah, sir! "you may live in obscurity, and fight your battles noiselessly; no historian may record your name; no monument be erected to your memory; you may bear the look of scorn and contempt, the world's sneers"—what of all that? A time is coming when the "intelligent universe will adjudicate aright;" when the man who masters an evil passion, battles a popular vice, fights a ruinous error, will be deemed worthy of higher praise than earth's greatest warrior. "The marble monument will crumble into dust; the very earth reel to and fro beneath the tread of the coming Judge; all the roll of historic records be consumed in the final conflagration; but the memory of the moral hero will be imperishable."

He will live in the grateful memory of those whom he has blessed, whose tears he has wiped away, whose wants he has relieved, whose gloom he has dispelled, and whose wandering feet he has brought into the paths of peace. There, yes, "there shall his memorial be reared, where the flames cannot reach, and where the rocking of earth's last convulsions shall not be felt."

CHAPTER XV.

KNOWLEDGE AND CURIOSITY—ABSURD BLUNDERS AND LAUGHABLE MISTAKES.

What is Knowledge?—Ignorance with a Library—Wisdom is applied Knowledge—George Cruikshank the Simon Pure—Blunders in Spelling—"Preshus Sole"—Laughable Mistakes—The Deacon who thought he could Preach—Anecdote of Robert Hall—Self-knowledge and Physical Health—Knowing Others—"Brass" no Test of Character—Misjudging Others—Knowledge through History—Goodness—Mental Cultivation and Moral Corruption—Inquisitiveness—"Funnels of Conversation"—How a Man Lost his Leg—Anecdote of John Randolph—Misapplied Labour—Dinner and Duel—How to Collect a Crowd—Van Amburg's Lion—Feats of Legerdemain—Sir Charles Napier and the Indian Juggler—Ignorance and Superstition—Whimsical Vagaries—Senseless "Omens"—Sowing for the Harvest—Immortality Revealed—De Quincey upon the Present—Faith a Necessity—The Story of Poor Joe.

MAN is so constituted that in acquiring new truths, in the pursuit of learning, or the search for knowledge, he finds enjoyment, a high degree of happiness. Sir Wm. Hamilton declares, with philosophic insight: "It is ever the contest that pleases us, not the victory. The hunter derives more pleasure in the chase than in the possession of the game." Malebranche declared: "If I held Truth captive in my hand, I should open my hand and let it fly, in order that I might again pursue and capture it." Lessing wrote: "Did the Almighty, holding in His right hand truth, and in His left search after truth, deign to tender me the one I might prefer, in all humility, and without hesitation, I should request search after truth."

"Truth," says Von Muller, "is the property of God; the pursuit of truth is what belongs to men." Jean Paul Richter says: "It is not the goal, but the course which makes us happy."

What is knowledge? is an important and yet difficult question to answer. It is not simply to gather information, or to furnish ourselves with certain facts. It is well to know all we can that is useful, and right to avail ourselves of other men's labours and investigation. God has given to a comparative few favoured ones the intellect and ability to discover truths; therefore it is lawful to gain, from the toils of others, general information and knowledge.

Men seldom become proficient or eminent in any one branch of science without personal investigation and thought. He who would be an astronomer, a natural historian, a geologist, a chemist, must himself make researches. Then again, men may collect an enormous library of books, and even read them, without intelligent curiosity. You may teach one to repeat their contents; still his real knowledge may be small. A parrot repeats wise words, but the bird is not a whit the wiser. Wisdom is knowledge made our own and properly applied. Knowledge and wisdom may have no connection. "Knowledge is proud that it has learned so much; wisdom is humble that it knows no more."

An old writer has declared: "'Tis the property of all true knowledge to enlarge the soul by filling it, to enlarge without swelling it, to make it more capable and earnest to know, the more it knows." He who has no ideas save those he borrows from other people may possess knowledge, but is not wise. It is possible for a man to learn, and not reason; to remember, but never think. Let no one depreciate true knowledge. Learn all you can, gain correct information from every source. For the want of real wisdom men sometimes make whimsical blunders. Some years ago the relative merits of George and Robert Cruikshank were contrasted in an English review, and George was spoken of as the real Simon Pure. A German editor begins his memoir of Cruikshank by informing his readers that he is an artist whose real name is Simon Pure; and in the index we read: "Pure, Simon,—the real name of George Cruikshank."

Very absurd blunders are made by the lack of a correct knowledge of orthography. I think the spelling-matches of some years since, that were so popular for a time, were very useful as well as enjoyable. How the beauty of a sentence may be marred, or the force weakened, by incorrect spelling! A young man told me that he was constantly receiving letters from a friend who was very anxious about his spiritual welfare. "But," said he, "they do me no good, for I am sure to get to laughing over some incorrect or absurd spelling. He will write, ' I send you this letter, not to intrude my views on you, but in the interest of your preshus sole.'" I often receive from secretaries of societies letters badly spelt, as well as from ministers, and men and women who ought to know better. One gentleman wrote that he was sorry to trouble me with another letter, and he hoped I would not consider him a "boar."

Some persons, through ignorance of the meaning of certain words, make laughable mistakes. I have a letter from a gentleman who desires me to reply by my own hand, as he wishes to preserve the letter as a "momentum!" A lady writes: "My husband cannot drink liquor without impunity." We are much amused at the reported misuse of words by the coloured people, —words that they do not understand. A gentleman told me of once going into a "coloured church" very neatly frescoed, except behind the pulpit; here the wall had been taken down to form a recess, and the plastering was left in a rough state. The minister wished to say, "Brethren, we shall have no more service here till we have raised by contribution sufficient money to fresco this recess;" but he said, "Bredren, de gospel will not be dispensed with any mo' till we have took up a contradistribution enuff to have dis yer abscess fricasseed!"

A very important branch of knowledge is self-knowledge. "Know thyself" is a maxim too deep for men in general. Men may toil through the intricacies of complicated systems, and know all about the characters of ancient heroes, and know but little of their own. But every man of common capacity may attain to this knowledge, if he will. He alone may follow the "autobiography of his heart," and see, as in a book, the indelible record of his life. What is my chief weakness? What is my predominant propensity? What gives me the highest delight? What are my prejudices against persons and things? What is my temper? What are my motives? What are my views of life? What is my faith? How few can answer these questions! yet every one who sets himself honestly to self-examination can answer; but men in general do not want to know. Some of us would be frightened if we searchingly asked ourselves these questions.

A man would become an awful fact to himself by thorough self-examination. A young man once said to me:

"I do not think I am a sinner."

I asked him if he would be willing his mother or sister should know all he had done, or said, or thought,—all his motives and all his desires. After a moment he said:

"No, indeed, I should not like to have them know; no, not for the world."

"Then can you dare to say, in the presence of a holy God, who knows every thought of your heart, 'I do not commit sin'?"

A knowledge of his characteristic weakness may help a man in his conduct through life; for, if guarded against, it will become his strength. It is this want of self-knowledge that leads men often into absurd positions; like the deacon, who thought he could preach, and teased the minister to let him try. He went through the preliminary exercises very comfortably, then took his text from one of the Epistles, and began:

"These words were written by Paul the apostle. They were written to the Church to whom they were addressed. Paul, the apostle—was an apostle—to the Epistle of the Gentiles—that is —the words of the Epistle of the apostle Paul were words—that if you read, you will be impressed with their importance. I have chosen for my text these words of Paul—who—when—in this apostle of the Epistles—hem—hem. If anybody in this congregation thinks he can preach, let him come up here and try it, for I can't."

A young man who had annoyed Robert Hall for permission to preach, afterwards received a severe rebuke upon asking Mr. Hall what he thought of his sermon. Wearied by his pertinacity,

Mr. Hall at length told him that the sermon had done him a great deal of good.

"Ah, I am delighted to think I could have said anything to benefit *you*. What particular part affected you most pleasantly?"

"Oh, all of it."

"Ah, indeed; in what way?"

"Why, last week I heard Dr. Mason preach, and I thought I could never preach again; but after hearing you, I think I can."

One important advantage of self-knowledge is, that when a man fully realizes what he is as a man, his wonderful and delicate organization, the complicated and yet harmonious arrangement of his system, even physiologically considered, he will more carefully avoid all self-abuse by the indulgence of appetite or passion. The knowledge that alcoholic drink is a poison, disorders digestion, inflames the mucous membrane, taints the springs of life at their source, impoverishes and depraves the blood, and deranges almost every function of his body, so "fearfully and wonderfully made," should suffice to induce every man to abstain; but when the realization comes that he is a man, with soul, mind, spirit, that his body may be the temple of the Holy Ghost, will he fill himself with all pollution and defilement, and make himself a child of hell, who might be an heir of heaven?

Another important branch of knowledge is to know others; and this is more difficult, and yet the desire for it is universal. Some men are so open and transparent, they seem to carry their hearts in their hands; while others are reticent and reserved. How little we really know even of the most intimate friend who walks by our side, and with whom we are in communion! How often we misjudge men—mistake them! I know of a man who exclaimed, on being told that a friend of his belonged to the Church, "Why, I have known him intimately for some years, but I never dreamed he was a Christian." Again you may say of another, "He has not a vice," when it is possible his whole composition is thoroughly vicious.

Bring two really honest men together, and each misjudging the other through difference in temper and manner, may prevent a recognition of their honesty; but bring two men together, both unprincipled, perverted, and bad, and they will recognize each other by instant sympathy. Men who pretend to be judges of character are often deceived. We should not always trust to appearances. "Oh, I do not like his looks," is an expression often heard at first sight of a man.

I heard a gentleman once say, "I never trust a man who cannot look me right in the eye." That is not a correct basis for judgment upon one's character. There are some timid, diffident souls, who are easily looked out of countenance, who cannot meet the stern eye of a person who is trying them by their brass. The very worse criminals can stare you out of countenance; and it is no criterion that the man who can outstare you is the virtuous, truthful man, and the diffident person whose eyes droop before your staring gaze is the vicious and untruthful one. I believe we may sometimes judge a man more correctly by his looks than by his words or actions, for professions may be false, but the face is generally true; and yet he may not be able to endure stolidly an inquiring stare. Some faces are so unmistakably rascally, it needs no great penetration to decide the character. It might be said of them, as was said to an individual who complained "I don't feel myself to-day," "I heartily wish you joy, for you must certainly be the gainer by the change."

We are apt to misjudge others, and distrust them. The world is bad enough, but we imagine men worse than they are. Take an audience anywhere, and composed as you will, and deliver to them a speech full of sordid, base, mean sentiments, and you will be hissed; but utter sentiments honest, lofty, chivalric, noble, and applause will follow. We find that, however men may live, there is an inherent sympathy with what is noble. Many there are who walk through life utterly unknown and unappreciated by their fellows,—"fine, sensitive natures, that encase themselves in a second or outer life, unseemly, having no beauty that they should be desired, and who will never be known for what they are by those who look only upon the outside. They live on, unprized, uncared for, until some one, skilled in the knowledge of other men, discerns beneath the surface the real nature of the man, and sees, hidden from other eyes, God's glorious handiwork." I believe there are many such walking side by side with us in the world, men of whom we are not worthy, whose real beauty and grandeur will never be fully known till, in eternity, God uncovers His own image, and bids us see them as they are.

There is a noble development of this desire for knowledge when a man possesses the power to bring before him in a living panorama the grand lessons of history,—mingling with the generations that are gone, his heart glowing at the "songs of bards two thousand years old," his nerves thrilling at the eloquence of men who can never die, his spirit kindling with "thoughts that have passed from soul to soul since souls have been," sympathizing in the struggles of nations battling to be free, joining them in their welcome to the light. He weeps at their griefs, rejoices when they are glad; his heart is affected by the "mighty utterances of humanity through the ages." He trembles in agony to behold nations losing their way, and groping in the darkness of despotism. He takes a part in all the progress of the race as knowledge opens to him a glorious world, and he "holds converse with the mighty dead;" or, "studying the heavens on the shore of that limitless ocean, he sounds the depths of the ether, gauges the visible universe, counts the myriads of stars that people it, measures their distances, unravels their most complicated movements, reveals their dimensions, evolves order from apparent confusion." Oh, it is grand! The crown of knowledge is brighter than a monarch's diadem; and yet a man with such a glorious heritage may not be one whit more moral, religious, or, in the highest sense, more useful. Why, knowledge itself, unless wisely directed, will even make a bad man more dangerous.

Knowledge, unless allied with goodness and wisdom and embodied in upright character, is naught. It is not how much a man may know; but the end and purpose for which he obtains knowledge is of the greatest importance. The great object must be to improve character, to make it better, more useful, benevolent, energetic and efficient in the attainment of high purposes. "One may be able to interpret the eloquence of nature, and look out among the stars with a feeling of exultation at the glories of the heavens; yet if he scrutinizes the universe with self only before his eyes, he lies buried in the earth alone with all his burning thoughts. But when in devoutness of spirit he gazes into the heavens, he himself becomes as nothing, as an atom of dust on the outskirts of a glory immeasurable." He perceives in everything the Presence that fills immensity, and crowds it with proofs of His power and wisdom. Then the Author of this beauty and majesty becomes the object of his desires, while in his self-abasement he exclaims, "What is man, that Thou art mindful of him!" and learns to trust Him in His faithfulness to all eternity, and finds that "the fear of the Lord is the beginning of wisdom." "The pillar of cloud and of fire which led the Israelites to safety drew the Egyptians to destruction. One saw the hand of God, the other but a phenomenon."

All the worldly knowledge a man can acquire will not make him a good man, or prevent him from falling into grievous sin. We may find great mental cultivation combined with moral corruption.

Knowledge is a trust, and brings with it a mighty responsibility. Few more awful sights are seen than a once cultivated intellect fallen,—a mind that has soared into the highest heaven of intellectual attainment, that has shone forth like the sun in his glory, and filled the world with its blessed beams, degraded and debased,—a mind that might have been like a Samson among its fellows, shorn of its strength, and only brought forth at times to make sport for the Philistines; like the eagle that might have risen to the firmament and drunk of the fountain of divine light, fluttering, broken-winged, and blinded, in the dust; or, like the fallen angels, taking refuge in the Gadarene swine from the presence of Him in whom they ought to have delighted —the divine spark fled from the human face, the soul gone, the beast everywhere grovelling in the thing that had once been man. Hear him, with voice thick and husky, a cracked laugh, talking rubbish and ribaldry, and in the midst of balderdash gleaming now and then a gorgeous sentence that drivels away again into a cadence almost idiotic. It is one of the most awful sights of earth.

The desire to know becomes paltry when it develops into mere inquisitiveness. Some one has defined inquisitiveness as an "itch for prying into other people's affairs, to the neglect of our own." The constant and genuine food of some minds is news. They seem to subsist entirely on this diet. "The news—what's the news?" Shakespeare says:

> "With open mouth, swallowing a tailor's news."
>
> "Ah, curiosity! the cause of all our ill;
> And yet the plague that most torments us still."

Some men delight in asking questions about affairs that are often not worth knowing; silence is torture to them, and by continual application they become masters of all kinds of queer histories; they never miss anything for the want of asking. Such can tell you of all the weddings that are to come off, and when; of all the engagements that are broken off, and for what cause; whose property is mortgaged, and for how much; who borrows money, and for what; and who lends it, and on what terms. They know the amount of everybody's income; can inform you what their neighbours eat, drink, wear, say, or do; when they sleep, walk, or ride; they watch the postman and the butcher; know how many letters and how much meat they have. They are fully acquainted with all domestic squabbles, and pride themselves on having the earliest information. To obtain this, they pass their time keeping a watchful eye upon others, gathering up chance remarks or inadvertent expressions, and weave them into a web of history, asking little innocent side questions, seemingly vague and unimportant, and then deducing conclusions by no means so unimportant, until they become entangled and ensnared in the cobwebs of petty inquisitiveness.

Such persons become the "funnels of conversation, taking in nothing for their own use, but merely to pass it to another.

They are the channels through which all that is spoken of others is conveyed; simply funnels." How amusing it is to see one of these inquisitive persons with a mystery! How he ponders it, lies in wait for it, scents all around it, fixes on it with a bull-dog tenacity, follows it with a persistence worthy of a nobler object. He will concentrate on it all the force of his will, fancying himself on the verge of discovery; and after all this expenditure of time, energy, and patience, becomes possessed of a piece of news—fresh news—yes, fresh; but, like the manna, "food one day, stale and corrupt the next."

We have no sympathy for these merely inquisitive ones in their disappointments, but rather laugh at them. That is a good story of one conversing with a very quiet person who had lost his leg.

"How did you lose it? When? Where?"

To all his questions he received evasive replies, until the itch to know *how* that leg was lost became so intolerable, and his persistence was so annoying, the gentleman said:

"If you will promise me on your word and honour that you will not ask another question—not one—I will tell you how I lost my leg."

"Agreed. Tell me."

"Not another question?"

"Not one more; only tell me that."

"Well, my friend, it was bit off!"

"Bit off! Oh—ah—hum."

I do not condemn utterly the asking of unimportant questions. Some men, for the sake of showing politeness or attention to a stranger, may border on the inquisitive, without being offensive, and may be very much hurt by a rude reception of the questioning.

John Randolph stopped once at an hotel where the landlord tried very hard to converse with him, but without success. After he had paid his bill, and was starting, the landlord said:

"Which way are you travelling, Mr. Randolph?"

"Sir?"

"I asked which way you were travelling?"

"Have I paid my bill?"

"Yes."

"Do I owe you anything more?"

"No."

"Then I am going just where I please; do you understand?"

"Oh yes!"

But when he had gone a little way, he came to a fork in the road, and sent his servant to ask the way. The landlord shouted out:

"Mr. Randolph, you don't owe me one cent; take which way you choose!"

There is often labour expended in obtaining information that is not worth the time and toil. At a trial, a lady witness was being questioned, when she stated a fact:

"He took me by the shoulders and pushed me from the room."

"What did he say?"

"We do not want to know what he said," exclaimed the opposing lawyer.

"Yes we do," said the other.

"What did he say?"

"I object to the question; it is not admissible;" and at it they went, arguing the case till night. The court adjourned; and next day books were consulted and arguments advanced, the court determined to decide the point; and after some consultation, and examining precedents, it was declared the question might be admitted.

"Then what did he say?"

The court was in breathless attention and suspense while the important question was asked, "What did he say?"

"Nothing at all."

Curiosity to know little things—unimportant matters—sometimes leads men into extravagance. An American and a Frenchman were taking a meal together. The American ate so voraciously, that the Frenchman said:

"Monsieur, s'il vous plait, is dat your breakfast or your dinnaire vat you eat?"

No reply.

"Pardon, monsieur, vill you dell me, s'il vous plait, is dat your breakfast or your dinnaire vat you eat?"

"Go to thunder!"

"Why you tell me go to thunder for ask you one civil question? Ah, you are not gentleman!"

A quarrel ensued; a challenge given and accepted; a duel fought; the American shot the Frenchman.

"Oh, I am very much kill! Oh, I shall die! Oh! ah!"

"My dear fellow, I am very sorry. What can I do for you?"

"Oh, monsieur, you can do great deal! Oh, ah! vill you tell me vas dat your breakfast or your dinnaire vat you eat?"

The developments of the elements of curiosity are almost illimitable. Some people seem to be possessed of a desire almost amounting to a passion to see rare things, or indeed anything bordering on the impossible.

Advertise that some impossible feat is to be performed and you will draw a crowd. In London a notice appeared that in the course of an entertainment a man would jump into a quart bottle, and sing a comic song. The house was crowded, and because the feat was not performed, which they knew was impossible, they nearly destroyed the theatre. A talking-fish—a mermaid—a monstrosity, will draw crowds. A man went every night to see Van Amburgh put his head in the lion's mouth. When asked why he went every night, he said he knew to a moral certainty that the lion would bite that man's head off some time before he had done with him, and he wanted to see it! If there were a certainty that Blondin would fall from his tight rope, it would draw a larger crowd than otherwise. Our curiosity is excited by feats of legerdemain, or prestidigitation, and I must confess I should like to know how some of them are performed.

There are many feats wonderful as well as very curious. When Sir Charles Napier was in India, a juggler visited camp, and among other performances cut in two with a stroke of his sword a lemon placed in the hand of his assistant. Napier doubted the feat, and held out his hand for the experiment.

The juggler looked attentively at the hand and refused. Napier thought he had found him out and laughed at him.

"Let me see your other hand," said the juggler.

The hand was submitted, and the man said:

"If you will hold it firmly I will perform the feat."

"Why the left hand and not the right?"

"Because the right hand is hollow in the centre, and there is danger of cutting off the thumb; the left is higher, and there is less risk."

Napier says if he had not laughed at him he should have refused, but putting the lemon on his hand he held out his arm. The juggler balanced himself, and with a swift stroke cut the lemon in two pieces. Napier said he felt the edge of the sword on his hand as if a cold thread had been drawn across it.

The desire of knowing coming events is one of the strongest inclinations in the minds of many. I think it is Dr. Johnson who says, "The quality of looking into futurity seems the unavoidable condition of a being whose motions are gradual, and whose life is progressive." We all are solicitous about events which lie hidden. The mind is not satisfied with objects immediately before it, but is always breaking away from the present, filled with conjectures about things not yet made real to us by outward existence, and longing to penetrate into futurity. To this cause is owing the success of astrologers, fortune-tellers, prognosticators, wise people, seers, spiritual mediums, biologists, and all pretenders to a knowledge of future events; the consulting of oracles, the noting of signs, omens, lucky days, and all the various arts of superstition.

It is a fact that the superstitious are generally ignorant. No head is a vacuum; some are circumscribed, some are capacious, and the more room is taken up with useful knowledge the less remains for credulity. "The more a man is acquainted with real things, the more willing he is to give up the ghost of things;" yet after all, there is a vast amount of superstition among us. The vagaries of some are very whimsical, and would puzzle the antiquary to discover how they have originated. What nonsense in examining the grounds of a coffee-cup to learn of your future husband; putting bride-cake under the pillow to dream of him (you do not suppose any one believes such absurdities! I cannot tell, but why do they do it? I hardly suppose that any young lady puts bride-cake under her pillow without a glimmering hope that she may in her dreams behold the coming man); throwing the apple-paring over the head that it may fall in the shape of the first letter of his name! How silly to stir the fire expecting to read in its bright flames the prophecy that you will have a bright husband!

Then note the multitudes of omens really believed in by many! If a hen crows it is a sign of bad luck. If a spark flies out from the fire a stranger is coming. If the cat turns her tail to the fire we are to have a hard frost; if she sneezes, all in the family will have colds. If you find a pin with the head turned towards you it is a sign of good luck. Spilling salt, or laying knives across each other are ill omens. I have known persons to be really annoyed at either of these occurrences. If the head itches it is a sign of rain; if the eyebrow itches you will see a stranger; if the right eye itches, you will cry; if the left, you will laugh; if your nose itches you will shake hands with a fool; if it is your right hand, you will pay money; if your left, you will receive it; if it is your back, butter will be cheap; if your side, somebody is wishing for you; if your knee, you will kneel in a strange church; and if it is your foot, you will tread on strange ground.

These are, to be sure, vagaries and extravagances, but it is curiosity that leads to them, curiosity to know the future. What would you give to know whether your speculation will be successful, and your marriage happy! Perhaps if I ask my reader the wish that is with you most prominent, you would tell me, "To know what is to come;" yet you cannot. "Trace a rainbow from the ocean, through the clouds, and back again into the sea, and find it there, and then perhaps you may be able to foretell what will happen in the future."

Our thoughts can have no influence on the future, but our acts will. What folly to be so absorbed in the desire to know the future as to neglect the present, dreaming out life, or worrying it away in vain conjecture! Such men become unstable, always planning, never executing; always commencing, never completing; always thinking, never acting; always proposing, never performing; with life before them, and its objects, pleasures, duties; but duties never fulfilled, pleasures never tasted, objects never attained. In the beginning, life seems a vast conception; at the end, an unsatisfactory, miserable failure. Such men float on the sea of life; they are boats without rudders, tossed by every wave of passion, caprice, or impulse; promising to do everything, doing nothing; within sight of the land of peace and comfort, but never touching its shores.

We can make our own future,—we are making it every day. It is a solemn fact, that "whatsoever a man soweth, that shall he also reap." Sow corn, reap corn; sow weeds, reap weeds: sow the corruptible, reap the corruptible; sow the imperishable, reap the imperishable.

The ruin of men is but the thickening of the harvest of which they have sowed the seed. They reap the fruit of their own husbandry; the same grain the sower scatters, the reaper collects. If the husbandry of wickedness goes forward, there is a harvest of anguish to be gathered. We reach the summit of all that is tremendous and awful in conception when we consider a man consigned to the tyranny of a passion never to be conquered, and never to be gratified. Milton puts these words into the mouth of Satan:

"Which way I fly is hell; myself am hell."

Sow envy, malice, revengefulness, covetousness, drunkenness, sensuality, and we must eat of the fruit of our way, and be filled with our own devices. What hell ever preached can surpass this? No need of fire, or rack? Who can imagine the agony of such a poor, torn, tossed creature, who has endowed every unholy passion with sovereignty, ploughed iniquity, and sown wickedness, only to reap the same. If we would make our future peaceful, let us sow righteousness, and reap life everlasting. "He that is unjust, let him be unjust still; and he that is filthy, let him be filthy still ; and he that is holy, let him be holy still."

But to know what shall be!—here curiosity is blocked, and we rest on faith. The future is known to God alone, and we can know no more than He has revealed, and that we receive by faith,—faith that amounts to certainty,—because He has said it. We believe in "a life which after myriads of ages will be still new, and still beginning." Immortality is revealed to us, and we receive it as an absolute certainty ; but the character of that unending existence depends upon ourselves, for God has said, "He who sows to the flesh, shall of the flesh reap corruption ; and he who sows to the spirit, shall of the spirit reap life everlasting." Our knowledge relates chiefly to the present, and what is that? We talk of the flight of time, but how limited is the space in which we can say "Now"? We do not comprehend how small that space is.

De Quincey, in one of his essays, presents this thought very vividly : "How narrow, how incalculably narrow, is the true and actual present! Of that time which we call the present, how small a part but belongs either to a past which has fled, or to a future which is still on the wing. It has perished, or it is not born. It was, or it is not. The true and very present in which only we live and enjoy, offers less capacity for our footing than the slenderest film that ever spider twisted from her womb. All is finite in the present, and even that finite is infinite in its velocity of flight towards death."

I quote the language of another writer: "All our ideas concerning a futurity of living, thinking, acting, are phantoms seen in the dark without revelation. There is nothing possible in the trackless future, but by faith. Faith is a necessity. By faith, we learn all things pertaining to the ways of the Almighty. By knowledge, we learn His works; by faith, we learn His ways in the life that now is, and that which is to come. Is not faith of more importance than knowledge? A man may know all mysteries, may understand all languages, may weigh the stars, may be profound in all sciences, filled with all the knowledge of the schools, yet as he stands on the confines of his life, with the consciousness of immortality, if he sees no star of hope to guide him, all is uncertainty and doubt. He stretches out his hand and grasps the darkness; his soul fluttering in the weakened body that fain would hold it, passes away into an eternity of which he knows nothing, and dreads everything. How poor he is! how miserably poor!"

Another, whose faith in God is the governing and actuating power of his whole being, knowing nothing of the learning of the schools, may talk but stammeringly one language, yet standing on the verge of eternity can say, "I know whom I have believed. I shall be satisfied when I awake in Thy likeness." How incomparably rich is he!"

Poor Joe could neither read nor write; he understood no doctrine but the one simple truth of the Gospel. Lying on his hard bed, he could say, "Joe only knows one thing: Jesus Christ came to save sinners. Joe is a sinner. Jesus Christ came to save him. Joe believe it, that's enough. Joe love Jesus Christ."

Some years ago, in Allen Street Church, New York, I related the little history of Joe, as I heard my mother tell it; and a man, rather shabby, and with the evident signs of dissipation, stood up in the audience, and cried out: "I am Joe, and I am a sinner; and if Jesus Christ came to save sinners, I want Him to save me."

Many Christian people that evening took him by the hand, and encouraged him. A long time after that, a man and his wife came to me. They were well dressed, and respectable. The man said, "Have you forgotten me? I'm Joe. Don't you remember, at Allen Street, Joe stood up, and said he was a sinner? Well, I am Joe, and this is my wife, and we are trying to serve Jesus Christ. I was a swearer and a drunkard, but now I am sober, and I love Jesus Christ; and I and my wife wanted to speak to you, and let you know that Joe meant what he said that night in Allen Street Church."

I occasionally hear of Joe and his wife as a couple united in one purpose to serve the Lord Christ, and who have persuaded others to walk in the same path.

Then give me faith, the ground of a settled hope, without knowledge, rather than all the learning of earth without faith; so that when the shadows of death fall on my eyelids, I may compose myself to sleep with the certainty of a coming morning, and a glory above the clouds, as undoubtedly as I close my weary eyes to sleep to-night with the assurance of a sunrise to-morrow.

Then let me say especially to the young, in the words of the wise man, "With all thy getting, get understanding. Wisdom is the principal thing; therefore, get wisdom; exalt her, and she shall promote thee; she shall bring thee to honour; she shall give to thine head an ornament of grace; a crown of glory shall she be to thee." Job tells us in his parable: "It cannot be gotten with gold; the topaz of Ethiopia shall not equal it; the price of it is above rubies; it shall not be valued with the gold of Ophir, with the precious onyx, or the sapphire. Whence, then, is wisdom? God understandeth the way therefore. He knoweth the place thereof. When He made a decree for the rain, and a way for the lightning of the thunder, then did He see it, and declare it. He prepared it, and stretched it out." "And unto man He said, Behold the fear of the Lord, that is wisdom; and to depart from evil is understanding."

CHAPTER XVI.

COMEDIES—THE HUMOROUS SIDE OF LIFE.

The Art of Putting Things—Illustrative Anecdotes—Macklin at the Theatre—The Smoker on a Coach—Mr. Parker's Preaching—Managing Others—The Scolding Schoolmaster—The Inhuman Teacher—Appeals to Honour better than Brutality—The Model Principal—The College President's Lecture on Spontaneous Combustion—The College President guarding his Hen-Roost—The Midnight Ride—Acknowledgment of Errors—Bonnie Christie—Matter-of-fact People—"Six-penny Caliker"—No Devils ever cast out of a Man—The Quaker's Answer—The Physician and the Stone-Mason—A Digression but not an Argument—Henderson the Actor—Difference between Settling down and Settling up—Wit of Dr. Samuel Cox—The Conceited Count—Practical Jokes—My Sacramento Acquaintance.

"IT'S not so much what he says, but how he says it." "It's not so much what he does, but how he does it," are remarks constantly heard. Some one has written an essay on the "Art of Putting Things." How many quarrels might be avoided, if we could learn the art of rebuking with courtesy and tact! Macklin, when a man stood before him and his friend at the theatre, completely shutting out all view of the stage, might have asked him to sit down, or with his cane struck him in the back, and probably given offence; but he simply said, "I beg your pardon, sir; but when you see or hear anything particularly interesting on the stage, will you please let us know, as we are entirely dependent on your kindness." That was sufficient. With a smile, and an apology that could hardly have been extracted by rudeness, the gentleman took his seat.

A man seated between two gentlemen on the outside of a coach, was smoking incessantly, when one of the gentlemen, nearly strangled, said, "Please, sir, would you have any objection to smoke in that other gentleman's face a little while?" The pipe was immediately, and with perfect good-humour, put out.

I was once visiting a lady, who told me that her son came home from church one Sunday, and said:

"Mother, I do not like Mr. Parker's preaching; and I do not intend to hear him any more."

To all her persuasions,—for she feared if he refrained to go with her to church, he would go nowhere else,—his reply was, "I do not like his preaching; he does me no good; and I shall go somewhere else."

Soon he dropped into the habit of staying away from church a whole or half a day; troubling her, because of the irregularity of his church attendance. One day, Edward met Mr. Parker in the street.

"How do you do, Ed?"

"How do you do, Mr. Parker?"

"Been out of town lately, Ed?"

"No, I've not been away."

"Ah! I've not seen you in church lately."

"Why, do you know whether I come to church or not?"

"Oh, yes; I have missed you for some Sundays past. Do you not go to church at all?"

"Not much."

"Why?"

"Well, Mr. Parker, I do not like your preaching."

"No more do I, Ed. You cannot have a poorer opinion than I have of my preaching; and if you can tell me how I can preach better, I shall be obliged to you. I do not blame you for not liking my preaching; I wish you could help me to preach better. I do not ask you to hear me; but do not stay away from church because you do not like me. Go and hear Mr. ——, he's a good preacher; or Dr. ——, he's a much better preacher than I am. Go and hear somebody; do not leave the church altogether. Good-bye, Ed, my dear fellow."

He went home, and his first words upon coming into the house were:

"Mother, Mr. Parker is a brick, and I'll go and hear him, like or no like, just as long as he and I stay in the city." And from that time he has been a regular attendant, and he and Mr. Parker are fast friends.

How few possess the faculty of managing others! How rare is the ability of ruling or controlling others! Yet some possess that ability in a large degree. There have been teachers who, by too much governmental discipline, have embittered their scholars for life; while others, who have been the strictest disciplinarians, have gained the love and respect of all whom they have taught. I have but little experience of schools, but remember one which I attended whose master—one of those uncertain men of whom you are never sure—ruled according to his feelings. If his breakfast disagreed with him, woe to the boys! If his wife had been cross, and perchance had scolded him,—and that was not seldom, for he was the meekest of the meek at home,—then he would emphasize his troubles upon the boys. How we suffered when he had dyspepsia! Scarcely any in the school but hated him, and yet he was successful in teaching, after a fashion. His was one of those independent schools of fifty years ago in England, when the master was supported solely by the charge to each scholar.

> "Full well the busy whisper circling round
> Conveyed the dismal tidings when he frowned,"

would apply most emphatically to nearly every morning;

> "Full well they laughed with counterfeited glee
> At all his jokes, for many a joke had he,"

would not apply at all. When he came into the school-room, every boy's head was bent to the desk after one glance at the dial of his face, which told the state of the thermometer. Suddenly a ruler would whirl through the air, aimed at some luckless boy; perhaps it hit him.

"Robert, bring that ruler to me!"

The boy walked up to the desk.

"Hold out your hand!"

And the palm soon tingled and was stung with half-a-dozen

blows, as if fire had touched it. What for? Oh, that was a small matter: perhaps the boy's head was not posed to suit the master. I have stood on a bench with a heavy book in my hand, compelled to hold it at arm's length till the sweat of pain would stand in beads on my forehead, and every nerve, from the fingertips to the hips, and down to the very toes, was throbbing with pain; and that for a trifling misdemeanour. Oh how we hated him! There were such masters years ago; thank God the race is extinguished!

A gentleman said to me, "I have the most agonizing pain in my head almost constantly. I have many a sleepless night tossing with pain. What is the cause? Schoolmaster. Yes, my schoolmaster would strike me on the head with his hand, and sometimes with a heavy book, and the result is these terrible headaches; and sometimes, when I am suffering so keenly, I almost curse the man that by his brutality has caused me so much suffering."

I do not believe in coddling boys, or remitting all punishment, nor in relaxing the strict government; but I believe boys can be governed by appeals to their honour rather than by brutality; and if punishment is needed, let the infliction be in proportion to the offence.

I was struck with the methods pursued in a large school, one of the best, for boys, in a neighbouring State. The principal entertained me for a few days. There was no flogging, no spying, no talebearing. There was subordination and an easy compliance with rules. Every delinquent reported himself. It needed some patience and skill and persistence to bring the scholars to this point. For instance, if the principal were disturbed by a great noise in one of the dormitories occupied by a dozen or more boys, he would go up to the room at once, and probably all would be still, every boy in his bed, some feigning sleep.

"Who made that noise?"

No reply.

"I ask, who made that noise?"

No reply.

The question was slowly repeated.

No answer.

"Young gentlemen, please dress yourselves, and come down to the recitation-room."

When they were gathered there, he would address them, telling them how mean it was that the guilty should permit the innocent to be punished for their fault; and dilating on the cowardice that would commit a fault and permit others to suffer the consequences, he would ask the young gentleman who originated the noise, or if there were more than one, to acknowledge it, and receive the punishment; that he should consider the whole class in disgrace until the culprit or culprits confessed. This experiment was generally successful, and he had but very little difficulty in ascertaining the cause of any breach of the rules.

The president of a college, whom I knew as a dear friend for many years, possessed a wonderful faculty for governing and detecting a culprit. On one occasion a good-sized haystack was burnt, evidently set on fire. Who did it? That was a mystery. Some one connected with the college, no doubt; but who? No remarks were made about it except those that were perfectly natural. A week or more after, the president announced that he would give an extra lecture on chemistry to the whole college of students. In the course of his lecture, the hall being crowded, he spoke of spontaneous combustion, and proceeded to explain scientifically the causes of spontaneous combustion; and with a glance of his keen eye flashing in every corner of the room, he alluded to the haystack as a very good instance of the effect of such a combination as he had described. In that one glance he detected the unconscious half-smile on one, and the almost imperceptible wink on another, and the involuntary change of countenance, or the furtive look on a third; and quietly finishing his lecture, he requested certain gentlemen to come to him in his study; to find, on asking them on their honour, that his ingenious plan, aided by his keen perception, had brought him to the correct conclusions.

Another story is told of a college president who suspected that some of the boys had planned to rob his hen-roost. Near the enclosure were two large apple-trees at the back of the house; so he quietly went out and waited till they came. Of the two, one ascended the tree, the other remained below. When they were ready to commence operations, the doctor made a slight noise, and the one below started off with an exclamation of surprise. The one in the tree asked in a whisper :

"What's the matter?"

To which the doctor replied, also in a whisper :

"All's right."

"Here, catch hold," said the upper one, handing down a rooster. "Here's old Prex."

And, handing down a hen :

"Here's Mrs. Prex."

"And here," handing down a chicken, "here's Miss Prex. I guess that'll do."

The doctor quietly got over the fence with the fowls, and went to his house.

The poor robber of the hen-roost descended to find his companion gone. What they said when they met will probably never be known; but in the morning the two young gentlemen received a polite invitation to dine with the president,—an honour they could not very well decline. Possibly they were embarrassed when, seated at the table, they saw three fowls roasted for the dinner; and we can imagine their sensations when the doctor said :

"Now, young gentlemen, will you have a piece of 'old Prex, Mrs. Prex, or Miss Prex'?"

How the dinner passed off, and how the young delinquents got off, deponent sayeth not. On that theme history is dumb; but nothing more was heard of the escapade, the doctor thinking that the mortification was sufficient punishment.

A very good story is told of the head of one of our celebrated institutions, who was the possessor of a very clumsy, old-fashioned vehicle, to which he was very partial, and which he constantly used in riding through the streets of the town to the disgust of most of the students. A plan was formed among some of the boys that on a certain night they would remove this offensive vehicle from the coach-house to a wood about half a mile from the college. Their intention was to run the carriage into the thickest of the woods and underbrush, and leave it there. But the principal by some means learned or suspected their intention. Accordingly, in the evening, he quietly went out to the coach-house, and, well wrapped up, crouched in a corner of the carriage, and waited. Soon the boys came, very stealthily, and, without looking into the vehicle, began their operations very quietly; and in whispers, and with many a "hush," and "take care," and "look out," they succeeded in getting it out of the house and yard, and into the road.

There they were all right, but they were puzzled to find the thing so heavy to haul; and amid grumblings and puffings and pantings, varied occasionally with a strong expression of disgust, they succeeded in reaching the woods, the principal listening to their complaints and rather enjoying the situation. Having with some difficulty backed the carriage into the brush, they began to congratulate each other on the success of their manœuvre. The old gentleman, letting down the window, to their utter surprise and alarm, very quietly said :

"Now, young gentlemen, just take me back very carefully, if you please."

It was rather a sharp lesson, but better than to disgrace a set of young men for a comparatively harmless joke.

Sometimes it is very hard to learn how to acknowledge an error. There are those who cannot understand that there is something manly and worthy of their dignity in acknowledging a mistake, or owning their ignorance.

When a lady asked Dr. Johnson how he came to commit a palpable blunder in his dictionary, he replied, "Ignorance, pure ignorance."

For a schoolmaster, or one in authority, it seems specially hard to confess to an error, and yet such a confession often raises him in the estimation of his subordinates, and binds him to them with stronger cords of affection and respect. I once read somewhere a very interesting narrative of such an experience by school and schoolmaster, illustrating this and also the beauty and nobleness of character and truth.

Two boys were in a schoolroom together, when some fireworks were suddenly exploded. When the master questioned them, one boy at once denied it; the other, Bonnie Christie, would neither admit nor deny it, and without further questioning he was severely flogged. When the boys were alone again, he who had escaped, said:

"Bonnie, why did you not deny it?"

"Because there were only we two in the room, and one of us must have lied."

"Then why not say I did it?"

"Because you said you did not, and I pity a liar, and will never tell of him."

When school resumed, the boy marched up to the master's desk, and said:

"Please, sir, I can't bear to be a liar; I let off the crackers," and then burst into tears.

After a moment's pause the master, hand in hand with the culprit, before the whole school, walked down to where young Christie sat.

"Bonnie Christie, lad," said the master, "he and I have come to beg your pardon; we were both to blame."

The school was so hushed they might have heard Bonnie's big-boy tear-drops fall on his copy-book, as looking up with the tears on his cheek,—such tears as the severest flogging would never have forced from his eyes, he gently said, "Master, for ever," and the glorious shout of the scholars made the rafters ring as the master's eyes grew dim with tears.

A good-tempered retort often accomplishes more than a long argument, in defeating an adversary. It requires tact and self-possession, with a quick apprehension to hold your own in an encounter of wit; but on the dull and literal it is almost impossible to make any impression. In such a case the wit must be heavy and blunt, or an explanation would be required of you. I have met the obtuse and literal, and been amused at their utter inability to understand a joke; they take you as you say, not as you mean.

Narrate to them some extravagant American story or jest; tell them of a man running round in a circle so fast that he could see his own back, and they will begin to argue the point and discuss the possibility, or impossibility, of such an operation.

We often find among the common people in this country, especially in New England, a class with whom it would be dangerous to perpetrate a practical joke; and woe betide if they suspect you are fooling them or dealing by them unfairly.

A lady told me that her brother, who kept a dry-goods' store, was rather glib in his talk, and inclined to be somewhat flippant to his customers. An old woman came to his store and said:

"I want to get some sixpenny caliker."

"Sixpenny, marm! Better not take a sixpenny calico; take a ninepenny. Sixpenny calico won't wash; a ninepenny calico will. A sixpenny calico is sleazy; a ninepenny calico is firm. Take a ninepenny calico, and you'll be glad you didn't take a sixpenny; take a sixpenny, and you'll be sorry you didn't take a ninepenny. Let me measure you off the ninepenny; it is heavier, will last longer, is cheaper in the end. Don't take a sixpenny, when only threepence more will give you a dress worth double. What do you say,—a ninepenny?"

The old woman stood perfectly still till he paused, and then said:

"A sixpenny caliker is good enough for a poor worm like me."

"Worm! worm, marm! don't call yourself a worm. I don't like to hear people call themselves worms. We are not worms; we are men and women. Worms indeed! I'm not a worm; you're not a worm. I'll tell you what we are made of: water, gas, lime;" and he went on with other items.

The old woman simply said:

"Law! is that so? Then I reckon the biggest part of you is gas. Now I'll take ten yards of sixpenny caliker."

A bantering acquaintance of the other sex remarked to a woman:

"I never heard of seven devils being cast out of a man."

"No," was the reply; "they've got 'em yet."

A Quaker, in giving evidence before a Board of Excise in

England, and being rudely treated, was rather pompously asked:

"Do you know what we sit here for?"

"Yes: one of thee for a thousand pounds a year, and the other for seventeen hundred."

A physician passing a stonemason's shop, bawled out:

"Good morning, Mr. D. Hard at work, I see. You finish your gravestones as far as 'In the memory of,' and then wait, I suppose, to see who wants a monument next?"

"Waal, yes," replied the old man, "unless somebody's sick and you're doctoring him, and then I keep right on."

An architect was asked in a slighting tone:

"You are a builder, are you not?"

"No, sir; I am an architect."

"Ah well, they are much the same, I believe."

"I beg your pardon, sir; they are totally different."

"Perhaps you can state wherein this great difference consists."

"Yes, sir. An architect is the mind; the builder is the machine; the architect is the power that puts the machine together and sets it going."

"Very well; perhaps you can inform me who was architect to the tower of Babel?"

"There was no architect, sir, and hence the confusion."

These are good; but rather the neatest I ever read was one by Henderson, the actor, who was seldom known to be in a passion. When at Oxford he was once debating with a fellow-student, who, not keeping his temper, threw a glass of wine in the actor's face. Mr. Henderson took out his handkerchief, wiped his face, and coolly said, "That sir, is a digression, now for the argument."

A man whose business transactions had been rather suspicious, and who had passed through bankruptcy twice, was boasting:

"I left business and settled down with a comfortable fortune," when a listener said:

"If you had settled up you wouldn't have had a cent."

A very self-important young man came to the turnstile at the railway station.

"Ticket, please," said the porter.

"Ah, my face is my ticket," was the reply.

"All right," said the porter; "my orders are to punch every ticket before I let it pass."

I once heard a very neat rebuke from Rev. Dr. Samuel Cox to a company of men, who understood it fully, and on whom anything keen or witty would have been lost. I was travelling on the Erie Railway. At Elmira three coloured persons, mulattoes, took passage. They were very neat, genteel, quite good-looking, and well-behaved,—two women and a man, who quietly took their seats near the door. Just before me sat four men, with their seat turned over. They were filthy and offensive, their language profane. They were drinking whiskey, and eating onions and cheese, leaving the odour of the car far from being agreeable; in fact, they were as repulsive as men could well be, and be permitted to remain in the car. There had been some audible grumbling at their coarse language.

The train-boy came into the car with water, and asked one of these coloured ladies if she wished some. She, with a smile, said, "Thank you," reaching out her hand to take the glass, when one of these dirty, blear-eyed, half-drunken creatures roared out with an oath, "They are giving a d—d nigger water!" The girl turned her face towards the wretch, and said, in a very sweet voice, "Perhaps this gentleman wants some water; you had better pass it to him before you offer it to coloured people." The deep pathos of her tone moved us all. Dr. Cox, who was sitting near me, and with whom I had been conversing, said, "That is well done, madam; thank you!" One of the men started up, and glaring at the doctor said, "Old man, mind your business, or I'll take care of you." Dr. Cox said, in that clear, bell-like voice that so many remember, "Sir, if you would take care of yourself, and live as cleanly as I have all my life,—if you live to be as old as I am, you may be as good-looking an old man as I am."

The contrast between the grey-haired, fresh-looking gentleman with the clear eye, the fine complexion, and the pure, sweet expression, and the bleared eye, the bloated face, the sensual mouth, the coarse skin of the brutal fellow who had dissolved his manliness in drink, was so striking that every one in the car seemed to be touched; and there followed a round of applause from hands and feet for a minute, to the utter discomfiture of the four ruffians, who were very quiet, and soon after left for the smoking-car. I thoroughly enjoyed this scene, as I always do the extinguishment of the impudent and overbearing.

It may sometimes be necessary to teach some men good manners by a little rougher treatment. On one occasion, while travelling, I saw a gentlemanly-looking man enter the car. I heard afterwards that he called himself a "Count," but he proved to be of very small account,—who illustrated the fact that looks are sometimes deceitful, and that a man may be very well dressed, and what the world calls genteel, and be but a slight remove from a blackguard. This person took a seat directly before a young lady, evidently travelling alone. After awhile, he took out of a morocco case a very beautifully-carved meerschaum pipe, then a small bag of tobacco. He filled the pipe, lighted it with a fusee, and opening the window, began to smoke.

Soon the lady said, "I beg your pardon, but the open window drives the smoke in my face, and I do not like tobacco smoke;" to which appeal he only replied by a shrug of the shoulders, and a long-drawn "Ah-h-h," and went on smoking. The lady again said, "I assure you, sir, that the smoke is very annoying to me; and gentlemen are not allowed to smoke in this car." The fellow said, in a drawling tone, "If you don't like the smoke you can take another seat, can't you?" A gentleman rose, reminding me very much of the late Judge McLean, and walking up to the smoker, said, very sternly, "Put that pipe out instantly." The reply was, "You mind your business." The gentleman said, "I will; this is every gentleman's business," and suddenly snatched the pipe from the man's mouth, and threw it out of the open window, and then remarked, "You may resent that if you please." Perhaps it would have been as well to call for the conductor, but by the applause that greeted him when he took his seat, the passengers evidently thought the punishment was just. The smoker seemed of less account than ever, and looked like a figure nine with the tail cut off.

I enjoy a joke, but practical jokes so called—though often exhibiting some ingenuity, and calling out our laughter at their absurdity—are one-sided, and the fun is generally for the perpetrator, and the misery and mortification for the victim. There is too often a vein of heartlessness, if not of cruelty, running through the whole transaction, and the life-long sufferers from a practical joke are not a few. I like fun without malice or heartlessness; and a sharp and well-deserved lesson may be taught by a joke. A man, in spite, once chalked the word "scoundrel" on a neighbour's door. The next morning, the neighbour called. The man was out; so he left his compliments with the servant, stating that he had returned the call as her master had left his name at the door.

When in Sacramento, I met the man who, when a boy, was the cause of my losing a good situation by an attempt to retaliate on him a practical joke he had played on me. I was working at my bench, and a tub of paste was by my side with brushes in it for use, when he took one of these brushes, heavily loaded with paste, and holding it near my face, said, "John!" I turned quickly, and got the paste on my face and in my hair. I was thoroughly vexed. He ran down the stairs. I took a sheet of paper, and putting perhaps a pint of paste on it, and holding it on the palm of my hand, waited at the door till he should come. I determined to wait there all day, or until I should catch him, as I knew that he must come back, and by that door. So there I stood, biding my opportunity, when I heard him, as I thought, stealthily creeping up the stairs. "Now," I thought, "my boy, you shall have it," and braved myself for the deed. I was excited at the thought of paying him in his own coin, when the door opened, and with all my might I dabbed the whole mass upon his face. Oh, horror! it was the boss of the shop! Never shall I forget how he looked, or how I felt. The joke was anything but a joke, for in a short time I was dismissed from my employment. There I learned that practical jokes, especially in cases of mistaken identity, are often expensive.

CHAPTER XVII.

VICTIMS OF DRINK—SCENES FROM LIFE.

Beer as a Beverage—Beer Drunkenness among Women—Great Britain's Curse—"Doctored" Beer—The Inside of a London Gin-Palace—What is "All Sorts"?—Kinahan's L. L.—The Landlord—The Bar-Maid—The Customers—Life in the Bar-Room—Disgraceful Scenes—"Fair Play"—What the London *Times* says—A "Genteel" Gin-Palace—Rev. Wm. Arnot on the Liquor Traffic—The Fratricide—A Hardened Woman—The Gambler's Suicide—A Horrible Sight—Suicide of McConnell—The Blood-Stains on the Floor—The Meanest Man in the World—The Rum-seller's Bargain—Result of the Trade—Dr. Guthrie's Testimony—That of Canon Farrar—"Fruits of the Traffic"—A Ghastly Story of the Prisoner at Dartmouth—The Convict's Story—Rum and Murder—Remorse—Waiting for Death.

THERE is in this country a growing tendency toward the commendation of beer as a beverage. This fallacy is built upon the misapprehension that drunkenness is caused altogether by spirituous liquors. The greatest harm from the use of beer is in its soporific effects, stupefying the drinker if he imbibe largely; consequently, the consumption of beer is alarmingly on the increase. If this tendency caused a diminution in the consumption of spirituous liquors, we should not be so much troubled.

It is an acknowledged fact that the drunkenness of England is mainly produced by beer. It is a fallacy to say that if we can induce men to drink beer instead of spirits, there will be less intemperance. The English Beer Act of 1830 was passed on this false theory, when it was received with almost universal acclamation. This measure was designed to supply what Lord Brougham called a "moral species of beverage," instead of immoral gin and rum, and was to prove an inestimable blessing to the British working-man, by giving him free access to this cheap and "wholesome" beverage. The express purpose of the Act was to encourage the consumption of beer, and discourage that of spirits. What was the result? Sydney Smith has given the whole story in a nut-shell: "The new Beer Bill has begun its operations. Everybody is drunk. Those who are not singing are sprawling. The sovereign people are in a beastly state." The scheme was a bitter disappointment to its friends. While the distillation of spirits has not decreased, beer-makers have become a power; and I believe there is no single power in Great Britain which so influences British character, and so sways the material and moral destinies of the British people, as the influence that sits enthroned on the beer butts of the brewers.

That "beer is the curse of Great Britain" is not my sentiment alone, but that of thousands who feel its truth in the growing demoralization of the people from its effects, and who are protesting against it. The drunkenness of England is something frightful. The first expression of surprise from an American or foreigner landing on the shores of Great Britain, is at the vast number of public-houses so well patronized, and at the proportion of women who frequent them.* The subject is overwhelming. With my voice I can speak, but on paper words fail me. By day I have walked in the brilliant metropolis, and the key-note in every street was drink. At night alone, or in the viler quarters accompanied by a detective, I have peered into the slums, and there beheld sights of orgy which compel me to believe that drunkenness in England among a section of the "lower classes" is more prevalent now than it was twenty years ago. I have stated the same impression in one of the London periodicals. This evident increase of intemperance, I believe, has startled a multitude of conscientious men and women to action in this matter; and I trust in God that the results of the uprising of the Christian philanthropists against this monstrous evil will be as successful

* 16,525 women were found drunk and disorderly in London, in 1878.

as the uprising of the North was against the twin curse to the world—Slavery.

Beer was to be introduced as a substitute for gin, but has become only an additional article for intoxication, demonstrating that the use of beer leads on to spirits. There are some who say that lager beer is not intoxicating. I heard a reformed man say that he got so drunk on lager that, to use his own expression, he "couldn't tell the difference between a two-dollar bill and Boston Common." Men drink for intoxication, and the beer only ministers to this desire. Let us look at a modern public-house, or gin-palace, in London.

There are some which are regarded more respectable than others, but this corner establishment is an average "palace;" is very gay, gaudy and glittering; its brilliant gas-jets gleaming through its windows of finest plate glass. There is no lack of French polish and gilding. Tier after tier of gigantic casks surround the room. Beer is sold a halfpenny a pint cheaper than at the beer-house. It is curious beer, half sweet and half acrid, black, muddy, brown in the froth, unpleasant to the taste, adulterated, cobbled up that the dealer may get rich and the customer drunk and poisoned. There is very little beer that is not "doctored" and made even worse than in its original state by deleterious drugs. Indeed, every kind of intoxicating liquors is adulterated. The manufacture of wines, brandies, whiskeys, and other liquors is a wonderfully profitable trade. I have a book, obtained with some difficulty, on the manufacture of these articles, and the revelation is somewhat startling. But to return to the public-house.

The area before the bar will hold seventy or eighty persons, allowing at the same time room for a stand-up fight. The gin-palace has not only a bar but divers boxes partitioned off from the general area. There is the wholesale bar entrance, retail entrance, jug and bottle entrance; but wholesale or retail, jug or bottle, it means beer and spirits. The bar is covered with pewter, perforated to allow the drainings, washings and outspillings of the glasses to run through,—all which is dealt out again, under the name of "all sorts." The drinkers being shaky in the hand, the profit from this source tells up at the close of the year. At the back of the bar are placards printed in colours and framed, telling of "Old Tom," "Cream of the Valley," "Superior Cream Gin," "Beer, Strong as Brandy, Tenpence a Pot," "The Dew off Ben Nevis," "Kinahan's L. L., the Right Sort." I was told, when in Dublin, that the origin of the mark on the casks of Kinahan's L. L. is that one of the Lord Lieutenants some years ago was very partial to a certain kind of whiskey made by Kinahan, and when the casks were sent to the government house they were marked "Kinahan's L. L., the Right Sort."

Look at the landlord, corpulent, hands in his pockets, his keen eyes fixed on the beer or gin-drawing gymnastics of his barman, who wears a cap and holds a piece of straw or the stalk of a flower in his mouth. See how viciously he bites the silver coin when suspicious of its genuineness. When he gives you change, he slaps it down on the counter with "'ere ye are," and to the next customer, "Now, then." There is generally a barmaid or two, and the number is increasing (for they are found more attractive than men), with a brilliant complexion, long ringlets, and necklace.

Look at the customers, for what you see in one gin-palace is seen in all, with some qualifications. There is a sickening sameness, for while some of them have a respectable appearance, a majority of the frequenters are thieves, beggars, hoary-headed old men, stunted, ragged, rickety children, blowsy, slatternly women, heavy-looking labouring men, gaunt, sickly, half-grown creatures. It is the same everywhere; the same woman giving her baby gin; the same haggard, dishevelled wife coaxing her husband home; the same poor girl sitting meekly in a corner with both eyes blackened, while her partner is drinking; the same pale, weary-looking little man, who appears as if he had come up out of his grave to get another glass of gin and has forgotten his way back; the same red-nosed man who disgusts you with his slang, and surprises you with his Greek and Latin quotations; the same thin spectral man who has no money, with hands piteously laid over each other, standing for hours, gazing with gin-hungry eyes at the liquor, licking his fever-white lips, smelling, thinking, hopelessly longing.

More dreadful than any, that same miserable girl, sixteen in years, one hundred in misery, with foul matted hair, ragged boots, cracked voice, tattered shawl, and hopeless eye; her haggard face stamped with the impress of death. See that man whitening his face to do the ghost in Hamlet! Here's a costermonger, with a basket, pressing his way up to the bar, and jostles that vendor of fish.

"Now then, stupid, vere are you driving to, eh? I say, I'm blessed if there isn't the werry same fish you vos a-wending a week ago last Monday!"

"Come, old fellow, I'll butter your muffins both sides for you, and throw in the pepper for nothing."

"Vill ye?"

"I kin and I vill."

Both set down their baskets. The slang is awful. One of the raggedest, dirtiest, and smallest of the boys climbs on a barrel and shouts out "Fair play!" An extensive "shindy" is kicked up, and the fighting becomes, as one of them tells us, quite "permiscus." The police are called in, the house cleared, the doors closed; the mob dispersed, the door opens and the game goes on.

Such is a fair specimen of a certain class, and by far the most numerous class of publics. In proof that my description is not overdrawn, I give an extract from the leading newspaper of England:

"In other parts of the world," says the London *Times*, "may be seen the frown of the African when excited by rum, the contortions of Arabs under the influence of 'hashish,' Malays furious from 'bang,' Turks trembling under the effects of opium, Chinese strangely emaciated from its inordinate use; but for a scene of horrid vice and filth and lust and fury, all drawn into one point and there fomenting, a man might search the world all over and not find a rival to a thriving public-house in a low, gin-drinking neighbourhood. Is it, then, astonishing that of such scenes as these an eminent judge should say that the working-man often enters the public-house respectable and leaves it a felon?"

While the Londoners have imitated the Americans in some beneficial respects, they have imitated them in a ruinous direction in the cafés and saloons that are springing up in the best thoroughfares,—many of them very gorgeous and attractive, most of them with private apartments, the customers of a higher grade in the social scale than those to be found in the common but less dangerous gin-palace. I have stood as a looker-on before some of these places to note the patrons. They come in cabs or hansoms,—young girls with their gentlemen friends, perhaps lovers. Nothing there to offend the eye: a policeman on special duty; no noise, no profanity, no ribald songs; it is genteel. Such places are by-ways to perdition. Then there are the music-halls,—many of them disgraceful, some more exclusive, others tolerably decent, all licensed by Act of Parliament,—of which I may speak on another page.

There is no trade so damaging to the community, so dangerous to the people, and so hardening to the dealer, as the trade in intoxicating liquors. Men naturally kind-hearted, who would help a fellow-being in distress, risking their own lives to save other lives, seem, in this trade, to lose all humanity or sympathy with the race, as far as their trade is concerned.

The late Rev. Wm. Arnot, of Edinburgh, at my request furnished me with his views on the liquor traffic. His manuscript lies before me, and I transcribe some of the principal heads. He says:—

"The liquor traffic stands alone, and has no right to rank with the ordinary avocations of men. Bring it at once and bluntly to the test of common-sense and conscience. Let there be five contiguous shops possessed by five separate shopkeepers. The first sells bread, the second milk, the third leather, the fourth dry-goods, and the fifth intoxicating liquor. The five men ply their tasks all day, count the contents of the till at night, and consider the prospects of trade for the morrow. The more they have sold, the better for their own pecuniary interests. In this they are all alike. But the more that the customers have bought from the first four, the better for the general interests of the public; the more that the customers have bought from the last, the worse for themselves and for society. The other dealers may, with a good conscience, pray for the increase of their sales; the fifth cannot pray, unless his conscience is seared as with a hot iron. He has seen many customers enter his shop to-day and spend money which he knows is worse than lost to them. He cannot desire that they should repeat their custom on the morrow without deliberately wishing ill to his neighbour. In short, his own pecuniary interests are at direct variance with the interests of his customers. The prosperity of his trade is the ruin of those who deal with him.

"A poor inebriate, with his mind weakened by frequent indulgence, demands a glass, pays for it, swallows it. He demands another; the dealer gives it: he gains a penny or two by the transaction; but the penny, he can but know, is wrung from the life-blood of a brother. When such a wretch demands his glass, it is the *experimentum crucis* for the dealer. If at that moment he love his neighbour, he will refuse; if he only love his own gain, he will give it. He stands helpless between these two dread alternatives: he must either abandon his own gains, or be the agent in the perdition of his neighbour. There is in practice seldom any mental struggle, because a man soon becomes case-hardened. Generally the liquor-seller pours out the glass to the drunkard without any uncomfortable twitches within; this, however, is due, not to the innocence of the deed, but to the hardness of the doer's conscience. We do not say the liquor-seller is worse than other men; but this business is so bad that he must either part with his trade in order to retain his humanity, or part with his humanity in order to retain his trade.

"A certain large village in Perthshire, the centre of an agricultural district, is, like its neighbours, dotted much with public-houses, one of which, at the least equal to others in respectability, is kept by a widow. This widow had two brothers: one, unmarried, resided under her roof; the other, the father of a family, was a farmer in the neighbourhood, whose brain had been permanently injured by long-continued habits of excessive drinking. The two brothers were wont to dine together, along with other relatives, in their sister's house, on the day of the weekly market of the village. One market-day the party had all assembled, and the dinner was not ready. The farmer was impatient; his brother tried to soothe him with gentle words, and then left the room to hasten the preparation of the meal. The man could not, with his damaged intellect, lay any rein on the fury of his passion; he followed fast, and in the lobby plunged a knife in his brother's breast. The wounded man was carried to his bed and died. The fratricide was tried for murder and found guilty, but on the ground of insanity was sentenced to perpetual imprisonment instead of death. The people pay the expense of that murderer's maintenance during the period of his natural life; and the widowed sister,—bereft of both her brothers, the murdered and the murderer,—what of her? She had her brother's blood washed from the floor, then tucked up her sleeves, and continued to sell whiskey in the same house and the same room. At this hour that sister trips across 'the spot that will not out,' with the server and glasses, to her jovial customers. She is not conscience-stricken, and her neighbours are not shocked.

"The traffic in liquor, as it is commonly conducted, soon withers a woman's soul within her. It has no rights to plead, and we must lay restraints on those who are engaged in it, and save them from themselves."

The liquor traffic is the same unrighteous trade everywhere; its hardening influence on the traffickers is as manifest here as in Great Britain. The trade is no worse there than here; indeed, I believe that, as a general thing, the liquor-sellers there are a better class than here. Years ago it was considered in many sections of our country a very disreputable thing to sell liquor; and whether we are "bravely" getting rid of that idea or not, the fact is, the business is as bad now as it ever was, and I am inclined to think, a little worse.

Some years since, in an hotel not far from Boston, a poor fellow who had been gambling nearly all night cut his throat in the room over the bar on the Sunday morning. The group round the bar were startled by a heavy drop of blood falling on the counter, and, looking up, discovered a large red stain on the ceiling, from the centre of which the drops of blood were gathering and falling on the counter, faster and faster, till they splashed on the floor. It was known that before the blood was cleaned from the bar and floor men were drinking and the trade went on, though it was the Sabbath-day.

When poor McConnell cut himself to pieces in a bar-room in Washington, it was stated, and never denied, that the saloon-keeper boasted he had cleared over one hundred dollars by the operation, as so many came in to see the blood-stains where the poor fellow had lain; and they could hardly come in without taking a drink.

The meanest men on the face of the earth are among the liquor-sellers in this country. I knew of a woman who had lost her husband by drink, and was left penniless, with four children. I do not say the drink-seller swindled him; but he had got possession of his little home, and all the poor sot had to show for his share of the bargain was the livery of the drunkard. The widow was left very poor, and took in plain

THE BLOOD ON THE CEILING.

sewing, which was rather hard to get. Some time after the loss of her husband the liquor-seller called and condoled with her, asked her kindly about her prospects, professed his desire to serve her, and proposed that she should make some shirts for him; he wanted a dozen at fifty cents each,—that would be six dollars. Gladly the poor widow accepted the proposal, and began to think the liquor-dealer was a humane man.

She toiled on, comforting herself with the thought of six dollars, and thinking pleasantly of what she should do with the money. She planned for a pair of shoes for the shoeless boy, a dress for the girl, and so worked on till her work was done; carried it to her employer, who found no fault with the work—all perfectly satisfactory. After examining the articles, he said, "I have always considered you an honest woman, Mrs. ——, anxious that all should have their dues. Now, I owe you six dollars, but I have a claim against you—that is if you are the honest woman I take you for. I have a note of your husband's for five dollars, given me about a month before he died. Now, if I pay you one dollar, that will make us square;" and actually returned her the note given by her poor, besotted husband, and the one dollar. The woman related this fact to me herself. Truly the "tender mercies of the wicked are cruelty."

The result of this trade is to multiply want, aggravate misery, to stimulate every evil passion into crime. The sufferings of the victim are not all; the poverty, hunger, nakedness, and cold; the battered body, with mind beclouded, and conscience destroyed. If that were all, it would be enough to call loudly for some remedy! but this is not all: the drunkard's curses grow into blows upon his wife, and his savage violence is expended on his children. Exaggerate the evil? Dr. Guthrie says: "It is impossible to exaggerate; impossible truthfully to paint the effects of this evil, either on those who are addicted to it, or on those who suffer from it; imbruted husbands, broken-hearted wives, and, most of all, those poor, innocent children that are dying under cruelty and starvation; that shiver in those rags upon our streets; that walk unshod amid winter snows; and with matted hair, and hollow cheeks, and sunken eyes, glare out on us wild and savage-like from patched and filthy windows."

This great curse cannot be ignored, and woe to those who, for profit or popularity, or any other motives, will not only not seek to repress it, but actually encourage it. I cannot believe that any Christian man can investigate this evil and its causes, without being stirred in his inmost soul to do something to stem the terrible tide. Much of the indifference is from want of knowledge; it is the apathy that springs from ignorance.

Canon Farrar says: "I must confess that it is only familiarity with the subject that can at all impress us with its magnitude. In the providence of God, my own life has been passed in quiet country places, and it was not till I came to London, and not till my attention was very deliberately turned by circumstances to it, that I saw how terrible was the curse which was at work in the midst of us. It seems to me nothing more nor less than a Fury, withering and blighting the whole fame of England. Every week in the organ of the United Kingdom Alliance is published a ghastly column called 'Fruits of the Traffic.' It is no invention; it is no rhetoric; it is nothing that is disputable, nothing that can in the least be questioned; it is nothing in the world but a series of horribly prosaic cuttings from the accidents and offences, the police and criminal reports of other newspapers; and it records calamity after calamity and crime after crime, disease, shipwrecks, conflagrations, murders, the kicking and trampling of women, the maiming and murdering of little children,—all of which are directly attributed to the effects of drink, by the declaration of judges, by the reiterated testimony of witnesses, and by the constant remorseful confessions of the poor criminals themselves."

Can we submit to be taxed to support all that this curse brings upon us? I have before spoken of crime; let me relate a fact. In the Dartmouth prison was a prisoner, a fine-looking, intelligent old man, who had been in a respectable position in society. He was under sentence of penal servitude for life. His nature was kind, courteous, and amiable; he was so child-like and simple-hearted you could hardly conceive of his committing an act of brutality and violence; and yet he had murdered his wife, who, he said, had been dearer to him than his own life for twenty years. He had gone out to spend the evening with some friends, had taken an unusual quantity of liquor, and came home drunk. When expostulated with at the door by his wife, in his madness he struck her a blow that laid her dead at his feet.

This reminds me of a case I met in one of our own state prisons. I was attracted, while speaking to the prisoners in the chapel, by the patient, gentle look of one of the convicts who sat before me, whose whole appearance was that of a mild-tempered, quiet man. After the service, one of the prison officers, in reply to my question, stated that this same man was serving out a life term. I asked what was the possible crime for which he was serving a life term in a state's prison.

"Murder."

"Murder?"

"Yes; he murdered his wife."

Having asked if I might have an interview with him, my request was granted, and I held a conversation with him.

"My friend, I do not wish to ask you any questions that will be annoying; but I was struck by your appearance, and was so much surprised when I heard of your crime, that I thought I would like to ask you a question. May I?"

"Certainly, sir."

"Then why did you commit the crime? What led you to it?"

Then came such a pitiful story. He said:

"I loved my wife, but I drank to excess: she was a good woman; she never complained; come home when or how I might, she never scolded. I think I never heard a sharp word from her. She would sometimes look at me with such a pitying look that went to my heart; sometimes it made me tender, and I would cry and promise to do better; at other times it would make me angry. I almost wished she would scold me, rather than look at me with that patient earnestness. I knew I was breaking her heart, but I was a slave to drink; though I loved her, I knew I was killing her. One day I came home drunk, and as I entered the room I saw her sitting at the table, her face resting on her hand. Oh, my God! I think I see her now! As I came in she lifted up her face; there were tears there, but she smiled and said 'Well, William.' I remember just enough to know that I was mad. The devil entered into me. I rushed into the kitchen, seized my gun, and deliberately shot her as she sat by that table. I am in prison for life, and I have no desire to be released. If a pardon was offered me, I think I should refuse it. Buried here in this prison, I wait till the end comes. I trust God has forgiven me for Christ's sake. I have bitterly repented; I repent every day. Oh, the nights when in the darkness I see her face—see her just as she looked on me that fatal day! I shall rejoice when the time comes. I pray that I may meet her in heaven."

This was said with sobbings and tears that were heart-breaking to hear.

Only one victim among the many!

CHAPTER XVIII.

DESPAIR AND DEATH—STORIES OF RUINED HOMES AND BROKEN HEARTS.

The Prisoner's Testimony—How Prisons are filled—the Offspring of Drink—Appalling Statistics—The Inhuman Father—Selling a Child for Two Pairs of Stockings—Getting drunk with the Proceeds—The Drunken Mother and her dying Children—An Affecting Story—Sufferings in the Best Circles—A Terrible Story—The Brutal Husband and his Dead Wife—Horrible]Brutality—Truth Stranger than Fiction—The Clergyman's Suicide—The Lawyer's Despair and Death—Rum unmakes the Gentleman—A Dreadful Domestic Scene—Th Beaten and Disfigured Wife—Destruction of Property—The Mountaineer Home—Rum-Madness—Driven from Home—The Night on the Mountain—Terrible Destitution and Sufferings—The Desolate Home—Enticed to a Grog-Shop—A Drunken Sot—The Winter's Night—Eaten by Swine.

IN the London *Times* is a letter from a very intelligent man who suffered six years' imprisonment for crime committed under the influence of drink. I give a few extracts. He says:

"During the whole of my stay in prison the question kept rising in my mind, What brings all these men here? Day after day I asked men with whom I came in contact what brought them to prison. I got as an answer the 'same dull, dismal, damnable old story,' over and over again.

After referring to special cases of young men who had become bankrupt in pocket and health, belonging to respectable families, bank clerks and shopmen, every one of whom traced their ruin to City and West-End drinking saloons, he says:—

"Now that I have passed a term of penal servitude as a consequence of similar folly, I seem scarcely able to understand in what the horrible fascination consists which keeps men day after day lolling over a refreshment public-house bar. The habit is confined to no class : mechanics, merchants, professional men, clerks, shopkeepers, and labourers are taking that wretched road. The convict prisons are crowded with men who, had they been abstainers from strong drink, would have been to-day the support and comfort of happy families. What their condition is, only those who have experienced the horrors of prison-life can understand; what the condition of many of their families is, is too fearful to contemplate."

It is useless to shut one's eyes to the fact that, but for the drink curse, the number of criminals would be so small that at least two-thirds of the convict prisons would be empty. The chaplain of the Clerkenwell House of Detention keeps an elaborate note of the cases which come under his notice, and he finds that seven-ninths of the cases which come to his prison come there as the result of drink. The chaplain of a prison for females—not himself an abstainer, and he cannot therefore be accused of partiality to his creed—states from his note-book that out of one hundred and forty-six persons brought to the prison in five days, one hundred and twenty-six came directly through the influence of drink. People can verify these statements as to the general result of drinking by a fair examination. Let me quote from the ex-convict's letter:

"I was compelled for six long years to listen to family histories, to stories of crime and poverty, wretchedness and horror. It was with no disposition in favour of total abstinence that I tried to probe the cause of it. I had never been a teetotaler; had I been so I should never have been in prison myself. But stern facts which came to my knowledge day by day forced me to the conclusion that a very large proportion of all the crime and all the poverty in the land is the direct offspring of intoxicating drink.

"Many of them inherited the vice from drunken fathers and mothers. They were taught to sip the drink in their babyhood, and took it from the hands of mothers who had stolen the money with which to purchase it. I learned day after day, from the admissions of these criminals themselves, that the poverty, ignorance, and want of proper homes had been, in nine cases out of ten, the consequence of drink."

It seems amazing that well-authenticated facts do not move the people. Our own judges are continually testifying to the crime produced by drink; yet how little do the great bulk of

A CELLAR SCENE—THE BRUTE AND THE LAMB.

the people feel the pressure of such terrible facts. A committee of the House of Commons of the Dominion of Canada, reporting in 1875, states that out of 28,289 commitments to the jails of the provinces of Ontario and Quebec during the three previous years, 21,236 were committed either for drunkenness or for crimes perpetrated under the influence of drink. It is the same everywhere.*

If hydrophobia should produce in this country one hundredth part of the crime, poverty, misery, taxation, and the multiplicity of evils that drink does, there would not be a living dog in the United States in six months. Every lady would give up her pet spaniel, the hunter his setter and pointer; even the very watch-dogs would be destroyed, or most carefully guarded against contagion.

The revelations of the results of the drinking customs are appalling. Let us take a few well-authenticated facts. We read statistics of pauperism, lunacy, and crime, and think no more of them than of a number of figures that mean nothing. But go where the shot strikes. Listen to the cry of that little girl as the sound rings out from that cellar. Enter, and see that mere child of seven years writhing under the heavy blows inflicted with a large strap by a brutal, half-drunken man; the poor little creature striving to defend herself, the blows fall alike on head, arms, and shoulders. Will a father beat his child so young, in such a brutal manner? Perhaps; but this is a child he has bought from a drunken mother, who had sold her for half-a-crown to that cruel, drunken wretch, and who had spent the money the same day in drink.

I saw an interesting little girl who had hip complaint, whose mother had sold her to a villainous tramp for two pairs of stockings. She sold the stockings, and got drunk with the proceeds. There is a man now in prison whose wife lost an eye some time since by his violence when drunk, and whose only child is deformed for life as the result of another drunken fit. He is now confined for depriving his wife of her other

* Read Judge Noah Davis' pamphlet on "Intemperance and Crimes," from which I have taken the above statement.

eye when they were both drunk. She is blind, he in prison, and the child is a cripple.

A woman had two children suffering from fever. One morning she received from some ladies in the neighbourhood all that had been prescribed by the doctor, together with money for their wants. The ladies went in the evening to inquire after the children, and found them alone in the agonies of death, induced by want and neglect. On being searched for, the woman was found drunk in a neighbouring tavern. She had spent the money and then sold the articles of clothing, given in charity, for drink. All that could be done for the children was of no avail—it was too late. In the night the ladies left her when she had become somewhat sober, she making all sorts of promises. When they called, the next forenoon, they found the little corpses lying unstraightened where their spirits had left them; and the comforts their hands had provided a few hours before had gone to the pawn-shop. The mother was again drunk in the nearest grog-shop.

Tell me of exaggeration in our statements! Talk of enthusiasm, fanaticism, and monomania in our protest against this horrible evil and its cause! Look at these facts! Do you wish any more? I can fill this book with the records of drink's doings. You say they are among the lower orders. There is more difficulty in arriving at definite knowledge of cases in the so-called upper classes; for while the poorer seem to live very much out of doors, and accordingly what they do is known, the habits of the other classes are so covered by the circumstances of their position that we only see and know what crops out on the surface.

But, oh, the revelations that come to me! If I should give you letters that I have received from mothers, sisters, wives, and daughters of education and refinement,—ladies belonging to the aristocratic circles, confiding to me the story of ruined homes, broken hearts, tarnished characters, the unnecessary sickness, the maniac's death, revealing scenes perfectly appalling, you would say that my book was a volume of horrors, and yet all stern truth with no exaggeration.

Bulwer says that "a wicked gentleman who has lost caste and character is more unreclaimable than a wicked clown, low born and low bred, that in proportion to the loss of shame is the gain in recklessness." A shrewd writer has said, "There is always hope for a dull, uneducated, stolid man, led by accident or temptation into guilt; but when a man of ability and education besots himself in the intoxication of dark and terrible excitements, and takes impure delight in slimy ways, the good angel abandons him for ever." I believe it, for in my experience I have found such a man the hardest to reach, generally the most desperate and reckless. He never takes his self-wrought ruin kindly; he cannot lie down in the ditch without shame and remorse; he has neglected opportunities, and he knows it; he compares the thing he is with what he was and might be but for his folly; he shrinks with disgust from himself; he gnashes his teeth at the retribution that must come, and takes his punishment with rage in his heart. Oh, yes, it is true in morals as it is in physics: the farther a man falls the deeper he goes.

Here is an extract from a letter, written by a lady moving in the higher circles of society, who refers to a well-known doctor of divinity for proof of the statement should it be needed. After giving some details of the course of intemperance into which a gentleman of education and fortune, occupying a high social position, had fallen, and the distress and weary agony of his wife, she writes :—

"Mary's heart broke. I was with her during her last illness, and never have I seen such patience as she manifested. S—— was gone nearly all the time, and when he did come we were obliged to lock the doors, and sometimes to send for help to keep him off, for he was furious when drunk, and once, when in drink, had fearfully whipped his sweet little girl. During her sickness I never went on my knees that I did not pray God most fervently to take her to Himself. At last she died. Having laid her out, we locked up the room, and left her in the chamber of death. That night S—— came home seemingly sober, and requested us to let him see his wife. So deceived were we by his well-assumed melancholy, that we gave him the door-key. In about ten minutes after he left us, a servant came to the door weeping, and begged us to go and 'take master away, for he was beating mistress.' We sent some of the gentlemen up. After they came back, we went to see what he had done, and there was my precious Mary, his own wife, who had never given him an unkind word; lying on the floor; all her burial clothes torn from off her body, and that bruised and mangled to such a degree that the ladies in the room were unable to endure such a scene. Her old nurse and I stayed and shrouded her again, and her body was in such a condition as to compel an immediate burial. The servant who saw him said that he dragged her from the bed on which she lay, and stamped on her, and then dashed her against the furniture. In a few months after S—— died drunk."

My heart sickens, as I turn to these letters which I have preserved. Such revelations! not fiction, not romance, but fact, and all produced by the use of that which, to say the best we can for it, is but a luxury. It is easy to talk of exaggeration, but I wish those who doubt the reality of such outrages could only once see for themselves.

I venture to give a few extracts from over three hundred letters from the victims of this terrible evil. I have selected only those where the statements could be corroborated, and where the correspondents were reliable, and I give them as genuine. Those who did not sign their name sent me cards of reference. Where I put initials I have the names. Some held interviews with me after I had received their letters. I have some communications well attested, but so fearfully horrible that I refrain from publishing them. A gentleman writes me from Pittsburgh, signed W. K.:

"In the year 18—, a clergyman belonging for some time to the Methodist Church, one whom I had often heard preach, cut his throat from ear to ear in my parlour in broad daylight. I was at tea in another room. When I came into the parlour, to my utter astonishment he had the knife in his throat, up to the handle. I attempted to stop him, and very narrowly escaped being killed myself. This man had been highly respected for piety and talents, but he fell by indulging in the moderate drinking of ale, until he became a drunkard. Remorse of conscience drove him to the horrid act. He seldom drank anything but ale."

Ale is a soporific and, according to authority, is a "good thing to sleep on."

A most respectable gentleman writes from Ohio:

"As a reminiscence for useful reference, allow me to narrate to you in short the life and death of an old friend of mine who lived in W—— County, in this State. His name was B—— C——, a brother of J—— C——, who at one time was one of the Supreme Judges of O——. B—— was one of the ablest jurists, and for many years a partner of one of the first lawyers in the State. He began to drink in early life, when it was fashionable for everybody, from the clergy down to the common labourer, to 'take a glass.' He continued to circulate around on the edge of the whirlpool, until he 'couldn't quit.' He became, with his mighty mind and masterly legal attainments, a great sot. At one time, I heard him make one of the most cogent legal arguments I ever listened to ; and he said, after he got through, that while he was speaking he could see toads squatting in the corners and along the walls of the court-room, and serpents were coiling all around before his eyes, and hissing in his ears, while all manner of imps were dancing about in the air, spouting their blue breath in his face. Such is but a brief description of things imagined, which he said tormented him so that he could hardly speak. And yet he recounted the evidence and applied the law and reasoning to the facts in the most masterly style, and more so than his partner, who was with him in the case. How can a man reason thus in delirium tremens?

"A few weeks after this, the unfortunate inebriate, in the endeavour to climb the stairway to his office, made a false step near the top, and fell backwards to the ground, the stairway being outside the house. He was taken up, and conveyed to the house of his brother, the judge, where he died in a week or two in that horrible state of mind and body—*mania-a-potu*. During his illness, he was attended by the kind hand of his amiable brother and tender friend. His brother he would often curse. Had it not been for drink, this man of excellent mind and manly disposition might have been yet living, an honour to his name, and of usefulness to his kind. He was a bachelor.

"Yours, etc., R. R. M——."

I received the following from a gentleman in Canada:

"My father is a Scotchman by birth. He received the education of a gentleman's son in his native land ; his abilities were of the highest order. He was, from his boyhood, of a fiery temper, and very easily excited ; of a majestic mien, and a great favourite. He married, emigrated to this country, purchased a farm, and settled on it, living there for twelve years in the enjoyment of peace, happiness, comfort, and prosperity. He at length thought that farming brought too meagre profits, and accordingly embarked in the mercantile business, dealing in liquors by wholesale and retail. He began to drink, and in less than two years became a confirmed drunkard, and has been so for the past eighteen years, becoming a miserable wreck. The influence of liquor upon his mind defies description, as it always produced a maddening effect. It never succeeded in destroying his locomotion, or laying him in the gutter, or numbing his tongue; but, on the contrary, it always gave buoyancy and strength to his step, elasticity to his feet, and eloquence to his tongue; while at the same time it made him a fiend to his own family, and particularly to his wife.

"Many times had my poor mother to flee out of her bed in her nightdress, in the coldest winter nights, and take refuge in the horse-stables and barns, and as frequently did her children throw her clothing out of the windows of her bedroom, to protect her body from the chilling northern blasts of the Canadian winters. On one occasion he locked her in her room, locked all the doors of the house, and then swore to my sister, who was about seven years old, that if she should make any noise while he was whipping her mother, he would murder her. He then retired to the room where my mother was incarcerated, and dealt her a ponderous blow, which laid her upon the carpet, weltering in her blood. He then leaped upon her with his feet, pounded her face until it was black, and the blood oozed out of her ears, nose, and mouth; when providentially a neighbour, hearing the alarm, burst open the door, and, shall I say, saved my mother's life.

"After he was released from the influence of alcohol, and saw what he had done to the wife of his bosom, whom he loved sincerely, he went almost distracted. For two months did he nurse her, and tried his very best to restore her face to its natural appearance, but alas! it could not be effected; she bears at this moment a long and deep scar upon her brow, done by the hand of her husband while under the influence of damning drunkenness.

"But notwithstanding the fearful and tragical end that this revel had almost led to, it was soon forgotten. The appetite was too strong, too deeply rooted within him to be resisted, or to be conquered, and a multiplicity of engagements, or at least pretended engagements, calling him frequently into company, revel has succeeded revel—spree has succeeded spree; and chasing wife and family with deadly instruments, and the destruction of household furniture, have followed as necessary consequences during these last years.

"My two brothers left him at the age of eighteen years, whom, on account of their being under age, he endeavoured to prosecute, but he could not, in consequence of his having abused them. I left at the age of seventeen. I shall never forget that gloomy morning. It was the morning that I was roused out of my slumbers by the rattling of the carriage-wheels, and the galloping of the horses up to the front door. I heard my father burst into the house, ripping and tearing like a madman, because the family were not out of their beds to salute him on his arrival home. He went into my mother's room, and seized her by the throat in her bed. When I heard her cry for help, I bounded out of my bed, and ran downstairs, and rushed into my mother's apartment, and took hold of him.

behind his back, and by some supernatural strength prostrated him upon the floor. As soon as mother made her escape, I made mine, although pursued by father and his gun, and left a last adieu to my father's abode, and have since directed my attention to a profession.

"His destruction of property has been exceedingly great. He has squandered thousands of pounds in drink; drove horses to death; broke carriages; consigned the most valuable clothing of the family to the flames; destroyed household furniture, such as dishes, chairs, sofas, sideboards, stoves, clocks; and all of which he would immediately replace, as soon as he would get sober, without counting the cost.

(Signed) "A. M. K——."

I had an interview with the writer, now following a profession in Canada.

The next extract is from a very long letter written by a friend, relating to circumstances well known in the county where he resided.

"Enos Cook resides, or his family does, upon the mountain side, about a mile east from our village, and far elevated above it, in a wretched hovel built of logs (a dreary, lonesome, desolate place); he has been for many years the miserable victim of intemperance. His family, poor and destitute, have been the subjects of want and misery, of destitution and untold suffering, for many a sorrowful year. Yet they bore it in silence, and submitted without a murmur to the blows and brutal violence of the oft-infuriated husband and father, to the present occasion.

"His wife, one of the most harmless, inoffensive persons, has all this time supported the family by hard work, away from home, at washing, house-cleaning, etc. (as all his earnings went into the liquor dealers' hands), often having to leave her little children at home alone, miles from her work; yet she murmured not. And when her husband came home in a rage from liquor, she as silently permitted him to devour or waste the whole of the proceeds of her labour, as she dared say or do nothing to offend him. He has even, on many occasions, carried from home such of the articles of her earnings as were available to him, and exchanged them for liquor with the heartless rum-seller, leaving her and her children in utter destitution. To such treatment the woman has submitted for years.

"This season has been, if possible, worse than former ones. She has been beaten frequently and dragged from the house, and on one occasion for several rods over the stony ground, for endeavouring to prevent him from murdering her son. On Thursday last, being destitute of liquor, he collected from the mountain a quantity of pine knots (such as are used for kindling fires), and took them to the village and procured liquor. He then went to work and made a couple of splint brooms, for which he procured two bottles of liquor on Friday. Returning home intoxicated, he secreted one out of doors, went into the house and demanded of his wife something to eat. She told him she had nothing in the house, when he struck her a blow that felled her from her chair almost senseless on the floor, and fell to kicking her most inhumanly. When she was able to speak, she intimated that she would go to the poor-master for relief from this brutality, but this only enraged him the more, and added to the blows and kicks she had already received.

"When his bottle was exhausted, forgetting what he had done with the other, he demanded it. The woman told him she knew nothing of it, when he turned to his daughter, about twelve years old, and ordered her to get his bottle or he would kill her. Alarmed for her life, the girl commenced looking about the room, but not finding it, the madman seized her by the throat and was strangling her to suffocation, when the mother endeavoured to prevail on him to desist. He then let go of the daughter, seized his axe, and flew after his wife, but she had escaped out of doors just in time to prevent him from burying it in her brain. He did not pursue her, but raged about the room, striking his axe into the floor, and threatening to murder the children. The few old chairs and all the furniture they had were smashed to pieces. He then opened a box containing all the clothing she or the children had, tramped upon the contents, and kicked them into the fire.

"In the meantime the woman went to the poor-master, and he told her he would do something next day. Toward night she ascended the mountain, and silently drew near her wretched home to learn the fate of her children. She heard her husband raving and swearing that when she returned he would maul her so that she could not get to the village again. Her youngest child, just old enough to walk, was outside the house. She seized it, and taking the miserable rag from her own shoulders, she wrapped it up and retraced her steps to a neighbour's house, where she spent the night of Friday.

"Next morning, his liquor being gone, he having found the other bottle and drank the contents, he took two fowls, which had been given his wife for her labour, and carried them away. One he sold to a liquor-dealer, and raffled away the other to another one.

"On Saturday, toward night, in the absence of her husband, the woman ventured home. But on his approach she retired, and when the officers went to arrest him, where was she? Gone to the village? No. She had taken refuge among the cliffs on the bleak mountain side. Beneath a shelving rock, upon that cold Saturday night, she and her infant were found, where she had gathered a few sticks and had succeeded in lighting a fire, thinking there to pass the night. This night would have been her last, had not the officers told her to return to her house, as they had secured him, and would protect her. He was taken to Kingston jail on Sunday.

"On that afternoon I went up to see the family, and the scene ex-

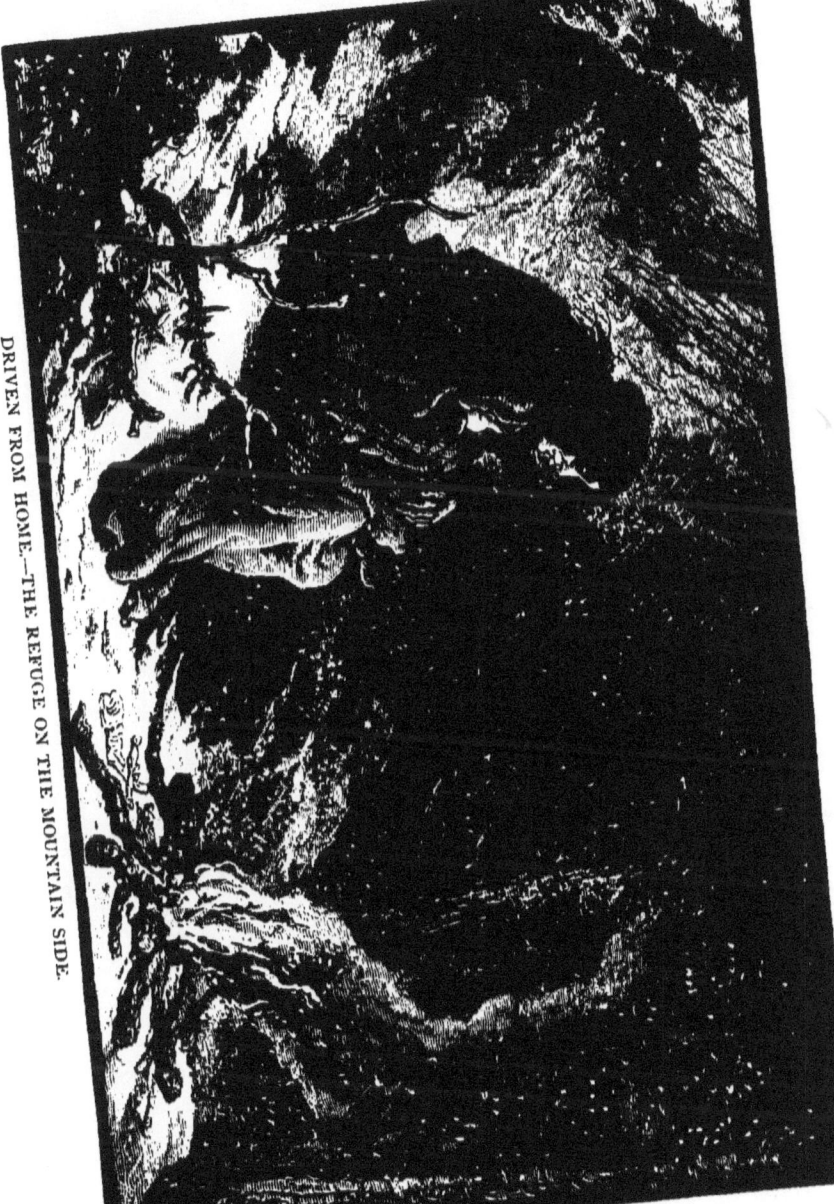

DRIVEN FROM HOME.—THE REFUGE ON THE MOUNTAIN SIDE.

ceeded my worst anticipations. The door, torn from its hinges, was leaning up to its place without being much protection from the cold wind, which around that pile of logs shrieked its shrill requiem over domestic happiness destroyed; and although the sun was still shining, all was darkness within save the feeble flashes of a scantily-fed fire. There was not a window in the house, or any aperture through which light could find admittance except at the doorway. The mother, with her infant at her breast, and three other small children, were occupying the remnants of the broken chairs. When my eyes had become regulated to the room I saw that there was nothing in it, save the axe, the empty box, a broom, an apology for a table, and two miserable bunks covered with old carpeting and rags. Such are the doings of rum, and such the home of the poor drunkard and his family.

(Signed) "G. A. D."

The gentleman who wrote the foregoing letter was well known to me.

I now quote from a letter sent me by a gentleman of New York, relating to a case in Albany.

"A worthy mechanic, I think a cooper by trade, had an interesting family, a fond wife and three children. For a long time he was industrious, frugal, and domestic in his habits. He was enticed from his usual path of virtue to a grog-shop by his companions; and from that time day by day he frequented that charnel-house of destruction, until he became an habitual drunkard. Night after night he would leave his family, and come home late, a perfect sot. His wife expostulated and did everything in her power to reclaim him, but in vain; he soon became lost to all obligations to his family. He was frequently so drunk that he could not reach his home until his poor wife had left her abode and her helpless children in search of him, and by the aid of friends had, night after night, brought him home a drunken sot. One cold winter evening, carousing with his bad associates, he left them, and in attempting to reach his room, he missed his way, and to find shelter he stumbled into an old hovel on Pearl Street, the basement of which was the usual retreat for the stray hogs of the city. In this filthy abode this poor creature made his bed for the night. Not reaching his home, late at night his wife, with a friend, started in pursuit of him. After visiting the dens he usually frequented, they gave up the search in despair. The next morning they continued their search, and, sad to relate, they found the mangled body of this once fond husband and doting father, half eaten up by this herd of swine, with whom he had unconsciously taken shelter from the inclement storm. H. C——, 7 G—— St."

CHAPTER XIX.

FOOTPRINTS OF RUM—STORIES OF RUINED HOMES AND BROKEN HEARTS (CONTINUED).

A Cry from Connecticut—Drunkenness worse than Death—Five Days with Delirium Tremens—Hope Deferred—The Drunkard's Adopted Child—The Murdered Babe—The Wife shielding the Murderer, only to be murdered herself—The Murderer's Suicide—Last Scenes in the Domestic Tragedy—The Drunkard and his Dead Wife—The Drunken Clergyman preaching Old Sermons—Stealing Postage-Stamps to buy Rum—Another Clergyman ruined by Drink—An Unfeeling Father—Stealing his Little Boy's Shoes to buy Drink—The Drunkard's Cry—Pity for the Victims—A Blasted Life—The Drunkard's "Ode to the Departing Year"—"What of the Ship?"—The Redeemed Man's Narrative—Evils of Social Drinking—Bitter Recollections—Maddening Desire for Drink—What is to be done?—The Dram-Shops of Birmingham—Sunday Drinking—Terrible Results.

THERE is not a commonwealth but has felt in many homes the terrific curse of rum. Homes blighted by its desolation are countless. Out from Connecticut, that "land of steady habits," comes this wailing cry. It takes the deepest suffering to call forth the anguish of woman's loving heart:

"I have never known but one sorrow. My father, a sister, and a brother have left me, and gone to their last home. I thought that was sorrow; but how mistaken I was! My loss was their gain. But I have a sorrow, a grief, a great grief; and it bends me down, and sometimes I feel that it is insupportable. I have friends that know in part, and they say with one voice, 'Leave the cause.' I ask them, 'Can I forget, if I leave?' I cannot make them understand how I can love a man that has forgotten to respect himself. Poor man! nature has done much for him, and, with an education that might have helped him through life pleasantly, all has been wasted, so far. He is but thirty-three years old, and yet many have been the nights that I have sat over him anxiously watching and fearing lest he should never wake again, and—I shudder when I think of it!—for five days I nursed and watched him through delirium tremens. I let no one but his father see him. How we both lived, God only knows, for he thought me an enemy.

"At one time after that he became a Son of Temperance; but through his acquaintances he fell. He was pleasing, and young men liked his company, and when invited he could never say 'No;' and now he doesn't seem to care what people say or think. Oh, he has fallen, fallen so far! So many times he has promised he would never taste again, and I believe he means it when he tells me so; but he has not power to resist temptation. He sometimes says none care for him,—he is of no consequence. I am afraid I have lost what influence I ever did have. We are told, 'Hope deferred maketh the heart sick.' I feel it is too true; for surely my heart is sick, and were it not for the consolation I find in the religion of Jesus, I should long ere this have despaired. Oh, that he could be saved! Can there be any help? His precious soul, what will become of that? If there is any advice you can give me for his benefit, no matter what it may be, it shall be followed as far as lies in my power. What would not a woman do for her husband? And I have a little son, my only child, just ten years old; and oh, how I tremble for him lest he will follow his father's example! He is a child quick and impulsive, and fond of his father, and has many times asked why he can't drink beer, if his father does. Oh, dear sir, you can't know the anguish of a heart lacerated as mine has been; but I know you can feel for a poor bleeding heart, and so I have trespassed on your time and patience. I beg you will pardon me; but if you think for one moment of a poor man falling lower and still lower, I believe you will both pity and forgive me.

"M——."

The following are extracts from a Philadelphia letter, revealing the scenes in a domestic tragedy which occurred in that beautiful city:

"Some few years ago I was in business at No. 30, Market Street, at which time a man named J—— C—— applied to me for work. He was quite genteel in appearance, and I gave him work, which was satisfactorily done. For some time I continued to employ him; but he seldom came himself for or with his jobs. His wife was in the habit of coming to the store, and on one occasion I asked her why John did not himself bring in the work, when she reluctantly told me of her fears to trust him out, if it could be avoided, lest in his weakness of habits he should drink to excess, when he was sure to abuse her. So long as he kept from liquor, however, he was affectionate, industrious, and as good a husband as any woman could wish for."

After relating scenes of distress, imprisonment, brutality

almost beyond belief, nearly murdering his wife—revelations of sickening and revolting cruelty,—he writes:—

"They had adopted a child, and John was very fond of the babe, and his wife became very much attached to it.

"He left home one morning early, came back about eleven o'clock; he was drunk, and he then said that it was time the child had gone after its mother,—that he was not going to be troubled with other people's brats. However, he soon went out again, and did not return home until just about dusk. When he staggered up-stairs, the windows in the room were raised, as the weather was quite warm. His wife was just in the act of lighting the lamp as John went over to the settee, upon which she had just laid the child. Without a single word, he picked up the child and threw it out of the window. The woman flew down the stairs to the street, and there she found the babe: it was dead; the head was smashed. She fainted at the sight. Oh, it was horrible! A crowd soon collected. She was, with the child, taken into the house. And now she was in a dilemma: her husband was a murderer, and yet she loved him still; for she knew, or felt then, that it was not his nature to commit a violent wrong, only when his action was controlled by rum. She therefore sought by stratagem to release him from any charge, and battled a little while with her conscience, and then, with grief and sorrow depicted on her countenance, she told those persons around her that she had been sitting at the window with the child in her arms, where she had fallen asleep, and that the child rolled out of her arms and fell to the pavement. Unfortunately for her, she was believed. The child was buried, and there was nothing afterward said about it. John sometimes spoke of it, but never without bringing tears in his eyes. She believed that he never forgave himself for having committed the murder."

This child was a little girl six months old. Some time after, the poor woman was compelled to separate from him, and for a while he could not discover her whereabouts. One Sunday evening the gentleman who writes me was at his home in North Fifth Street, when the man called, as described in these closing words of the letter:—

"He appeared to be sober, and upon my invitation he came in. After sitting a while, he apologized for calling upon me on Sunday, but he wished to know if his wife still worked for me, or if I had seen her lately. I told him that she had done no work for me for many months, and that the last time I saw her, she told me that she was living in Jersey. He then said that he met her in the street the night before (being Saturday night), and that she would not speak to him; and that if he could find her, he would kill her. He appeared much irritated. I then talked to him, and tried to convince him that he alone was in fault; that if he would only entirely abandon the use of rum, there was no doubt of much happiness still in store for him. I made use of every argument to induce him to become a sober and industrious man. I offered him every encouragement to do so, by promising to give him employment, and at the same time tried to convince him that if he could keep sober and industrious, she would find it out, and would be glad to come back to him.

"I suppose he stayed with me for an hour, and before he left, he became softened, and promised to reform. After expressing an everlasting obligation to me, he left.

"On the following Sunday, about noon, I was walking in the neighbourhood of the Exchange, and observing a crowd around a bulletin-board in front of a printing-office, I crossed over, and judge of my surprise when I read as follows: '*Horrid Murder!* Last evening, at nine o'clock, a man named John C——, a tailor by trade, followed his wife into a house in Front Street, below South Street. She had been out in the streets for a bucket of water; he followed her up into the third story, when he stabbed her in forty different places. The screams attracted persons to the spot; and when they attempted to take hold of him, he with a long knife cut himself across the stomach, and died in a few minutes, having committed a double murder.' At the inquest held immediately afterward, it was proved that he was under the influence of *Rum*."

I have witnessed scenes that have haunted me for days. In company with a friend, I once called on a man who had formerly been a gentleman of position, but who was now living on an annuity of $500 per year—a comparative pittance saved from the wreck of his fortune. His wife was very ill. When we arrived, we found the man drunk, sitting by the fire smoking, and the wife lying dead on the miserable pallet in the room. The drunkard was making a great noise, and declaring she was not dead. The gentleman with me laid his hand on him, and said:

"Now, you keep still; your wife lies there dead, and I will not permit this noise."*

The drunkard sprang to his feet, exclaiming:

"I'll let you see whether she is dead or not."

Before we could prevent, he sprang to the bedside, and dealt on the upturned face of the dead woman a terrific blow with

* See Illustration.

his fist. Oh, I heard the sound of that blow for weeks, at night and by day!

Rev. Charles Garrett, of Liverpool, tells us that he saw a man, under whose ministry he once sat with profit, in a low public-house, with his face blackened, preaching some of his old sermons to degraded men and dissolute women for twopence; while his wife, refined, educated, and delicate, was struggling with the newsboys for the last edition, that she might get bread for her suffering children.

A poor creature, half naked, was dragged from under the bench of a music hall, who proved to be a clergyman of the Church of England, and one of the best Greek scholars in the United Kingdom. He was taken to the house of a Good Samaritan, and kept there four weeks. He would steal postage-stamps of his benefactor to get drink; and when started again in life, with a good suit of clothes, hat, boots, and all necessary for respectability, he was seen ten days after, ragged and wretched, asking for alms.

A gentleman was so reduced by drink as to bring his aristocratic wife to one room. No furniture; a heap of rags in one corner, and an old box for a table. When the gentleman whom I had sent visited them, there was a cup of weak tea and a bit of dry bread on the box, and three orange-boxes turned up for seats. There were the wife and six children; the youngest fourteen days old; and that morning the husband and father had stolen the last blanket they had, and sold it for a shilling. Afterwards, when charity had helped the family, and provided his poor boy with shoes, he stole them in the night, and got drunk with the proceeds. He considered himself so much the gentleman, that upon his complaining of having nothing to do, when a situation was offered him as conductor on a street-car, he refused, alleging that he never would stoop to a menial occupation. But why try to record cases that are unrecordable and innumerable?

How many of the victims of this vice are struggling for freedom! how earnestly they plead for help! how eager they are to lay hold of any straw that will help to save them, may

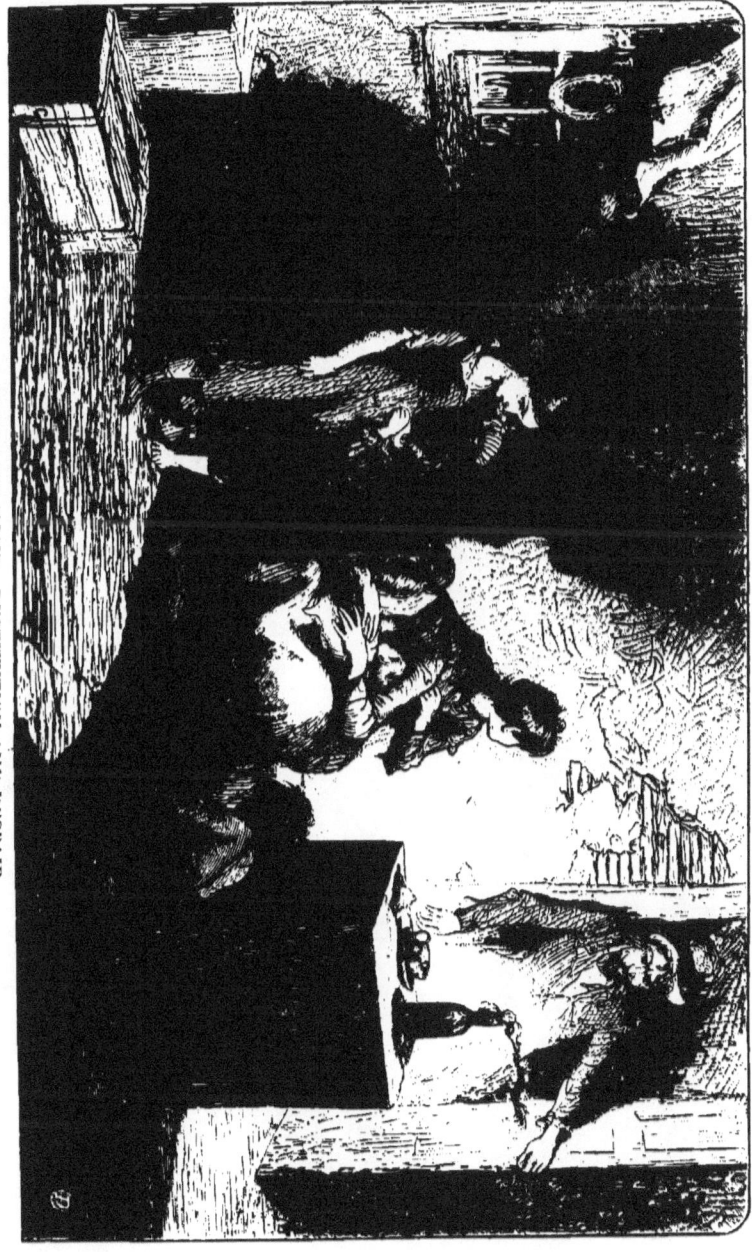

A HOMELESS HOME—DESTITUTION AND DESPAIR.

be known by the despairing cry coming up from the depths. Read this:—

"My object in addressing these few lines to you is, to ask if you can tell me how or by what means I am to do away with the excess of drink. My medical man, knowing my habits, distinctly says that after accustoming myself to spirituous and other liquors for so many years, it would be my death to give them up. My inclination is to sweep the use of them away altogether. My appetite is so craving, that if I give them up for one day, my life is not only rendered intolerable, but my nervousness is so *great*, GREAT, as to completely crush out my inclinations to the pleasures of this world.

"My means hitherto have been sufficiently ample to gratify my passion, or inordinate appetite, for strong drink; but if this strong drink is indulged in, my means cannot last. Would to God that you may be the instrument enabling me to trample under foot drink, that is already getting master over me! I shall hear (God willing) your next discourse; and I sincerely hope that you may be the means of converting a poor, wretched, and intemperate man."

One cry among thousands. I have not the heart to transcribe them.

How thoroughly we often condemn the drunkard, considering him only reckless and wilful! Some may be so; but did we know all the struggles and yearnings to do better, all the aspirations in the lucid moments for a higher and nobler life, we would pity the victims, rather than denounce them as reprobates. Young men, who now despise the drunkard in his weakness, God grant you may never be enchained and enslaved by the fearful appetite which, gratified, becomes at length a master-passion, and is a power that can never be understood or explained. To gratify it, men have sacrificed all that makes life desirable. Look into the inner heart of many a drunkard, and you will pity him.

A man of education, with whom I was brought in contact, was a victim, and though he died miserably, there was something in him at times very attractive. From his manuscript in my possession are the following portions of two little pieces he wrote. I omit several stanzas, and begin with the fifth, upon an

"ODE TO THE DEPARTING YEAR.

"Old Year! what hast thou taught me?
Old Friend! what hast thou brought me?
What good or ill hast wrought me?
   Hath bliss o'er-balanced pain?
What messages art bearing
For the Eternal's hearing,
At the last day's appearing?
   Oh, questions wild and vain!

"Since thy dim dawn, Old Year,
How much of hope and fear!
How many a bitter tear
   Hath fallen from sorrow's eye!
How many lithe and bright,
Who hailed thee with delight,
Have bowed before Time's might,
   And laid them down to die!

"Love hath been changed to hate;
Friendship to formal state;
Youth—with its dreams elate,
   Its hopes—how fondly cherished!
Hopes of renown, of fame,
Its ardent toils to claim
The glory of a name,
   Each after each have perished.

"Billow of time, sweep on!
Go, join the ages gone,
Where earth's sun never shone
   To gild the shadowy shore;
Farewell! but not for aye;
Thou'lt meet me on that day
When sun and stars decay,
   And time shall be no more!

"Yea, when the trump sounds clear,
When all the dead appear
Before the Judge severe;
   When heaven and earth shall flee;
Oh, then, Old Year! I feel
Conviction o'er me steal,
That thou, for woe or weal,
   Wilt a 'swift witness' be!

"Dead! the Old Year hath died!
The new one by my side
Stands in his jocund pride,
　　Heedless of woe or crime.
New Year! what dost thou bring
Upon thy radiant wing?
Methinks I hear thee sing
　　A glad 'To-morrow' chime.

"To-morrow, false to-morrow!
We consolation borrow,
Whilst suffering present sorrow,
　　From thy perpetual dawn!
Time—bright time—coming ever;
We wait, but greet thee never!
Fruitless each wild endeavour
　　To have thy veil withdrawn!

"Haste onward, Year, new-born;
I laugh, this natal morn,
Thy promises to scorn!
　　I scarcely welcome thee.
Past years are but past pains;
My years but galling chains,
Whose scars this heart retains;
　　And such, too, thou wilt be!"

He was at my house at the time when the country was deeply anxious to know the fate of the steamer "Pacific," many years ago, and he wrote the following. I copy from his manuscript, which lies before me, entitled,

"WHAT OF THE SHIP?

"OR, SHIP WRECKS AND MIND WRECKS.

"A 'PACIFIC' RYHME.

" 'There is gloom in each eye, and a tremor of lip,
As the question sounds dolefully, 'What of the ship?'
Through long days of doubt we have hoped, but in vain,
To see her return to her haven again.
And through each dark night we have longed for the morn
For with every new dawning a new hope was born;
Loving eyes gaze afar through the mists of their tears,
But no trace of the missing 'Pacific' appears.
"Ah, she yet may be safe!' lingers still on the lip,
For the heart of affection won't give up the ship.

"Ran she foul of a berg? Did the ice-fields close round her?
Did she drift with the 'pack' or at once did she founder?
'Midst the fogs of 'the Bank,' and the waves' ceaseless dash,
Was there heard, when ships met, a wild shriek and a crash;
And, crippled and staggering, still ploughs she the wave;
Straining eyes from her deck seeking aught that might save?
Or in some sheltered cove of the isles of the West,
Hath she found, from the strife of the elements, rest?
Though such questions may hopefully leap from the lip,
The cry of suspense is still—'What of the ship?'

"It is thus, ever thus, when some palpable woe
In the great city's heart robs the blood of its glow;
A public catastrophe all men deplore,
Though they heed not life's tragedy acting next door!
Even now, while anxiety, anguish, dismay,
Is felt for the fate of the steamship away,
There is near us full many a once gallant bark,
Drifting hopelessly on, or going down to death's dark!
Vessels straining and leaking; and yet scarce a lip
Asks hopefully, anxiously—'What of the ship?'

"For, oh! there are wrecks on humanity's sea,
More fearful than any on ocean can be!
Once with far-streaming pennons they floated along,
While hope lent its sunshine, and music its song;
Ever cloudless the skies, ever azure the seas,
Ever favouring the currents and joyous the breeze!
Passion hurried them on, and in beauty's bright smile
They basked on the shores of each Eden-like isle;
And regarding life's voyage but pleasure's gay trip,
They abandoned the helm, nor thought—'What of the ship?'

"And the wine-cup was filled, and again filled the bowl,
Till madness crept into the heart and the soul.
Care was flung to the winds; hope ne'er whispered again;
And pleasure, unmasked, showed the visage of pain!
On rushes the doomed one; no pilot to guide,
As helmless, and chartless, he floats o'er the tide;
Driving on, driving on, urged by passion's wild throes,
Ruined, raving, yet onward he recklessly goes.
To end with death's draught, what began with a sip;
And then—fearful question—'Oh! what of the ship?'

"Aye, what of the ship? They are scouring the wave,
In hope the 'Pacific' to find and to save;
But what of the human wrecks? Shall we not send
To aid them in peril a brother—a friend?
Forlorn and despised, on they drift to their doom,
O'er the world's raging sea, to their refuge—the tomb!
Let them feel that, though tempest-tossed, shattered, distrest,
Hope its torch may relume, that they yet may be blest,—
That smiles may yet play upon brow and on lip,
If the angel of Temperance but charters the ship!"

Now read a few words from one who has escaped:

"I will not trouble you with a long account of my career in the service of rum; were I to do so it would fill, not one, but many sheets. I am a young man, just entering my twenty-ninth year; thirteen years ago I came to this city from the country to engage in business. I came poor but honest, with the warning voice of a Christian mother (who had gone home to that Saviour whom she loved) fresh in memory. Would to God I had adhered to her counsels; had I done so, rum would never have crossed my lips. For nine years the prospects before me were bright and promising. I enjoyed the respect and confidence of my employers, and was beloved by all my friends; but a dark cloud came over me, which well-nigh proved my destruction.

"At the age of twenty-four, the seeds sown in the social circle began to develop themselves (for it was in the society of friends that I was first induced to touch the intoxicating cup). Oh, how little do friends think when offering the wine-cup to the young man, that they may be planting in him the seeds of a destruction that will ultimately consign him to an eternity of woe! And here let me protest with yourself against that accursed custom of social drinking, which is opening wide the flood-gates of destruction, and educating young men by scores for the rum-shop. The work of reformation must begin at home. Let men become teetotalers, bring up their sons the same, and banish from their homes all that intoxicates; then there is some hope for the rapid advancement of the temperance cause. Take from the rum-seller his customers, and he will soon abandon a business that fails to enrich him. Much as I now love the temperance cause, and firm as is my determination to adhere to it, looking to God for strength to sustain me, my heart bleeds for it when I look around and see the stumbling-blocks thrown in its way by the so-called politeness of society.

"From the social circle I took to the bar-room, where I drank with friends and acquaintances. From this point my course was downward. I would give worlds to-day, did I possess them, could I wipe out for ever the bitter recollections of the past. For more than four years rum held me its slave. In that time I lost my situation in business; all my friends, with a few exceptions, deserted me, and gave me up as hopeless. On my last spree I put up at an hotel, kept out of the way of my friends, and for four weeks was constantly drunk; ate scarcely anything, drank incessantly; sleep was to me a stranger, except when rendered totally unconscious by liquor. All the energies of my waking moments were concentrated in the maddening desire for drink. A friend found me at a fortunate moment; had I remained a day longer as I was, the hand that pens these lines would this day be mouldering back to its mother earth, and over the sod that covered me might have been written 'A Drunkard's Grave.'

"My friend took me to his home and nursed me through a spell of sickness that brought me to the brink of the grave. I had an attack of *delirium tremens*. I need not detail to you the horrid sufferings I passed through—you know too well its horrors; your own description of this horrid disease is true to the letter, for I have experienced it all. God mercifully spared my life and restored me to health. Blessed be His name. When I did recover, there was one fixed and determined resolution formed,—that was to cast from me for ever the firebrand that had been consuming my very vitals. Five months have now rolled round since that time, in which I have adhered strictly to my resolve."

I thank God for the rescued, but with all our efforts the disease is spreading; and being so constantly brought in contact with the results, must be my excuse,—no, I will erase the word "excuse,"—I need no excuse for speaking or writing—the iron has entered my soul, and, as sitting in my library, I recall the past and remember the scenes I have looked upon, the harrowing facts that have come under my own observation, I feel ashamed that the thought of an apology entered my mind for one moment.

The question ought to arise, What is to be done? What can I do to stem this awful tide? To quote the words of an eloquent speaker:—

"Are we to pass from chamber to chamber of this great temple of abominations, and look at what we see, as though it were a cabinet of curiosities, and gaze coldly on all these scenes of shame and horror that are painted on its walls; or are we to be aroused by these facts merely to talk the vague language of philanthropy, and to sigh over wretchedness, while we do not so much as lift a single finger to help the wretched?"

This whole country ought to be flooded with facts. Let us

have committees formed to investigate. Have we no men of standing with patriotism sufficient to move them to some sacrifice that they may ascertain more fully the extent of this evil? In Birmingham, England, one Saturday night, Major Bond, superintendent of police, had thirty-five public-houses watched for three hours, and on the average each house turned out twenty-five drunken people,—or a total of eight hundred and seventy-five within three hours. The people were startled by such a revelation; but such a disclosure cannot be made without self-sacrifice.

One great agency in obtaining the Sunday Closing Bill for Scotland was the persevering efforts of individuals to obtain just such statistics with regard to Sunday drinking; and when the police failed to do the work, or were not permitted by the authorities, many gentlemen of high standing took the work upon themselves, and, in spite of insults from those interested in the traffic, continued the work, and scattered broadcast the results of their efforts, until the people were frightened at the revelation.

These are the statistics that the people are forced to accept. The cry of "exaggeration" fails to affect them. I have heard men ridicule the idea of 50,000 drunkards dying each year in the United States. Let us have a thorough investigation, and we shall find that it is simple fact.

Dr. Farre, of England, who has evinced the opposite of favour to teetotalers and to teetotalism, has confessed to 53,000 annual alcoholic deaths in the United Kingdom, with a population 14,000,000 less than in the United States; they expend 140,000,000 pounds sterling (or about 700,000,000 dollars), and we $750,000,000 with our greater population, every year on drink. The same terrible results are to be seen the world over.

CHAPTER XX.

"SECRETS" AND "TRICKS" OF THE LIQUOR TRADE. A GLANCE BEHIND THE SCENES.

Rum is Rum the World over—Drunken Mohammedan is said to have "gone to Jesus"—Speech of Canon Farrar—Ludicrous Side of the Question—The Connoisseurs of Liquors—Wine-Drinkers humbugged—The Secret of Success in the Manufacture of Liquors—Ingredients—How "Imported Cognac Brandy" is made—How Schiedam Schnapps and Common Gin are made—Champagne Receipt—"Native Catawba Wines" made without Grapes—"Fine Old Port —Receipts for making Porter—"Ale" good to sleep on; how made—To the Uninitiated—How to bottle neatly—Sugar of Lead as a Sweetener—Filthiness no Hindrance to the Drinker—The Effect of these Revelations—The Slaves of Fashion.

ALCOHOL, the product of civilization, has become the curse of civilization. It accompanies the first rude settlers on the desolate frontiers, as a curse; it follows in the wake of or precedes the pioneer of Christianity in the deserts of heathenism, as a hindrance. The missionary finds it the greatest obstacle to his work. It is the universal testimony that the introduction of alcoholic drinks among pagan nations has been an unmitigated curse to the population. By it the Indian of our own country has been swindled, deceived, and reduced far below the original state in which he was first known to civilization.

I have letters from many parts of the world,—the same story, whether from civilized Europe or pagan Africa; whether from Asia, with its millions of Orientals, or from our own country, and we know what it is, and what it has been to us.

In a letter from Australia the writer says: "Intoxicating drink is the curse of our young colony."

The following facts are from a letter received from a British officer in India. After saying that the Mohammedans are abstemious and do not drink intoxicating liquors, as a rule, the writer says:

"The remark is often made by the natives, when they see a Mohammedan drunk, 'He has left Mohammed and gone to Jesus.'"

On one occasion, while he was urging a native to examine the claims of Christianity, two drunken English soldiers passed.

"See," said the native; "do you wish me to be like that? As a Mohammedan, I could not; as a Christian, I might."

At a ball given by the officers a request was made to the general that rations of spirits should be served to the military band. The general objected, on the ground that they were Mohammedans. The reply was, "No; they are Christians;" and the spirits were ordered.

This is the evil we mourn over. Shall we do no more? Many tell us we exaggerate, or select the worst cases. Again I say, let such investigate. Pardon me, if I give a short extract from a speech of Canon Farrar in the Sheldonian Theatre, Oxford,—a place which, twenty years ago, no one could have imagined would ever be opened for a temperance lecture; the very proposal would have been hailed with a shout of incredulous derision. He says:

"Gentlemen: I look around me, not here in England only, but also through all the world, over dependencies upon which the sun never sets, and I see the frightful, the intolerable evidences of the devastation wrought by one fatal sin—the sin of drunkenness; and that sin caused by one fatal product—alcohol diluted in intoxicating drinks. I am unable, I have not the heart, to-day, to touch on one-tenth or one-hundredth part of the proofs which demonstrate to every serious mind at all acquainted with the facts, the awful importance of this question. Focus the lurid gleams which flash upwards from this pit of destruction, and you will see how frightful is the glare. Track the subterranean ramifications of this evil, and you will see how the whole nation, the whole empire is undermined; how every tread we take is over fire, ever bursting through the treacherous ashes.

"It is matter not of assertion, but of sternest demonstration, that the drink traffic causes the most amazing waste of our national resources: that to it are due, mainly and almost exclusively, the worst phenomena of pauperism; that it causes seventy-five per cent. of those melancholy cases of domestic ruin which fill our police-courts: that it contributes enormously, both directly and indirectly, to the hideous social evil; that but for it, on the testimony of nearly every judge on the bench, crimes of violence would well-nigh disappear; that it is the cause, both directly and indirectly, of a most terrible mortality; that it chokes our prisons, madhouses, and penitentiaries; that it creates an hereditary taint which makes life a curse to a stunted population; that because of it, thousands, ay, tens of thousands, of miserable men, and yet more miserable women, and poor little children, most miserable of all, lead lives of such squalor and anguish, as only they who have witnessed can conceive; that it devastates the humanity, and blights the bodies and the souls, not only of 600,000 drunkards, but of the millions which their ruin drags down to shame; that it frustrates our religious efforts at home, that it destroys and ruins our mission efforts abroad; that it is the chief bane and ruin of our homes; that it is the darkest stain on the glory and prosperity of our nation.

"Exaggeration, gentlemen! There is not one word of this indictment which is not true to the letter; not one word of it which is not capable of the most rigorous proof which evidence can establish and statistics contain. And unless it be exaggeration to say twilight when we mean midnight, then it is none to say the blackness of its darkness could only be represented in such colours as when some mighty painter dips his pencil in the hues of earthquake and eclipse. Those who know nothing whatever about the subject—those who are so unhappy as to be blinded by the possession, in some shape or other, of a share, or a freehold, or an interest in the production or the sale of that which is the cause of all this iniquity—may call this impeachment exaggerated; but they have never shaken, they have never even attempted to shake, the damning evidence on which it is founded, and to which concur, with startling unanimity, the testimony of every person, and every class of persons, that has in any way studied or come across the subject. That evidence has been produced in the most public way, and in every possible way, again and again; it has been produced before committees of the House of Lords, and before committees of the House of Commons; it has been gathered for the Northern House of Convocation, and the Southern House of Convocation; it has been collected by statesmen, and collected by political economists; it has been furnished from sources the most opposite and the most unsuspected; it is derived from clergymen and from judges, from jailers and from policemen, from the heads of work-houses and asylums, from physicians and from publicans; and it stands not only unshaken but absolutely unchallenged. And more than this, it is constantly admitted, at unguarded moments, by the very agents and the very writers who detest teetotalers, and who leave no stone unturned to defeat Sir W. Lawson, and to overthrow the Alliance. Language which, if used by a temperance reformer, would be angrily set aside as

RUM'S FOOTPRINT—DEATH AND DRINK.

exaggerated, is quite freely used at unsuspected turns by such grave and moderate organs as the 'Quiver,' the 'Standard,' and the 'Quarterly Review.'"

Though the consequences of drinking are so terrible, yet when we turn to a certain class of drinkers, there is something ludicrous in their assumptions of importance and style, and their pride at being considered connoisseurs of the various brands of liquors they consume. There is no class in this country so swindled and humbugged as the wine and spirit drinkers, and the wonder of all is, that they know they are cheated. How many in this country do you suppose think for a moment that they are drinking what the label or brand on their bottle purports it to be? The gentleman who drinks his "fine old port" must know that there is more "fine old port" sold in New York than there is made, purely from grapes, in all the region professedly the port-wine region. He will submit to such barefaced swindling in reference to no other article he uses.

I have good authority for this statement, that, "Of the port shipped for the English market as vintage wine, from nine months to two years old, at least two-thirds is manufactured or adulterated in Oporto."

In a book which I obtained with some difficulty, entitled "The Manufacture of Liquors, Wines, etc., without the aid of distillation, arranged and prepared expressly for the trade," the author says: "For bars, hotels, etc., the following directions will ensure a saving of from forty to two hundred and fifty per cent. per gallon, and the most critical examination will scarcely detect the genuine, a chemical test alone being able to indicate the difference of the one from the other." And again: "The great secret of success in the manufacture of liquor consists in imparting to the imitation the precise aroma of the genuine, and thus obtaining an article as near reality as possible, at a far less cost." I give his list of articles used for the manufacture of these liquors. "Neutral spirit: When alcohol is cleansed of grain-oil, it is then called neutral spirit. Tartaric, citric, and sulphuric acids, alum, amylic alcohol, or fusil-oil, heavy oil of wine, ammonia, ambergris, sweet and bitter almonds, oils of sweet and bitter almonds, cardamom, bone-black, namely, animal's bones burnt and ground, balsam of Peru, catechu, caustic potassa, cubebs, slippery-elm bark, eggs for fining, sulphuric, nitric, and butyric ether, flax-seed, grape-sugar, flour, gamboge, gentian, honey, molasses, oak-bark, oatmeal, long, cayenne, and black pepper, pellitory and grains of paradise (powerful acrimonious substances used for giving false strength to liquors), tinctures of musk and tolu, snake-root, sweet spirits of nitre, tea, quassia, olive oil, oils of cara-way, cloves, cedar, juniper, lavender, lemon, mace, rosemary, roses, sassafras and wintergreen, creosote and turpentine." These are all used for the manufacture of liquor; and for the colouring, the author gives "alkanet root, red beets, Brazil wood, cochineal, indigo, logwood, red sanders wood, and saffron."

How absurd it is to see men drinking their cognac brandy and boasting of its purity, "for it is 'imported.'" I have before me a method for giving age to new casks, and branding barrels and casks with marks that are not exactly custom-house. Let us see how your brandy is made, though perhaps I should say other people's brandy. First, the French method, practised in France :—

"Clean spirit, containing 50 per cent. of alcohol, 100 gallons; honey, 7 gallons, dissolved in 3 gallons of water, having first bruised $1\frac{1}{2}$ ounces of cochineal and allowed it to macerate in the water for a few days. Then add 8 ounces of catechu, 5 gallons of rum, 12 ounces of acetic ether, then add clean burst sugar; colour to suit the fancy or the particular market it is intended for."

This is your "pure" French imported cognac brandy. Now we will see how cognac is manufactured here :—

"25 gallons of whisky, 14 gallons of water, 1 gallon tincture of pepper, $1\frac{1}{2}$ gallons of strong tea, 6 drops of oil of orange dissolved in a wine-glass of alcohol, 1 pound of acetic ether; colour with burnt sugar or sanders wood." *Note*: "This can be made at from 12 to 20 cents per gallon, according to the price of whiskey, 20 cents per gallon being the estimated price."

Hurrah for the swindle! Who are the biggest fools, those

who will not touch the stuff, or those who are cheated with their eyes open?

Some prefer Schiedam schnapps to cognac. How is it made?

"Common gin* 30 gallons, strained honey 4½ gallons, water 2 gallons, sulphuric acid 1 ounce, sweet spirits of nitre 8 ounces, spirit of nitric ether 3 ounces, 10 drops of oil of wintergreen dissolved in 2 ounces of acetic ether."

The comment after the receipt is, "Really a fine liquor, and cheaply made." When I observe gentlemen, and often ladies, ordering wine at the hotel, looking so very wisely over the list, and gravely choosing champagne as the most fashionable wine for drinking, I am very much inclined to laugh, while I am saddened at what may be the result of their folly.

Champagne! Let me give you a receipt for making champagne—*genuine* champagne; for while you know there is more champagne bought, sold, and drunk in New York than there is manufactured of the pure article in the world, you—whether at home or abroad, in Paris, London, Berlin, or New York—always obtain "genuine champagne." Here's the receipt:—

"Fifty gallons of water, 2 gallons of honey, 5 ounces of bruised ginger, 5 ounces of ground mustard. Boil this mass 30 minutes, add a quart of yeast, and let it ferment from 10 to 14 days. Add 6 ounces of bitter almonds bruised, spirits and grains of paradise to suit convenience. The more spirit the champagne possesses the greater will be its body. For colouring use cochineal half an ounce to the 50 gallons."

There you have it, and in addition we have the direction for bottling, laying on the Dutch metal, and printing and placing the labels to prove that you get it pure and genuine, direct from any firm you choose to select. Oh, I forgot—for *pink* champagne add "a little more cochineal."

"Ah," say you, "but I only drink *native* wines, sparkling Catawba." Well, here you have it:—

"Receipt for sparkling Catawba: 100 pounds of raisins, 35 gallons of

---

* The receipt for making common gin is 25 gallons of clear whiskey, water 10 gallons, oil of juniper dissolved in a gill of alcohol (sometimes a small portion of turpentine is added), 1 gallon of grains of paradise of double strength, fine, with alum.

sweet cider, 100 gallons of water, 3 pints of yeast; ferment for 12 days; then add 12 gallons of honey, 12 gallons of clean spirit, 1 grain of ambergris rubbed well with 2 ounces of sugar; then 4 gallons of Jamaica rum, 12 ounces of orris-root, and fine the whole with 3 quarts of boiled milk added while hot."

Very fine sparkling Catawba!
"Well," say some, "I only drink claret." Here you have the receipt :—

"Claret Vin de Bordeaux :—Five gallons of boiled cider, two gallons of spirit, 5 gallons of water, 2 ounces of powdered catechu, or 2 drops of sulphuric acid to the gallon to suit the taste. Colour with tincture of logwood."

Do you prefer sherry?

"Ten gallons of cider, 4 ounces of bitter almonds, 1 gallon of honey, 4 ounces of mustard. Boil for 30 minutes; then add one-half pint of spirit of orris-root, 2 ounces essence of cassia, 3 quarts of rum."

Then we have this additional piece of information: "Jamaica rum is preferable, as this wine is often prepared for the auctions, but the amount of spirit becomes an important item, owing to its cost; therefore when this is kept in view, tincture of grains of paradise should be substituted for spirits."

But here is the receipt for the port which is used so freely by the gentlemen of the old school, who "always get the best,"— the port prescribed so freely by physicians, who should not dare to tamper with any deleterious substance without knowing something of the ingredients, and who are bound to get it *pure*. I only ask when the country is flooded with such stuff as is sold for "port wine" (and the manufacturers whisper that we cannot tell the difference between that and the genuine), how do these doctors, who so freely prescribe, know what they give to their patients? I give you a receipt for making "good port wine" :—

"Twenty gallons of cider, 2 gallons of honey, 12 ounces of carbonate of soda, 1½ gallons strong tincture grains of paradise, 5 ounces of powdered catechu. Colour with logwood or burnt sugar. A small portion of spirit would improve it. The carbonate of soda is to neutralize the acid in the cider, which, if allowed to remain, would present too large a proportion of acid for good port."

How careful they are that drinkers shall have "*good port!*"

In addition to these receipts, published "for the trade," are receipts for manufacturing seven kinds of brandy, besides the cognac, some of which might frighten you, seven kinds of whiskey, two kinds of gin, five kinds of rum, and ten different kinds of wine.

Now, to the porter and ale drinkers we have something to say. The following is a receipt for making porter:—

"Boil 3 quarts of wheat bran, 1½ pounds of hops, and 8 ounces of bruised ginger, in 12 gallons of water, for one hour. Then strain through flannel, and, while warm, add two gallons of molasses, 1 quart of yeast, half a pint of brandy-colouring, and half a gallon of tincture of grains of paradise, which will be formed by digesting 8 ounces of the grain in half a gallon of whiskey."

If you prefer ale, here's a receipt :—

"Four pounds of brown sugar, 1 pound of hops, 2 ounces of quassia, and 12 gallons of water. Boil for three-quarters of an hour. Then add 1 gallon of molasses, 1 pint of yeast, and continue the fermentation until the froth ceases to rise on the surface. Then add half a gallon of tincture of grains of paradise, and strain through flannel. Add 3 ounces of butyric ether, and boil *immediately.*"

To avoid the costly price of hops, the small dealer of ale and porter, as a substitute for the bitter of the hops, makes use of quassia, nux vomica, or strychnine, aloes, catechu, pellitory, long pepper, wormwood, gentian; and for a false strength similar to alcohol, uses cocculus indicus, copperas, and grains of paradise.

The following receipt for giving strength and body to beer and ale is given :—

"2 pounds of quassia, 2 pounds of gentian bruised, 1 pound of aloes, 10 gallons of water. Boil to 5 gallons. Then add 1 pound of copperas, and boil to 4 gallons. Add this to the ale to suit the taste."

I will conclude with the following interesting statement to

the uninitiated: "It may be necessary to state, for the benefit of the uninitiated reader, when and how this kind of porter and ale is disposed of to form a remunerative investment. This consists in bottling and labelling this *fluid* with neatness. The labels should be obtained from the lithographers, and should be executed in the highest style of art. The same articles are sold under the names of London porter, Scotch ale, India pale ale, pine apple ale, etc., etc.; and the ale receives all the names of the different varieties of that article that have acquired any celebrity in commerce. The bottles are packed in barrels or boxes, and are disposed of at auction. This ale is usually manufactured at a cost varying from four to eight cents per gallon."

"It is not an unusual occurrence in commerce to meet with porter (or so called) that has been made from the fermentation of molasses, yeast, and water. This, after becoming sufficiently acidulated from fermentation, has the further progress of the fermentation checked by the addition of alcohol, and a small portion of ground mustard-seed. It is then strengthened with aloes, pellitory, pepper, quassia, catechu, and burnt sugar, and has a rough, bitter, acidulous taste, and leaves a disagreeable *after*-taste in the mouth."

A gentleman writes me: "About a year ago, a dealer in paints told me that a man came in to purchase sugar of lead. He had none, except some that was rather dirty, which he alluded to. The purchaser said it would suit his purpose; he did not want it to mix with paints as a dryer, but to sweeten sour wine."

Now, to what end is this revelation? What effect will it produce? Very little, if any, to prevent some men and women from drinking. Those who have the appetite, and are determined to gratify it, will not be deterred from drinking by a knowledge of the poison or the nastiness of the liquor which they crave. Men have been known to drink alcohol out of bottles containing specimens of vile things, snakes, scorpions, etc.; have been known to drink the spirits in which a corpse has been washed; to drink camphor, cologne, camphine, anything however vile, offensive, or filthy, containing the alcohol to start the stagnant blood in the diseased vessels of the stomach.

Many who are the slaves of fashion, who drink because they are afraid to refuse, will pooh, pooh! such revelations, and profess not to believe; and so all that we can say, all the flood of light that can be thrown on the subject, fails to convince sufficiently to induce the people to abstain. So the manufacturer and dealer, rolling in his wealth, or striving to make money, can laugh us to scorn in all our attempts to reveal the truth to the victims either of appetite or custom. But whether men hear, or whether they forbear, God helping us, we shall do our best to warn, entreat, and save.

CHAPTER XXI.

SOME OF MY EXPERIENCES WITH BRAZEN-FACED PEOPLE.

The Life of a Public Man—Peculiar Annoyances—Kind Treatment of the Press—"Interviewing"—An Unfortunate Little Notice—"John B. Gough lying dangerously ill"—Mistakes in Reporting Lectures—Amusing Specimen—Applications for Help—Begging-Letter Writers—Tramps preferable to these—Extracts from Begging-Letters—Young Man's Strange Request for Fifteen Hundred Dollars—Request for One Thousand Dollars—What the Lord is reported to have said—One Thousand Dollars wanted to educate two Nieces—"I am taken in"—Notes and Promises to Pay—A New Method—A Curious Plan of Professionals—Begging "Mediums"—Letter purporting to come from my Mother—An Incident in Scotland.

THERE is in the life of a public man, especially of one who is constantly before the people, a monotony of change, when the necessity for constant travel becomes exceedingly wearisome, and the mere thought of rest is a comfort. Still there are compensations in the knowledge that your aim is to make men better, and that you are not absorbed in the selfish ambition that seeks your own, independent of others' welfare; and again, in the delightful associations that ripen into life-long friendships, and the companionship of the good, the true, and the pure—the very nobility of humanity.

Every public man is often exposed to annoyances, some serious in themselves; some more trifling, yet serious in their results; while others are almost imperceptible to sight or touch, like the red bug of the south, inserting its almost infinitesimal self under the skin to irritate and inflame; or the mosquito of the north, that persistently hums his defiance in your ear, till you wish he would *bite,* and end the music.

In speaking of annoyances, I have no desire to complain; but if the relation of some of them may induce any who unintentionally annoy to be more thoughtful, this will not be a wasteful expenditure of time or paper.

Far be it from me to criticise or speak unkindly of the press, for I have been most kindly treated by newspapers for thirty-eight years. Seldom in all that time have I received an unfair criticism from any respectable paper, much less any personal injustice. I have been criticised, and occasionally with a sharpness that made me wince; but I have endeavoured to profit by every criticism, so far as has been in my power. Every public man must acknowledge to have been occasionally treated unfairly by one portion of the press, that can hardly lay claim to respectability. In the United States and in Great Britain, most kind and liberal notices have been given of my work, although I have never asked for a notice; and only twice in thirty years have I been in an editor's office, besides having never once sent a press-notice to the committees employing me, though often urged to do so. All the kind notices—and they have been many—have been entirely voluntary on the part of the press, and never sought by me.

One annoyance is experienced in the system of interviewing. No statement made of a man's personal history or opinions should ever be published, without submitting it to his perusal and revision; for one word, either in addition or subtraction, may make a tremendous difference in the whole meaning.

I remember but one occasion when I could fairly state that I was interviewed, and then I was so sadly misrepresented that it made a former friend a strong enemy, and put me so wrongly before a large section of temperance reformers, that I have not been fully righted up to the present time.

A gentleman called on me at the hotel where I was stopping, in a Western city. The conversation was in substance this :—

"I wish to get your opinion on the women's temperance crusade. What do you think of it?"

"I have seen scarcely anything of it, and am not qualified

to give an opinion without further knowledge of the work. From what I have heard, I should judge it to be a new departure which promises to wake the people up to some interest on the question."

"What do you think of the women praying and singing in the street?"

"With regard to that, I am rather dubious, and should hardly like to give any opinion. I have not seen that phase of the women's work; but it seems to me I should hardly like to see my wife or sister singing and praying in saloons, or in the public streets."

"Do you not think Mr.—— is a mere sensationalist?"

"As to that, I can only say I have not the dread of sensationalism that afflicts many very good people. I think we need something to waken us up; and I do not object to, but rather welcome, some excitement. I certainly prefer a little sensationalism to the dull, heavy apathy, that is so hard to interest. As for Mr. ——'s sensationalism, I know nothing about it. I believe he has been very enthusiastic in his advocacy of the women's crusade."

This, I think, was all I said of importance; and when I saw in the morning paper the report of the interview, I felt my cheek burn, for I at once saw that it would put me in a false light before the people who might read it, and was an injustice to a man who was my friend. This was the report of the interview:

"Mr. Gough is not very much in favour of the women's crusade. With regard to the praying and singing in the streets, Mr. Gough would not like to see his wife or sister doing such work; and his opinion is that Mr. —— is a mere sensationalist."

I received many letters of inquiry, and found myself compelled publicly to take a position decidedly for or against the women's work; and after becoming acquainted with and interested in it, attending some of their meetings, I was rejoiced most emphatically to approve their efforts, which I did continually in every speech, when I could consistently introduce it. The mistake of the "interviewer" caused me some annoyance.

On another occasion, the wrong done to me, or perhaps I should say, the inconvenience to which I was subjected, arose from an incorrect statement made to an interviewer by a gentleman who I know would never willingly have caused me any annoyance; and if his statement had been submitted to me, I would gladly have revised it; but the article was extensively published, with no revision. Several of the answers to the interviewer's questions were quite correct, some of them slightly incorrect, but of no material consequence; but there was one assertion that was made on no authority but a supposition, that "John B. Gough has an annuity, and is worth $100,000;"—a statement of no particular importance to any one; to me it would have been very gratifying if true; but the fact is, I have no annuity, and am not worth in available property one-half the sum stated.

"Well, how can such a report injure you?"

Only by the annoyance of being compelled to refuse applicants for help. They have come, since that item was published, from all quarters of this country, from persons who never saw me, from remote places I have never visited, and for sums varying from $1,200 to "what you think you can afford." These applications are generally prefaced by the announcement that they have read in the papers so and so. The item was published in an English paper; and from the other side of the Atlantic I have received several applications for help on the ground of being possessor of £20,000 and an annuity. On another page I shall speak fully, and give my opinion of these beggars.

At one time, in the midst of a season's work, I was taken ill at Scranton, Pa. The physician said it was a severe cold, and I must rest a few days, or it might develop into pneumonia. So I gave up two appointments, and remained in Scranton from Friday till Tuesday. On Wednesday I commenced work again; and, while travelling to an appointment on the Thursday, saw in a daily paper this item of news: "John B. Gough is lying dangerously ill at Scranton." That small item cost me several dollars, and gave me much annoyance. First came the telegrams to the Bureau, inquiring if I should be able to meet my engagements, or would they furnish another lecturer in my place; then letters to me forwarded from Scranton; and in several instances I was told on my arrival at the town to fill my appointment, "We cannot sell the tickets, for the people do not believe you will come, as the item stating your illness has been copied into our paper; and we must get out extra handbills announcing your arrival, and that you will lecture this evening." Thus that unfortunate little notice plagued me, and diminished my audiences for more than a week.

I mention one other annoyance, and that may be considered a very small one,—but the small things are sometimes the most perplexing,—just as a small hair in the nostril will irritate worse than a pain, and the tickle of a feather may cause convulsions if persevered in, and a drop of water constantly falling on the head may produce madness. I refer to the mistakes in reporting what is said in a lecture, very often quite absurd— so much so that no possible harm can be done by them. At other times the mistake in a word may completely alter the tone or meaning of the whole sentence, and we are reported as stating views directly the opposite of our convictions and former utterances.

But some things, to use the New England expression, "are too funny for anything." I give you one from a report of a five-column speech in an English paper. I had said:

"Come with me to the Yosemite Valley. Yonder stands El Capitan, a mile away; it seems so near you could strike it with a stone. Approach it nearer—nearer. How it grows and widens and looms up! Nearer yet —nearer. See those shrubs! Shrubs? They are trees, one hundred feet in height and three to four feet in diameter. See that dent in the face of the rock. That is a fissure seventy-five feet deep. Soon you stand under the shadow of El Capitan. A plumb line from the summit will fall fifty feet from its base. Now look up—up—up—thirty-six hundred feet right up. How grand! Two-thirds of a mile. A perpendicular rock. There it stands, anchored in the valley, seared and seamed with the storms of centuries. Your nerves thrill, your lips quiver, and your eyes fill with tears. You are impressed with the grandeur and sublimity of the magnificent surroundings. You feel your own littleness, that you are but as the small dust of the balance in comparison, and remember that the inhabitants of the earth are but as grasshoppers in His sight, who is the great Creator."

This is a description not worth much perhaps, but it is better than the report which I copy from the paper that lies before me :

"Come with me to the great Yosemill Valley in California. The land will rise before you miles and miles away. But approach it nearer and nearer. How the land looms up before you ! See in the distance a shrub. No ; it is a tree, twenty feet high and three or four feet in diameter. Come nearer yet. There's a dent yonder. No ; it is a fissure in the rock seventy-five feet deep. There is El Capo, thirty-six hundred feet from the base to the summit. Stand and look up at the inhabitants on the top of it, and they appear no bigger than grasshoppers, and the people look down on you as the small dust of the balance."

That is verbatim. In the same report were several absurd things, but this was the most ridiculous.

Another annoyance is the increasing number of begging-letter writers. When in England twenty-five years ago I boasted that I knew nothing in America of the system of writing begging-letters, so prominent there ; but I really think we can now fairly challenge competition in that line with any country in the world. I rather think it is an imported nuisance and not indigenous to the soil of America.

A tramp who comes to my house and tells me he wants food or money, or help of any kind, is preferable to the whining, begging letter-writer. The tramps are not half so rasping to me as is the writer of a letter from which I give an extract :

"Having heard that you were a very benevolent man, and knowing you were not a poor man, for I saw it stated in the paper the other day the amount of your income, I make bold to ask you a favour. My folks are respectable, though not very well off, and I wish to go to a music school for three years. My father has a rich uncle, whom I wrote to help me, but he thought himself too poor. The cost will be 500 dollars a year. I wish you would send me a check for 500 dollars for three years, or a check at once for 1500 dollars. Pardon my boldness, but I do so much wish to go, etc., etc.

"P.S.—A check payable to bearer."

I will not copy long extracts, but give a few of the cases. One writes:

"You talk of serving the Lord. You will serve Him by helping me. I want $1000 to get a home."

Another:

"I asked the Lord where I should get $100, and He whispered your name. Now if you go to the Lord, perhaps He'll tell you to send it to me."

Another:

"If you only knew how happy $100 would make me, you would send it, for you are abundantly able."

Again:

"I want $1000 to educate two nieces, and I write to you."

The most annoying class among the so-called respectable beggars are those who apply to you personally, and by appeals to your sympathy obtain money they never mean to repay.

A young American in England begged me to lend him £10 for a passage home. He could be sent home by steerage, but he could not endure a steerage passage; spoke of his relatives, and said, "I can give you an order on my mother." The money was lent and two pounds additional for some comforts for the voyage. The order on his mother was given. I have it now. When the gentleman reached this country he had the coolness to write me not to present the order to his mother, as it would be of no use, for she had no money, and that is the last of that transaction. Over and over again have I declared that I will lend no more money to persons unknown to me; but they make such fair promises that I think "this must be a real case," and, like Mr. Hartop, "I am taken in."

These people, many of them, never intend to repay. I write as a sufferer; for from 1845, when they began on me, till now, the game has been going on,—a losing one for me, for I have notes and promises to pay to an amount that would hardly be believed of one in my circumstances. All I can say is, that the amount might be put down in five figures, and the figure five at the head of the sum, not one penny of which amount do I ever expect to receive; for of all the loans I have made—and they are hundreds—I have received only in four or five cases the amounts borrowed.

I would not utter one word to discourage the benevolent in giving to real objects of charity, for I have given freely to such; but it is the regular harpy who thrives on the benevolence of those who possess means, or it is the young man—and the number of this class is increasing—who depends, not on his own exertions, but on the help he can obtain from others, for a start in life. The whining cry, "I want a little help," from able-bodied, healthy young men who are not ready to endure hardship and some privation to make their way in the world is contemptible. I sometimes think of adopting a plan to shame these beggars, if they have any shame left; and that is to publish in a pamphlet the letters, with their names, and, circulate it through the country, and offer their notes for sale at a discount.

A very curious plan adopted by some of these professionals is to take advantage of the credulity of their intended victims. I give portions of a letter received, purporting to come from my mother, who has been dead forty years.

Poor, dear woman! she has forgotten how to spell, for she writes that this letter is to be attended to "immegertely:"

"John, I, your mother, can speak to you through a medium in Bath, Maine." (She seems to have learned something of geography; for when she was a denizen of this earth, I doubt if she knew there was such a place as the above.) "You and this medium are strangers; but if you will come to her, my dear boy, I can convince you that I still live to enjoy my son's prosperity." (No necessity to go to Maine to know that the dear mother lives.) "Do not think or believe your mother does not help you and bear you up," etc., etc. "John, my son, fear not; God has given you great gifts, and He has given great gifts to the one I am controlling to-day. I wish you would help her to come out of the poor condition she is in. If you knew what a gem she is, I know you would help her. Come and see me. I, your mother, send this. Come and talk to me through this medium. If you feel disposed to help her, do. From your mother to John."

This reminds me of an incident that occurred in Scotland some years ago.

I was on the platform of a railway station waiting, with my wife, for a train, when a gentleman approached me, looking very solemn, and said, rather lugubriously:

"Mr. Gough, we have had a communication from your dear mother."

"My mother?" I said; "why, she has been dead these twenty years."

"Yes," he said; "she is in the spirit land, and oh, so happy! Would you not like to hear her message?"

"That depends; how did you get your message?"

"We had a *séance* last evening, and communicated with your dear mother. Would you not like to hear her message?"

"No; I want to hear nothing about it. If my mother, who knows I love her dearly and treasure every little relic she left behind her, and who knows that I would be glad to see her and hear her speak, will not communicate with me except through mediums, and *séances*, and table-rappings by a parcel of people who know nothing about her and care as little, I do not wish to hear anything; for I think my mother must be deteriorated to descend to such tricks to communicate with one who loves her as well as I do."

CHAPTER XXII.

AMUSING EXPERIENCES WITH LETTER-WRITERS, BEGGARS, AND ASPIRANTS FOR FAME.

Letter-Writers and their Wants—A Lady "wishes to get married;" full Particulars—Specimen of a Class of Oddities—What "the Simple Son of a Carpenter" desires—An Unappreciated Benefactor of his Country—A "Big Thing to be accomplished—Applications for Old Lectures—The Ambitious Young Man with a "Hobby"—An Aspirant for Fame—Newspaper Man wishes two "Wornout" Lectures—Request for a "Moddle" Lecture—Receipt for a "Moddle" Lecture—A Few Hints to the Ambitious—Requests for Autographs—Levying Black-mail—Take Warning—Dr. Chalmers on Autographs—Demand for Photographs—"Very like a Bore"—Not limited to Friends—Comical Arrangements of these Pictures—Side by Side with the Gorilla.

PUBLIC men are liable to receive communications containing inquiries on all kinds of topics, asking questions on all kinds of abstruse subjects, or making the most absurd propositions. I give a portion of a letter I received from a lady:

"I will state my circumstances and wishes as briefly as possible. I come to the point at once, and inform you that I wish to get married, and I hope you will think none the worse of me for thus making my wants known to one who must have a large circle of acquaintances, like yourself. When a lady finds her hair fast becoming threads of silver, and the crow's-feet deepening in her face, it is time for her to begin to look out for herself, if she would not spend her declining days in loneliness, 'unloved and unloving,'—a prospect that I do not at all relish, unless I find that it be God's will. If so, I must make the best of it. I am thirty-five years of age; very unprepossessing in appearance, having a dark complexion, plain, sad features; only four feet ten inches in height; weight ninety to ninety-eight pounds; and health quite variable, still good. Physicians have told me that I am just as likely to live forty years as any one.

"My father's home is in ——, away back in the country, where there is not a gentleman of my acquaintance that I would marry, even if they wished to marry me. I wish to get a kind, honest man, about fifty years of age, possessing common intelligence and refinement, and at least property sufficient to take care of himself and me ; and he must be between forty-five and sixty-five years of age, and a total-abstinence man ; widower preferred ; also one who would care more for home and wife than society. And I, on my part, think I could be a true and affectionate wife, capable of managing a household, and willing to dress and live either in a plain and economical style, or luxuriously, as our mutual views and circumstances might seem to require. . . . .

"And now, if you know of any gentleman that answers to my description who would like to make my acquaintance with a view to matrimony, please furnish him with an introduction and recommend from yourself, and I shall be happy to commence the acquaintance at once, either by correspondence or personally." . . . .

After giving references, the lady requests that—

"If you write them concerning me, I beg you will sign a fictitious name, for they would think it about as wild in me to write to you as it would be to write to the King of France. I trust, should you be so fortunate as to bring about an acquaintance between two temperance people, that it will be so managed that the part I have taken in it may be kept a profound secret. Should you aid me in this matter, I presume that in time you will be rewarded. Yours faithfully, ———."

I give extracts from a series of queer letters received from a gentleman, as a specimen of a class of oddities with whom we have to deal. He first proposes an interview.

"Dear Friend Gough,—The lecturing field, which is white already to harvest, I, the uneducated, unsophisticated, simple son of a carpenter of the nineteenth century, conscious of the powers that are in me, am desirous of entering. You have had a large experience therein, and may render me valuable aid in the way of advice, hints, and suggestions ; and may possibly point me to an opening, if you will thus kindly volunteer your services on my behalf, provided it can be done without discommoding yourself, or hindering your own work. If I could see you at your own home when you have leisure, or some other place you might appoint, and have with you some half dozen or so of your lecturing or literary friends, I would in an unembarrassed manner, or as much so as possible, read to you a couple of lectures that I have in my possession, and shall remodel, entitled, one of them, ' Our Country and its Brilliant Prospects and Possibilities.' This lecture is descriptive of the country, and of the people, and of some of their great interests, and one more especial than the rest, their mining interests. And its peroration is a glowing description of the grandeur and glory that surely awaits the American people, if they only retain in each other *unbounded confidence*, and exercise patience and perseverance in all well-doing, and the wealthy out of their abundance see to it that the destitute and the helpless are provided for until business can be started. Friend Gough, we must marshal 'the hosts of God's elect' from the four quarters of the earth, *i.e.*, the eloquent orators and reformers of the day, and exercise the evil and ultra spirits that run so many off into a tangent of weird, wild fanaticism, and clothe them in their right mind, and show them their proper sphere. Then we'll evolve out of the present miserable chaos, *harmony*. Yes, this *we must do*. And in so doing we will fuse the wills of the American people into one. This work accomplished, this nation then shall demonstrate itself to all the world as the chosen people of God, to still continue leading on civilization, science, art, invention, philosophy, government, poetry, commerce, agriculture; and above all, the noblest aspirations and highest aims in each individual of the nation, after purity of life and character, and an increasing intelligence, that shall know *no* stopping-place, as we avail ourselves each for himself of a careful perusal of the life and characters in their biography of the illustrious of all ages. *That* in that very act, their virtue, intelligence, lofty principle, and exalted aims may from them, who being dead (yet thus to us speak, come, or), flow into us as their living spirit through the dead letter that in or by others as a substitute they have left behind for us. And in this way, as the American people, we shall render ourselves and the continent and our institutions as the true Archimedean lever that shall lift a world from its degradation."

Soon after the receipt of this letter, I received another, from which I give the following extracts:—

"Friend Gough,—I must see you if I can, and shake hands with you, and look you in the eye, and listen to the tones of your voice in your own home, and if you have time, to read two lectures that I have. I have a mission to accomplish. The American people must be quickened into a higher life, into a *closer unity*, a stronger sociality, a deeper feeling of interest in each other's welfare. The conscience, the enthusiasm, the aspirations, and the will of the nation need at this particular juncture greatly quickening, need fusing into one, and fanning into a red heat, that the exalted destiny of the nation may, in the right direction, be speedily carried forward; that genuine intelligence and virtue, and a true love of art and science, political economy, literature, agriculture, commerce, finance, philosophy, invention, and all that tends to promote a high and true state of social unity, may be promoted. And we indeed become the chosen people of God to redeem the earth—the Archimedean lever to lift the world from its degradation. We want to rid ourselves from all undue love of fashion, and pride, and aristocratic notions;

from false ornament, and an excessive love of wealth, purely for a display; and seek to be giants in virtue and intelligence, in invention, art, science, and philosophy. Now, this is a big thing on ice to be accomplished. Of course it is. 'But there is a flood taken at the tide leads on to fortune.' 'There is a fulness of times' that in nations every now and then happens. There is a period when the pear is ripe, and must fall. There are individuals who, like Timothy, inherit from their mother Lois, and grandmother Eunice, an unusual quantity and element of the true Promethean fire direct from the throne of the third heavens, so to speak, and who have the metal that constitutes an intellectual and moral battery, marvellous in its capacities to become highly surcharged; who have an ocean of enthusiasm, emotion, sensibility, and a corresponding voice of tone, modulation, flexibility, pathos, power, unction, and thrilling sensation that all rivets attention, and quickens feeling, and kindles and brightens in the soul of every one that listens aspirations after a higher, holier, purer, truer life of virtue and intelligence. There is every now and then a Peter the hermit, that comes forth from a life of austerities to wrap the continent in a blaze; a character simple-hearted, earnest, and burning with a zeal to see all men united in an indissoluble band of brotherhood, and genuine heartfelt fellowship, to see sorrow and suffering depart if we will.

"I am in my 49th year; the youngest son of a carpenter; was born of respectable parents in a beautiful valley between two mountains. Inherited a delicate constitution, and throughout nearly my whole life have been much afflicted. In my young days I suffered from a seven years' spinal disease, and from the terrible effects of that broken-down constitution have never fully recovered; have had, in addition, many serious seasons of sickness; came once near dying with a typhoid fever, and once with two large carbuncles and a succession of boils, covering a great portion of the body; have had the itch, and have been l—y; and have had almost countless colds and curious fevers, indigestion, pain of back and kidneys, sore eyes, sleepless nights, and rush of blood to the head. Have been from early youth wonderfully exercised in mind over the tangled snarl of theological, philosophical, metaphysical, social, political, agricultural, commercial, scientific, inventive, and artistic problems of the race, that from birth have confronted me in every conceivable direction, and that still in a great measure do confront me with curious wonderment and profound questionings, but through which of late I begin more clearly to see; and as I earnestly gaze, the clouds scatter, and the cheering rays of a celestial sun reach me, and the heavens are spanned with a rainbow of hope that brings peace and assurance to the soul, and bliss unutterable to the whole man. The waters of trouble are subsiding and sinking into the porous soil beneath my feet, and my tread is felt to be solid as I touch *terra firma;* and I am assuming the air and aspect of a conqueror that approaches the burnished spires and gleaming turrets of the celestial city, and coming streaming in the sunlight upon his eager vision, through an atmosphere redolent with the odour of exquisite flowers and ambrosia."

I will omit the remaining portion of this letter. My wife wrote to him that I should probably be away from home at the time he proposed calling on me; and even if I should not be, I was so busily engaged that I could give him but very little time, and therefore I thought it would hardly pay him to travel so many miles for so small a result. I give you his reply. After stating that the letter was received, he says:—

"This letter of M. E. Gough gives me an insight into the life of my friend Gough that I had not until now been as fully impressed with. Can it be possible, dear friend Gough, that your time and attention is thus *completely occupied, absorbed*, and that you are being driven, as it were, with a whirlwind of duties from the face of the earth? Oh, my God of Infinite Majesty, love and truth! Is this the natural consequence of success? Why, I start back in horror at the thought! A man is not happy until he gets at that that he has a faculty for, and then because he can do that thing well, forsooth must everybody hunt him down as though he were a wild hyena? Now I do most earnestly protest against all this nonsense that we have got agoing on upon this planet. The fact of it is that our American people want to be preached and preached and preached, and lectured and lectured and lectured to, until they are preached and lectured to death and the devil; and get to be as lazy as they can stick in their hides, morally and intellectually lazy. They want to imbibe and imbibe and imbibe, like a huge sponge, and give nothing forth. In a word, they have become moral and intellectual misers, moral and intellectual effeminates, babies, great grown calves, who will have you continually a-chewing their food for them, putting it into their mouths and a-wabbling their jaws, and a-rubbing their blood into circulation, and thus ever keeping them babies that can communicate nothing. Now I move that we go to work to stop this thing, in order to save our public teachers from the most abject drudgery, slavery, oppression, tyranny, cruelty. Who wants to succeed as an orator if he must be hounded off of the face of the earth by the public, who can't talk themselves because they are too infernal lazy to make the effort? Do you know that such a state of things, if I was a successful orator, would make me as indignant as the prophet Elijah! Well, you can just bet your life it would, and I know full well that I'd have to hold as tight fast to my old armchair as I could to keep from going off half-cocked, a-cussing like a blue streak. Well, you see, the idea is just this: When men and women have read and listened for a long time to earnest teachers and books, they should be able to communicate their ideas as well as the next one. They should have become splendid conversationalists. What has God given them a tongue for? There is plenty around them steeped in ignorance, who labour under such disadvantages of birth, education, and circumstances of poverty, that they can't find out what is the best for them in hardly anything; and these lazy imbibers of knowledge and oratory can do nothing for these poor souls, who are as sheep without a shepherd, because they won't put forth a solitary effort to waggle their own tongues glibly as they might, if they would only give themselves that practice that makes perfect; but they must go on oppressing, and make unrighteous demands upon the public orators of the day until they push them into the grave. The idea of a public's inexorably demanding of its orators to *go on, go on, keep right on*, pandering to their great big morbid mouth and unnatural appetite for sweetmeats that false custom has given them, just because they (the orators) have cultivated with success their oratorical powers. I don't see the point, and I wouldn't see the point had I climbed to the very highest summit of success. No, sir. 'All that a man hath will he give for his life.' 'Necessity knows no law.' All institutions were made for men, not to defeat their own object and crush men. If there is anything on earth that would come any nearer (than this crushing of my soul, brain, and body) to making me fall from grace, I don't know what it could be. The idea that a great set of grown calves and baby imbeciles who were too lazy or too proud to use their own tongues should want me to talk myself to death! Now do you know that I couldn't be put upon that way: my wrath would boil over when such animals came after me, and ten chances to one, as good-natured as I generally am, if I wouldn't suddenly forget myself and bawl out before I knew it, 'Go to—Huckleberry Hill! you infernal, lazy scoundrels! You think my stomach's lined with copper, and my throat with brass, and my lungs with iron, do you? Well, if you don't, you act as though you did. Mercy is not in your vocabulary or creed; you don't seem to know anything about such an article; with you it's one of the lost arts. Well, I'll kick a little into you, you unmerciful Shanghai Shysters!' .... I had thought of getting you to help me to get started as a lecturer, for I am burning up with the burden of a mission. But, O heavens! I now start back amazed at the thought. I would like to see you, and have a pleasant chat with you," etc., etc.

I suppose every lecturer has applications for his old lectures, but probably very few are applied to for their name. Here is an aspirant for fame, who desires to gather inspiration and gain a name at the same time. He says:—

"Is there a chance of my making arrangements to travel with you? I want to lecture, and I must be a good one or none at all. I do it for charity's sake more than money. I have some written lectures on hand.

I am only twenty-two years in age, but forty in mind. I wish to travel with you, and adopt your name and style, and perpetuate it. I am very ambitious, and it would save me twenty years' hard labour if I could get an introduction through you.... My hobby is to be a lecturer. My phrenology says I would make a good lecturer. I am a good composer; will give you all particulars when I receive your answer. Excuse haste. Please give this your kind attention. I should like to take your place as you are turning over the last page of your life perhaps. In haste, Yours, etc."

Very flattering!

A gentleman writes that he is about to start a newspaper, and shall commence canvassing for it, and if he could deliver lectures as he passed through the country it would be a help to him. Would I send him two of my worn-out lectures, as they would be fresh in the region in which he should canvass, and I should never want them any more, and he will never let anyone know they are mine. Flattering again!

Another writes for a "moddle lecture." He says:

"Being in need of a moddle lecture, I send to you for assistance. My request is, that you will please compose a moddle lecture from the *extracts* of your old lectures, and give it a subject—a lecture that will take about one hour to repeat it. I have heard of no man that can tie a lecture together with choice anecdotes such as you can, and indeed, sir, eloquence has distilled her choicest nectar upon your lips. I have spoken several times on temperance. If you wish any recommendations as to character apply," etc., etc.

Now, as to a "moddle lecture," I hardly know how to prepare one. I will here give a few hints to any who may be fired with the same ambition. Your subject might be "Reminders." You can introduce it by stating briefly or at length, according to the time you have, that for a conversation it is necessary to start a theme, and then all is easy. Describe a company of people sitting dull and silent, with nothing to say; no subject to interest them. How shall they engage in a stirring game of conversation? Let some one tell a story, no matter what it is, and it will be sure to remind some one of the company of something else. There you are—"that reminds me" of a man who had but one story, and that was about a gun. He would impatiently watch, when in company, for a chance to repeat his story. When all was still, he would let fall a book, or stamp with his feet, then start and say: "Oh dear, how it startled me! It reminded me of a gun. Talking of guns, 'reminds me,'"—and then came the story.

"This story of a gun reminds me of a famous hunter, who had shot tigers in Africa. Conversing with a German about sport, he said, 'I care nothing for sport, unless there is an element of danger in it.' The German replies, 'Ah! you vant danger? Vell, you go shoot mit me, dere vill be de danger. Vy, I shoot my brother in his stomich, t'oder day!' Talking of shooting reminds me of the man who had a heavy charge in his gun, and taking aim at a squirrel, fired. Over went he, and the squirrel ran twittering up the tree. 'Oh!' said he, as he picked himself up, 'if you had been at this end of the gun, you would not have run so fast.' That reminds me of two negroes, who were out shooting, and coming to a wolf's hole, one said, 'Dar's a wolf's hole.' 'I reckon dar is,' said Jem. 'I wonder wedder de ole un's in dat hole.' 'Dar ain't no wolf in dat hole, it don't look like dar was a wolf dar. I reckon dar's young uns.' 'Reckon dar may be young uns: s'pose you go in dar, Cuff, and see wedder dar is or not.' 'Go in yourself, Jem. I'll stand at de hole and watch for de wolf. If I see him coming I'll let you know.' 'All right;' and Jem crept into the hole. Soon the wolf came up with a swinging trot, and made straight for the hole. Cuff was too late, and could only seize the wolf's tail, and then it was, pull wolf and pull Cuff, the wolf's body completely filling the hole. Jem said, 'Cuff, what makes de hole so dark?' 'Is de hole dark?' 'It's all darkened up, what makes it?' 'Well, I reckon, if dis wolf's tail comes loose, you know what makes de hole so dark?' Talking of negroes reminds me of a coloured man who, when asked whether he knew the way to a certain place, said, 'I wish I had as many dollars as I know where dat place is.' This mistake of the negro reminds me of a Dutchman, who wanted a man to go out of his store, and said, 'Go out of my store. If you don't go out of my store, I'll get a policeman vot vill.' Talking of Dutchmen, reminds me of two who went into Delmonico's and got lunch. The price was higher than they expected, and one of them was very angry, and began to swear. 'Vot's de matter?' 'Matter enough; noine tollars for a lunch,—I vill swear!' 'Ah, nefer mind,' said the other, 'nefer mind. The Lord has punished dat Delmonico already, very bad.' 'How has He punished him?' 'Vy, I've got my pocket full of his spoons.' Talking of spoons reminds me of a politician,"—and so you get into politics and finish your lecture *ad lib.* I think these are suggestions for a "moddle" lecture.

To some men, the practice of requesting autographs is a nuisance and a bore. I have never had any objections to giving or sending an autograph, when a stamped and directed envelope is enclosed with the request. I regard it as very small to send for an autograph without the stamp. Yet, I have learned to be careful in the reply, especially if more words are sent than the mere signature. I was in the habit of writing, "I cheerfully comply with your request," till I received a letter thanking me for a sum of money sent, and requesting a further remittance. The letter was so very plain in the statement that I had sent a certain sum on a certain date, and stating that nothing would be said about it if I sent another sum, but that if I did not, I might hear of something unpleasant, it startled me, and I asked a friend connected with the police what he thought of it (after I had satisfied myself that the letter was intended for me, and for no one else). He said,—

"I think it is a trap. Let me see—do you ever send autographs by mail?"

"Yes, I send very often."

"Do you write more than the signature?"

I then told him that I generally wrote, "I cheerfully comply with your request."

He said: "Never do that again, unless you know the person you send to. Always insert the words 'for an autograph.'"

When I asked, "Why?" he said,—

"Don't you see, if any person wished to make a charge

against you for sending money for any purpose not very reputable, they have you at a disadvantage by the possession of your letter? They may say, 'I sent a request to him for a hundred dollars, and I take my oath that I received a hundred dollars in this envelope with these words, 'I cheerfully comply with your request;' for any person who would attempt such a game as that, would not hesitate to take a false oath."

Since then I have sent autographs in such a shape as to preclude the possibility of their being used for improper purposes.

To many, the application for autographs is considered as impertinent. Dr. Chalmers wrote the following letter to a gentleman who had requested an autograph:—

"EDINBURGH, 17*th September*, 1846.

"Sir,—I received both your letters. The first I laid aside, because of my great aversion to any direct application for my autograph, and in virtue of which it is my general practice to leave all such requests unanswered. Your second letter, of May 6th, I placed among the letters to which I might reply, because I felt a wish at the time to let you know the grounds of my antipathy to a practice which I think is not in accordance with good taste. I find, however, that I have not time for the full statement of these grounds, and shall only say, in the general, that I feel as if, on the one side, the making of such a request implies a certain degree of indelicacy, and, on the other side, that in the granting of it there must be a certain sense of awkwardness, as the very act involves at least the semblance of vanity. And yet the desire of having autographs is legitimate and natural; but the right way to go about the formation of a collection is to seek, and not from the person himself, but from any of his correspondents, such letters or fragments of his handwriting as can anywhere be found. I should imagine that, to every man who feels as he ought, a naked request for his autograph must be extremely distasteful. In sending you this autograph, it is a relief that I should have something to write about; and all the more so, that along with the autograph you have my testimony against the method in which they are sometimes sought after, both by individuals and by such public bodies as you represent. With the best wishes for the prosperity of your museum, I have the honour to be, sir,

"Yours truly, THOMAS CHALMERS."

The demand for photographs is "very like a bore." There is a pleasure in giving these to relatives and real friends. We all fancy there are a few who really care to possess our likeness for the regard they have towards us personally. But the demand for photographs is not limited to friends, or even acquaintances. One who has ever seen you, or has seen anybody that *has* seen you, or knows any one who says he has seen you, or thinks he may have seen you, considers himself entitled to make you pay twenty-five cents, more or less, for a photograph to · put in his book. He may not care a straw about you or your likeness; he has a book and means to fill it, and your picture will help accomplish the desired object. When these photographic albums were first introduced, the demand was almost intolerable. Men were asked to exchange, and a picture of some one you knew nothing about was sent, demanding yours in return. But now I am thankful to say that the novelty has worn off, and the demand is much less than heretofore.

I do not condemn the system utterly: I think it is useful, ornamental, agreeable, delightful, and all that; but it may be too much of a good thing, and it is hardly fair that you should be accounted a bear, or uncivil, because you do not send to all and everybody, known or unknown, who choose to ask your photograph. I have seen some comical arrangements of these pictures in the books. Think of Canon Farrar face to face with Maud Somebody in character, or Dean Stanley with Miss Violante in costume, or Dr. Taylor of New York face to face with Madame What's-her-name of the *opera bouffe*, or Mr. Spurgeon *vis-à-vis* with Sarah Bernhardt, Frederick Douglas face to face with Toombs, and so on! And the mere collectors of photographs will place you side by side with Tom Thumb or the Gorilla. Now, I have an idea that all men possess the right to some consideration as to where they shall be placed even in a photograph album. We all have our tastes; and, without being invidious, I must confess that I should rather not be mixed up even in an album with the ladies of the variety shows, or the singers of the *opera bouffe*.

CHAPTER XXIII.

UNENDURABLE BORES—MY EXPERIENCES WITH THEM—AFFECTION AND "STYLE."

A Class of Bores—An Aggravating Case—Its Sequel—Incident of a Lecture—Two Hingham Callers—The Brilliant Young Man in a Joking Mood—The Conundrum, "Canaan"—"Old Dog Tray"—President Woolsey and the Joking Boy—Cultivation of Affectation—Indifference—Imitating Enthusiasm—Affectation turning into a "Lithp"—Unstylish Persons in Style—Tarts "Fourpence a-Piece, Ma'am"—Late-Comers in Church and Lecture—"Who art Thou?"—An Officer of Her Majesty's Service—Making Puns—Dealing with the Superlative in Conversation—Common Mistakes—Petty Expressions—"Lor', how cunning!"—Exaggerations in Speech—Trivial Faults mar the Enjoyments of Life.

THERE is a class of bores that are almost unendurable, that are self-sufficient, confident, obtrusive, and annoying. They will call upon you and insist on an interview. Perhaps, having set yourself at a task for the day, you are interrupted by some vexatious person who will hinder you in your work, taking up your valuable time with his absurdities. Patronizing in his demeanour, he seems to feel that he is conferring a great favour by detaining you from important avocations. So exacting is he in his demands on your time, that to get rid of him you must be guilty of positive rudeness.

I remember one instance among many. I was quietly reading, one summer day, under the trees, when the servant announced that a gentleman wished to see me.

"Who is he?"

"I don't know."

"Did he give his name?"

"No, sir."

"Where is he?"

"At the front door, in a buggy."

So, hoping that he would not keep me long, I went to the front door; there sat a young gentleman in an open buggy.

"How do ye do, Gough?"

"How do you do, sir?"

"Don't know me?"

"No, sir."

"Don't know me? Look at me."

I looked at him.

"Now don't you know me?"

"No, sir; I do not recollect you."

"Why, you stopped at my father's house once, when I was a boy. Know my father?"

"No."

"Don't know my father? Well, I do. Ha, ha! that's a joke. Well, how do you do? I got a buggy in Worcester, and drove out here on purpose to see you."

"Will you walk in? I will see that your horse is hitched."

He walked with me into the parlour.

I have a framed picture near the door, entitled "The Return from the Deer-Stalking:" a woman is rowing a boat across the loch, while a gentleman in a hunting cap and dress is in the stern.

When he saw it, he said:

"Ah, a picture!" holding his half-closed hand to his eyes to get a good sight. "That's a good picture. Queen Victoria and Prince Albert, I suppose?"

I said, "Hardly! Queen Victoria would not very likely row a boat across the loch."

"Ah, I dare say; but you've been to England, and it struck me that was the Queen."

Turning to another picture called "Langdale Pikes," he said,—going through the same motions with his hand,—"Ah, a very pretty farm scene."

I said, "That is not a farm scene; that is a view of Langdale Pikes in Cumberland."

"Yes. Well, I see some cows there, and didn't know but it was an English farm scene. Been to England, you know. By the way, I want to see your library."

I took him into the room.

As he looked around, he said: "What a lot of books! Here's where you cook up your lectures, eh? read 'em all?"

And so he went round the room, talking nonsense, till he came to the two volumes of the "History of British Guiana."

"Oh, there, I knew you were a practical man! I like practical men. You're a farmer, and here's the book! I see you are practical."

I said, "What has that book to do with farming?"

"Why, don't you see, the 'History of British Guano'? That's practical—learn its history before you use it!"

And so for three mortal hours did that gentleman nearly drive me wild.

A circumstance occurred some years after, in connection with this visit, and I give it as a sequel. It is so ridiculously absurd that one can scarcely believe it to be possible, but I record the simple fact. I give no names; and if the individual should happen to read this, he would not probably recognise the picture as any representation of himself. I was stopping in the hotel of the town where I was to lecture that evening, when this gentleman called, who said he had come to town to hear my lecture. We chatted a while, and he left me. While I was speaking, I saw him in the audience. Soon I came to a point where I needed an illustration of the stolidity or stupidity of a regular bore, when the idea seized me—"Why not use this gentleman's visit at my house? Ah, it would be too barefaced." The temptation grew on me, and as I was speaking I argued the point. "I do not believe he will take, yet it will hardly do." Still I seemed to be seized with an almost irresistible desire to use the circumstance of his visit. Perhaps it was impudent, but I did it. As I looked on his face, and remembered him at my house, the risk of his taking it grew less, and I told the whole story through. He seemed to enjoy it, for he laughed when others laughed. After the lecture was over, he called on me at the hotel. Now, I thought, I shall catch it; but to my utter surprise, he said:—

"Well, Gough, I enjoyed your lecture firstrate; but the best part of the whole was about that man who called on you; for don't you remember I called at your house once, and I remember your library and pictures. It was firstrate."

It is almost past belief that any man should be so obtuse, but so it was.

Many years ago, during my residence in Roxbury, and before my wife had learned to refuse me to all and any who might call while I was resting for the evening's work, two ladies called, and wished very much to see me.

My wife said, "Mr. Gough is resting."

"We will keep him but a minute. We came from out of town, and very much wish to see him."

So I was called, and came into the room half asleep and in not very good-humour. There were two large ladies seated on the sofa, who looked at me, and then very complacently smiled on each other.

"Ladies, did you wish to see me?"

"Yes, we called on purpose to see you."

"What did you want?"

"Oh, we do not want anything. We live in Hingham, and we've heard you lecture, and we was in Roxbury, and we found out where you lived, and we don't want anything, but we thought we would like to see how you looked in the day-time, for we've never seen you except in the evening!"

"Is that all?"

"Yes, that's all we wanted."

"Good afternoon, ladies."

And I went back to my room with my rest completely broken by the curiosity that desired to see how I looked in the day-time.

A very disagreeable person, often met in society, is the young man who has an idea he is very brilliant. Woe be to the party he patronizes. He will interrupt the most interesting conversation with his inanities. He has an idea he is original, and will bore you with puns, jokes, or conundrums, worked out with laborious effort at his leisure, and brought forward at the most inopportune occasions as a fresh scintillation of his wonderful genius. Think of a dunce like this interrupting a pleasant social chat with—"Ah, here you are! I've got something for you, perfectly original. I made it last night—that is—I thought of it last night. It's a conundrum—perfectly original, I assure you. Would you like to hear my conundrum? You never heard any one like it, and never will. It's my own —perfectly original. I have not even had a suggestion. It came to me last night like an inspiration. There was no shape to it when it came, but I have rounded it out and filled it in till it has become a symmetrical conundrum, perfectly original. Would you like to hear my conundrum? You will never be able to guess it."

Not at all discouraged by the evident annoyance of the party he is boring, he goes on: "Now I'll tell you! Prepare to be astonished; it's perfectly original. What town in New York is like — is like — Pshaw! now I had it all right. What town in New York state is like — What town is like — m — m — dear me! how strange! I had it all right. Oh, ah, yes! What town in New York State is like the promised land? That's it! Do you give it up? Can't you guess? No? I knew you couldn't. Now for a surprise. You never could guess it. What town in New York State is like the promised land? Why, Canandaigua, to be sure. Don't you see it? No? That's because it's original, and an entirely new idea. Canandaigua. See! cut the word in two, and throw away the daigua, and there you have it: Canan. Only pronounce Canan, *Canaan*. Ha, ha! is not that original?" All this without a word being spoken other than by himself, he being sole talker, both in questioning and answering. Hearing no reply, he passes on, thinking they must be overwhelmed by the originality of the conundrum, and he approaches another group, to disturb, it may be, another conversation. He will appropriate any person's story, and attempt to tell it, generally failing in the point; for he has no idea of the joke, except that the listeners have laughed, and he thereby suspects there is a joke somewhere.

Once, in a party, where I was present, there were groups gathered both in the drawing-room and library. In the former, a gentleman was amusing the company with some jokes that seemed to take, as the roars of laughter testified. One thing he said was: "Poets do not always tell the truth. Many of their sentiments are false; for instance, 'Old dog Tray's ever faithful.' That is not true: it may be poetry, but it's not fact; for how can old dog Tray be faithful, if he betray?" "Ha, ha! very good," was the response; and a genial chorus of laughter filled the room. One young gentleman caught the idea in part, and knowing it had pleased one party, rushed into the library, and cried out, "Oh, I've got something for you: it's very good—capital! 'Old dog Tray's ever faithful' is not true: it's poetry, but not fact; for how can old dog Tray be faithful if his name is Tray? Ha, ha!"—laughing almost frantically himself, till he sees the sober faces of the group, when he went back to the gentleman who had told the story, and interrupted him by saying, "Oh, look here; your story doesn't take in the other room!"

Some persons neither appreciate nor repeat another's joke correctly. I was told that in New Haven a gentleman of this class was walking with President Woolsey, of Yale, when a boy fell down.

"Boy, how did you happen to fall down?" asked President Woolsey.

The boy's reply was, "Notwithstanding."

"Very good," said the President; "don't you think so?"

"I didn't see anything in it."

"But did you not hear what the boy said?"

"Yes, but I did not see any point."

"But I did, and thought it was very good."

They separated, and the obtuse gentleman said soon after to a friend, "A little thing occurred on the street just now that seemed to please President Woolsey, but I didn't see anything in it. A boy fell down, and the President asked him how he happened to fall down, and the boy said 'Nevertheless,' and I didn't see the point."

Some one has said that affectation is a "deformity acquired;" and many young people cultivate affectation till it grows into a habit; and some begin with being ridiculous, and often end in being immoral and vicious. Hamlet says to the queen, "Assume a virtue if you have it not." But there are men who will assume an absurdity, and even a vice. You can comprehend how a man may pretend to be witty, frank, honest, amiable, generous, or even pious, but not so easy to understand why one should pretend to weaknesses, defects, or demerits. What an extremely insufferable affectation is that of indifference or insensibility—interested in nothing. Ask such an one if he saw the Alps when abroad.

"Ah, I believe I did see some mountains somewhere with snow and ice, and that sort of thing, with glaciers, I think they call them."

The opposite extreme is an affectation of enthusiasm, going into raptures on the slightest occasion. Laman Blanchard tells of a lady throwing up her eyes and clasping her hands, as she exclaimed, "Oh, I have such a passion for roast veal!" They will *adore* a bonnet, or give all the world for a new fashion.

Some indulge in the affectation of defective utterance till it grows into a confirmed habit, "introduthing a lithp, ath if there wath a muthical charm in a lithp;" or a drawl to make the most of the few words at their command.

Others cultivate the disagreeable and absurd affectation of introducing a giggle after every sentence, and often in the midst of one.

There is an affectation of style that is very ridiculous. How some people will force themselves into a circle and style of living for which they are not fitted! They must get into a fashionable house in a fashionable quarter, take a pew in a fashionable church, a box at the opera (for that is style), engage a staff of servants to swindle and laugh at them, give dinners for the purpose of informing their guests the cost of every dish, and to display their plate and vulgarity to a class of people who eat their dinners, and serve them up in a spicy dish of ridicule at the next party. They pretend ignorance of all domestic details, for that is fashionable; their sons go to ruin; their daughters make fools of themselves. We may say of them,

> "Oh! wad some power the giftie gie us
> To see oursels as others see us."

But "Where ignorance is bliss, 'tis folly to be wise," you know.

I once heard of a lady of this class, who, having a sudden call of hungry visitors, not being prepared for them, sent to the confectioner's for some tarts to help out the dinner,—the propriety of which we do not question. All would have gone off well, but the lady, wishing to show off by exhibiting ignorance of the contents of the said pies, said to the servant,

"Ah, John, what are those tarts?"

"Fourpence a-piece, ma'am."

Some of this class grow supercilious and important. Notice their coming into church, or concert, or lecture-room. They seem to think they are the observed of all observers. They will make a point of coming late; and with what an air they will strut to their seat, imagining they produce a sensation, reminding you of the officer in full regimental uniform, who strutted up the aisle of the church just as the minister uttered the words, "Who art thou?"

"I am an officer in Her Majesty's service, attached to the Light Dragoons, and am here on recruiting service, thank you;" and sat down, amid the titter of the congregation.

Some men acquire the disagreeable habit of making puns on all occasions, and will sit gaping for an opportunity to jingle their nonsense with whatever happens to be going on. Such a one will catch at some detached bit of rational conversation, and pervert its sense, continually interrupting what might be intellectual intercourse by absurd distortions, ill-timed and ill-placed. He will store in his memory words that are alike in sound, but differing in signification. He probably once made some hit that took, and gained him some applause, which encouraged him to try again, until he has acquired the habit, and become a punster,—a regular hard-going thick-and-thin punster—a character that Theodore Hook once described as "the dullest and stupidest companion alive, if he could only be made to think so." Remember, I refer to the inveterate punster. If one speaks of an electrical machine, "Ah, that is a shocking affair;" of worshipping idols, "That is an idle custom." If he sees a man grinding an organ, "That is music by Handel." A man stands up to urge his horse, that is "rising to propose a motion." Another leading a pig, that's "pig lead." A man firing a gun with his eyes shut, that is "shutting his eyes to the consequences. Hot-house fruit is "forced to be agreeable." You cannot buy a pair of boots when they are "half-soled;" and so on, *ad infinitum*.

There may be wit in a pun, of course, and they are not to be condemned indiscriminately. Some of Foote's, Quin's, Sheridan's, Hook's, Jerrold's, and a few others, are full of it.

Goldsmith once said that "even wit was in some measure mechanical; and that a man long habituated to catch at its resemblance, may at last possess the substance."

The power of language is often destroyed, its force weakened and its beauty marred, by the habit of using unnecessary words. There is a simplicity and power in "I went alone;" but "I went away all alone by myself" is weakness. "I saw it" is decisive and striking; but "I saw it myself with my own eyes" adds words which weaken the force.

"I must go" is far preferable to "I've *got* to go;"—and, by the way, how absurdly we use that little word *got*. "I've got to go to the store." "I've got to go and get my lessons." "I've got to go and get this bill settled;" and so on. Cases might be multiplied, for the habit is almost universal. Think of this for a sentence: "I went there my own self, and saw him as plain as anything with my own eyes. He said, 'I've got to go and get the doctor.' I heard him say that with my own ears, but being that I did not care about his seeing of me, I went away all alone by myself, and thinks I that *beats all* I ever saw before in the whole course of my life. Well, then I came right straight home and I never said a single word to nobody. I was pretty considerable kind of tired out, and you'd better believe I was about used up."

Then the absurdity in dealing with the superlative in conversation, making such use of high-flown exclamations on the most trifling occasions; never using the positive or comparative, always using the superlative. A mouse running across the room will call forth as strong an ejaculation as the thunderstorm. A landscape is "perfectly splendid;" a sunset "perfectly splendid;" a frosted cake, "perfectly splendid;" a sleigh-ride, "perfectly splendid;" Niagara, "perfectly splendid;" a wedding, "perfectly splendid;" a young man, "perfectly splendid."

The opposite absurdity is in the use of petty expressions entirely inappropriate. A landscape is *nice;* a sunset *pretty;* a frosted cake is charming; a sleigh-ride is lovely; Niagara is elegant; a wedding, sweet; a young man is beautiful; etc.

I once showed a fine engraving of Raphael's Holy Family to an affected young lady who had been using these petty expressions in reference to almost every surrounding, expecting to hear some appropriate exclamation, when I was struck dumb by hearing this remark, "Lor', how cunning!"

Then the exaggeration in speech which is so common among a certain class, such as, "he ran like lightning;" sometimes it will be, "he went quicker than lightning;" "my feet are colder than ice;" "he is as strong as a horse;" "Oh, I shall die;" "I laughed fit to kill myself." I once heard a person say several times in a few minutes, "I never laughed so much in all my life." A friend once said to me in reference to a call I was proposing, "If you only go to see him he will be tickled to death."

These things seem too trivial to mention, and yet much of the enjoyment of life is marred by these extravagances and puerilities of speech.

CHAPTER XXIV.

THE SPEAKER AND HIS AUDIENCE—ANECDOTES AND INCIDENTS.

Dread of an Audience—Personal Physical Suffering—Mutual Sympathy required—Incident in the Church of Dr. Joseph Parker—Efforts at Reading a Hymn—Experience with President Finney at Aberdeen—The Minister's "Supplication"—Involuntary Selection of Persons in every Audience—My Stolid Hearer—Method of Preparing Lectures—Five Thousand Temperance Addresses in Seventeen Years—Interview with the Actor Macready—His Method—My Early Experience with Books—"Rollin's Ancient History," and "Putnam's Library"—Incident at Rhinebeck—Illustration from Niagara Falls—Taking down the Scaffolding from my Temple—"Gough is a Story-teller"—The Wonderful Story—"Gough a Retailer of Anecdotes"—Value of Incidents.

"SOME feel it a cross to speak, and others feel it a cross not to speak; I would advise both to take up their cross," was the remark of a shrewd writer.

Whether this be sound advice or not, I have for thirty-seven years been a cross-bearer as a public speaker; but have never known the time when I did not dread an audience. Often that fear has amounted to positive suffering, and seldom am I called on to face an audience when I would not rather by far run the other way, and as I grow older this suffering is increasing. A very large assembly depresses me at first sight. I have often begged the chairman to make an address, and give me time to recover.

There are occasions when without the relief of the chairman's remarks, I should commence my speech falteringly and with tears. In my suffering, trembling seizes upon every nerve; my throat and tongue become dry and feverish; my voice hoarse or husky, until the first few minutes have passed. At one time the painful sensations may be much stronger than at another, but the occasions are very rare when I am in any good degree unembarrassed, and never am I at perfect ease in sight of an audience.

There are some persons who consider this affectation. I have been told that it was impossible that any man who had faced over eight thousand audiences should be nervous, or apprehensive, or troubled at the sight of the people. From the first speech I ever made, when my heart beat like a trip-hammer, and after uttering the half-dozen sentences I sat down shaking in every limb, to the last in Philadelphia on the 15th of April, I have more or less suffered from this unaccountable dread at every public address.

I think in my whole experience I never volunteered a speech, and never asked for an invitation to address an audience. After the first nervousness has passed, I have but little sensation, except the desire to make my audience feel as I feel, see as I see, and to gain dominion for the time being over their wills and affections. If I succeed in this, or think that I have their sympathy, and especially should they be responsive, the fear is all gone; then comes a consciousness of power that exhilarates, excites, and produces a strange, thrilling sensation of delight.*

When placed in circumstances new and strange, I have been asked suddenly to perform some public service, through a nervous timidity I have been utterly unable to comply with the request. During my recent visit in London, I frequently heard Dr. Joseph Parker. On one occasion at the close of one of his powerful sermons, to which I had listened with intense interest, I was startled to hear him say:

" I see my friend John B. Gough in the audience. Will he please come into the pulpit while they are singing the anthem, and conclude Divine service with prayer?"

* I should not have introduced this topic into my book, but one or two dear friends, for whose judgment I have a high regard, have earnestly requested me to do so.

I turned to my wife and said,—

"Mary, what *shall* I do? I can't go up there to take part in the service."

She said very quietly, "You had better go into the pulpit and explain to Dr. Parker."

So, with head bent, I passed down the aisle, crept up the stairs, and entered the desk, where Dr. Parker sat waiting for me. His pulpit, a very beautiful one, presented to him by the corporation of London, is large, and rather high. As I half stooped I could hardly be seen by the congregation.

There is a small platform on which the Doctor stands.

I said, " I cannot pray here."

"Oh yes, you can."

"But I cannot *here*. If I were alone I could, but here, after that sermon, I cannot lead the devotion and worship of this people. Indeed—indeed, I cannot. Please excuse me."

He very kindly excused me, and asked me to give out a hymn. I told him I would try to do that. He told me to give out the twenty-seventh hymn, and only read the first verse. I had just commenced when he bade me stand on the platform, as not much more than my head could be seen by the audience below. That added to my embarrassment.

I stood on the platform, and said, in a very husky voice, "The twenty-eighth hymn."

He corrected me: "The twenty-seventh hymn."

More and more nervous, I said, " The twenty-seventh hymn," and blundered through the four lines, but how I know not.

Now this was real suffering, and I suppose I ought to have been in the spirit of prayer, for we are told to "continue instant in prayer." But to me it has ever been a task and a cross to lead the devotions of others; for I consider it the most solemn exercise in which a man can engage. I cannot help it, and I cannot overcome it.

When the Rev. Mr. Finney was in Aberdeen, Scotland, I heard from him a wonderful sermon. The next morning he with his wife called on us at the hotel.

In the course of our conversation I said, "Mr. Finney, I fear I am in the seventh chapter of Romans."

"What?"

"I fear I am in the seventh chapter of Romans."

He instantly said, "Let us kneel down."

When we were on our knees, he said, "Pray."

I told him I could not.

"Pray," he repeated.

"I cannot."

"Pray," again he bade me.

"I cannot pray, and I will not."

Then he said, "O Lord, have mercy on this wiry, little unbeliever," and offered a prayer himself.

Some have the gift of praying in public, and are able to do it without embarrassment. I think if I were a minister, that leading the devotions of my people would be much more difficult than preaching the sermons. At one of our meetings in London a minister was asked to open with prayer, and he prayed for almost everything—for the Zulus, for the Afghans, for the government, for the country, other countries, for the audience, for the speaker, for those that were instrumental in obtaining the chapel for the lecture,—and at the conclusion of the long petition of nearly fifteen minutes he turned to the secretary of the meeting and asked him if he was satisfied with his supplication. Such a person must have a very strange idea of prayer.

Many questions are put to me in reference to my experience of public work. "Do you see your audience as individuals in detail, or in the aggregate?" When I rise, there is an involuntary selection of the persons to whom I shall speak; my will has nothing to do with it. Glancing over the assembly, my eye rests on certain individuals in different parts of the house, and to them my speech is largely addressed. I seem compelled to speak to them, and to no others. The rest of the people are in the aggregate; these are the individuals. If I move these, I move the rest; if these are sympathetic, I feel it; if they are unmoved, I am distressed. I have more than once talked for some minutes exclusively to one person who seemed stolid or indifferent, trying all methods to move him.

One occasion especially has its vivid recollections. A very stolid man sat before me, one of those I had selected; but he was so very obtuse, apparently, that I soon concentrated all my energies on him. The conviction impressed me, "I must move that man to an interest in me and my theme, and until I can move him I shall accomplish nothing." I well remember the sensation of relief I experienced when, at a funny story, I saw a slight twitch of the mouth, and an almost imperceptible twinkle of his eye, as he passed his hand with a rapid motion over his face. My thought was, "Now I have you." Sure enough, at the next story, which came very quickly, he laughed; I felt a positive friendship for him, an interest in him, and would have been pleased to shake his hand. During the rest of the speech, after that laugh, he appeared to be the most interested auditor I had. All this I cannot explain, but so it is. I have no control over the selection of these individuals, and when once chosen I have no power to change them.

How do you prepare your lectures? This is rather a difficult question to answer without going into some analysis of myself, and stating some facts in reference to the position I occupy.

For the first seventeen years of my public work I spoke entirely on temperance, delivering more than five thousand addresses on that theme; eleven hundred and sixty of these in Great Britain and Ireland. I never wrote one of them, or composed one in my thoughts; I never, except on perhaps six occasions, have taken with me a slip of paper to the platform, and then only some figures I needed, or one or two passages of Scripture I thought I might want; for, though I composed no speech, I sometimes had an idea of the course I should take. Usually I have known no more what I should say, except in the general idea, than the audience I was to address.

Some years ago, after a lecture I had delivered in Sherborne, England, Mr. Macready, the celebrated actor, who spent the last years of his life near that town, came on the platform and invited me to breakfast with him the next morning. I regretted being unable to accept his invitation, being compelled to leave in the early morning.

He then asked, " Do you commit these speeches to memory, and recite them ? "

I said, " No, sir."

"Then you have them arranged in your mind, so that, although you may not strictly memorize, you know what you shall say, having studied them ? "

"No, sir. I knew this evening, when I came to the platform, no more what I should say than you did. I knew I was to speak on temperance, and I knew I must draw on the stores of material I have been gathering in my memory for years; but how I should arrange thoughts, or facts, or incidents, I could not tell when I began. If you remember, I began by stating a simple fact, that drunkenness is an evil, and our duty is to remove the evil ; then from that I went on."

"But," said he, " do you not deliver the same lecture at different times ? "

" I use the same material, but not the same arrangement."

He said, " Excuse me ; but I felt desirous to ask you these questions, and trust I have not been impertinent."

I assured him I was glad to meet him, having been present in New York when the rowdy element assailed and mobbed him. He further told me that if he was requested to make a speech at a dinner, or on any public occasion, or in reply to a toast, he must gather his material, write the speech, and commit it to memory. He never could produce an entirely extemporaneous speech. I was very much interested in his statement.

Twenty-five years ago I bought an index-book for jotting down thoughts that might occur to me, or selections from authors. That book to-day has not a score of selections or thoughts, and the pages are, for the most part, as clean as when I purchased it at the book-store. My early life, as is well known, was one of privation. I longed for an education, but was blocked at every turn. It was not so easy then as now for a young man to obtain a liberal education. Till I was twenty-five years of age I had positively read no book of history or science, except those I might have read when a mere boy at home. My life was work without holiday. I read novels in what leisure I had. From my twelfth birthday I was without a home and its restraints. My mind had never been subjected to discipline or training, but was, like an untamed colt, very active, but with no direction. Desultory reading of novels and frequent attendance at theatres, with an irregular Sabbath service, was all the intellectual food I obtained, and at twenty-five years of age I was fearfully ignorant, as the world terms ignorance. My library in which I am now sitting is the history of the development of a desire for better things when I threw off the fetters of habit, and was inspired with an intense desire for a better life, and to redeem in some degree the useless past.

I well remember, and I sometimes think of it with tears, bringing to my lodgings "Rollin's Ancient History," in six volumes. I wanted something to read. I had no one to advise me to a course of reading, so I pitched on Rollin. Next I obtained a number of Wiley and Putnam's "Library of Choice Reading," and there I found essay, and biography, and history; but for the lack of a system, my reading was desultory. My time was soon fully occupied in speaking, day and night, in school-houses, vestries, and halls, so that the opportunities for intellectual culture were limited. Still, I read a great deal to small profit, owing to the lack of advantages, such as I might have obtained, by the training which an education would have imparted.

My earlier addresses were without any preparation, and no material but my experience. The first speech after my signing the pledge I have given in my autobiography, with a brief account of my entering into public life as a speaker. But what has this to do with the question, "How do you prepare your speeches?" If you mean my temperance speeches, they are not prepared at all. For seventeen years I was constantly on the look-out, in travelling, conversation, reading, strolling the streets, in society, for illustrations, incidents, or facts, that I could use for temperance lectures; not exactly storing them in my mind, but letting them float on the surface, ready at the moment when required.

I knew nothing of grammar or rhetoric. Logic was a term to me that I could not define. I had occasionally an idea, when I went before an audience, that I should relate some story, or use some illustration, but when, where, or how, I could not tell. When I had a fixed purpose to relate some particular incident, it became a burden and hindrance to me till I got rid of it. I have been requested to repeat some story, or anecdote, and have promised to do so, when the remembrance that I had a certain thing to do would perplex me so much, and so check the flow of thought, that I have more than once stopped in my speech, and said, " Ladies and gentlemen, I have been requested to give you such or such an anecdote, and I must give it now, or I shall be compelled to give up, for I can make no progress till I get this out of the way." Then after relating the anecdote, or incident, I have gone on with my lecture.

A little incident will serve to show how I would appropriate what I saw or heard for my purpose. At Rhinebeck, many years ago, I was entertained by Mr. Freeborn Garretson, who then resided on a beautiful estate near the Hudson River.

We were walking through the grounds one morning, when he said to me : " I am sorry you do not see us in the summer time : we look very barren and desolate ; the trees are so utterly without foliage, they might be dead trees for all the evidence they give of life. It is winter time with us now ; but come to us in the summer, and under the shade of these grand trees you may enjoy a cool and exquisite refreshment."

I went in the evening to the lecture, and as I was passing into the church, a gentleman said to me: " I am glad you are come to help us, for the temperance cause is dead in Rhinebeck."

During my speech, I said, " A gentleman said to me on the threshold of this house this evening, ' The temperance cause is dead in Rhinebeck.' No, it is not dead; it was born in the church of Christ, and can never die."

Then Mr. Garretson's remarks in the morning flashed into my mind, and I said, "If I should say to you as I passed through the streets of your village, 'Cut down these dead trees,' you would say, 'They are not dead.' If I tell you there is no evidence of life, there is no bud, no blossom, no leaf, and ask you to cut them down, and plant living trees, you might tell me: 'It is winter time with us now. There is neither bud, blossom, nor leaf, but the sap is in these trees; and by and by the warm spring rain will water the roots, the sun will shine on the branches, and they will bud, blossom, and leaf out, and as

"The tree-tops stir not,
But stand and peer on Heaven's bright face, as though
It slept, and they were loving it."

You may stand under their deep shade, and enjoy the cool refreshment thereof.' So with our temperance tree. There may be but few, if any, signs of life. It may be the winter time with us; but the sap is in the tree, and by and by the refreshing rain of public sentiment will water the roots, and the warm sun of woman's influence will shine upon the branches, and it will bud, and blossom, and leaf out; and the branches, hanging heavy with foliage, shall touch the earth, and spring up again, like the banyan-tree, and cover the land, and under its shade every poor victim of this vice shall find a refuge."

Now, when I commenced my speech I had no idea I should use Mr. Garretson's remarks, and the line of poetry I had read a few days before in Festus.

Perhaps some person may say, "Did I not tell you that Gough was a plagiarist? Here is an illustration of it. He used Mr. Garretson's remarks without giving him credit for them. Why did he not quote the words as Mr. Garretson's?" A question easily answered. Mr. Garretson was present at my lecture, and it would have been impertinent in me to allude to him publicly without his permission. I shall in another place say a few words about the charge of plagiarism.

I never wrote or studied an illustration. Upon my first sight of Niagara, and while standing by the rapids, I had no thought that I could use them; but that same evening, in Buffalo, I introduced the simile of the rapids, which has become so familiar to my hearers, for when once uttered, I use them again and again, altering the phraseology, but keeping the main features intact. These illustrations are all worked out on the platform.

Remember, I am speaking of the purely extemporaneous lectures on temperance. This remark does not apply to the written lectures of the past twenty years. Occasionally, some thought has flashed into my mind in the midst of a speech, the germ of an illustration, and I have commenced with no idea how or by what means I could bring it to a successful climax— an awful risk before an audience.

In the Broadway tabernacle, one evening, I suffered such an exhaustion at the close of one of these attempts, that, though nearly thirty years have passed, I remember it as distinctly as if it were yesterday. I commenced to build a temple, and, with no preparation or material, laid the foundation-stone, by workers, under the surface, out of sight, toiling in the deep, damp trench. When I had brought it to the surface, then came the struggle, appropriation and rejection, a double, or I might say, a threefold operation in my mind. The temple must be finished somehow; and as the materials came to me, I must instantly reject or select; and with pillars, capitals, architrave (oh, how I needed some knowledge of architecture!) I became wonderfully excited. I lost sight of my audience. All apprehension vanished; I could feel my nostrils quiver. I clenched my hands so tight that I bore the marks of my nails for days. The scaffolding was introduced something as follows: "We do not see the glory of the temple yet, for the scaffolding is all round it; ropes, and poles, and ladders hiding or marring its beauty." How to get the ropes and poles and ladders down, I did not know. Swift as lightning, the thought flashed across me: "John, you will fail! That scaffolding, what shall I do with it!" Then came another thought: "Let a trumpet's blast be heard, and the scaffold will fall." Then it came: "A trumpet's blast is heard ringing through the clear atmosphere; the scaffold falls with a crash; and the glorious superstructure is revealed in all its wondrous beauty before an astonished world; and the last drunkard shall go into it, leaving his broken, burning chains behind him." It was fortunate this was the close of my speech, for I was terribly excited, and somewhat exhausted. The illustration may have been very crude, and not at all symmetrical in the eye of a critic, but it was given as I have stated; and it will not be egotism to say that the audience received my efforts on that occasion very generously.

It has been said, "Gough is a mere story-teller." That may be true in a certain sense, so far as my temperance speeches are concerned. I have no wish to defend myself from any such silly charge as that. When I first began, I only told a story. I had no literature, no scientific knowledge, no beautiful thoughts clothed in beautiful language. I had a story to tell, and I told it. It was a story of privation, of suffering; a story of struggle, and final victory; a story of gloom and brightness; a story of life: a story of hope and despair; a story of God's mercy; a story every word of which I felt in the deepest depths of my own soul. Yes, I am a story-teller!

I have related the stories of other experiences than my own. I have tried to tell the story of the cross; and I thank God to-day with my whole heart that there are so many who have been moved at my story to make the remaining chapters of the story of their own lives better, nobler, higher. I am content to be a story-teller, if I may win a soul from vice to virtue; warn the unwary, encourage the desponding, or strengthen the weak. And I have the cheering evidence, by letters and personal interviews, that my story has been harmful to none, and helpful to many.

Yes, but "Gough is only a retailer of anecdotes—that's what we mean." I have a keen sense of the ridiculous; and when I find a good story, I appropriate it, and use it. Some of these I make, by putting some funny thought into a narrative, or dialogue; some I find in the newspapers; some are related to me by others; and some occur in my own experience. I use them all. They are public property; and I have known persons sit before me, jotting down every story I tell; for what purpose? I do not inquire, and do not care. I think the public will not charge me with introducing a funny story except to illustrate a point; and, besides, I think a good story, *well told*, will relieve an audience wonderfully. I have evidence, by the laughter, that my stories do please; and I expect to continue the practice of "retailing" a few stories, either original or borrowed, with but little regard to the adverse opinion of critics.

CHAPTER XXV.

WHAT OPPOSITION WE MEET—FALSE CHARGES AND MISREPRESENTATIONS.

"Gough not a Thinker"—Unexplainable Knowledge—Plagiarism and its Meaning—Satire on Plagiarism of "The Little Busy Bee"—Gough's Apostrophe to Water, and that by Paul Denton—History of its Inception—Reply to a Shameless Attack—Increased Consumption of Beer—Our Pullman Cars and Liquor-drinking—Increase of Intemperance in Thirty Years—Worcester as an Example—1843 and 1880—Washingtonianism—Drinking among Ministers—Drinking among Women—Murder as excited by Beer—Hereditary Effects of Beer-drinking—Paper circulated by Life Insurance Men—Reported Interview with the Oxford Students—The True Story, and the Scene—The Happy Conclusion.

IT has been said, "Gough is not a thinker." He never professed to be very profound, and indeed how many profound thinkers are there in the world? You can count them on your fingers nearly. Yet I *think* occasionally. I do not always jump to conclusions, or arrive at them by intuition. I think a little, but I do not pretend to be a teacher, or instructor of the people. It is not my fault, and I hardly suppose it is a great misfortune, that I am not a profound thinker, for there must of necessity be some commonplace people in the world, and I have no objection to rank with them.

The man in the Gospel knew not who the Healer was, but he could say, "One thing I know: whereas I was once blind, now I see." It requires no great amount of thinking to realize that, and to endeavour to lead the blind to the same great Healer, that they too may know they see. I do not depreciate thought or profound thinking, though it may be so profound that with my short line I cannot plumb its depths. I only think it absurd to bring as a reproach on a man, that which he cannot help, and which perhaps he would remedy if he could.

But "Gough is a plagiarist!" (noun), one who purloins the writings of another, and puts them off as his own, a plagiary. "Plagiary (a noun), a thief in literature, one who purloins another's writings and offers them to the public as his own." We might as well have a correct definition. Coleridge says a plagiarist is the most sensitive to plagiarism. The cry of plagiarism is often very absurd. I have read somewhere a capital satire on those who are always uttering that cry. The *Athenæum* had accused Alexander Smith of plagiarism, and the satirist defends him by enumerating several specimens of the crime overlooked by his accuser. He says: "Certainly Smith is guilty of plagiarism, for there is scarcely a word he has used but is purloined from other authors; but there are instances strangely overlooked by the *Athenæum*. Mr. Smith speaks of the 'busy bee.' He must have stolen that from Dr. Watts, for whoever revealed the fact that the bee was busy till Dr. Watts wrote his immortal lines? But there is a glaring instance that could hardly have escaped the notice of the reviewer. Smith's line reads,

"'A sigh and a curse together,'

evidently plagiarized from Walter Scott, whose line reads,

"'He draws his last sob by the side of his dam.'"

I have but few words to say in reference to this charge. In a very abusive and unjust article in the *Rutland Herald and Globe* the writer very coarsely accuses me of reckless falsehood, palpable exaggeration, calls me a mountebank, a demagogue, and professional sensationalist; says that I have fastened myself to the skirts of a great cause, I am guilty of amazing untruthfulness; intimates that I am a man of base and depraved habits, and states that no intelligent or candid man ever listened to Gough without a feeling of disgust; and much more of such rubbish. While he accuses me of gross plagiarism, he can only fasten on one instance, and that is what is called "An Apostrophe to Water," which he says was originally written by a man named Arrington, now dead. This elegant writer and critic (?) may have it all his own way, and I mention the charge of plagiarism that I may do what I have always intended to do since I was first accused of appropriating what was termed "Paul Denton's Apostrophe to Water." When any person feels particularly spiteful and venomous towards me, he reiterates this charge of appropriating another man's thoughts.

In the early days of my temperance work we had at our meetings often sections of the Cold Water Army of children, who sang for us, and one of the favourite songs was:

"Sparkling and bright in its liquid light
Is the water in our glasses."

Another was:

"Give water to me, bright water to me," etc.

Long before I ever heard of Paul Denton I spoke at my meetings of the beauty of water, and holding the glass in my hand, would say: "Is not this beautiful? Talk of ruby wine. Here is our beautiful beverage,—water, pure water; we drink it to quench our thirst. There is no necessity to drink, except to quench one's thirst; and here is the beverage our Father has provided for His children. When Moses smote the rock the people were thirsty, and it was water that came gushing forth —not wine, or rum, or ale. Were you ever thirsty, with lips dry and feverish, and throat parched? Did you never lift the goblet of pure water to your lips and feel it trickling over the tongue and gurgling down the throat. Was it not luxury? Give to the traveller on the burning desert, as he lies perishing with thirst, a goblet of cold water; and he will return the goblet heaping with gold; give him wine, ale, or rum, and he turns away in feverish disgust to die. Our beverage is beautiful and pure, for God brewed it,—not in the distillery, but out of the earth, and wherever it is, it is always beautiful." Then

I described it in the white mantle over the wintry world, as rolling up the valley in the cloud-mist, settling on the mountain top, in the waterfall and in the streamlet, in the rainbow, in the hail and rain, beautiful always and blessed; no curse to it, no heart-broken mother or pale-faced wife, no starving child, nor dying drunkard ever cursed it. It is always beautiful:

> "'Give water to me, bright water to me,
> It cooleth the brow, it cooleth the brain,
> It maketh the weak man strong again.'

"Tell me, young men and maidens, old men and matrons, will you not dash from your lips the drink that maddens and destroys, and take as your beverage the beautiful gift our Father in Heaven has provided for His own children?"

I had for years occasionally used this apostrophe, or bits of it, before I heard what purported to be Paul Denton's. I first saw that in Glasgow, in 1854, and noticed some similarity in its construction to mine. He used more beautiful language than I did, for he speaks of the "Iris," of the "Seraph zone of the sky," or the wonderful power of refraction, etc. I adopted a few of his illustrations of the beauty of the water, and incorporated them with mine, always saying when I came to quotations from him, "As Paul Denton has said." I was the first to draw attention to the fact of the similarity of his "Apostrophe" to water and mine. I quoted him until I changed the whole structure of the passage, for I was continually changing it in detail, and as I left out his sentences I left off his name. I have not used this apostrophe for several years except on one or two occasions, and have forgotten, and could not repeat it to-day. If this is plagiarism, then I am guilty and confess, but will not say, "I won't do so any more."

I have received several communications in reference to an item that has been the rounds of the papers: "John B. Gough says that drunkenness in this country has increased in the past twenty-five or thirty years. There are more ministers drinking, more women drinking, than ever before. Twenty-five years ago you never saw a woman drinking in the cars, but now you see it every day, and that, too, out of flasks. The cars in these days are made regular grog-shops." This is the heading of the article in the *Rutland Herald*, containing the most shameless attack that I have had for thirty years. In this quotation from the reports there are some things I did say in several places, and some things I did not say anywhere.

I was speaking of the temperance reform in England, and said the curse of Great Britain is beer, and in this country there is an alarming increase in the consumption of beer; that beer was not a substitute for spirits, but an addition; that beer was a feeder to intemperance; and that I *believed* there was more intemperance now than there was twenty-five or thirty years ago; that we saw more of it on the cars and at hotel-tables; that I *feared* the use of ale and lager-beer was on the increase among ministers and women; that twenty-five or thirty years ago you would see but little drinking in the cars, and very rarely, if ever, among the women, but now it was a common sight. I stated that the porters would furnish ale, and, I *believed*, anything you required, in drawing-room coaches; for I had known brandy to be furnished to passengers by porters. Some one has said, "Our Pullman cars are getting to be travelling grog-shops;" and I *fear*, if the use of ale is increased, we shall see what is occasionally seen in England,—ladies drinking out of flasks in public conveyances. For every one of these statements I am ready to give a reason.

We note the increase of intemperance in the past thirty years. Take Worcester as an example. In 1843 she had a population of 20,000, and a meeting was called to see what could be done to suppress the traffic known to be carried on in twelve or fourteen places. Now, in 1880, the population is 58,040. There were over 200 licences granted two years ago, and between 100 and 200 are granted now. Then only one hotel sold liquor; the United States, and that was constantly prosecuted. Now every hotel, I believe, but one sells liquors.

The Worcester Temperance Society held meetings every

Monday night in the Town Hall; now there are no weekly meetings in the City Hall, and the Temperance Society is defunct.

In Boston there were four or five temperance houses; now I know not of one. There were no licences granted in Massachusetts except in one county; now there are some licenses in every county. We had Cold Water Armies in every town; now there are but few, if any. In 1843 Washingtonianism was a wonderful power, and it is my belief there was a stronger sentiment against the drink then than now.

We know there is an amazing increase in the consumption of ale and beer, and very little, if any, diminution in the consumption of spirits.

For the expressed fear that there is more drinking among ministers, I would state that I could name those whom we once considered our staunch friends who now are using ale, some even defending it; others who were with us are gone out from us; and I am told by some ministers who have long been considered total-abstainers that they have been in the habit of taking beer by the advice of their medical men, etc.

In reference to the drinking of women, Dr. Hargraves, the temperance statistician, said, in a speech in Philadelphia in 1876: "Intemperance is on the increase among women. I contend there is as much intemperance now as in 1867. It may not be seen among the men, but I know it is seen among the women. I see them repeatedly drunk along our streets. I see the cans and pitchers running from morning till night; and you will find it in every part of this great State."

About the drinking in the cars. It is well known that until the drawing-room coaches were introduced, there was no sale of liquors on the cars. Now travel from Boston to Buffalo and you may obtain what you wish. Only the other day I saw a party furnished with six bottles of wine; and a little while since I saw a lady, on the journey between Boston and New York, drink four glasses of ale. At another time a gentleman drank three bottles, and was so *sleepy* when we arrived in New York that it required a sharp push to wake him. These are the reasons for saying what I did; and I maintain I had a right to say it without calling down on me such low abuse and vituperation.

A gentleman of large experience and observation, who has travelled in the United States twenty thousand miles each year for the past six years, to whom I read the above statement, tells me that he knows there is a large increase in the consumption of liquor on the cars, and he has several times remonstrated with the conductor and porter for furnishing drink to persons who made themselves quite offensive by its use. He asserts that he has seen ladies drink from bottles they have carried with them, etc.

I have in another place spoken of the increase of the use of beer, and its deleterious effects. Let me here introduce the contents of a paper that is being circulated among life-insurance agents by one of the prominent companies of New York:—

"The fashion of the present day in the United States sets strongly towards the substitution of beer for other stimulating liquors. An idea appears to be gaining ground that it is not only nutritious, but conducive to health; and further, that there does not attach to it that danger of creating intemperate habits which attends the use of other drinks. The subject is one of great magnitude, and deserves the attention of medical men as well as that of the moralist.

"Many years ago, and long before the moral sense of society was awakened to the enormous evils of intemperance, Sir Astley Cooper, an undisputed authority in his day, denounced habitual beer-drinking as noxious to health. Referring to his experience in Guy's Hospital, he declared that the beer-drinkers from the London breweries, though presenting the appearance of most rugged health, were the most incapable of all classes to resist disease; that trifling injuries among them were liable to lead to the most serious consequences, and that so prone were they to succumb to disease, that they would sometimes die from gangrene in wounds as trifling as the scratch of a pin.

"We apprehend that no great change, either in beer or men, has taken place since the days of the great surgeon.

"It may also be said of beer-drinking that there is less limitation to it than to the habitual use of other drinks. It does not produce speedy intoxication. When the drinker becomes accustomed to it, it will scarcely produce active intoxication in any quantity. It makes him heavy, sleepy, and stupid. Even in moderate quantities, its tendency is to dulness and sluggishness of body and mind. Beer-drinkers are constant drinkers;

their capacity becomes unlimited. The swilling of the drink becomes a regular business; it has no arrest or suspension, like whiskey-drinking, to admit of recuperation. The old definition of a regular beer-drinker was true: 'Every morning a beer-barrel, every night a barrel of beer.'"

Of all intoxicating drinks it is the most animalizing. It dulls the intellectual and moral, and feeds the sensual and beastly nature. Beyond all other drinks it qualifies for deliberate and unprovoked crime. In this respect it is much worse than distilled liquors.

"A whiskey-drinker will commit murder, only under the direct excitement of liquor; a beer-drinker is capable of doing it in cold blood. Long observation has assured us that a large proportion of murders deliberately planned and executed without passion or malice, with no other motive than the acquisition of property or money—often of trifling value—are perpetrated by beer-drinkers.

"We believe further, that the hereditary evils of beer-drinking exceed those proceeding from ardent spirits. First, because the habit is constant and without paroxysmal interruptions, which admit of some recuperation; secondly, because beer-drinking is practised by both sexes more generally than the spirit-drinking; and, thirdly, because the animalizing tendency of the habit is more uniformly developed, thus authorizing the presumption that the vicious results are more generally transmitted.

"It will be inferred from these remarks that we take no comfort from the substitution of malt drinks for spirituous liquors. On the contrary, it is cause of apprehension and alarm, that just as public opinion, professional and unprofessional, is uniting all over the world in the condemnation of the common use of ardent spirits, the portals of danger and death are opening wide in another direction."

It is strange how a report will change in a very little travel. One story was, that I said there was more drunkenness among ministers and women than there was twenty-eight years ago; and another, which I received the other day marked, was very much abbreviated. This stated, "Gough says there are more ministers and women in this country than ever before."

I saw in a recent paper a queer account of my interview with the Oxford students in 1854. I give you the genuine and the spurious, just for the "fun of the thing." This strange version is headed:—

"GOUGH'S CONTEST WITH OXFORD STUDENTS.

"An amusing story is told of John B. Gough, when he went to Oxford to address the students on temperance. The students sent word to Mr. Gough that they 'would not have any temperance,' and advised him not to persist in lecturing; but he went to the hall. For twenty minutes he spoke in pantomime amid the deafening cat-calls of the boys. Finally, he stepped forward, demanded British fair play, and offered to whip every one of the five hundred students singly.

"His offer was loudly cheered and promptly accepted, and a big six-foot athlete was sent up on the stage. Gough, who is a little man, backed off as the big fellow approached him, and explained, 'My friends, you evidently misunderstand me. This is to be an intellectual contest, not a prize-fight.' The students cheered again at this evidence of the American's shrewdness, and ordered the debate to proceed. The college lad was, therefore, obliged to discuss with the temperance champion. He was at a disadvantage, but he quoted Scripture, and reminded the plucky lecturer that it was one of the apostles who wrote to Timothy—a young man too, like themselves—to take a little wine for the stomach's sake and for his often infirmities. The lads shouted vociferously at this.

"Gough slowly examined the six-footer from top to toe, and then said, 'My friends, look at this athlete; this fellow with muscles like steel, who can wield the club of Hercules, who can bend an English yeoman's bow, who could knock down an ox with the blow of a hammer, he is the personification of health and strength, but he thinks he needs a little wine for his stomach's sake!' Gough's inimitable manner of saying this had a tremendous effect. The students fairly yelled with delight, and their defeated champion retreated.

"Another was sent up. He was the intellectual giant of his class, in contradistinction to the six-footer. He, with much self-confidence, made a finished argument for liquor-drinking, based on Christ's changing the water into wine at the wedding-feast. His comrades cheered him to the echo, and thought his argument unanswerable, and Gough was chaffed for his defeat. 'Young men,' said he, solemnly, 'I admit that your champion has forestalled me. He has said to me just what I came here to charge you to do. Drink all the wine that you can find that is made entirely out of water.'"

The original statement I extract from my autobiography:

"The Committee of the London League were very desirous that I should speak in Oxford. On proposing it to the friends of temperance in that city, they stated that it was doubtful if such a meeting could be held. A certain class of students had been in the habit of disturbing concerts, lectures, and the like, and it was thought they could not resist the opportunity of having some 'fun' at a temperance lecture,—a subject held in contempt by a majority in the class to which these Oxford students belonged,—and their 'fun' was occasionally rough. They had smoked out a gentleman who came to lecture to them on tobacco. Some scores of pipes and cigars were in full blast. The Oxford friends stated also that though they would do all they could to assist in the arrangements, and promote the success of the meeting, no person known in that city would venture to preside, and the project had better be abandoned. The London committee were determined to make an attempt to get a hearing for me there; and I having consented, and a gentleman from London having agreed to preside, the evenings of Wednesday and Friday, June 13th and 15th, were appointed.

"I went down to Oxford with three or four gentlemen of the League. On entering the hall I found a large number of students, distinguished by their flat caps and gowns. The introduction passed off quietly, and I was received with noisy demonstrations, not exactly complimentary. I proceeded in my speech. The majority seemed to be looking at me curiously, as I supposed a pugilist looks at his antagonist, watching the first opportunity to give him a 'settler.' At length I said, 'What is the cause of the intemperance of Great Britain?' when a thin squeaking voice called out, 'Tempewanth Thothietieth.' At this there was a universal laugh; but I happened to catch the exact tone of the speaker, and replied, 'I beg your pardon, sir; but it is not 'Tempewanth Thothietieth' at all.

"Then there was another laugh, and the noise began,—laughing, whistling, crowing, braying, but no hissing. They were good-tempered, and simply wanted the 'fun'—and I sympathized with them in that. A little harmless fun will hurt nobody.

"The scene became so irresistibly ludicrous, and the young gentlemen went into it with such a perfect abandon, and such evident enjoyment, that, though I felt compelled to maintain my dignity, (such as it was,) I was thoroughly amused, and internally chuckled while striving to keep my face straight. The volley of questions that were hurled at me—some of them ridiculously personal, and some bordering on the profane—were incessant for some time. There was no abuse, but simply rollicking fun. I kept my position on the platform, though I could not be heard. At every lull I would say, 'Gentlemen,' and then would come a storm of cheering. Look which way I would, I saw laughing faces. I turned to the chairman, and was amused to see him with a broad grin, and his mouth wide open, enjoying it hugely, till he saw me looking at him, when his mouth closed instantly, and he made futile efforts to look grave and serious; but in spite of his sober face, his eyes were twinkling with merriment. What was I to do? It would never do to give it up so. Their questions became, after a while, more serious and answerable.

"One called out, 'Who turned water into wine?'"

"To which I replied, so that they could hear me, 'We have no objection to wine made of water.'

"Then came a string of Bible questions.

"In one of the pauses of the din, I said in a loud tone of voice, 'Gentlemen, fair play is a jewel.'

"At this they cheered, and some shouted, 'Fair play!'

"I said, 'What's the Englishman's motto?—Fair play.'

"'Yes, fair play!'

"'Down in front!'

"'Hats off!'

"'Caps on!'

"'Hurrah!'

"'Fair play!'

"Again I shouted, 'Fair play!' and then said, 'Gentlemen, I have a proposition that I think will please you—and I like to please my audience.

"'Let's have it!'

"'Proposition! proposition!'

"'Hush-sh-sh!'

"I said, 'We all believe in fair play, and this surely is not fair play; so many of you attacking one, and he a little one. My proposition will give us all fair play.'

"'Proposition! proposition!'

"'Stop that noise!'

"'Hush-sh-sh!'

"'Down in front!'

"The proposition is, that you choose your champion, and he shall take the platform, and he and I will take it ten minutes—turn about—and the rest of the audience shall judge who is the victor in this contest—he, or I. That's fair.

"'Yes, yes, that's fair;' and there were some comical proposals as to champion, and, as I suppose, personal hits; for there was loud laughing where I could not see the point. But after a little confusion, no champion appearing, I was permitted, with very slight interruption, to continue to the end of my speech, and received hearty cheers at the conclusion.

"The next evening my wife and I attended, by invitation, a rendering of *Œdipus* by Vandenhoff and his daughter, the choruses being sung by the choirs of the cathedral, assisted by amateurs among the students. It was very fine. I was recognised with a smile by some who were at the meeting the night before."

CHAPTER XXVI.

ON THE PLATFORM—PERSONAL EXPERIENCES AS A PUBLIC SPEAKER.

The Judge's Speech—Power of his Example—" Give it to him, Old Man "—Self-Possession necessary under Embarrassments—Man in Faneuil Hall, and Story for his Benefit—Woman and her Crying Child—" Did he lose his Eggs ? "—One Handkerchief for Two—Power of Audience over the Speaker—The Man with the Newspaper—How the whispering Young Ladies were stopped—Cultivation of the Voice—Power of Sarcasm—The Donkey at Snowdon—Sarcasm of O'Connell on Benjamin Disraeli—John Randolph and the " Vacant " Seat—Tom Marshall's " Demijohn " all but the Straw—Personal Experience under Trying Circumstances—" Here's one of your Cigars, Mr. Gough "—Quotations from Locke and Walter Scott which were not Quotations.

THE following expresses the contrast between what is genuine and the reported. I find in a paper the following :—

" At a great meeting at which Mr. John B. Gough spoke, in America, the card of a gentleman, a judge in the place, was sent up, as he desired to speak.

" 'I beg to differ *in toto* with everything said by the lecturer. I began with nothing, and worked my way up to the top of my profession, and have been a moderate drinker all my life ; and if people would only follow my example there would be no drunkards.'

" A man in the gallery called out, ' Hear, hear !'

" As the judge went on speaking, that ' Hear, hear ! ' was changed into ' Go it, old chap !' ' Hit him again!' ' Get your name up !' ' Sit upon him !'

" And while this was going on, everybody saw that the poor fellow was drunk.

" The chairman jumped up and said, ' Let us turn that man out.'

" Away rushed three or four to seize him by the neck, and were pulling him outside the meeting, when somebody came up and whispered a word, Let him alone ;' and then he held out his hand to support the judge's own son."

The original is as follows:—

At a meeting in a large town in Pennsylvania, at the close of the lecture a gentleman rose and was announced as Judge So-and-so, judge of the quarter-sessions. He said:—

"Ladies and gentlemen: Before the audience is dismissed I wish to say a few words in defence of myself and the class I represent. Now, it is very hard to have it publicly stated that I set a bad example."

The speaker had not said that the moderate drinker set a *bad* example, but that he did not set a *good* one.

"Now," said he, "I am a moderate drinker. Everybody knows me. I take my glass at home; I take it abroad. I am a moderate drinker,—a respectable, moderate drinker. Who dares say anything against me? Who ever saw me the worse for drink? Who ever saw me out of the way by drink? If young men followed my example they would be as I am, respectable and respected. I challenge the town in which I live, I challenge the county, to say whether my example is a bad one. Let young men follow my example, and they will be as I am."

A man in the audience cried out, "Give it to him, old man; give it to him! Put a head on him!"

Some one said, "Put that man out!"

Another gentleman said, "No, let that man remain; he is the only son of the judge."

His only son tried to follow his example, and there was the result—he was so drunk that he would disturb a respectable meeting.

I have made a long digression, and will now return to the relation of some of my experiences as a public speaker.

Like all other speakers, probably, I have been placed in embarrassing circumstances, and a certain amount of self-possession has been necessary to overcome an unexpected difficulty or opposition, especially such an interruption as often occurred in the earlier days of temperance work. On such an occasion I lost all fear, and became self-possessed, watching for an opportunity to retaliate. The secretary of the National League in London once told me that he was tempted to induce some one to hiss me, as the sound of a hiss seemed to stir me up to a more vigorous speech.

I was never utterly put down by an opposition in my public addresses. I have been sorely tried. On more than one occasion I found it was of no use to employ arguments with those who were determined to annoy me, but if possible would think of some apt story to get the laugh on them; and then I always succeeded in maintaining my ground.

A man in Faneuil Hall had troubled me by interruptions, with insolent and profane remarks, for some time, until I felt the necessity of quieting him. My indignation was roused by seeing under the gallery some liquor-sellers enjoying the fun hugely, and aiding the man by loud laughing at every impudent remark he made. I also discovered that the man was slightly under the influence of liquor. So, pausing in my speech, I said,—

"My friend, I pity you; for you are doing the dirty work of men who dare not do it themselves. You are serving your masters and employers, who sit here in this audience encouraging you in doing what you never would dream of were you not set on by others. You look like a sensible man, and I should like to tell you a story of which you remind me."

The man said, "Let's have the story."

"Well, you listen and I'll tell it to you.

"A certain merchant, who was sadly afflicted with stammering, had one joke which he related to every one who would listen to him. His clerks had repeatedly heard this joke, and were familiar with it. One day a stranger came into the store. The merchant accosted him with, 'Can you tell me wh-why it was th-h-at B-B-B—why it w-was that—that B-B—wh-wh-why it was th-that B-B——' One of the clerks, seeing his employer's difficulty, said, 'He wants to know if you can tell him why Balaam's ass spoke.' 'Yes,' said the stranger, 'I guess I can. I reckon Balaam was a stuttering man, and got his ass to do his talking for him."

The man laughed with the others, and in a few minutes got up and left the hall.

On another occasion I silenced a man who was quite noisy, when the audience cried, "Put him out!" by saying, "Do not put him out; let him remain; he reminds me of the woman who was taking her squalling child out of church, when the minister said, 'Do not take the baby out; it does not disturb me.' 'No,' said the woman, 'but you disturb the baby.' This baby does not disturb me, but I probably disturb him."

There are some persons in every audience on whom your best illustrations produce no effect. They are interested in the material or main chance, and care but little for romance or poetry.

I have a curious letter from a student in one of our Western colleges, which I copy here:—

"Dear Sir,—Several years ago, while attending college in the Michigan University, I had the pleasure of hearing you lecture. During your lecture you related a thrilling incident about a man being let down from the top of a perpendicular cliff of rocks to a great distance below, over the waves of the sea, by means of a basket and rope, for the purpose of gathering the eggs of sea-birds in the ledges below; and that when being drawn up he was attacked by an eagle, and, in striking at it with a knife, cut the rope very nearly in two; and that when he was finally drawn up, his hair had turned perfectly white from terror.

"The next morning after your lecture a young man related the incident at the breakfast-table of his boarding-house to a number of students, the landlord and lady, and the landlord's mother, who was far advanced in age. When he had finished the story, and had told how the man was frightened gray by his perilous situation, the old lady raised her spectacles and inquired, with much curiosity, 'Well, did he lose his eggs?'"

Occasionally, the most practised speaker will be thrown off his guard if not self-possessed, and even with all his self-possession may be considerably disturbed. As he sees all before him, some trifling incident, some untoward accident, may upset his gravity.

At one time, a couple were seated before me on the front seat. They had evidently come to hear what was to be said; just the people one likes to speak to. They were not critical, but came to the hall to be pleased (and it depends very much on the audience whether they are pleased or not).

Sit cold, critical, determined not to be moved, and let the

speaker see the slight sneer on your face at his efforts. Look at him, as much as to say, "What are you going to do next?" and you will so destroy the elasticity of any speaker, that, if he has not the ability to turn from you, he will be seriously embarrassed. But take your place with the desire to be interested, look at the speaker as if you would say, "We have come expecting and desiring to be pleased: now do your best, and we will show our approval," and you encourage him to do his best.

There are audiences that are positively cruel to a speaker, and who, without intending a wrong, may do essential and permanent injury to a timid speaker, who by a little encouragement might be a splendid success. The audience can hardly understand how much life an occasional expression of approval may put into a speaker.

But to return to my couple. They were a middle-aged pair, who attracted my attention at once. As I arose, they greeted me with a smile, and evidently settled themselves to listen. As I proceeded, I found them growing more and more interested, and at every point I made, one would nod at the other. At a funny story they laughed heartily. By-and-by I related a very pathetic incident. Then the smiling face was changed to a sober, then to a sad, expression. Soon the man began to sniff a little, feeling at the same time for his handkerchief, which he did not find, having probably forgotten it and left it at home. He felt in each of his pockets, then he wiped his eyes with his hand. Seeing his wife's handkerchief in her lap, he took it and began using it. The wife soon began to sniff, and felt for her handkerchief. Missing it, she found her husband using it; and so, with a loving, wifely motion, she leaned toward him, and taking one end of the handkerchief, she wiped her eyes with it. The sight of that pleasant couple wiping their eyes with the same handkerchief, so excited my sense of the absurd, that I had hard work to keep my face sober, and was compelled to look in another direction to maintain my gravity.

Then again, a speaker may be considerably annoyed and

perhaps vexed by the conduct of some one person in his audience. A man once sat before me, who, in the midst of my speech, ostentatiously drew out a newspaper, opened it, and began to read, turning it over with a very unpleasant rattle. I bore it as long as I thought it best, then I said a few words requesting him to bear with the speaker's lack of power to interest him, and to go to sleep rather than to disturb those who desired to listen.

Once a couple of young ladies had taken a seat directly in front of me, and I had hardly commenced when they began to whisper and giggle, and became so excited in their conversation that they were evidently annoying others. I did not like to tell them to stop talking, so I said: "A minister told me that he regretted very much rebuking two young ladies who were disturbing him and others by talking during his discourse, for he was told that one of these young ladies had just secured a beau, and that she was so exceedingly tickled about it, she could not refrain on all occasions when she could get a listener from expatiating on the dear young man's perfections: there seemed to be so many of them she could never exhaust the enumeration; and when she began to talk about her beau, she went on interminably. Just so whenever I see two young ladies talking together in a church, or at a lecture, I imagine one or the other, or both, have got a beau, and it would be hardly fair to disturb them, so I let them talk." The whisperers troubled me no more.

Endure all you can before putting any of your audience to shame. There are a few cases that deserve the punishment, but it is best to avoid it as far as possible.

I would advise every aspirant to eloquence to carefully cultivate the voice, to acquire a perfect command of that organ if possible. By careful, earnest, and frequent training, a defective voice may not only be improved, but an astonishing mastery be gained over it. A naturally harsh voice, which without cultivation would grate upon the ear of others, may be so brought into subjection as to become musical in its modulations. A power may be gained of uttering loud, clear, prolonged, trumpet tones, or sounds as sweet and penetrating as the echoes lingering about the soul long after it has ceased haunting it—as some voices will for ever.

No man with an incurable defect in his voice should seek to become an orator. Think of a speaker attempting pathos or sublimity, if he pronounces m like b, and n like d. "O by bother, by bother!" "My dabe is Dorval!" "Freds, Robads, cudtrybed!" The power and beauty of language are utterly destroyed.

I once heard a man who preached occasionally, and who invariably pronounced n like l. For instance: "My brethrel, pass roul the coltributiol box, but dolt put rusty lails or buttols ill, but mully. If you put ill bottols, put 'em ill with holes ill 'em, lot with all the holes jalled ilto wull!"

But, seriously, a cultivated or a naturally good voice is one great essential. It is said that when William Pitt uttered his torrents of indignant censure, or withering sarcasm, his voice assumed an almost terrific sound.

The power of sarcasm should be used with great discretion and moderation. A man may utterly lose his cause, and even excite hostility, by a too free use of this dangerous and yet powerful agent. There are cases where sarcasm, as in a retort, may be withering to an opponent, and gain for you the sympathy and applause of your audience.

A friend of mine in London possessed this power in an eminent degree. Any officious person who interrupted him was sure to get the worst of it. On one occasion he was speaking to a large audience, and said:

"You remember, Mr. President, when we visited Snowdon we saw the tourists on their donkeys ascending the mountain."

A man in the audience shouted out:

"There ain't no donkeys in Snowdon!"

"Ah!" said the speaker; "a gentleman tells us there are no donkeys at Snowdon."

"There never was a donkey in Snowdon," replied the man.

"How do you know, sir?" was the question from the platform.

"Because I've been there myself," was the reply.

"Oh!" said my friend. "Now, ladies and gentlemen, this individual tells this respectable audience there never was a donkey in Snowdon, and in the same breath informs them that he has been there himself."

The man was utterly crushed, though he was right, and the speaker was wrong, for there are no donkeys used at Snowdon, as the ascent is made on small ponies.

I think one of the most terrible sarcasms on record is that made by Daniel O'Connell on Benjamin Disraeli. Disraeli had left the party of the Liberator, and had indulged in severe personal attacks on O'Connell, who replied in a tone of unexampled bitterness, and concluded with these terrible words,—

"I cannot divest my mind of the belief that if this fellow's genealogy were traced, it would be found that he is the lineal descendant and true heir-at-law of the impenitent thief who atoned for his crimes on the cross."

Disraeli being of Jewish extraction, this struck him like a poisoned arrow.

I suppose that John Randolph was the most sarcastic of human beings, and made himself many enemies by its too free use. He could select at will, and at once, the very word that would sting. On one occasion, a gentleman, who had been elected in the place of a colleague of Randolph's, who had died, made a furious onslaught on him. He never looked from the paper before him while his opponent was speaking, but soon after arose, and in the course of his remarks paid a glowing tribute to the memory of his departed friend. Then, with his long finger pointed toward the seat that was occupied by his opponent, he said,—

"Mr. Speaker, when I look at the seat so long and ably occupied by my honourable friend, my heart is sad to find that seat *vacant*."

I believe it was Tom Marshall who, during a speech at Baltimore, when interrupted by a half-drunken man, with, "You're a demagogue," turned quickly to the man and said, "If you had a wisp of straw around your neck you would be a demijohn."

The only instance of embarrassment I could not overcome, occurred many years ago. It was my own fault, and proved a sharp lesson to me. I was engaged to address a large number of children in the afternoon, the meeting to be held on the lawn back of the Baptist church in Providence, R. I. In the forenoon a friend met me and said:

"I have some first-rate cigars, will you take a few?"

"No, I thank you."

"Do take half a dozen."

"I have nowhere to put them."

"You can put half a dozen in your cap."

I wore a cap in those days, and I put the cigars into it, and at the appointed time I went to the meeting. I ascended the platform and faced an audience of more than two thousand children. As it was out of doors I kept my cap on, for fear of taking cold, and I forgot all about the cigars.

Towards the close of my speech I became much in earnest, and after warning the boys against bad company, bad habits, and the saloons, I said :—

"Now, boys, let us give three rousing cheers for temperance and for cold water. Now, then, three cheers. Hurrah!"

And taking off my cap, I waved it most vigorously, when away went the cigars right into the midst of the audience.

The remaining cheers were very faint, and were nearly drowned in the laughter of the crowd.

I was mortified and ashamed, and should have been relieved could I have sunk through the platform out of sight. My feelings were still more aggravated by a boy coming up the steps of the platform with one of those dreadful cigars, saying:

"Here's one of your cigars, Mr. Gough."

Though I never afterwards put cigars in my cap or hat, when going to a meeting, I am ashamed to say it was some time after that before I gave up cigars altogether.

As already recorded, I have always avoided committing any portion of a speech to memory; that is, the phraseology. I get the idea, and perhaps may use the same words at every repetition of the sentence, but never charging my memory with the words, allowing the opportunity of changing at will.

When I attempt to make a quotation it often ends in a blunder.

I attempted once to quote the sentence: "Locke says we are born with powers and faculties capable of almost anything."

I began very confidently with my quotation. "Locke says, 'We are born.'"

There I stuck fast, and could not remember another word.

So I said, "We are born; I suppose we *are* born; but what we are born *for* in this connection, I am sure I do not know."

Before a very dull audience, at one time, I caused the only laughter that was heard during the address, by a confusion of syllables.

I intended to say, "Walter Scott once, on hearing his daughter say of something that it was *vulgar*, asked her if she knew the meaning of the word 'vulgar.' 'It is only common, and nothing common except wickedness deserves contempt.'"

I began all right. "Walter Scott once, on hearing his daughter say of something that it was *vulgar*, asked her if she knew the meaning of the word 'vulgar.' 'It is only common, and nothing except wicked—commonness—nothing wicked except commonness—nothing except common wickedness—nothing deserves wickedness. Dear me! nothing except contempt deserves wickedness."

I finished by saying, "I do not know what the man said to his daughter, and I am sure I do not care!"

I have been sometimes embarrassed by an introduction. In Lockerbie, Scotland, a chairman thus introduced me:—

"I wish to introduce to you Mr. Gough, who is to speak to us on the subject of temperance and I hope he will prove far better than he looks to be."

In my Autobiography I have narrated many curious incidents

of my public life as a speaker, which I will not repeat, only to say, that however faulty my speeches may be in their construction, I know they have been useful to many. In England, they have been recited, read at meetings hundreds of times, and hundreds of thousands of printed copies have been sold there. Extracts have been published, and selections in the form of leaflets, illustrated, have been scattered broadcast. It is estimated that the penny edition, containing one lecture to each number, has been sold to the extent of one million copies. Thirty-six different lectures have been published.

When in England, three reporters from London followed me for weeks. Four London papers published my speeches in full; and extracts from them were published in several other metropolitan papers, besides reports in local papers. My Autobiography was published and circulated to the extent of over a hundred thousand copies. I write of these facts not in egotism, but thankful that my utterances on temperance were received with favour, and that I enjoyed the privilege of speaking to so many thousands by the powerful aid of the press.

CHAPTER XXVII.

MEN I HAVE KNOWN—PULPIT AND OTHER ORATORS OF GREAT BRITAIN.

Public Speakers—Lectures I have heard—Personal Experience as to Public Occasions—Ministerial and other Acquaintances—Thomas Gutarie, D.D.—The Audience—Guthrie's Philanthropy—His Appearance in the Pulpit—Not a "Weeping Preacher"—My first Impressions—Power of his Utterance—William Arnot, D.D.—Appearance and Manner—"Figs of Thistles"—Newman Hall, D.D.—Lincoln Tower of Christ Church—Mr. Martin, of Westminster Chapel—Strange Texts—"Man of One Book"—Cowper's Model Preacher—Some of my Chairmen—Lord Shaftesbury—John Bright—Bright's Speech at Henry Darby's Feast—Sir Fitzroy Kelly; his Style and Manner—Joseph Parker, D.D.—Immense Power—Pulpit Apologetic Manners out of Place—Dr. Parker at Home, and as a Preacher—First Impressions of the Preacher—Vividness of Description—"God's Testimony against Sin"—Sins of Presumption—Where do Texts come from?

PUBLIC speakers have few opportunities to hear others speak. If a lecturer, he is busily employed during "the season;" if a minister, he has his own pulpit to fill. Lawyers and members of Congress are exceptions, I suppose. Many of them hear more speaking than is perhaps desirable or profitable for them. For my own part I may say that I have literally heard no public speakers except in the pulpit. I have no recollection of ever attending a political meeting but once.

I have heard but four lectures in my life; one from Rev. Wm. Arnot, more than twenty years ago, in Exeter Hall, subject, "The earth fitted and framed for the habitation of man;" one from Clara Barton, in Crosby's Opera House, in 1867, on her "Work in the Army during the Civil War;" one from Miss Willard, in Mechanics' Hall, Worcester, in 1876, on the "Women's Temperance Reform;" and one, in 1878, from Dr. B. W. Richardson, in Exeter Hall, on "Moderate Drinking."

I have heard several temperance speeches at conventions or anniversaries, when I was to speak myself. I have never heard a literary lecture in America. I have never attended a religious anniversary except to speak myself, when I have occasionally heard short speeches. At Sabbath School and Bible conventions I have enjoyed brief addresses, but only under the pressure of my own coming speech. I have never attended a meeting of the American Board of Foreign Missions. I have never heard a speech in Congress, except on two or three occasions, for five or ten minutes at a time. Therefore I can give no opinion of any speakers except the pulpit orators I have heard; and, from the fact that I have generally travelled eight months in the year, though I have listened to some hundreds of ministers for a single sermon, I have rarely been privileged to "sit under" the preaching of any one man sufficiently to enable me to form an opinion worthy of record. But I will endeavour to recall my impressions of some I have been privileged to hear, and perhaps allude to some of my chairmen I have omitted in a former chapter.

The ministers I have heard in Great Britain are Revs. Dr. Guthrie, of Edinburgh; William Arnot, of Glasgow; Newman Hall, of London; and Mr. Martin, of Westminster Chapel, London, on my first visit. I heard Mr. Spurgeon and Rev. Dr. Parker, on my second visit. With the exception of Mr. Spurgeon, whom I heard only twice, I was a frequent attendant on their ministrations. I heard occasionally single sermons from notable men. In the United States I have heard Rev. Dr. E. N. Kirk, of Boston; Rev. Dr. Taylor, of New York; Rev. George Gould, D.D., of Worcester; and Rev. D. O. Mears, of the Piedmont Church, Worcester—the latter church being the place of my attendance, when at home, for the past four years.

One of the most fascinating preachers I ever heard was Dr. Guthrie of Edinburgh. In 1853-55, 1857-60, I listened to him often. It was difficult to get into the church, every inch of room being occupied that could be made available either for sitting or standing. The doctor kindly gave me a pass, and my wife and myself always found a good seat.

The audience was composed of the literary, philosophical, scientific, and intellectual, with a fair show of the commonplace; for the preacher had a marvellous power of adapting his discourse to the gratification of the intellectual and to the understanding of the common mind. The Duke of Argyle was often there, and professors from the University. Truly the rich and poor met together, for Dr. Guthrie was almost worshipped by many of the denizens of the closes on High Street, and no wonder; for while he rebuked their sins, he sympathized with the sorrows of poor humanity.

It is well known that in his earnest desire to ameliorate the sufferings of poor neglected children he was the founder of the Ragged School system. He was also instrumental in introducing a pure water supply into Edinburgh, a great boon to the poor tenants of those lofty houses on High Street and the closes of the Lawn Market, and the Canongate. It must be often distressing to find those you seek to benefit utterly oblivious of their advantages. It is related that having asked a woman how she liked the water introduced into the city, she said: "Aye, not so well as I might; it's not like the water we had before, it neither smells nor tastes."

His appearance in the pulpit was very striking, and his manner was indescribable. I have seen him stand, bending over the pulpit cushion, with his hands stretched out toward the people, and heard him talk with such amazing power, combined with such sweetness, as drew all hearts towards him. I have never liked to see a preacher cry in the pulpit, but tears filling Dr. Guthrie's eyes seemed to be so appropriate that at certain passages you would feel they were necessary to the full effect of his utterances.

After the preliminary exercises, which were very solemn and tender, the people seemed to settle down to listen, and then he would take his text. The first time I heard him he said, when the audience was still: "We all do fade as a leaf." Then there was a pause amid the breathless silence of the congregation. See him with his noble forehead; those magnificent eyes, as he tenderly looks over that great assemblage, his heart overflowing with tender sympathy and affection for those who were travelling to that "bourn from which no traveller returns!" Then with that wonderful voice he repeats, with a deeper pathos and a stronger Scotch accent, "We all do fade as a leaf." Then he told us where to find his text.

The first words of his sermon were : " And the earth helped the woman." I was wondering what connection he could make with that and his selected theme. It was to show that the Bible used everything in nature as an illustration—the "lily of the valley," the "grass of the field," and the falling leaf; and then he went on, and on, with that magnificent voice, sometimes like "a thunder psalm among the hills," then like the sigh of the wind among the autumn trees ; again like the sound of a trumpet, then like the Æolian harp ; again sharp, staccato, and then seeming to struggle through a "mist of unshed tears." Your eyes would fill in spite of yourself by the power of his pathos.

One sentence he uttered that strangely moved me, not by what he said, but by his method of saying it. The sentence might have been written and spoken by a schoolboy, but uttered as he uttered it only by a genius. He had been speaking of the great law that prohibits this wonderful combination of the machinery of the human system working on for ever. Then pausing a moment, and with his finger pointing downward, he said, " No, it goes slower, and slower, and slower, —and then—it STOPS," his voice growing deeper in tone at every pause, till at the word *stops* it seemed to me to be a deeper and more musical bass than I ever heard from the highest artist. It seemed as if I felt " the skin lift from the scalp to the ankles, and every hair stand up and shiver," not by what he said, but by his power in saying it.

I always hoped he might visit this country ; but it was not so to be. One of the delightful reminiscences of my first visit to Britain was the acquaintance and friendship I was permitted to enjoy with Dr. Guthrie. His admirable biography has been published ; so I have given only a few of my own impressions of him. He presided several times at my meetings, and I remember how amused he was when the secretary said, "The Rev. Dr. Guthrie, author of the 'Sins and Sorrows of the City,' will preside; and Professor Miller, author of 'Alcohol,' will preside to-morrow evening."

Another of the Scotch preachers was Rev. Wm. Arnot, whose biography has been published in this country. He entertained us for some days in Glasgow, and called upon us when he visited London. He was very different, in almost every respect, from Dr. Guthrie, yet not one whit below him in his influence and power. He appealed to the intellect rather than to the feelings, and yet at times he was very tender in his appeals. His appearance I need not describe; he has been seen often in the pulpits and on the platforms of this country. His manner in the pulpit was rather heavy and somewhat unwieldy. I know I had a sensation of uneasiness when I first heard him. His motions were not graceful, his gestures were awkward, his pronunciation rather broadly provincial. He distressed me at first by the jerking of the elbow, the shrugging of the shoulders, the hesitation in his utterance.

His text was, "Figs of thistles." I was held fast, though the enjoyment was marred by his strange motions, and I said to my wife as we came out of the church, "That was a grand sermon; but I wish he had kept still, and had not jerked his elbows so strangely." But as to the effect of that sermon I can truly say that for months after I heard it I turned in no direction but right before me seemed to be the words "Figs of thistles." Did I purpose entering into my engagements or making any plans, "Figs of thistles. He had the power, in spite of his peculiarities, to drive the truth into the hearts and consciences of those who heard him. He was one of the men I learned to love, and that with no effort on my own part.

When in London we heard the Rev. Newman Hall and Rev. Mr. Martin. Of Mr. Hall I say but little; he has been heard extensively in this country. On hearing him preach one is impressed with a consciousness of his sincerity and large-heartedness. In his appeals you feel that he is in earnest, meaning what he says; and yet withal there is the beautiful simplicity that has made his immortal work, "Come to Jesus," so full of interest to thousands. I was his guest when he was a pastor in Hull, before he came to London. I heard him often in "Surrey Chapel," and on the last Sabbath spent in London in 1879 it was my privilege to speak in his new "Christ Church," for the tower of which he gathered funds in this country. It is a beautiful edifice, and "Lincoln Tower" is worthy of the noble name it bears.

Rev. Mr. Martin of Westminster Chapel, at the time I heard him, had become a power in the pulpit. We were fortunate in obtaining a seat, which we occupied, when in London, for two years. This chapel was built amid many disagreeable surroundings in Westminster,—a very disreputable neighbourhood, the sights and sounds in the vicinity repulsive; yet in spite of all this the chapel was crowded. The locality is gradually changing for the better. Mr. Martin was very solemn and devout in the pulpit, yet with an exceeding sweet expression. At first he seemed cold and rather commonplace; but that was only in the introduction. As he unfolded his subject he fired up, and with flashing eye he warned his auditors of the consequences of sin, of the realities of the world to come; using the plainest terms, and but few illustrations, either hard logic or facts; but with tenderness and earnestness winning his way to the hearts of those who heard, till they were convinced of his strong desire to bring them to the truth. Occasionally he would select the strangest texts, and you would feel disappointed, in view of the conviction in your own mind that nothing could be made of such a passage. Once he took the passionate cry of Job, "Am I a sea or a whale?" and from that he preached a most impressive sermon on God's care for us, even in discipline. He was a fine reader, and one morning I heard him read that very difficult Psalm, the hundred and thirty-sixth, of twenty-eight verses, each verse ending with, "For His mercy endureth for ever." There was no monotony in his reading, but rather a sweet monotone of musical cadence that was fascinating.

As a writer has said, "A man of one book is always a formidable foe;" and Mr. Martin was emphatically a man of one book. He sought for no notoriety; was seldom heard out of his own pulpit; his only aim appearing to be, and was, to make men feel that the Bible is true, and to induce them to shape their lives by its precepts. I spoke twice in his chapel, and on my last visit to London missed him as one would miss an old friend, remembering with gratitude the few interviews I had with him, and thankful that I knew and loved Samuel Martin. Ritchie says Mr. Martin might have sat for the portrait of Cowper's model preacher.

"Simple, grave, sincere.
In doctrine uncorrupt; in language plain,
And plain in manner; decent, solemn, chaste,
And natural in gesture; much impressed
Himself, as conscious of his awful charge;
And anxious mainly that the flock he feeds
May feel it too; affectionate in look,
And tender in address, as well becomes
A messenger of grace to guilty man."

These four preachers I heard and knew on my first and second visit to great Britain. When I returned they were all gone but the Rev. Newman Hall.

I recall some of my chairmen of those days, among whom was Lord Shaftesbury, who presided on several occasions, who still is a power for good in England, one of the true nobility, a noble Christian gentleman, whose kindness to me I shall never forget. He was not a fluent speaker, but his presence was mightier than speech, since all recognized in him a self-denying servant of the Master.

Another of my chairmen, on three occasions, was John Bright, almost as well known in this country as in England. I heard him speak for nearly an hour at Brymbo, in Wales. We were the guests of William Henry Darby, of Brymbo Hall, and during our stay, Mr. Bright, with quite a large and very pleasant party, was with us for nearly a week.

Mr. Darby gave a feast to the workers in the extensive

mines and iron-works, at which gathering several speeches were made. Mr. Bright spoke on the question of "labour and capital," showing how necessary the one is for the other, and how suicidal to create division between them, or to bring them into mutual antagonism. The speech was incisive and clear as crystal; no redundance of words, but each word necessary and appropriate. It is now twenty-six years since I heard that speech, yet there remains a very vivid recollection of its power. Often have I wished I could hear him again, but the opportunity has never been given.

Another of my chairmen, claiming more than a passing notice, was Sir Fitzroy Kelly, now Lord Chief Baron of England. When holding the office of Her Majesty's Attorney-General, Sir Fitzroy entertained me as his guest at his beautiful seat, the "Chantreys," near Ipswich, and presided at my meetings on two occasions. He has a very fine countenance, expressive of deep, earnest energy. There was a wonderful power in his delivery. He stood perfectly still, no gesture, the thumb of his right hand in his waistcoat-pocket, and he simply talked. I could have listened to him for hours. His fine voice was like the rippling of water on the bed of some pebbly brook; and then suddenly changing his tone, without moving from his position, his words came with deep emphasis. He was a great Chancery lawyer. He is a man of iron energy, and is by nature and character keen, watchful, and wary. His demeanour is marked by great gravity and dignity. As a host he was genial, understanding thoroughly and practising the most graceful method for the ease and comfort of his guests. I have always felt grateful to him for his kindness to me twenty-five years ago.

One of his guests, when I was at the Chantreys, asked him how long he had ever spoken at one time. The reply was, "I once spoke eight hours in a case before the Lords. Their Lordships agreed to hear the case argued that day, provided it could be done at one sitting; so I continued for eight hours, and nothing passed my lips during that argument but the juice of two oranges."

The Rev. Joseph Parker, D.D., is a most remarkable man, and a preacher of great power. I heard him often, and always with great delight and profit. So many and varied have been the opinions of Dr. Parker, that I am induced to record my impressions as to his power. I am not qualified to review him critically, nor shall I claim to analyse his methods scientifically.

I have heard the remark, "Dr. Parker is an egotist." What man conscious of great power, with an influence sufficient to establish and maintain a church so complete in all its appointments, and with the ability to keep an audience week after week, and year after year, filling the spacious edifice, with no diminution but rather an increase, till the place is becoming too strait for the accommodation of the crowds eager to listen; sustaining a Thursday noon lecture, attended by thoughtful men who crave and can only be satisfied with strong meat, and being able to meet the demands of the intellectual throngs who attend his ministry,—I ask, what man conscious of all this, must not necessarily be self-confident, or rather self-reliant, and that not offensively? There are some men so painfully conscious of their defects, shortcomings, and failings, as not to realize and be thankful for the gifts God has given them, but are so excessively humble that their superfluity of humility is as painful to witness as the egotism of another.

Dr. Parker never enters the pulpit with an apologetic air, as if he would say, "I come to tell you what I think, diffidently to give you the result of my guessings, and to submit with deference the result of my studies, in all humility, to the test of your superior judgment;" but he appears as "one having authority;" as if he would say to his people, "I come to instruct, to tell what I know, and what I have attained by close study. I have given to this subject my best thoughts; and, by hard searching, have obtained the best thoughts of the wisest men. Having condensed all this into the compass of a half-hour's discourse, I invite your closest attention, that you may be wiser at the close of my sermon than when you entered this house."

For my part, I prefer the teacher who will lay his hand on me with an authority, and say, "Listen to me, and you will be a wiser man," to the other who approaches me with a humility that will lessen my confidence in his ability to instruct. I believe an affectation of humility is one of the most offensive forms of egotism, and Dr. Parker will never sin in that direction.

No one who has seen Dr. Parker in his home would judge him to be an egotist. One day's charming visit at his house can never be forgotten. No restraint was laid upon us in the society of himself and wife in their genial and hospitable home. They gave us a most cordial greeting. It would hardly suit the ideas of some persons if I should say that Dr. Parker was childlike—I do not mean childish. It was simplicity with dignity, no assumption of superiority; he was not there the teacher, but the friend, manifesting a deference to others' opinions that surprised me. I have known some men, supposed to be great men, who seemed to be seeking an opportunity to exhibit their ability by drawing you out just far enough to afford them the chance of humbling you. I have been, on more than one occasion, so contradicted, snubbed, put down, by some self-important, imperious egotist, that I have lost respect for my tormentor, and indulged in a little retaliation as my defence.

With Dr. Parker, at his own house, there was not the slightest assumption of superiority, although he knew that in intellect he was a giant in comparison. During the course of conversation I remarked, "You exhibit many striking peculiarities in your pulpit delivery." He said, "I should not be Joseph Parker if I did not, but" (laying his hand on my shoulder) "come here, my dear fellow, and tell me of my peculiarities;" and we sat together, and talked for a long time with perfect freedom.

"What do you think of Dr. Parker as a preacher?" I have heard no preacher like him. He is different from all others; he has marked out a path for himself; he is an original. I cannot compare him with other great pulpit orators, since I have not heard them sufficienty to institute such a comparison. I have walked twice on the Sabbath from Piccadilly to Holborn Viaduct, a distance of two miles each way, and been amply repaid for my eight miles' walk.

Let me give my impressions on hearing him for the first time. He was not an entire stranger to me, as he had very kindly taken the pains to call at my "Hillside" home with his wife, when they were in this country some years since, and I have always been grateful to him for the trouble he took to see us in the midst of many pressing engagements in all directions. When he rose in the pulpit he stood motionless, his face almost rigid as marble, no expression,—reminding one of the "silent oracle." His first words revealed a magnificent voice. The reading of the hymn convinced you that he had studied elocution. The impressive manner in which he uttered the sentence, "Let us worship God," showed his perfect control over every intonation; and the reading of the Scriptures manifested his knowledge of the power of appropriate emphasis. The prayer was beyond and above criticism. God was the Father, ready to bestow; man was the needy one; Christ was the Mediator, through whom all petitions must be offered, and all blessings must flow. The phraseology of the prayer was to me rather unusual, but so perfectly intelligent and appropriate that the heart responded to every utterance.

In the beginning of his discourse I was disturbed and annoyed by his manner, entirely new to me—thoroughly different from anything I had ever seen; but I soon forgot his manner in the intense interest awakened by the sermon. I will not attempt a description, except to say that he introduced that scene where the servant of Elisha in his trouble said, "Alas, my master, how shall we do?" And the prophet answered, "Fear not, for they that be with us are more than they that be against us. And Elisha prayed that the servant's eyes should be opened, and he saw, and behold the mountains were full of chariots of fire round about Elisha." His description was so vivid and took such hold of me, that on the next evening, while speaking to a large audience, I felt compelled to use it. I told the people that having heard Dr. Parker the day before, he had so revealed to me the beauty and grandeur of the event, that I could find no better illustration of the faithfulness of God to His people, and the certainty of His unseen protection in the midst of enemies when we are engaged in His work.

Dr. Parker's utterances of sentences occasionally are wonderful in their power, often startling and very impressive, producing a permanent effect on the mind. I heard him once describe hell according to the biblical description. "The worm that dieth not, the fire that is not quenched." "I will not," said he, "abate one word, or explain away the awful meaning of the 'weeping, and wailing, and gnashing of teeth;' of the 'bottomless pit,' for it must be bottomless if the soul is immortal. I will bring them all before you,—this fire, this weeping and wailing, this undying worm, this bottomless pit;" and then with an indescribable gesture, with his finger pointing as if towards this aggregation of horrors, he said, "There— there is God's testimony against sin." At another time he was speaking of sins of presumption. "Deliberate, wilful sin —what is it? It is a shut hand, a clenched fist, an upraised arm, the muscles to their full tension, and the object God Almighty's face!" A thrill passed through that audience; there was a deep-drawn sigh audible in every direction; and I must confess that never before had I such an idea of sin, presumptuous sin against God, as in these two striking passages.

On one occasion, after repeating his text from Jeremiah vi. 16, "Thus saith the Lord, Stand ye in the ways and see and ask for the old paths, where is the good way, and walk therein, and ye shall find rest to your souls," he said, "Would you like to hear the old preachers? Yes. *Once!*" and that word once was uttered with an amazing power. Then he went on most fearlessly to condemn the milk-and-water preaching of half truths, etc. Another time he commenced his discourse by asking, "Where did Jesus Christ get His texts?" when he gave us a beautiful illustration of the adaptation of Christ's words to every phase of human character that He addressed.

Once, speaking of the bulwarks that were being broken down in these days of lax living and lax doctrine in the Church, he said of one doctrine after another, "*Gone!* the Devil, *gone!* and God—*going!*"

No one can imagine the power and force of the utterance of the words I have italicized but those who have heard him. As a preacher he stands apart from all other men. In this country he produced a marked sensation. The more I heard him, the more I desired to hear him. What I have said has been simply the recording of my own opinions; for whatever criticisms there may have been of him and his preaching, I have never seen them.

CHAPTER XXVIII.

MEN I HAVE KNOWN (CONTINUED)—SPURGEON—AMERICAN CLERGYMEN.

C. H. Spurgeon : Early History—His First Sermon—"Who is this Spurgeon ?"—Park Chapel and Exeter Hall—The Metropolitan Tabernacle—Publication of Fifteen Hundred Sermons—The Man a Miracle—Public Institutions for Missions and Benevolence—The Beautiful Work of Mrs. Spurgeon—Pedigree of Pulpit Story—Ministers must be "Thick-skinned"—Anecdotes—Spurgeon a Total Abstainer—Boys' Orphanage at Stockwell—Reception of Mr. Spurgeon—The Little Consumptive—True Greatness—Sources of Power as a Preacher—The Book of Books—Comments on Proverbs—Tale-bearers and Dissemblers—Mr. Spurgeon and the Dog—Edward Norris Kirk, D.D.—Oratory and Elocution—Our Last Interview—Elocution sometimes a Hindrance—George H. Gould, D.D.—Rev. David O. Mears—William M. Taylor, D.D.—Power with the Scriptures—Helpful Themes—Theodore L. Cuyler, D.D.—Preacher and Correspondent.

ONE of the most remarkable men I have been privileged to know is C. H. Spurgeon. His has been a career thus far unparalleled in the history of ministers. His educational advantages were very limited: four years in a common school in Colchester, and a few months at an agricultural college at Maidstone. After he had begun to preach he was strongly advised to enter Stepney College, to prepare more fully for the ministry; and an appointment was made to meet Dr. Angus, the tutor. Mr. Spurgeon went to the place appointed,—that of Macmillan, the publisher,—and after waiting in a room for two hours, rang the bell, and asked the reason of the delay. The servant informed him that the doctor had waited in another room till he was tired, and had gone away. Thus ended all efforts for a classical education.

His first sermon was preached under peculiar circumstances. In 1851 he was asked to walk with a young man, whom he supposed to be the preacher, to a village four miles away. While on his way, the young man expressed the hope that God would bless him in his labour.

"Oh, dear," said he; "I never preached in my life; I never thought of doing such a thing. I was asked to walk with you, and I sincerely hope you will be blessed in your labour."

"Nay, but I never preached, and I don't know that I could do anything of the sort."

So they walked on, as he says, his soul all in a trouble as to what would happen. But when they found the congregation assembled, and no one there to preach—though he was but sixteen years old—he did preach from the text, "Unto you that believe, He is precious." A gentleman who heard him then, says, "he wore a round jacket and turn-down collar."

He continued to preach after that, constantly, and was settled over the little church at Waterbeach, on a very meagre salary. One of the deacons of Park Street church, Southwark, in which Dr. Rippon had preached for sixty-three years, heard Mr. Spurgeon deliver an address at a Sunday-school anniversary, and such was the effect produced that he soon after received a call to Park Street church. His first sermon was preached to about two hundred people in a church with sittings for twelve hundred. Before three months, the question in London was—and I remember it well in 1854—"Who is this Spurgeon?"

In one year Park chapel was enlarged, during which time he preached in Exeter Hall. It was in this hall that I first heard of him as a young man drawing immense audiences. He had secured the ear and attention of the people. In 1856 Park chapel was entirely inadequate to receive the crowds who flocked to him, and the Royal Surrey Gardens' Music Hall was engaged. Here he preached to ten or twelve thousand persons every Sunday morning, until his present spacious edifice was finished.

The "Metropolitan Tabernacle" was formally opened in

March, 1861. It seats five thousand five hundred persons, with standing room for a thousand more. When the church removed from Park chapel, it consisted of eleven hundred and seventy-eight members. In 1877 the membership was five thousand one hundred and fifty-two. The immense amount of work performed by this one man is astonishing. He has published fifteen hundred sermons in volumes, and more than a hundred singly. He has also published a commentary upon the Psalms in five volumes, called the "Treasury of David." In addition to these he has issued sixteen other works, besides compiling a hymn-book, conducting a monthly magazine, and writing prefaces and introductions to scores of other men's works.

People say, "Ah, he is not an educated man." Speaking to a lady of title about him, she said, "But is he not quite vulgar?"

Let the experience of a quarter of a century demonstrate! Let the list of his works determine! No man of education has done more for the extension of the kingdom of Christ by the publication of valuable and instructive books than he; and the uniform testimony of the press confirms the high excellence of his writings. In short, he is—and I told him so—a miracle to me.

I should fill a volume were I to speak of his Pastors' College, his Orphanage for Boys, where he has two hundred and forty, and an orphanage just opened for girls; his Colportage Association; his Tabernacle alms-houses; then the institutions connected with the Tabernacle; the Building-fund to help poor churches to build; a German mission, supporting two missionaries; a mission to the Jews; missions in Golden Lane, Richmond Street, Green Walk, James' Grove; a blind mission, a mother's mission, a Baptist country mission; Evangelists' Association; the Loan Tract Society; General Loan Tract Society; the Rock Loan Tract Society; the Ordinance Poor-fund; the Ladies' Benevolent Society; Home and Foreign Missionary Working Society,—all at work, and all alive.

Then I must not forget the beautiful work of Mrs. Spurgeon,

who has been an invalid for years; but who in her weakness and pain has instituted and carried out a plan for providing destitute ministers with books, and occasionally with money.

Mr. Spurgeon has had a reputation for eccentricity fastened upon him, in common with many other popular preachers. As he says, "Throw mud enough, and some of it will be sure to stick." It is interesting to trace the pedigree of a pulpit story, though it is not often possible to discover its actual parent; like Topsy, they may say, "I growed." He says, "These same anecdotes occur from age to age, but they are tacked on to different men. Liars ought to have good memories, that they may recollect that they have already assigned a story to some one else."

I once asked him in reference to several tales I had heard of him, whether they were true—whether he ever said, on entering the pulpit, "It's d——d hot this morning." He said, "Never, never;" and yet some time after I heard a clergyman relate this story, and when I told him of Mr. Spurgeon's denial of it, he said, "My friend heard him say it, and I believe my friend." He was once represented as sliding down the balustrades of his pulpit! and he says he never gave even the remotest occasion for the falsehood, and yet he hears of persons who were present when he did it, and saw him perform the silly trick. Mr. Spurgeon says that "a minister who is much before the people has need to be thick-skinned." A literary gentleman sent me what he called authentic stories of Mr. Spurgeon. When I was with him, I asked him about them. Not one of them was true.

He is very fond of a joke, and there is a comical twinkling of the eye when he perpetrates one, that is irresistible, reminding you of Sam Weller's winks that always cause a laugh, though we are utterly ignorant of the cause of the winking.

On one occasion an artist had drawn a sketch of him, and brought it for his inspection. Looking at it, he said:

"Ah, this is very well; but women and fools are, they say, the best judges of these things, so I must hunt up somebody."

Just then up came one of Mr. Spurgeon's deacons.

"Ah, brother, you are just in time; what do you think of this sketch of me?"

Another artist wished to make an engraving of him.

"I hope," said Mr. Spurgeon, "you will not make it an expensive one; the public would not give more than twopence for me. A friend of mine, to do me honour, published a photograph of me at eighteen pence, and he lost a lot of money by it."

I think these anecdotes show that he is one of the most natural of men, with no false pride or starch about him. He says just what he thinks in the most natural and homely manner. He is a troublesome customer to pompous people who fancy themselves somebodies, when they are nothing of the kind.

The strangest stories have been in circulation with regard to his drinking. I am glad to be able to say, that I know he is at present, and has been for some time, a total abstainer; and that when he took stimulants, it was by his physician's prescription. When he took it he made no secret of his course, but freely spoke of it wherever he might be.

Personally, he is fascinating. He may not be called prepossessing; there is nothing finical about him, not the shadow of a sham. Some one has said, "His face is heavy," but when illuminated by a smile, it is beautiful. His first greeting captured me. I think the few hours spent with him were as delightful and profitable as any in my life. He is full of genial humour. His laugh is infectious. Yet with all his wit and fun, with the keenest faculty of seeing the ludicrous side of things, there is no unbecoming levity. It would not shock you if after a hearty laugh he should say, "Let us have a word of prayer."

I would like to give you one incident to illustrate the man in his greatness and simplicity. He wished me to visit his Boys' Orphanage, at Stockwell. I could go only on Saturday, and his note to me was characteristic:—

"Beloved friend,—Although I never go out on Saturdays, my horses being under the law and not under grace, keep the seventh day Sabbath, yet we will arrange to visit," etc.

A beautiful day it was for London as we rode together, chatting all the way. The history of the Orphanage is intensely interesting. The commencement was a sum of £20,000 to Mr. Spurgeon, from a lady, to commence an orphanage for fatherless boys. All the money that has been expended has been raised by voluntary contribution, and the £20,000 is invested as an endowment. When we entered the grounds, the boys set up a shout of joy at the sight of their benefactor.

I asked, "What are the requirements for admission?"

He said, "Utter destitution. Nothing denominational. We have more of the Church of England that of the Baptists. We have Roman Catholics, Presbyterians, Methodists—all sorts."

After the boys had gone through their gymnastic exercises and military drill, I spoke a few words to them. Mr. Spurgeon was like a great boy among boys.

He said, "There are two hundred and forty boys—only think! How many pence are there in a shilling?"

"Twelve."

"Right. How many shillings in a pound?"

"Twenty."

"Right. Twelve times twenty, how many?"

"Two hundred and forty."

"That's a penny a piece for each boy.

"Here, Mr. Charlesworth," handing him a sovereign, "give these boys a penny apiece;" when a shrill hearty hurrah was given, as Mr. Spurgeon turned away with a laugh of keen enjoyment.

"Will you go to the infirmary? We have an infirmary and quarantine; for sometimes the poor creatures we take in need a good deal of purifying. We have one boy very ill with consumption; he cannot live, and I wish to see him, for he would be disappointed if he knew I had been here and had not seen him."

We went into the cool and sweet chamber, and there lay the boy. He was very much excited when he saw Mr.

Spurgeon. The great preacher sat by his side, and I cannot describe the scene. Holding the boy's hand in his, he said :—

"Well, my dear, you have some precious promises in sight all around the room. Now, dear, you are going to die, and you are very tired lying here, and soon you will be free from all pain, and you will rest. Nurse, did he rest last night?"

"He coughed very much."

"Ah, my dear boy, it seems very hard for you to lie here all day in pain, and cough all night. Do you love Jesus?"

"Yes."

"Jesus loves you. He bought you with His precious blood, and He knows what is best for you. It seems hard for you to lie here and listen to the shouts of the healthy boys outside at play. But soon Jesus will take you home, and then He will tell you the reason, and you will be so glad."

Then, laying his hand on the boy, without the formality of kneeling, he said, "O Jesus, Master, this dear child is reaching out his thin hand to find Thine. Touch him, dear Saviour, with Thy loving, warm clasp. Lift him as he passes the cold river, that his feet be not chilled by the water of death; take him home in Thine own good time. Comfort and cherish him till that good time comes. Show him Thyself as he lies here, and let him see thee and know Thee more and more as his loving Saviour."

After a moment's pause he said, "Now, dear, is there anything you would like? Would you like a little canary in a cage to hear him sing in the morning? Nurse, see that he has a canary to-morrow morning. Good-bye, my dear; you will see the Saviour perhaps before I shall."

I had seen Mr. Spurgeon holding by his power sixty-five hundred persons in a breathless interest; I knew him as a great man universally esteemed and beloved; but as he sat by the bedside of a dying pauper child, whom his beneficence had rescued, he was to me a greater and grander man than when swaying the mighty multitude at his will.

I need not describe Mr. Spurgeon's preaching; very few Americans visit London without hearing him. So much has been written and published in the United States of him and his sermons that the people of this country are familiar with him as one of our own people. I am most impressed with the simplicity, freedom, fearlessness, earnestness, and naturalness of his preaching. He has more heart than eloquence, and illustrates the truth of his own words, " Eloquence of the most lofty kind is mere sound unless there be love in the speaker's heart to give weight to his words—better to have a loving heart than to speak twenty languages."

He has a powerful, rich, and melodious voice under perfect control. Twelve thousand people have heard him distinctly in the open air, and twenty thousand in the Crystal Palace. He does not aim to be a great preacher, but is a man of wonderful attraction and marvellous power.

The first time I heard him he preached from the passage " Who forgiveth all thine iniquities." The sermon was remarkable for directness, simplicity, and earnestness. When he quoted the passage, " As far as the east is from the west, so far hath He removed our transgressions from us," he said, " How glorious is this statement! If it had been as far as the South is from the North it would have been an immense distance; but no, it is as far as the East is from the West, an immeasurable distance." From the first sentence to the last he held the attention and left an impression not easily effaced. I think I never met a man who seemed more in this world and less of it. He feels that his work is among men, and while his associations here are with the earth, yet his conversation, his citizenship, is in Heaven.

His various institutions show his worldly wisdom in all their managements; and in their inception and maintenance they manifest in truth the wisdom that cometh down from above—that "layeth up treasure where neither moth nor rust can corrupt, and where thieves cannot break through nor steal." I regret not having heard more of his pulpit ministrations; but among my library treasures are the twenty-four choice volumes of his sermons, all the more prized because personally given by him. We have his " Treasury of David," and use at our family devotions his "Interpreter." We enjoy and profit by his comments on the passages selected for reading. They may not be profound, but they are simple and enlightening. The children may understand them, the language often of every-day life, bringing the Bible near us as the book to be read and understood and believed,—not to be read once or twice a day in a constrained tone and with ceremony, but a book for every day,—a book not given to bewilder, but to comfort and instruct, yet withal a book so deep and profound that the highest intellects on earth find it worthy of their earnest study, while the "wayfaring man though a fool need not err therein."

Many of his comments are pithy, striking, quaint, and full of marrow and instruction. Take the comments on Proverbs xxvi. 17-28. I read this the other evening at family worship, and was so pleased with his running comments that I cannot refrain from inserting here a few specimens :—

20*th verse.* " Where no wood is, there the fire goeth out ; so where there is no tale-bearer the strife ceaseth." His comment is : " Do not talk about it and it will die out. No hurt ever comes from holding our tongues ; silly tattling causes much sorrow. If we will not reply, those who slander us will tire of their dirty work, or will be powerless for mischief. Evil speaking seldom injures those who take no notice of it. Do not find fagots for your own burning. Let the tale-bearers alone, and their fire will go out for want of fuel."

21*st verse.* "As coals are to burning coals, and wood to fire, so is a contentious man to kindle strife." His comment is : "Wherever he is, quarrelling begins, or being already commenced, it is fanned to a fiercer flame. He is a stoker for Satan's fires. Let us never grow like him."

24*th verse.* "He that hateth dissembleth with his lips, and layeth up deceit within him." His comment is : "He is brooding mischief, and storing up revenge, yet he speaks fairly. He hangs out the sign of the angel, but the devil keeps his house."

25*th verse.* "When he speaketh fair, believe him not, for there are seven abominations in his heart." His comment is : "All kinds of evils lurk in a dissembler's soul. The man's heart is a hell, full of evil spirits, the forge of Satan, the workshop of all mischief. Whenever any one flatters us let us fly from him at once, and avoid him for the future. He would not spin so fine a web if he did not wish to catch a fly."

28*th verse.* "A lying tongue hateth those that are afflicted by it ; and a flattering mouth worketh ruin." His comment is : " It is the nature of ill-will to hate those whom it injures. Hurt another, and you will dislike him, benefit him and you will love him. Above all things abhor flattery, for he who uses this detestable art is surely plotting your overthrow. Young people should learn this lesson early, or their ignorance may cost them dear."

His illustrations are very simple, principally drawn from real human life, or incidents that are constantly occurring, or in experiences to which all are liable. I give one on " Trust," how impossible to scorn or turn away from any that trust you. He describes a garden in which he took great delight; but a neighbour's dog would occasionally burst through the hedge that separated the grounds and do no small damage at such times. He was thoroughly vexed as one day, while he was enjoying the garden after planting some fresh seeds in one bed, and anticipating a fine crop of flowers in the other, this dog bounded through the hedge and tore over the newly-seeded beds to their great damage. He was quite angry at this, and seizing a stick, hurled it at the animal. The dog stopped, looked at Mr. Spurgeon, and, wagging his tail, picked up the stick in his mouth, and trotting up to him, laid it at his feet, and looking in his face pushed his nose in his hand. "Now," said Mr. Spurgeon, "could I punish that dog, or drive him out of my garden? No; I patted him, and said, 'Good dog, come into my garden when you will,' because he trusted me."

I have spoken of Mr. Spurgeon at length, for " take him for all in all, we ne'er shall look upon his like again," and I rejoice in the privilege of such a friendship. In a recent letter to me he says: " May the Lord ever bless and keep you and yours, and may the divine appointment arrange us somewhere near each other in the land where sinners washed in blood behold the face of the Well-beloved. Yours very heartily and gratefully, C. H. Spurgeon."

When a boy, I had heard Dr. Nathan Bangs, Dr. Durbin, Rev. Wilbur Fisk, President of Middletown College, Bishop Waugh, and other celebrated preachers of the Methodist church, forty-five years ago, and to this day I have clear recollections of their style, appearance, and mode of preaching. But the preacher who first interested me in my early manhood was Dr. E. N. Kirk, of Boston, with whose church I united in 1845, and on whose roll of membership the names of my wife and myself are still left. Though we reside so far away that we can hardly be numbered with the congregation, we hold the most friendly relations to the present pastor, Rev. Dr. Herrick.

It is not my purpose to speak of Dr. Kirk as a preacher, since his biographer, in his admirable "Life of Edward Norris Kirk, D.D.," has given an analysis of his power as a minister, which is complete and exhaustive, supplemented by the testimonies of others, prominent among which is a sketch by Leonard Bacon, D.D. This chapter, the 15th, is exceedingly interesting. I could not add one word to it. It was written by one who was his intimate friend, who knew him well, and whose ability to portray the great preacher, and present to us a vivid picture of the popular pulpit orator, is manifest on every page.

To me Dr. Kirk was a loving friend and faithful pastor. In my darkest experience, in the sickness nigh unto death that prostrated me, he stood by, full of purest sympathy, unfolding to me the words of Christ. For many seasons he was a frequent visitor at Hillside. On such occasions we often arranged his writing-desk on the piazza, that he might prepare his sermons amid the singing of birds and the odour of flowers, with the hills and woods in the distance.

He was a natural speaker, having little or no need of elocutionary training; still he had almost a passion for oratory and elocution. He often encouraged young men in their studies in that direction. The last time I ever saw him was when, at his invitation, I went to his house to hear a young man read. He sat in his chair, hardly able to distinguish objects in the room, and listened intently to the young man's reading, and then asked if I could not encourage him by giving him a favourable opinion of his powers.

When the young man had departed, he said, "Now, John, come near me, that I may see you better. How are you?

How is your soul's health? Is Jesus precious? Oh, as this world grows dim, and I strain my poor eyes to discover objects, how bright and glorious is the New Jerusalem, where the Lamb is the light thereof." He gave me his benediction, and I saw him no more, but his last words to me were very precious.

I spoke of his interest in elocution. I think his study of that art was a hindrance rather than a help; it modified his naturalness, and gave him what appeared a somewhat stilted manner, and diminished that "abandon" which was always such a power. In proportion as he followed closely the rules of oratory or elocution, did he fail in effectiveness;—at least, this was my opinion. I remember that, on more than one occasion, while listening with interest,—impressed perhaps more by the beauty of his diction, his grace of gesture, and studied intonations, than by the subject,—he would suddenly lift up his face, and in the forgetfulness of all rules would for a few minutes pour out his soul in pleading, or in rapt inspiration tell of the glories of Christ. Losing sight of himself he became absorbed in his theme. He appeared as God's messenger to dying men, and the full power of the truth took possession of every heart. His natural oratory seemed to me as much preferable to his studied elocution, as the natural waterfall is to the artificial cascade. But if this was a blemish, it was only one that was simply a foil to his marvellous excellences. He did a great work, and has gone home to his reward, with many stars in the crown of his rejoicing.

In 1856, I first met Rev. George H. Gould, D.D., and was fascinated by his preaching. He is emotional, with no sensationalism; he speaks with an earnestness that convinces you he believes all he utters, with a deep pathos revealing the tenderness of his own nature, an eloquence perfectly natural, a face radiant at times when he utters some lofty thought. He has no monotonous repetitions; there is nothing stale or conventional in his preaching. He reaches the intellect, the heart, and were it not for his health he would be one of the widely-known popular preachers of the day.

Rev. D. O. Mears, of Worcester, who is my home pastor, is a man who strikes right out boldly and fearlessly at sin in all its forms. Affectionate and genial in his nature, he is a stern rebuker of evil. He tells the truth with plainness; he is profitable to hear; he preaches as a man to men; he shows that Christianity is for the counting-house as well as for the prayer-meeting, for the week-day as well as for the Sabbath, for the world as well as for the church. He wrote the biography of Dr. E. N. Kirk, a work which has been very favourably received.

I could speak largely of the Rev. Wm. M. Taylor, D.D., of New York, but he is extensively known by his public ministrations, and by his published works, so that nothing remains but to give a few personal impressions. I have often timed my visit to New York, that I might spend the Sabbath there, and hear him preach. No man ever opened up the Scriptures to me as he does. By the emphasis of a word, he reveals to you the deep, true meaning of the passage. His sermons are adapted to the wants of humanity; the human soul craves sympathy, the human heart needs help and comfort and encouragement to be lifted, to be led upwards toward the divine. I have been tried and tempted, or troubled and oppressed, by unexpected cares; I am disappointed; I have been in darkness all the week; yet groping for light; I have human wants, desires, hopes, fears. I cry out for help, human help. I go to church. Of what value to me is a discourse on heroism, patriotism, the Jews, or the Catholics, at such a time? Merely husks to a hungry man. Whenever I go to the Tabernacle, I am helped and comforted. The prayer is from a human soul experienced in the trials and temptations of human life. I am led in the devotional exercises out of my own dreary thoughts to the throne of the heavenly grace, into the presence-chamber of the King, to talk with Him who is my surety, and thus I am in a measure prepared for the sermon, which is often a feast of fat things to my soul, in which there is a portion for every one in due season. As a friend who has counselled me wisely for years, and as a minister of Christ who has helped me so essentially in my Christian life and experience, I reverence and love him, and to me he is above all criticism. The remembrance of my indebtedness to him will never fade. His numerous published works are a valuable addition to any library.

Dr. Theodore L. Cuyler is an attractive preacher. I have known him for thirty-six years. In 1844 I first met him, at Princeton, when he was a theological student. I visited him in his first manse at Burlington, then many times in Trenton, afterwards in New York, when he was at the Market Street church, and since his settlement in the Lafayette Street church, Brooklyn. Though for years I have known him intimately, I have seldom heard him preach.

There are some ministers who commence their sermons in so striking a manner as to give promise of an intellectual and effective discourse. It is disappointing to find that in the first few sentences you have heard the best of the sermon—all there is of it worth remembering; for the preacher soon begins to drift out into a sea of platitudes, and the conclusion becomes so lame and impotent that the effect is discouraging and unprofitable. Others begin in a puny style, and reach the height of their discourse about midway, and then descend to the puny style of the beginning, reminding you of the

> "King of France with twenty thousand men
> Marched up the hill and then marched down again."

Dr. Cuyler secures the attention of the people at first, starting, perhaps, by a stirring illustration, or the relation of some fact or an allusion to some current event; but he holds his congregation to the end; and the conclusion only serves to impress on the heart and memory the truths he has uttered, and the peroration is often more striking than the exordium. I once heard him preach on Charity, when he began thus: "There was a mob at Jerusalem;" and after very graphically describing the martyrdom of Stephen, the dragging him out of the city, the stoning, until you almost saw the whole tragedy, he spoke of the bruised, broken body; and then most impressively said, "Hear him, 'Lord, lay not this sin to their charge.'

That's charity!" Then he gave a forcible exposition of the power and beauty of charity, riveting the attention of the audience to the last word of the discourse.

Dr. Cuyler is better known to me personally as a correspondent than as a preacher. I have read many of Horace Walpole's letters, all of Cowper's that are published, a large proportion of Charles Lamb's, but in my opinion, Dr. Cuyler's letters, of which I have a large package, are superior to them all. If selections from his correspondence with different individuals for the last thirty-five years were published, they would constitute one of the most readable books of the season. I often read passages from his letters to my friends, who always listen with delight. One I have nearly memorized by frequent perusal, written to me from his dismantled study in Trenton—the last letter he wrote in it; in which, calling up the precious memories connected with the place he was leaving for ever, he paints a charming picture of the faces of the dear friends who had been his guests, and with whom he had held sweet converse. From 1844 till now he has been my faithful friend, through evil as well as good report, in storm and sunshine, always loyal and true, and never failing in his fearless defence of the right. I hold him in my heart as a brother beloved.

CHAPTER XXIX.

OLD-TIME AND MODERN PREACHERS—WORDS WITH AND WITHOUT SENSE.

Sheridan Knowles—Varied Pulpit Ministrations—Old-time Discourses—Quaint old Books—Travesty on the Little Busy Bee—The Plagiarized Sermon—Sermon on the Slothful Man—"Awake Psaltery-tree and Harp"—"Who were the Patriarchs?"—Grandiloquent Oratory—Exordium upon Intemperance—"Wrecked on the Tempestuous Sea"—The Baneful Upas-tree—The Drunkard's Career on the Broad Road—Peroration—The Nobleman's Speech and Observations—Speech of an Agitator—"Bruce the King of England"—"Battles of Greasy and Potters"—"Pass round the Hat."

SHERIDAN KNOWLES has been described as "a shrewd, sharp-looking old gentleman, who takes a text but remotely connected with his discourse. You listen with great interest at first. The speaker is apparently very argumentative, and nods his head at the conclusion of each sentence in a most decided manner, as if to intimate very considerably the best of the argument. Now this is all very well for five minutes, or even ten; but lasting an hour—with no heads for you to remember—you naturally grow very weary. His sermons are bundles of little bits of arguments, tied up together as a heap of old sticks, and just as dry. He was but a very moderate preacher."

How faithful a portrait of some of the preachers at this day, let some of the sufferers testify. I have occasionally heard from pulpits a string of common-places and bald truisms with no application. I have heard sermons dry, without one word of help or comfort, without one particle of spiritual food to allay the heart-hunger, with no suggestive thoughts; barren of ideas, as a dead stick is barren of leaves; and I have felt if

I heard no preaching but that, my life would become a dull, dreary monotony, never rising above the plodding existence so utterly earthly. I have heard sermons from men entirely oblivious of grammar, who never studied the construction of a sentence, who were only learned in Bible lore, who had been taught in the school of Christ, that were as marrow to my soul; for it was a presentation of the simple gospel from one who had experienced the results of its application.

After all, no one can please everybody. Some require learning and polish, a classic finish, lofty, stately, majestic; others, again, fancy piquancy, pathos; others prefer solemnity, grandeur, splendour, clear and commanding, or fire, fervour, passion, unction; while others again require the deep, profound, massive, logical style.

I suppose in the old times those who had been in the habit of hearing their divines preach two, three, and four hours, would not be content with a sermon of twenty or thirty minutes. Bishop Hall, with the eighty heads to his discourse; Baxter, with his one hundred and twenty; Mr. Lyle, with his thirty particulars for fixing his theme on a right basis, and fifty-six more to illustrate it; and Mr. Drake, with one hundred and seventy parts to a sermon, in which he says he has passed over many very useful points, pitching only on those which comprehended the marrow and substance, were all popular preachers. And yet in these days they would preach to empty pews, and, as Dr. Beecher once said to a very sparse congregation, the church would appear "like a burnt district."

Many of those old divines were very quaint and witty, their sermons a treasury of good things; while there were some whose quaintness and oddity led them into absurdities. A list of the titles of books and tracts circulated in the time of Cromwell we should consider ridiculous. I give a brief selection :—

"A Most Sweet, Delectable, and Perfumed Nosegay for the Saints To Smell At."

"A Pair of Bellows to Blow off the Dirt cast on James Fry."

"The Snuffers of Divine Love."

"Hooks and Eyes for Believers' Breeches."

"High-heeled Shoes for Dwarfs in Holiness."

"Crumbs of Comfort for the Chickens of the Covenant."

"A Sigh of Sorrow for the Sinners of Zion, breathed out of a hole in an earthen vessel, known among men by the name of Samuel Fish."

With all this absurdity, the men who wrote these discourses possessed power, but we have occasionally the absurdity without the power. I would not ridicule any attempt of any man to do good who was at all qualified for his work; but those men who are utterly unqualified to become teachers of the people, and assume the responsibility of such a position, are fair subjects for criticism.

I remember going to church on one occasion, expecting to hear a celebrated preacher. To our great disappointment we were told that he was unable to be present, but that a minister who was in the town on a visit would preach. I shall never forget my sensations when this gentleman came into the pulpit. He was very tall, his hair brushed straight up from his forehead. He had a very long neck, rather red in colour; a pair of green spectacles with side glasses, and a boil on his nose. As he rose to his almost interminable length, we could hardly repress a smile. The text was, "For it is appointed unto men once to die." There was not a suggestion, nor a thought; no intellectual stimulus, but a dreary platitude, with no more connection of ideas than in the youth's essay on "Elocution." The boy was told not to be diffuse, but to lay down his proposition fairly, and come to the point at once. He delivered himself of this splendid effort: "Elocution is a good thing for boys: hence the immortality of the soul!" But this man was diffuse, without any points, as if he had taken for the basis of his remarks, "How doth the little busy bee improve the shining hour," etc., and treated it thus:—

"My friends, the subject under consideration is a bee. Not only is it a bee, but we are informed it is a *busy* bee. Not only is it a *busy* bee, but it is a *little* busy bee. Not only is it a little busy bee, but, my friends, it is a little busy bee that *doth*. Mark, it is a bee, not a swarm of bees, of which the poet writes. It is a *busy* bee, not a drone in the hive. It is a little busy bee, not a great bumble-bee that knocks his head against the window. Then the little busy bee *doth*. What doth it ? is an important question. First, it improves. What doth it improve—itself or some other person ? It improves an hour. What hour? A shining hour. What shining hour? moonshine, or sunshine, or starshine, or all hours ? It cannot be all, for we are informed it is a shining hour; singular, not plural. We must step a little in advance to settle the question. Ah, here it is: 'He gathers honey all the *day!*' Therefore it must be in the sunshine." And so on, to the end of the verse. And then: " Hence we perceive." I would as soon hear the boy's proposition and conclusion.

I once asked a minister who was rather celebrated for his poetry, how he could find time for so much rhyme, and prepare two sermons each week for his people. " Oh," he said, " my sermons don't trouble me; I just think of a text, and then I have my references, you know."

Once, after hearing a sermon, I asked some friends who were with me to listen while I read them some portions of a very interesting work. As I proceeded, some one said, " We heard that this morning ; " and we found the morning sermon was taken bodily from the work I was reading.

I heard a sermon from the text in Proverbs, " I went by the field of the slothful, and by the vineyard of the man void of understanding;" and we had twenty minutes of suppositions: " Solomon might have been riding in his chariot; he might have been going to Gilgal; he might have been in the company of his courtiers; he might have been taking his exercise; he might have been on horseback;" and so on, to an interminable and unprofitable extent.

A gentleman told me of a minister who boasted that he never studied, but was always *led*, who constantly quoted: " It shall be given you in that day what ye shall say." He never selected his text beforehand, but always took the first passage his eye rested on after he opened the Bible. On one occasion, when he opened the Book, his eye rested on the text: "Awake psaltery and harp!" And he pronounced the *p*, and added a couple of syllables to it, and read:—

"Awake pesaltery-tree and harp."

He had never heard of such a thing before, and hardly knew what to make of it; but there it was, and he put a brave face on it, and said:—

"Yes, my friends, it is a pesaltery-tree. This was a tree that growed in the region where David lived. It had branches and leaves and roots. I do not know whether it bore no fruit, but it was a pesaltery-tree. Now, the circumstances under which this 'ere text was writ was just this 'ere: David was very fond of laying in bed in the morning, which is a very bad practice, my friends. And one day he told his man to call him up at four o'clock in the morning, and he called him; and he got up, and it was a beautiful morning; and he opened the winder, and there was a pesaltery-tree a-growing outside; and he got out of that winder, and sat on one of the branches of that 'ere pesaltery-tree; and while he sat there, he told his man to bring him his harp; and when he got it he played, 'Awake pesaltery-tree and harp;' and that's the origin of this 'ere text." Then came a discourse on the advantages of getting up early in the morning.

I was introduced to a man who, when he preached and had no ideas, would shout and roar, and use his voice to the utmost extent of its power. Once he was at a great loss for ideas, and he shouted out with violent gestures: "There were the patriarchs; yes, the patriarchs, my friends. They were the patriarchs. Who were the patriarchs, I ask, who were they? Who were they—these patriarchs? Again I ask, who were they? Why, my friends, Jacob was one of them—Jacob was. Jacob was a patriarch—a patriarch,—and he had twelve sons; and every one of these 'ere sons was a boy, my friends!"

These may be very ridiculous specimens, and perhaps over-drawn. I did not originate them; I give them as they were related to me.

I here insert two specimens of oratory, one the grandiloquent, the other the effeminate.

I have a volume entitled, "Orations and Poetry on Moral and Religious Subjects," printed and published at Albany, with a portrait of the author, from which I make some extracts.

Here is the exordium to the oration on intemperance :—

"Man, ever since his fall in the garden of Eden, has been inspired with a spirit of deviation from righteousness, which often increases his misery. His imaginations are only evil continually,—laying structures of wretchedness and woe; and hewing out vessels that can hold no water. Such is his digression from the requirements of God, that he is a stranger to virtue, and lies buried in the open field of his pollution. But among all his wicked inventions, King Alcohol is the topmost stone."

Of the drunkard, the author says :—

"The strong man became palsied, and began to reel to and fro under the influence of the scourging waves. Their frail barks were now tossing on the tempestuous sea of life. At last their vessels sprung a leak, and foundered in liquid flames.

"This is the rock on which thousands split, and their frail barks plunge into the awful cataract of death. The losses by intemperance are almost supernumerary, and past the description of man. . . . The element in which he moves is poisoned by his noxious breath, and he spreads malignant contagion wheresoever he leaves his meandering vestige."

Of the liquor-seller, the author says :—

"Those dealers in alcohol will yet, for the love of gold, sell to their brethren the baneful Upas-tree, and keep up the stool-pigeons of mortal attraction, that they may destroy the unwary and feast on the purchase of their blood."

The drunkard's career is thus forcibly described :—

"The drunkard's career is on the broad road to ruin. The stream in which he first embarks may appear small, and but little dangerous; yet it empties into a boundless ocean, and conveys her votaries to the wailings of the second death! The intemperate are seldom reclaimed. Their condition is almost hopeless; for when they begin their voyage, they seldom cease, until they launch into the dark profundity obscure, from whence no traveller returns. Their consciences are seared with perfect inveteracy; they bid defiance to all men, although admonished with deepest commiseration and sensitive gratitude. They are governed by an enemy that knows of no condescension; who is fettering them stronger to that hold, which shall prove a baseless fabric, sinking beneath her builders, and leave them as fuel for that flame of wrath, which survives the dissolution of worlds, and is perpetuated by the vengeance of an angry Deity."

The peroration contains the following sentences:—

"Seed-time and harvest shall come and pass away. The hill and the valley shall smile with the luxuries of man. The cargoes of emporium shall float on the blue waves, and waft along the shores of the sublime highlands. The bells of minarets and bastions shall chime the midnight peal. The drunken revelries shall increase the history of death; and the baneful Upas-tree shall spread over all lands. The retreats of pollution, where King Alcohol waves his banner, shall swell the dirge of woe. The sound of the harp and viol shall chant the passions of youth; and the chandeliers of theatres, like terrestrial suns, shall deceive the unwary traveller. The card, and the throw of the dice, where souls are stamped for eternity, shall tell man's future history. The army of inebriates shall increase, ere they plunge the Jordan of death, to wait the resurrection fires and the direful woes of the final judgment. In all these scenes of pollution, man seems silent, as if at death he closed his eyes in eternal sleep. But suddenly the voice of the archangel splits the sapphire vault above, and comes trumping down the eternal avenue with a mighty clangour, such as the world never knew."

I give the reported speech of a nobleman who was requested to offer a toast at a dinner given for the benefit of a free hospital. He rose with the yearly report of the institution in his hand, and said:—

"Gentlemen! Ahem! I—I—I rise to say. That is—I wish to propose a toast. Gentlemen, I think that you'll all say—ahem! I think, at least, that this toast is, as you'll say, the toast of the evening—toast of the evening. Gentlemen, I belong to a good many of these things, and I say, gentlemen, that this hospital requires no patronage; at least, you don't want any recommendation. You've only got to be ill—got to be ill. Another thing, they are all locked up—I mean, they are shut up separate—that is, they've all got separate beds."

Then putting up his eye-glass, and looking at the paper, he continued:

"Now, gentlemen, I find by the report which I hold in my hand,—I find, gentlemen, that from the year seventeen—no, eighteen,—no—ah, yes—I'm right, eighteen hundred and fifty—no, it's a three—thirty-six—eighteen hundred and thirty-six—no less than one hundred and ninety-three millions—no—ah! eh! What?—oh yes!"

Some one whispered to him:

"Thank you, thank you! Yes! one hundred and ninety-three thousand two millions,—no—two hundred and ninety-three thousand two hundred and thirty-one. Gentlemen, I beg to propose 'Success to the Institution.'"

Some thirty years ago a speech was reported as delivered by an itinerating orator to a mob of rioters assembled in front of a gentleman's mansion in Warwickshire, England, where they had gathered for the purpose of committing violence and doing damage in the days of mob outrage and riot. I give it as a reported specimen, whether exaggerated or not I do not know :—

"Gents, partisans, and much-suffering hoperatives,—I would say to you what Julius Cæsar said to the Romans after he had stabbed Mark Antony in the cause of liberty at the siege of Troy—'Lend me your hears.' This same sacred cause of liberty has brought me 'ere, has brought you 'ere, has brought your wives 'ere, has brought your little uns 'ere. Let us do or die, as Robert Bruce the king of England said to Mary Queen of Scots, at the battle of Bannockburn. That battle was fought for liberty; and, gents, we 'ave a battle to fight too, against the 'eartless harristocracy. Gents, you are now on the right spot. The foe you 'ate is before you, as Tom Moore says in his 'Pleasures of 'ope.' Look at his proud castle frowning o'er—ahem—the deep —ahem—that is—I mean—frowning o'er us all. Within its walls is titled hinsolence, bloated vealth, and hoverbearing hextravagance. Gents, we must, we shall be 'eard. Our 'aughty tyrants shall bite the dust. They conquered us at 'Astings, when the Black Prince invaded Hengland at the Revolution, and brought in Norman hinsolence; but, gents, who have been the hassertors of Hengland's freedom but men of our class? Who was it forced King John and his runagate barons to give us *Magna Charta* but honest Jack Cade? Who was it shot a harrow at King Richard—the curdy lion—but Wat Tyler the blacksmith? Who fought under King Hedward the battles of Greasy and Potters but the cooks and scullions of Hengland? Who delivered our children and wives from Crook-backed Richard, who smothered 'elpless hinfancy in the Tower, but Mr. Henry Tudor, a gent from Wales—not much better than us? Who hindered the Pope from burning 'Enery the

Eighth and his six wives for bigamy, but Cardinal Volsey, a butcher? Who was Holliver Cromwell but a brewer, and did not he cut off King Charles's 'ead ven he had pulled him by the hears out of the royal hoak vere he vos a-hiding the *Magna Charta* from the people? Vos not Bacon a lord, and didn't he pick a gent's pocket? Vos not Shakspeare a poacher, and didn't he write sermons in stones? Vos not Burns an Irish ploughman, and didn't he write the 'Loves of the Hangels'? Gents, these are facts from the wollum of our country's 'istory. These show the degeneracy of the harristocracy. They may stand on a 'aughty helevation, and may cry in the words of 'Omer, the Greek poet, '*Hodi profanum wolgus et hareco*,' which means, 'The Common sort may go and be hanged;'—but we will hanswer them with a line found by Mr. Layard on the left paw of the winged lion, during his recent exhalations among the ruins of Nincom-something, in Abyssinia. This line is in the Chinese language, and runs thus, '*Wox populi wox Dei.*' It was written by King Belshazzar the night his palace was burned by Alexander the Great, when he was drunk. These words signify, 'Down with the Peerage, and hup with the people!' Men of Warwick, I have done. Never say die till the banners of Liberty, Confraternity, and Equality—cheap beef, bread for nothing, and beer for the asking, float over your 'appy 'omes and 'ouses. '*Wox populi, wox Dei!*' The hat will now go round for a collection."

CHAPTER XXX.

CHURCH SERVICE—IRREVERENCE, BUFFOONERY, AND CANT.

Ridiculous Side of Negro Preaching—Absurd Mistakes—The Plantation Preacher—"Glad Tidings and Hallelujah"—The Dirty Boy—Church Services—Singing in Mr. Spurgeon's Tabernacle; and in Dr. Parker's Church—The D.D.'s Stratagem—The Scotchman's Experience—"Don't sing, Sir"—Hymns of my Boyhood — Mutilated Hymns — Irreverence of Hymnology — Revivalists' Buffoonery—The Name above every Name—Christian Irreverence—Pious Cant—More Puritanism needed—The Christian Ideal and its Opposite—Possible Future Pulpit Notices.

A SERMON or a lecture may contain much that is absurd, and yet not be altogether unprofitable. Some of the negro preaching has a ridiculous side, while there are few persons who might not profit by the lessons taught. I heard a plantation preacher some years ago, who used the most extravagant expressions, and mispronounced and misplaced his words, forcibly reminding us of the negro, who said, when some one threw a brick at him while preaching, "Dat man what frowed dat brick is guilty ob an act ob moral turpentine;" or of another, who said of a little girl who had fallen down stairs and struck her head violently: "She getten on; de doctor has had her japanned!" A preacher has been reported in one of our religious papers as reading the line,

"God moves in a mysterious way,"

as,

"God moves in a mischievous way;"

and,

"Judge not the Lord by feeble saints,"

instead of "feeble sense." Not a very improper alteration.

But to the plantation preacher. He began by saying:—

"Bredren, I shall take two texes,— 'Glad tidings,' and 'Hallelujah!'" Soon he asked, "What is glad tidings, bredren? I'll tell ye what glad tidings am. Suppose dar was a king in a chariot, and six caliker hosses, like wat dey hab in the sukkus, a-prancing and a-tossing up dar heads, and de soldiers and ossifers marching by de side ob de chariot, and dar's a little boy standing on de corner ob de street as de percession goes by. Dish 'ere boy is ragged and dirty; his har sticking frough de holes in his cap; he ain't got no shoes,— nobody keers for dat boy; he ain't got no fader, no mudder, no aunty; and he's looking on to see de king, and de caliker hosses, and de ossifers, and de soldiers;—when de king he stops de chariot, and says to one ob dem ossifers, 'Bring dat boy to me!'

"'Dat boy's all dirt.'

"'Bring dat boy to me!'

"'But you'll ketch sumfin off dat boy.'

"Den de king got mad, and his *face lifted up on de top of his head like a coffee-pot lid*, and he hollered as loud as he could holler,—

"'Bring dat boy to me!'

"Den de ossifer bring dat boy, and de king say:—

"'Take dat boy and git him measured for some clothes, and get him a cap, and some shoes, and cut his har and wash him, put him in de barf, and den send him to de school like de white folks go.'

"Wall, all dis is done 'cording to de king, wat he tell de ossifer; and when dat boy was clean, and his har comb, and he got de eddification, den dat king come by again, wid de caliker hosses, and de soldiers and de ossifers, and he says, 'Where's dat boy?' and dey bring de boy, and nobody knowed him; but de king *he* knowd him, and say,—

"'My child, come up into de chariot. I 'dopt you; you is my heir.'

"Now, wouldn't dat be glad tidings to dat boy?"

Then came the application: God's love to sinners, cleaning

them, teaching them, and making them heirs of God, joint-heirs with Jesus Christ, by adoption. And when he came to the climax, he said,—

"Now, bredren, is de time for de second tex, 'Hallelujah;' and ye may jess shout much as ye're amind to."

With all the oddity of that discourse, I never heard a plainer exhibition of gospel truth, one better adapted to the comprehension of the hearers than this.

Discussing ministers leads naturally to church services. I venture my opinion. I prefer congregational singing to selected choirs, and especially to quartettes. This may be but a matter of taste, and some persons may say bad taste at that; but still to me there is something grand in the union of a thousand voices in a song of praise. At Mr. Spurgeon's Tabernacle, in London, there is neither choir nor organ; but the singing of six thousand persons is very impressive. At Dr. Parker's church, in the same city, there is a choir for occasional pieces, and to steady and lead the singing of the people. I think this is all right; but the people should be encouraged to sing as part of divine worship, in which they may profitably and delightfully partake. Dr. Chalmers, preaching in a fashionable church, once complained because no one in the congregation sang the praises of God except those who were paid for it.

A celebrated Scotch doctor of divinity was invited to preach where no singing was heard but by the choir. He gave out to be sung the Hundredth Psalm:—

> "All people that on earth do dwell,
> Sing to the Lord with cheerful voice;
> Him serve with mirth, His praise forth tell,
> Come ye before Him and rejoice."

To the doctor's surprise, nobody but the choir opened their lips, and when they had concluded the performance, he rose, and good-humouredly said: "The choir have done very well; let the congregation and me try it next." And so saying, he raised in fine style the solemn tune of "Old Hundred." The result was that before the first stanza was ended, the whole congregation had caught the enthusiasm of their leader, and sent up a very shout of praise to heaven in the appropriate words of the psalm; and they found it to be so heart-stirring an experience, when compared with their previous habits of being mere listeners, that they never afterwards abstained so generally from joining in the psalmody.

A Scotch gentleman, on a visit to England, thus gives his experience: "I was taken on Sunday by an English friend to one of the national churches. The first sounds that saluted my ears were the solemn peals and 'grave, sweet melody' of the organ. It is probable that at no distant period this instrument will be introduced into some of the Presbyterian churches in Scotland, where there is a growing taste for good music set in. The opposition to it surely cannot rest on scriptural grounds, so long as the Psalms of David form a part of the sacred volume. The singing in this place of worship was also very beautiful; and as I knew something of the tune that was first sung, I began to accompany the band, or choir, but had no sooner made my voice audible—which is not considered disagreeable in my own country—than the man who sat next me gave me a hard punch in the side with his elbow, accompanied by the command, 'Don't sing, sir;' and at the same time I was frowned upon by the portly, gowned seat-keeper, who happened to pass at the time, which I had no reason to doubt conveyed to me the same unreasonable rebuke. I thus understood that my business here was to be a listener, as in a theatre; and before the assembly was dismissed, a female, who I was informed is a performer in the opera-house, stood up alone, and sang a song to the admiring crowd."

When I was a boy, I learned a large number of hymns, so many that I could repeat them for hours. I suppose I had committed to memory three hundred hymns. They became to me old friends. When alone, I occasionally repeat them. They have often been my companions in the night-time, and I grieve to meet one of these hymns of my boyhood mutilated as I would to see an old friend scarred and deformed. To show how shamefully some of the precious hymns have been mutilated, and their beauty and almost their sense have been destroyed, I give specimens from three of my favourites.

> "Look how we grovel here below,
> Fond of these earthly toys;
> Our souls how heavily they go
> To reach eternal joys,"

has been mutilated thus:—

> "Our souls *can neither fly nor go*
> To reach eternal joys."

The person who changed that must have been grovelling here below.

Another specimen is in that fine old hymn—

> "My God! the spring of all my joys."

The second verse, as I learned it, and as my mother sang it, was:—

> "In darkest shades, if *Thou* appear,
> My dawning is begun;
> *Thou art* my soul's bright morning star,
> And *Thou* my rising sun."

Some irreverent meddler has changed this to—

> "In darkest shades, if *He* appear,
> My dawning is begun;
> *He* is my soul's *sweet* morning star,
> And *He* my rising sun."

Who ever heard of a sweet star, any more than of a sweet cataract, or the sweet sun! To me it is lackadaisical.

That beautiful hymn—

> "Jesus, and shall it ever be,
> A mortal man ashamed of Thee;
> Ashamed of Thee, whom angels praise,
> Whose glory shines through endless days?"—

is outrageously mutilated; the grandeur and beauty utterly destroyed in the first verse. Think of this and weep:—

> "Jesus, and shall it ever be,
> A mortal man ashamed of Thee?
> *Scorned be the thought by rich and poor,*
> *Oh, may I scorn it more and more!*"

Here I fail in utterance when I would express my contempt for such a change. I cannot do justice to the subject. Why will not these hymn-tinkers practise on something less sacred and precious than the old-time noble hymns?

Another objection to a certain style of hymnology is its irreverence,—the sacred name of Jesus so flippantly used, with absurd repetition of that name, to meet the requirements of some jingling rhyme.

> "I am so glad that Jesus loves me, Jesus loves me, Jesus loves me;
> I am so glad that Jesus loves me, loves me,"—

is a specimen. I express my own opinion, contrary perhaps to the opinion of others. But I believe the singing of such doggerel, in which the Saviour's name is introduced in useless repetition, tends to foster an irreverence which is unbecoming. Then the pointless repetition,—

> "Come to Jesus, come to Jesus, come to Jesus
> Just now. Just now come to Jesus;
> Come to Jesus just now."

I heard from good authority that a certain revivalist, at the commencement of a series of meetings, proposed that while some of the brethren retired for some consultation, he would interest the people by singing, and he commenced singing this doggerel. The conference was longer than he expected; and, growing weary of the singing, he called out to the friends in the vestry,—

"Hurry up, hurry up, brethren; I can't keep the people coming to Jesus all night!"

I protest against such irreverence.

Who is this of whom he speaks so flippantly? Read the description of Him:—

"His eyes were as a flame of fire, and on His head were

many crowns, and He had a name written that no man knew but He Himself, and He was clothed with a vesture dipped in blood, and His name is called the Word of God." Again: "He hath on His vesture and on His thigh a name written, King of kings, and Lord of lords," "His name shall be called Wonderful, Counsellor, the mighty God, the everlasting Father, the Prince of Peace;" and He is "the mystery of Godliness, God manifest in the flesh." "At the name of Jesus every knee shall bow, and every tongue confess Him to be Lord, to the glory of God the Father."

And this is He whose name is introduced into doggerel, and sung to a jingling tune. I prefer Wesley's hymn:

> " Jesus, the name high over all,
> In hell, or earth, or sky ;
> Angels and men before it fall,
> And devils fear and fly."

I have been told that we should recognise the humanity of Christ, that He is our elder Brother. Most fully do I accept Him in His humanity as my sympathizing Saviour and friend, who was tempted as I am. He was all this to His disciples, who lived and walked with Him; but they called Him "Rabbi," "Master," " Lord." At the last feast He said to His disciples: " Ye call me Master and Lord, and ye say well, for so I am ; " and this when He had just washed their feet. The disciple whom Jesus loved, while lying on His breast on that memorable occasion, in all the intimacy of personal friendship, called Him "Lord." I cannot but consider the flippant manner in which some use His sacred name to be irreverent.

Then there is a religious phraseology that amounts to cant. When I receive a letter saluting me as "My fellow-sinner," I always expect four pages of cant, introducing "The Lord " as if the writer were familiarly acquainted with Him. I could give you many specimens of this religious gush, but I forbear. A gentleman who "dear-brothered " me, and talked about the Lord in a whining tone till I was weary, told me he had not committed sin for six months. I told him I did not believe it, when he became quite angry, and I thought came very near sinning in his expressions of wrath.

While I am not inclined particularly to what is called Puritanism, I have an idea that if we had a little more of the spirit and practice of Puritan times, the churches would be stronger and more successful in their warfare on sin. We can hardly attack that with which we fraternize. I wish neither to be critical, nor to set up my judgment in reference to the laxity of church discipline, but I fear we are spending more time in discussing what we may or may not do, than in considering what we ought to do; how far we may conform to the customs and amusements of the world without violating our covenant vows, or how much we may compromise with the world and hold our position in the church.

Jesus Christ said to His disciples, "I have chosen you out of the world." We seem to be ignoring that; and I ask, what amusement or pursuit is there followed by the unbeliever that is not followed or defended by some Christians? Cards, dancing, theatres, operas, wine and liquor drinking, gambling, all these are patronized and defended by some who are members of Christ's body—the Church. I have witnessed the solemn service of admitting new members into the Church, and heard those received assent to the doctrines and covenant, in which act they promised to follow the Lord Christ; and I have sometimes imagined them at the theatre, at the card-table, or in the ball-room, notwithstanding their solemn vows in this impressive service; and the idea seemed so inconsistent as to become revolting.

Perhaps we are becoming more liberal and less scriptural; but I own it would be a strange thing to hear from among the pulpit notices one read like the following:—

"There will be a prayer-meeting next Wednesday evening, at half-past seven, to last an hour, after which there will be a social dance in the church parlours.

"The Whist Club will meet at Brother White's. Wine, spirits, and cigars will be furnished. Only whist, euchre, and seven-up will be permitted: for we must draw a line somewhere.

"On Saturday afternoon, the Dramatic Society of the Sunday school will rehearse, previous to giving a public exhibition. The play will be the '*School for Scandal*,' revised by the superintendent.

"We propose omitting our usual Thursday lecture, as the opera company from New York will give a grand performance, and the members of our choir are engaged for the chorus at the theatre on that evening.

"Our usual monthly lottery for the Sabbath-school library will be drawn at eight o'clock on Tuesday evening. All are invited to attend.

"A fair will be held on the 15th inst., in our church parlours, to raise funds for a new billiard-table in the gymnasium of the church. There will be several attractions: raffling for some very elegant articles; also the grab-bag particularly provided for the children. We hope to see a large attendance. We will now resume our service by singing,

"'Far from my thoughts, vain world, begone.'"

This may be an awful exaggeration of what might be. Very well; let it be so. I give a verbatim bill of the performances for the organ fund of a Congregational church in England. It is prefaced by a letter to the editor of the *Fountain*, from which I copy it. The letter is as follows:—

"Sir,—I send you a copy of a programme of an entertainment for the organ fund of a Congregational church, in the north of England.

"I do not know how you may look upon it; but I, in common with several friends, regard it as a very questionable way of raising money for the support of a Christian Church.

"The distinction that ought to exist betwixt the Church and the world is entirely ignored, and for the time being the maxims and policy of the world reign supreme.

"The true Church possesses the only remedy for the woes and sorrows of sin-stricken humanity; but this remedy will not be found in entertainments more suitable for a low music saloon than for a Christian church.

"Hoping you will use your pen in reproving the evil, and show church-members and ministers their true work and mission in the world, I am, yours respectfully, ———— ————."

"CONGREGATIONAL CHURCH.

"The public are respectfully informed that there will be held in the Town Hall, a Sale of Work, Wax Work, Entertainment, Promenade Concert, High Art Exhibition, and 'Trial by Jury.' Admission: To Sale of Work, 6d.; to Wax Work, 6d."

"GRAND WAX-WORK EXHIBITION.

"Under the distinguished patronage of General Holiday, General Laughter, General Uproar, and the General Public, will be exhibited the most marvellous collection of Living Wax Works in the world never shown out of London, in the preparing of which every expense has been spared.

"The whole figures are too innumerable to mention, but the following —wind and weather permitting—will be some of the first to arrive:

"The Prince and Princess of Wales (in native costume), from a photo by Blackhead, taken in Mary Land.

"Mary, Queen of Cullercoats, singing 'Buy my Caller Herring.'

"Professor Edison, the inventor of the electric light, discoverer of the Edison Lighthouse, and other edifying animals; with brilliant examples of the light.

"The pale-faced author of Cockle's pills.

"Mrs. Allan (the anti-fat one), not the hair-restorer.

"Signor Frioline (English 'Bill Fry'), or man-fish, recently sold at Tynemouth Aquarium; together with the kitchen-utensils and season-ticket holders, kindly lent by a defunct director for this night only.

"Girl of the period.

"Geordie, in full evening dress.

"Guy Fawkes (not of gunpowder renown).

"A jubilee singer (composer of 'My Grandfather's Clock').

"John Pitch, alias Jack Tar, doing a real iron-clad break-down hornpipe, with tobacco accompaniment.

"Widows of the late Brigham Young.

"The Japanese juggler, or jumping Jesuit of the jointless jungle.

"Doctor Spruce, author of 'Notions of Motions of the Oceans,' 'Durham Gas Pipes,' etc., etc.

"Little Zulus, in birthday suits.

"Dick Whittington and his cat, with a catalogue of their catastrophes, and an account of the mice she catched. Lewis Paine, the spiritualistic murderer, and the painful results arising therefrom.

"A father's blessing, one penny. A mother's warning, tuppence.

"*Notice*.—This marvellous exhibition, bear in mind, will not parade the town each day at one o'clock, headed by a cracked brass band, but will discourse sweet music from a really playful organ-man during the entertainment.

"Telescopes, opera-glasses, weather-glasses, wine-glasses, and spectacle-cases, on hire, by application at the door.

"*Admission.*—Tickets to be obtained at post-office, police-office, register-office, telegraph-office, or by payment at the door, especially the latter. Reserved seats (which persons are requested to bring with them), 1s. Second seats, 6d. Gallery free. Cabs (Brown's, or any other man's), wheelbarrows, perambulators, milk carts, to be ordered at 11.60 P.M.

"*Trains.*—The local trains will be run as usual, and the railway station ought to be thoroughly cleaned for the occasion. Jokes not seen during the entertainment will be explained at 6 A.M. next evening.

"The highly instructive explanations of the figures will be given by Professor Talkey, of Torkee (Torquay)."

CHAPTER XXXI.

MY VIEWS ON THE TEMPERANCE QUESTION.

Drunkenness a Sin and a Disease—Is Moderate Drinking a Sin?—My First Intoxication—Rum and Water in a Temperance Meeting—"Gentlemanly Inebriation"—The Intoxicated Boy—Pathology of Drunkenness—Testimony of Dr. Richardson—Destructive Effects of Alcohol on the Mind—Statement of Joseph Cook—Legend of the Triple Choice—The Sin is in the Cause, and not the Effect—Statements of Wm. Arnot, D.D.—Two Ways of keeping a Nation sober—Total-Abstinence as an Unfailing Remedy—Prevention better than Cure—The Giant's Hand—Drunkenness unnatural—Testimony of Distinguished Physicians—Case of the Hon. E. C. Hannegan—His former Useful Life—The Terrible Fall and Dissipation—The Murder.

OWING to some misapprehensions as to my position in the temperance work, it becomes my duty to record somewhat fully my opinions and define my position in reference to the temperance question. I may differ widely from some with whom I am glad to work; but my views are my own. Certain conclusions, after thirty-seven years' experience, have been forced upon me. I shall not be dogmatical, or profess infallibility; but I shall express my views, opinions, and sentiments so that there can be no doubt where I stand.

I consider drunkenness a sin, but I consider it also a disease. It is a physical as well as a moral evil. Sin is defined by Webster as "Transgression of the law of God; disobedience to the Divine command; any violation of God's will, either in purpose or conduct; moral deficiency in the character; iniquity." Webster defines drunkenness as "The state of being drunken, or overpowered by alcoholic liquor: intoxication; inebriety." Taking these definitions as correct, I ask, When is drunkenness a sin? I speak of an actual sin, which is "the act of a moral agent in violating a known rule of duty, and to depart voluntarily from the path of duty prescribed by God to men; to violate the divine law, in any particular, by actual transgression."

We will suppose a case. You are a Christian moderate drinker. You scout the idea of moderate drinking being a sin. To take one, two, or three glasses of wine a sin? No, certainly not! You sustain your practice by holy Scripture; and I will agree, if you wish, that you do it conscientiously, and that you can ask God's blessing on the wine. You have it daily on the table. The minister of the church to which you belong countenances its use. You have a son who has never tasted wine during his childhood. He is now fourteen or fifteen years of age, and you give him the wine. He becomes drunk, viz., "overcome by drinking, intoxicated, inebriated." Does he commit sin? "Certainly not," you say; "he did not know what its effect would be, nor did I!" Very well; then it is a physical inability to drink without inebriety. The first time I was intoxicated I drank with others; I had no more idea of doing wrong in that act of drinking than in eating bread. I did as others did. It went to my head. I was inebriated.

In the early days of my work, I was holding a series of meetings in a village in New England. It was my custom then to speak for an hour or more, then sing temperance songs, and invite signers to the pledge. I used often to become excited. One evening I was very warm in the crowded room, and became thirsty. There was neither glass nor pitcher in the desk, and I asked, "Would some one be kind enough to procure some water?" After waiting some minutes, a full pitcher was handed me. There being no glass, I hastily lifted the pitcher to my lips, and detected the odour of alcohol, and found it was a mixture of rum and water, and not very weak. Suppose in my excitement I had failed to detect the smell of the spirit, and not dreaming of such a cowardly trick, had drunk the mixture and become inebriated? There would be no sin in the drinking; but if I had detected and wilfully drunk it, knowing the results, the act of drinking would have been a sinful one.

You say, "A man who cannot drink moderately should let it alone." Granted; but how will he know that he cannot drink without inebriety, unless he experiments; and in the experiment, if he becomes intoxicated, does he commit sin? "No," you say. "But to get drunk is a sin." Now, I believe that when a man knows that the use of intoxicating liquors, or any other thing, is detrimental to his health, injurious to him in body or mind, hinders him in his useful labour, or is hurtful to him in any other way, and will, solely for his sensuous gratification, use it, then he commits sin.

The difficulty may be, that your son, if he is of the nervous, susceptible temperament, may be so fascinated by the exhilaration and temporary exaltation, that when the remembrance of the pain and reaction has faded, the recollection of the enjoyment becomes more vivid, and he determines with caution to obtain again the pleasure, without making a "fool of himself by getting drunk." So he tries it again, and for the fleeting enjoyment he runs an awful risk, the risk being in proportion to the fascination of what is often termed "gentlemanly inebriation;" for every time he indulges, he loses power to resist, and therefore becomes ensnared.

A gentleman at my house told me that when he was ten years old, a young lady, out of fun, gave him some diluted whiskey, and enticed him to drink it. He drank, and became intoxicated. Said he: "I shall never forget coming out of that stupid sleep; I felt awfully. That is fifty-two years ago, and nothing could tempt me to touch a drop in all these years." A very wise decision. Did that boy commit sin?

A dyspeptic who knows that a certain article of food is injurious, and who will for the sake of gratifying the desire for that article of food, partake of it, commits sin. The sin is not in the dyspepsia, but in the wilful aggravation of the disease by self-indulgence.

Perhaps this is what is termed splitting hairs, but our opponents are constantly endeavouring to puzzle us by hair-splitting. Rheumatism is not a sin, but if I wilfully expose myself for my own gratification, when the suffering comes I must or ought to bear it patiently, as a penalty for violated law.

Do you compare drunkenness with dyspepsia or rheumatism? I make no comparisons. If you mean the simple act of drunkenness in endeavouring to ascertain whether you can drink with impunity, or the wilful perpetuation of dyspepsia or rheumatism by self-gratification, I should say that the least sin was in the simple act of inebriety; but if you ask whether habitual drunkenness is to be compared with these other evils, I say, a thousand times, that habitual drinking, with the knowledge that drunkenness will ensue, is a tenfold greater sin than any habit or act that brings on these other diseases. I say that the voluntary drinking is the sin, drunkenness is the result of the act; the cause of it is the drinking.

Let no one suppose for a moment that I would palliate the evil of drunkenness—occasional or habitual; but while we condemn the effect, let us condemn also the cause. The whole civilized world is groaning under the awful results of intemperance in the use of intoxicating liquors; a large proportion of the crime, lunacy, suicides, pauperism, being caused by it. Look at its effects on the victim! "Wilson's Pathology of Drunkenness" is a most vivid and fearful revelation of the progress from conviviality to casual and habitual intoxication, and the constitutional and mental results. He tells us that disturbance of the circulation, disorder of the functions of digestion, disease of the liver, of the kidneys, of the lungs, tubercular degeneration, *mania a potu*, hiccough, an acute progress of decay, brain-disease, and apoplexy, are some of the constitutional results; and "loss or confusion of memory, mental aberration, delirium, lunacy, and suicide are some of the mental results. The springs of life are tainted at their source, and their currents diffusing themselves everywhere through the system, the one as the basis of vitality, the other as the origin of its leading phenomena, leave the traces of their altered qualities everywhere apparent."

Dr. Richardson says:—

"If I were to take you through all the passions that remain to be named,—love and lust, hate and envy, avarice and pride,—I should but show you that alcohol ministers to them all; that, paralyzing the reason, it takes from all these passions that fine adjustment of reason which not only places man above the lower animals, but, when celestially attuned, places him little lower than the angels.

"The demonstrative evidence of alcohol in its influence on the mind is then most clear.

"From the beginning to the end of its influence it subdues reason and sets free passion. The analogies, physical and mental, are perfect. That which loosens the tension of the vessels which feed the body with due order of precision, and thereby lets loose the heart to violent excess of unbridled motion, loosens also the reason, and lets loose the passions. In both instances heart and head are for a time out of harmony, their balance broken. The man descends closer and closer to the lower animals. From the angels he glides further and further away.

"The destructive effects of alcohol on the human mind present, finally, the saddest picture of its influence. The most æsthetic artist can find no angel here. All is animal, and animal of the worst type. Memory irretrievably lost, words and very elements of speech forgotten, or words displaced to have no meaning in them. Rage and anger, persistent and mischievous, or remittent and impotent. Fear at every corner of life, distrust on every side, grief merged into blank despair, hopelessness into permanent melancholy. Surely no Pandemonium that ever poet dreamt of could equal that which would exist if all the drunkards of the world were driven into one mortal sphere."

Joseph Cook says:—

"Harden the brain by drenching it with alcohol, and you harden the moral motive; and whatever disorganizes brain disorganizes character."

Every one of the thousands of victims who are, we fear, descending to the drunkard's grave, began with the first glass, and the whole evil is caused by drinking intoxicating liquor. It is an awful sin above all others. It is the promoter of all that is evil, of all that is vile and abominable. It solidifies and crystallizes, and makes chronic, every evil passion of depraved human nature.

I have read somewhere an old legend, in which a man was offered his choice of three voluntary acts: to murder his father, burn down his house, or get drunk. Laughingly he chose the latter, as that could not be very harmful. He got drunk. While in that state he became furious. Enraged at his father's attempt to control him, he struck him a blow with a hammer that lay near, and killed him; then, filled with horror at the deed, he set fire to the house, thus to destroy the body and hide his crime.

Drunkenness is a sin unlike others, in that it carries its penalty with it in the suffering and enslavement of its victim. It is but the penalty for violated law; the sin is not in the penalty, but in the violation of law. Now, is there no wrong in drinking, unless it produces what we call drunkenness or intoxication? If you mean by drunkenness a persistent use of alcoholic beverages, knowing all the consequences, then it is always and ever sin against the body, the mind, the soul, and society, and a grievous sin against God. But is there no sin in the intoxication that consists in mere exhilaration, elevation, or excitement; or even the slight confusion of thought, without staggering or stammering? If the brain is disturbed in its action and the power of the will weakened, or if the self-control is affected, the perception stimulated while its accuracy is destroyed; if the judgment is perverted, if the drinker will go where he would not go without it, say what he would not say without it, think as he would not think, and do as he would not do without it; though his utterance may not be thick, his eye may be clear, his gait steady, and no outward appearance giving evidence,—is he not in some degree tipsy, inebriated, drunk?

Can a man steal a little, lie a little, swear a little, and be innocent? Are there any degrees by which you may measure the enormity or the veniality of these practices? Is it a trifling thing to be tipsy, and a serious thing to get drunk? Where does the sin commence? I confess I am puzzled to get any reply to these questions. But what does it all amount to? Just this: I desire to fasten the sin where it belongs—*on the cause*, not the effect.

As I have stated on another page, the Rev. Wm. Arnot, at

my request, gave me his opinions on the liquor traffic, and I quote again from his manuscript :—

"There are two possible ways of making and keeping a nation sober. The result might be attained by the people voluntarily abjuring the use of intoxicating liquor, or by the legislature authoritatively prohibiting its manufacture and sale. The one is the principle of abstinence societies; the other is the principle of what is called the Maine Law. Under the one method, if fully carried out, there would be no drinkers; and under the other, there would be no drink. Either operation, if complete, would effect a cure. If one instrument were thoroughly driven home, both would not be required.

"If a choice were offered, we would prefer the former. We would rather see the blot of drunkenness wiped off by the spontaneous self-denial of the people than by an application of the ruler's power. This would indicate a better moral condition of the community, and the exertion would react to increase the moral power that produced it. But in the present ruined and imperfect state of human affairs, it would be foolish to refuse a portion of the coarser material, when the supply of the finer article falls short. We are glad, on all accounts, to take in the first instance as much of voluntary abstinence as we can get; but after all that this best method has yet done, or is likely to do, the Demon Vice possesses still a great multitude of the people, and deprives them of their right mind. For these circumstances, when we cannot get him cast out by the power of a people's virtuous will, we own we should be heartily glad to see him driven out by the strong arm of the law.

"We have no desire to see a prohibitory law suddenly enacted before the people are prepared to support it. We do not desire to go before public opinion; but we do desire to urge public opinion forward. People need not be afraid of a prohibitory law being enacted over the heads of a remonstrant community. Such a law will not be passed by the legislature until the majority of the community desire it, and a good while after that. But whatever may be the prospect of an entirely prohibitory law being desired by the people of this country and enacted by Parliament, there are various degrees of partial limitation possible and desirable in the meantime. It is the part of practical wisdom to look to these. A greater number of persons may be induced to unite in obtaining them, and they will diminish the evil which they cannot eradicate. There may be limitations in the kinds of drink, in the number of sellers, in the duties imposed, in the price of license, in the terms of conducting the traffic. It is the duty of all good citizens, if they cannot knock the wild beast on the head, to join in the effort to give him a short and aye a shorter tether.

"A great boon in this direction has been obtained for Scotland in the recently enacted law for the regulation of public-houses. The measure deserves not absolute, but comparative praise. The thankfulness with which we receive it is caused less by its own inherent qualities than by the enormities which it supersedes. It is the exceeding badness of the former state of things that makes the present appear so good. Our rejoicing under the Public-House Act is like the rejoicing wherewith the inhabitants of a Turkish province learn the appointment of a new pasha who will only strip them of their treasures, and the dismissal of the old one who skinned them alive. A very execrable tyrant was that pasha who sat astride of the Scottish people to regulate the spirit traffic, previous to the 15th of May last.* Practically there seemed to be no limit to the number of public-houses. Every man got a license who wanted it, every proprietor who thought his shop would let better for the sale of whiskey than for doing other business, contrived to get a friendly justice to attend to his interests on licensing-day. At every corner the spiders spread their webs, and the community had no voice and no redress, any more than if they had been so many blue-bottles."

I quote these words as the expression of my own opinion in reference to the remedy for the terrible evil of drunkenness. I shall first propound my views on total abstinence as a certain, effectual cure. It never fails; it cannot fail. It stops the supplies, and the evil must cease; it dries up the spring, and there can be no stream.

Prevention is better than cure. It is worth a life-effort to save a drunkard, to lift a man from degradation. It is worth some self-sacrifice to free a man from moral slavery and debasement; but to prevent his fall is far better. We may reform a man from drunkenness, but I believe no man can ever fully recover from the effects of years of dissipation and intemperance. You put your hand in that of a giant, and he crushes it. You shriek in your agony, and after long struggling, with a desperate effort you extricate your hand from that fearful grip; it is torn, crushed, mangled, and bleeding. That hand may at last be healed; but it will be mutilated as long as you live. It may become a useful hand, but its beauty and symmetry is gone for ever. So a man may be cured of drunkenness; but the marks are on him, and will be to the day of his death. You cannot take the stain from snow, nor restore the bloom when once rubbed from the fruit; no more

* This refers to the Sunday-closing Act of Scotland.

can you remove from the man the marks and stains produced by long-continued habits of self-indulgence and intemperance; but we can save the children.

No child was ever born with a natural appetite for intoxicating drink, any more than with an appetite for tobacco; except, perhaps, in those cases where the sins of the fathers are visited on the children, and the child or grandchild of the drunkard seems to possess a natural appetite for drink. I shall allude to this more fully on a future page. If he ever wants it, it is because he has used it. The use of it produces the desire for it. We have hundreds of lifetime abstainers who have never tasted it, and they have never wanted it.

I believe that no reputable physician of common sense will admit that alcoholic stimulants are necessary in health, but, on the contrary, will declare them to be positively injurious. Dr. Richardson, Sir Henry Thompson, Sir Wm. Gull, Dr. Edmunds, Dr. Norman Ker, and scores of the best physicians in Great Britain, and many in our own country, have publicly testified by their words and their writings that alcoholic drinks are never necessary in health; so that total abstinence is the safe, sure, and absolute preventive for every child who adopts it. So my theory is, "*Prevention is better than cure.*" This act of abstinence is perfectly easy for the child who has never tasted, comparatively easy for the moderate drinker, and positively hard for the excessive drinker.

There are many men who cannot drink intoxicating liquor in moderation; if they drink at all, they become crazed by the first glass, and rush into excess. I give one case. The facts as to the killing of his brother-in-law by the Hon. E. C. Hannegan were widely known at the time, many years since. Mr. Hannegan had been a member of the legislature, both houses of Congress, ambassador to Prussia. John Wentworth, of Chicago, who served with him in Congress, thus commented on his case in the "Chicago Democrat":—

"Every man who has seen Mr. Hannegan when under the influence of liquor, as we have, can believe the above (viz., the statement of the homicide); and every one who has seen him and lived at the same house with him and his family, as we have, when he was a total-abstinence man for months together, will indeed pity him.

"When sober, he is as pure, as upright, as kind, and as generous a man as there is in this country. With him there can be no middle state. He is a brute when drunk; when sober, he will compare in all the elements of goodness with any man living. But he cannot drink without getting drunk. Mr. Hannegan entered the Lower House of Congress many years ago, a perfectly temperate man, and in point of talents, integrity, and popularity, his prospects were as flattering as those of any young man in the United States; but Washington habits and fashions were too much for him.

"Dissipation drove him to private life. He reformed, became a temperance lecturer and an exemplary member of the church. His exhortations in times of great revivals are said to have equalled those of the most eloquent divines living. At length his old habits were forgotten, and he was sent to the Senate. He took his seat an exemplary 'Son of Temperance' and a Christian; but again the temptations were too great for him. His struggles with himself were gigantic, and the assistance of one of Nature's noblest of women, his wife, secured for him the sympathy of everybody. But he would have his sprees, and he lost his re-election. Like most politicians, he left office miserably poor. At the close of his term and of Mr. Polk's administration, to keep so popular and so good a man from despair and ruin, the senators unanimously—Whigs and Democrats—signed a call for Mr. Polk to send him to Prussia, and he was appointed to that mission. His unfortunate career there is well known. Since his return we have heard nothing of him until this melancholy affair.

"We have seen many a young man enter Congress perfectly temperate, and leave it totally ruined; but we never knew one who had so many efforts to save him, so ineffectually, as Mr. Hannegan. We now have in our mind three, in our own term, who killed themselves. Mr. Hannegan has tried to do so several times; but he lived to kill his wife's brother, the best friend, save his wife, he had in the world. That he wishes he was in poor Duncan's place, we have no doubt. What an awful comment, this, upon the evils of intemperance! It was the first drop that ruined Hannegan. He is now about the middle age of man, and may yet live to be a very useful man; but there is greater probability that he will commit suicide."

CHAPTER XXXII.

TEMPERANCE AND "THE GRACE OF GOD"—MY OWN EXPERIENCE AND THAT OF OTHERS.

Is Reform possible without Religion?—Grounds of Appeal—Total Abstinence does not renew Nature—My First Pledge without the "Help of God"—The Memory of the Garret Bedroom—My Second Pledge under the Grace of God—Does the Grace of God take away the Appetite?—Poison Kills the Christian and the Hottentot—The Grace of God includes Voluntary Total Abstinence—Is the Drunkard's Appetite left?—My Disgust at the Drink no Proof that Appetite is gone—Communion Wine; its Effect—Wines in Cooking—Religion removes the Desire, but not the Appetite—Self-deception on this Point—Thrilling Letter of a Clergyman—The Converted Rum-seller's Experience—The Fallen Minister—The only Safety is in Total Abstinence—"The Pledge and the Cross."

CAN a man, who is a drunkard, abstain without the special grace of God, or, in other words, without being a Christian? Can he break his chains, when he has been fettered for years, by the power of his own will? In answer to this, I will say, that I would never admit to a man that he could not stop drinking unless he became a Christian; that is, as we understand it, received the new birth—became converted, according to the scriptural interpretation of that term.

He may be a sceptic, an unbeliever, a man who rejects the gospel, who has no faith in prayer. Can I tell him that he must continue a drunkard unless he becomes a believer? Love of the drink may be, as it often is, the hindrance to his belief. If my appeal to him to give up the drink on the ground of its being a sin against God, produces no effect, may I not urge the personal advantage in the restoration to society? May I not plead with him to give it up for his own prosperity, comfort,

MEMORIES OF THE GARRET BEDROOM.

and respectability, and tell him he can abstain if he will? Suppose he will give up no other sin,—that he will profane the Sabbath, take the name of God in vain, just as he is doing now,—is it not right and expedient for him to give up that one sin, even if he purposes to give up no other? While I believe that drunkenness hinders more men from coming to Christ, from hearing and accepting the gospel, than any other agency, am I not doing a good work as far as it goes?

Total abstinence from drink, or abstinence from theft, or lying, or profane swearing, will not open for him the kingdom of heaven; nothing but the power of the grace of God can renew him in his nature.

When I signed the pledge, I was an unbeliever. The appeal to me was on the ground of personal advantage: "How should you like to be respectable, esteemed," etc. The nearest approach to anything of a religious nature in the appeal was in the question, "How should you like to be well dressed, and go to church?" In the speech I made, on affixing my name to the pledge, I said, "I am resolved to free myself from the tyrant Rum." There was not a thought of God; my motive in that act and declaration was a mere selfish one. In all my struggle I never uttered a prayer. I had not prayed for years. I said during the struggle, "Oh, my God! I shall die;" and after Jesse Goodrich had encouraged me, I said, "By God's help, I will keep up a brave heart." Yet I had no thought of asking God's help. I heedlessly used a term.

I fought that battle alone for six days, and though nearly thirty-eight years have passed away, that garret bedroom, my bed, my broken trunk, the window in the roof, the little strip of carpet, the water-jug, my shabby clothing as it lay on the one chair in the room,—are so vividly present before me, that, were I an artist, I could reproduce the scene in all its detail on the canvas. When I had obtained the victory, there was no thought of thankfulness to God; it was a sensation of pride in the consciousness of the power of my will; and I often boasted that no human being helped or encouraged me in that struggle, with the sole exception of Jesse Goodrich. Do I undervalue the grace of God in all this? No; I simply wish to state that a man may abstain, if he will.

To return to my own case. I continued for five months an abstainer from drink. I entered the field as a lecturer, self-reliant and boastful. Then I fell, covered with shame and mortification. After a week's absence, I returned from Boston to Worcester, where I was living, and re-signed the pledge, giving up all expectation of any more public advocacy. I have related all this at length in my autobiography.

It was after that lapse that I cried out, "Oh, my Father! may Thy hand support me, and my prayer ever be, 'Hold Thou me up, and I shall be safe.'" Yes, thus I would tell the drunkard, he can stop drinking by the power of his will; but every day he abstains in his own strength, in the midst of temptation and the slumbering appetite, he does it at a risk; but when he puts forth all his energies, and then trusts in God's mercy and grace, he is safe.

In my experience, I have found illustrations of this fact. One gentleman told me that for years after he signed the pledge, he would walk around a square rather than pass a certain saloon— he had such a horror of going back to his past degraded life. "But," said he, "when the grace of God came into my heart, I was no longer afraid. I could say, 'Lord, help me!' and was safe."

I have been asked, "Do you believe that the grace of God can take away the appetite for drink?" When a man tells me the appetite is all gone, I think he is mistaken; when he tells me the desire to drink is gone, I believe him; but, in my opinion, that is a different thing. I may have no desire,—in fact, the drink may be hateful to me, the smell of it offensive, I may loathe it with an absolute loathing, and yet the appetite be then in my system.

A lady wrote me once: "Will you dare to say that the grace of God will not take away the love of sin?" I say, if a man has the grace of God in his heart, he will hate sin, and that which tends to or produces sin; but the appetite for drink may smoulder in his system. That is physical, not moral; something that may be removed or relieved by medicine perhaps,* not by the grace of God, except by a miracle. The grace of God has certain functions, but the grace of God will not prevent drink from affecting the brain and nervous system, if a man drinks. You can poison a Christian as quickly as you can a Hottentot. If two men—the one brimming over with the grace of God, and the other who does not believe in the grace of God—take prussic acid, they will both go down together.

We are accused of putting total abstinence before the gospel in the reformation of the drunkard. I reply, the total-abstinence pledge *must* reform the drunkard, whether he be a subject of the grace of God or not. Every child knows that if the drunkard ceases to drink, he ceases to be a drunkard, and the grace of God will not save him unless he abstains. It is a physical impossibility for a confirmed drunkard to drink intoxicating liquor and continue a sober man, except by such a miracle as the world has never seen. The appetite for intoxicating liquors, when once fastened on the system, produces, in frequent cases, a certain something—a mystery to us who have no knowledge of physiology, and even to those who have—that responds to the first touch of alcohol, and the man has no power to prevent it. I will speak of what I know by my own experience.

I am sometimes asked, "Have you the appetite now?" My reported replies are, some of them, very absurd, and positively wrong. A very dear friend says that I cannot pass a place where liquor is sold, without a return of the old appetite in all its force. Another says that I never see it without wanting it. Some one writes: "John B. Gough was a hard drinker for perhaps fifteen years (this is a mistake; only seven years from my first drinking to my pledge of abstinence). We know scores of men who have been perfect sots for twice as many years, and to-day they are *free;* they have no more appetite for liquor than a babe, and the very sight of it is disgusting. Now, why should not Mr. Gough be entitled to all that comes with the grace of God as well as they? Certainly God is not disposed to leave this old warrior, whose locks are whitened with thirty years'

---

* I have little faith in quack nostrums

campaign, to fight the enemy in his own bosom still ; and yet we believe he confesses that this is true ; " and the writer states, in addition : "These men are free, and he is in bondage."

Let me in reply to these statements say, that the only effect produced on me by passing a saloon is disgust ; and the appearance of it at the table, in the cars, or anywhere, is unpleasant to me. It is not with fear I look at it, but with distaste. I may say with others, the appetite is all gone, and I have no more desire for it than a babe; but if I take a swallow of it—what then ? will it produce no more effect on me than it would on a babe ? This is the point to decide. Can I, who was once an intemperate drinker, ever be a moderate drinker?

When I first began a Christian life and united with the church, in 1845, I partook of the communion when intoxicating wine was used. I have reason to suppose it was the wine of commerce. I once told the minister that the church smelt like a grog-shop after the ordinance, and that the odour of alcohol was on every communicant's breath. I partook of that wine. Did it stir up in me a raging appetite for stimulants ? Not at all; but soon after, I gave up the use of intoxicating wine at the communion, and have passed the cup whenever I had the slightest idea that alcoholic wine was used. Was I afraid of it? I can hardly say that. What was its effect on me ? The small draught of that wine warmed my stomach. It brought back to me vividly the old sensations, though it did not mount to my head and affect my brain ; yet it was a reminder of the old bad times, and called up the associations connected with the use of this very article in another way than as a religious ordinance. I must acknowledge that the glow and warmth was to me a gratification; and I was startled at the pleasant sensations produced by the alcohol, even in so small a quantity, in my system. I could not help that if I took it, and I determined to use it no more.

So with the use of it in cooking—in jellies, custards, and so on. The effect on me was not at once to rouse the appetite, but to produce a sensation of pleasure in a slight degree, and with that sensation an inclination to try it again. Thus I gave up its use in cooking, and in every way, shape, and manner. Not that I felt I must become a drunkard, but the sensations, while in one sense disagreeable, were associated in my mind with exhilaration, and the delicious thrill of the nervous system, that to me was once so fascinating—which a man of different temperament knows no more of than a deaf man knows of music.

This is what I call the appetite; and if I, or any other person with a similar experience, should reason that the appetite was gone, and the grace of God would keep us from falling into sin, —that we might use this article so many good Christians were using with no detriment, only using it in moderation,—I firmly believe it would be a physical impossibility, and that I or any other person would drift again into drunkenness. So, instead of boasting that the grace of God has taken away the appetite, I say the grace of God enables me to abstain from drinking, and I thank Him that out of His abounding mercy the desire for it is taken away; and at the risk of coming under the condemnation of a Boston D.D., who says that "a man who cannot partake of alcoholic wine at communion without arousing his appetite, is neither fit for the communion nor benefited by it," I shall as long as I live, refuse positively to partake of the wine of commerce, or alcoholic wine, when offered at the ordinance of the Lord's Supper.

I honestly believe that if I wilfully used it in cooked food, or even at the communion-table, knowing what I do, I should commit sin. I often pleasantly and profitably partake of the Lord's Supper in churches where unintoxicating wine is used, and I hope to see the day when alcoholic wine will be banished from the table of the Lord, and the pure juice of the grape will be substituted.

The idea that I cannot pass a grog-shop without a desire to partake of liquor, or that I take with me a travelling companion as a precaution, is simply absurd. I saw, the other day, in the *Congregationalist*, a report of two cases in which the appetite had been entirely taken away; one where the person had been for years a confirmed drunkard, and the appetite was taken away entirely, *with no effort of his own.* Now I do not deny that, but simply say, if such is the pure fact, it was a miracle; it was contrary to physical law. Do you believe that the inflamed state of the stomach as shown to us in Sewall's plates,—the congestion, the thickening of the coats, the complete disorder of the whole nervous system,—and all the irritation that causes the desire, can be removed with no inconvenience and no effort, and that the whole system shall become as free from all appetite as when the first glass was taken? I do not believe it, except by a miracle; and I say to those who assert that such a miracle has been performed, "You of all others should be thankful to God, every hour of your remaining life, that with no effort you have been spared the struggle and the fight that so many of your less-privileged brothers have endured. If such an assumed entire removal of the appetite be true, and you ever fall, with no remains of the appetite in your system, redeemed from all necessity of a battle that often leaves your less-favoured brother weak for days,—I say, if you ever drink again, you deserve no sympathy from men or forgiveness from God." To-day I thank God for the experience of the few days, yes, the few months, after I signed the pledge; for perhaps, had I not gone through that awful fight, I might have looked with contempt at the conflict of others, and despised them that they did not reach the heights of perfect freedom with no effort on their part.

These cases are very frequently recorded. I would say to my struggling brother: "Do not be dismayed; pray on, fight on. Remember when Paul prayed that the thorn in the flesh might be removed, the answer was, 'My grace is sufficient for thee,' while even the thorn was not removed; and remember also that He will not permit any who trust in Him to be confounded or put to shame." Often have I been compelled to reply to some poor struggling souls who are discouraged because the appetite is not gone, who listen to the story of those who are rejoicing in perfect freedom with no effort of their own, and are doubting whether they are outcasts from God's mercy or not. I would hardly refer to this, were it not for the sake of such, and with my whole heart I sympathise with and pray for them.

When a man says, as one did in a public meeting, "Gough

has been thirty years a teetotaler, and he has the appetite yet; I was in jail a year ago, and now I am free, for the appetite has been taken away," I can only reply to such a statement in the words of the King of Israel to Benhadad's messenger: "Let not him that girdeth on his harness boast himself as he that taketh it off."

"This kind goeth not out but by prayer and fasting," said one of these privileged ones to me. "I prayed and fasted, and the appetite was taken from me in a moment."

Read portions of a letter I received from a sincere Christian man in the ministry:—

"My grandfather died of delirium tremens. My mother was a drinker all her life. I have a natural appetite for drink. When a boy of ten, I determined never to drink. I went through college; studied for the ministry. When ordained, I sought the hardest work I could find, and engaged as a home missionary on the Western frontier. I am very much worn with hard work, and this cruel desire for drink is my torment. Whenever I see it I want it; if I think of it I want it. I have covered my whole life with prayer as a garment. I have fasted; I have abstained from animal food for two years. I have spent hundreds of dollars out of my meagre income at water-cure establishments; and, for all this, I tremble every day on the awful verge of the precipice of indulgence."

That man is an hero whom I honour; and it seems to me that the angels look with interest on such a struggle. Shall I discourage him by intimating that he has none of the real, genuine grace of God in his heart? No! a thousand times no! I will tell him, as I did in a letter I wrote him, not to be dismayed, but to "fight the good fight," "looking unto Jesus."

Dr. Henry A. Reynolds said at the International Conference in Philadelphia, in 1876:—

"I am one of those unfortunate men who have an inherited appetite for strong drink. I love liquor to-night as well as an infant loves milk."

Who will say that Dr. Reynolds has not the grace of God in his heart? But he says:—

"The love for intoxicants is as much a part of my make-up as my hand."

But he also says :—

"I stand here to-night believing myself to be a monument of God's grace."

I conversed, not a month since, with a converted drunkard and liquor-seller, who has an inherited appetite. With tears in his eyes, he told me how he struggled ; how the smell of it affected him ; how, when despondent and weary, his thoughts would turn to the drink. But he said :—

"I believe God will keep me ; for though He does not take the appetite away in answer to my prayers, He has given me grace to resist the temptation for years, and I believe He will to the end."

Another said to me :—

"I have fought the appetite for sixteen years. I dreamed the other night that I drank a glass of liquor, and, God help me ! I liked it ; and I like it now, waking or sleeping,—at times I long for it."

These men are all men of prayer, and perhaps pray more earnestly than you or I ever did; but they are left to fight, and, thanks to the Great Captain of our salvation, they will fight to the victory.

I have a letter before me from a minister of the gospel, who lost his church by his intemperance. A few of his members clung to him, and choosing him for their minister, started a new enterprise in a hall. Many put confidence in his repentance and reform. The new church was prosperous. The pastor was earnest and sincere. The Sunday-school was flourishing. The prospects were bright. Gradually he was gaining the confidence of the people of the town, as the increasing congregation declared. This went on for a year or more. The minister was appointed on a committee for procuring a Sabbath-school library, and was deputed to go to the city to select said library, the other gentlemen of the committee having perfect confidence in his judgment. I now quote from his letter :—

"I had no desire for drink ; the appetite was all gone. I was perfectly free. I went to ——, and called on an old classmate for information as to the best method of procuring the books I needed, as I was to pay cash for them to the amount of one hundred and fifty dollars which I had with me. My friend invited me to dinner. He was a wine drinker—strictly moderate. He asked me to take a glass of wine. I had no desire for it; and thinking I might take one glass, and feeling perhaps a little sensitive at the thought that my classmate might suppose I could not take one glass with him, I did take that glass, then another. How I got out of the house I cannot tell; but I woke from a drunken sleep four days after, ragged, penniless; the money held in trust for the books all gone; and now I am ruined. I dare not go back to ——. What shall I do? Where shall I go? I am heartbroken."

Speaking from a deep experience and wide observation, I would say to you, my reformed friend, "Let him that thinketh he standeth take heed lest he fall." All the powers of earth and hell, combined, could not have wrecked this man, had he not drank. All the rest was the consequence of that act, and the grace of God did not prevent it. He said he had no desire for it, and thought he could take one glass with impunity. There is the mistake,—*the desire for it was gone, but the appetite remained,*—just as the crouching pet tiger licked playfully the man's hand till the blood was tasted; and then hold him who can? The only safety for the reformed drunkard is total abstinence, let others say what they will. Pray God to keep you from drinking, then the drink has no power over you. But if you drink, the grace of God cannot save you, unless by a miracle. The days of struggling will soon be over, and we shall say, "Thanks be to God who giveth us the victory through our Lord Jesus Christ."

Since writing the above, I have seen extracts from a work written by Mrs. S. M. J. Henry, one of the most devoted and active of the noble army of Christian women now engaged in the cause. I commend most heartily the book published by the National Temperance Society, 58, Reade Street, New York, entitled "The Pledge and the Cross." The author presents the case fairly and most lucidly. I give but one sentence. Speaking of a man who had fallen after his conversion, Mrs. Henry says:—

"Now what was the trouble? The failure was not in God's grace, nor in the sincerity of the man, but in an unsound doctrine—a simple human claim for God's grace which He has nowhere seconded : in claiming that it will do a work which is just as much out of its province as to straighten a crooked bone, or eye ; or to hew stone, and draw lumber to supply the needy with a home. The bone or eye may be straightened, the stone hewn, the house builded, if the right means are employed ; so the man may be carried over the crisis of his reformation, if God's good and abundant grace can find a channel ; if His spirit can find a medium in some loving, patient, Christian heart and hand that will furnish the practical help just at the time it is needed—in the man's hour of extremity"

CHAPTER XXXIII.

MODERATE DRINKING AND TOTAL ABSTINENCE.

The Moderate Drinker—The Moderate Drinker of Stockholm—Gough and his Moderate-drinking Friend—Dr. B. W. [Richardson on Moderate Drinking—Alcohol not included in the Scheme of Life—The Most Helpless Period passed without it—The Four Stages of Life—Voice of Science—Stimulation Harmful to Health—Foods and Alcohol—" The Alcoholic Stages "—" The Devil and the Peacock "—Wine and Civilization—Wine-drinking Nations—Wine only Dirty Water—Total Abstinence for the Sake of Others—" Abusing the Moderate Drinker "—A Dinner without Wine—The Right, the Wrong, the Doubtful—A Touching Story—The Idolized Son—Wine at New Year's Calls —Misnamed Friends.

I PROPOSE giving several reasons why I commend total abstinence to the moderate drinker. A moderate drinker is a person who can drink without intoxication. A gentleman once said to me, " Six glasses of whiskey toddy in a day is not excess, if I can stand it." There is no virtue in moderation, if this is the criterion by which we judge. Where can you draw the line between moderation and excess? I have spoken of this on another page, and will only state a few facts illustrating the various opinions or judgments of moderation.

Dr. Most, a German physician, in the "*Encyk. Med. and Chir,*" gives the case of a man in his seventieth year, who for twenty years had drunk, daily, upwards of a quart of rum, or nearly forty hogsheads in all.

Professor Huss thus describes the ordinary life of a *moderate drinker* among the labouring classes of Stockholm :—

" Rising at five or six in the morning, according to the season, he takes a cup of coffee mixed with a glass of brandy, containing from two to three ounces of the spirit, which is there usually prepared from potatoes. He then attends to his occupations till eight o'clock, when he takes breakfast and a second glass of brandy. At his dinner, at noon, he has another glass, or more—usually a glass and a half. At five or six he again has a glass; and, lastly, with his supper, at eight or nine, still another. He thus consumes from five to five and a half glasses regularly every day, enjoying all the time a character among his comrades as a person of great moderation, who scarcely takes what is requisite for an individual in his station. Even if he becomes intoxicated on two days of every week, the Saturdays and Sundays, he does not acquire the reputation of a drunkard."

Men have been know to swallow from sixteen to twenty glasses daily, without showing signs of intoxication. I have known men who could and did consume a quantity of liquor every day, one-half of which would make me drunk and incapable, while they were perfectly sober, apparently; at any rate they were moderate drinkers, and it would have been termed a libel to call them drunkards. I once met a man in the streets of Boston, who hailed me with—

"Well, Gough, how are ye?"

"Quite well; how are you?"

"Oh, I'm going on in the same old jog."

"Are you drinking yet?"

"Yes, just about the same as I did in the old times. You see, Gough, I had a mind of my own. I could always drink you down, and I do not think I was ever drunk in my life."

He was one of my old drinking companions, and could always consume double, yes, treble the quantity I could. I became a wreck in trying to do as he did; and he, at the time I saw him, fifteen years after I had signed the pledge, was a reputable moderate drinker; drinking in all those years, day after day, what would have destroyed another, body and soul.

On moderation, I cannot speak to you in the language of science, but I rejoice there are so many who can and will. Among the foremost is Dr. B. W. Richardson. To him and his admirable work, "Moderate Drinking, for and against, from Scientific Points of View," I refer you. I can commend total abstinence for the moderate drinker on the ground that every drunkard began by moderation, and became what he is by attempting to be a moderate drinker and failing. On the ground of its being utterly useless for a healthy system, I refer you to the scientist, and quote a few extracts from Dr. Richardson's work:

"Science declares that alcohol is not included in the scheme of life. Try a man by himself. Every child of woman born, if it be not perverted, lives without alcohol, grows up without it; spends—and this is a vital point—spends the very happiest part of its life without it; gains its growing strength and vitality without it; feels no want for it. The course of its life is, at the most, on an average of the best lives—sixty years; of which the first fifteen, in other words the first fourth, are the most dangerous; yet it goes through that fourth without the use of this agent. But if in the four stages of life it can go through the first and the most critical stage without alcohol, why cannot it traverse the remaining three? Is Nature so unwise in her doings, so capricious, so uncertain, that she withholds a giver of life from the helpless, and supplies it only to the helpful? Impossible! She provides for the helpless at once a food and a drink—their mother's milk.

"Further, there have been many men and women, millions and millions of them, who have gone on through the four stages of life, from the first to the last, without resort to this agent for the support of life. Some men, forming whole nations, have never heard of it; some have heard of it, and have abjured its use. In England and America at this time there are probably nearly upon six millions of persons who have abjured this agent. Do they fall or fail in value of life from the abjuration? The evidence, as we shall distinctly see by-and-by, is all the other way. There are, lastly, some who are forced to live without the use of this agent. Do they fall or die in consequence? There is not a single instance in illustration.

"On all these points, science, when she is questioned earnestly and interpreted justly, is decisive and firm; and if you question her in yet another direction, she is not less certain. You ask her for a comparison of alcohol and of man, in respect to the structure of both, and her evidence is as the sun at noon in its clearness. She has taken the body of man to pieces; she has learned the composition of its structure—skin, muscle, bone, viscera, brain, nervous cord, organs of sense. She knows of what these parts are formed, and she knows from whence the components came. She finds in the muscles fibrine; it came from the fibrine of flesh, or from the gluten or albumen of the plants on which the man has fed. She finds tendon and cartilage and earthy matter in the skeleton; they were from the vegetable kingdom. She finds water in the body in such abundance that it makes up seven parts out of eight of the whole; and that she knows the source of readily enough. She finds iron; that she traces from the earth. She finds fat; and that she traces to sugar and starch. In short, she discovers, in whatever structure she searches, the origin of the structure. But, as a natural presence, she finds no ardent spirit there in any part or fluid. Nothing made from spirit. Did she find either, she would say the body is diseased, and, it may be, was killed by that which is found.

"Sometimes in the bodies of men she discovers the evidences of some conditions that are not natural. She compares these bodies with the bodies of other men, or with the bodies of inferior animals, as sheep and oxen, and finds that the unnatural appearances are peculiar to persons who have taken alcohol, and are indications of new structural changes which are not proper, and which she calls disease. Thus, by two tests, science tries the comparison between alcohol and man. She finds in the body no structure made from alcohol; she finds in the healthy body no alcohol; she finds in those who have taken alcohol changes of the structure, and those are changes of disease. By all these proofs she declares alcohol to be entirely alien to the structure of man. It does not build up the body; it undermines and destroys the building.

"One step more. If you question science on the comparison which exists between foods and alcohol, she gives you facts on every hand. She shows you a natural and all-sufficient and standard food. She calls it milk. She takes it to pieces; she says it is made up of caseine, for the construction of muscular and other active tissues; of sugar and fat, for supplying fuel to the body for the animal warmth; of salts for the earthy, and of water for the liquid parts. This is a perfect standard. Holds it any comparison with alcohol? Not a jot. The comparison is the same with all other natural foods.

"Man, going forth to find food for his wants, discovers it in various substances, but only naturally, in precisely such substances, and in the same proportions of such substances, as exist in the standard food on which he first fed. Alcohol alien to the body of man, is alike alien to the natural food of man."

On the "Alcoholic Stages," Dr. Richardson says :—

"A man or woman sitting down, or standing up, if you like, to drink wine or other stimulant, always starts on the way that leads through four stages toward an easily realizable destination. Stage one is that gentle stimulation called moderate excitement, or support. Stage two is elevation—whatever that may mean. It is not elevation of character; of that I am satisfied. Stage three is confusion of mind, action, and deed, with sad want of elevation. Stage four is complete concatenation of circumstances,—all the stages perfectly matured, the journey completed, with the traveller lying down, absolutely prostrated in mind and in body. The destination is reached, and found to be a human being dead drunk and incapable."

Some years ago I received a letter from a friend that seems

so apposite to this as to be quoted for an illustration. It is as follows :—

"QUEBEC.

"Dear Sir,—There are persons whom it is difficult to persuade that the *first glass* drank by an individual who will be drunk by taking *any* larger quantity affects such individuals so as to produce any degree of drunkenness. I differ with such people, and think the following, from a small work on the natural history of birds, in possession of one of my little girls, an apt illustration, of which you are at liberty to make such use as you please. I am, etc.,
———."

"THE DEVIL AND THE PEACOCK.

"The Arabs, says Bochart, denominate the peacock as a bird of ill-omen, for the following reasons: it was the cause of the first entrance of the Devil into Paradise, and the expulsion of Adam and Eve. They also relate that the Devil watered the vine with the blood of four animals: first, with that of a peacock; and when the vine began to put forth leaves, with the blood of an ape; when the grapes began to appear, with that of a lion; and lastly, when they were quite ripe, with that of a hog; which is the reason, say they, that the wine-bibber at first struts about like a peacock, then begins to dance, play, and make grimaces like an ape, then rages like a lion, and, lastly, lies down in a ditch like a hog."

In reply to the statement that wine has been the promoter of civilisation, and the source of inspiration to poet and artist, Dr. Richardson says :—

"It is said that the use of wine and its allies has been the source of the power of the most powerful nations. It is said that the wine-cup has been the fountain of that wit and poetry and artistic wisdom, if I may use the term, which has made the illustrious men of the world so illustrious and so generally useful as they have been to the world. Take away the wine-cup, it is argued, and the whole intellectual life must needs become 'flat, stale, and unprofitable.' It were indeed a pity if this were the look-out of total abstinence, a second deluge of water, with not so much as a graceful dove and an olive-branch to cheer the trackless waste. It were indeed a pity of pities if this were the final look-out of total abstinence in the intellectual sphere. Can it be that all intellectual energy and hilarity must die out with the abolition of the wine-cup ? . . . . .

"Science, ever fair, says that some nations and wonderful peoples that have lived have been wine-drinkers at certain periods of their history. But she draws also this most important historical lesson, that the great nations were, as a rule, water-drinkers purely, until they became great; then they took to wine and other luxuries, and soon became little. Up to the time of Cyrus, the Persians were water-drinkers; they became all-powerful, and then also became such confirmed wine-drinkers that, if they had some great duty to perform, they discussed the details of it when inflamed with wine, and rejected the judgment or revised it when they had become sober, and *vice versâ*. Surely this was the acme of perfection as a test of wine. Curiously, it didn't answer. With its luxury Persia succumbed, fell into the hands of less luxurious conquerors, and, like a modern rake, found its progress anything but promising in the end.

"The Greeks in their first and simple days were clothed in victory over men and over nature. They grew powerful; they sang and danced, and all but worshipped wine; but it did not sustain them in their grandeur, as it ought to have done if the theory of such sustainment be correct. The Roman rule became overwhelming out of the simplicity of its first life. It rose into luxury, and made wine almost a god. But Rome fell. Wine did not sustain it. It is all through history the same. There is not an instance, when we come to the analysis of fact and circumstance, in which wine has not been to nations, as to man individually, a mocker. It has been the death of nations. It has swept down nations, as it sweeps down men, in the prime of their life, and in the midst of their glory."

And thus Dr. Richardson destroys the poetic dream of sparkling, ruby wine:—

"Science tells us that when one or two disguises are removed, even blood is water; as to wine, that is mere dirty water,—sixteen bottles, or cups, or any other equal measures of water, pure and simple, from the clouds and earth, to one poor bottle or cup of a burning, fiery liquid which has been called ardent spirit, or spirit of wine, or alcohol, with some little colouring matter, in certain cases a little acid, in other cases a little sugar, and in still other cases a little cinder-stuff.

"It is a pitiful fall, but it is such, and science not only declares it, but proves it so to be. A pitiful let-down, that men throughout all ages who have called themselves wine-drinkers have been water-drinkers after all; that men who have called themselves wine-merchants have been water-merchants; that men who have bought and still buy wines at fabulous prices, have been buying and still are buying water! A dozen of champagne, bought at a cost of five pounds ten shillings, very choice,—I am speaking by the book,—consisted, when it was all measured out, of three hundred ounces (or fifteen pints) of fluid, of which fluid thirteen pints and a half were pure water, the rest ardent spirit, with a little carbonic acid, some colouring matter like burnt sugar, a light flavouring ether in almost infinitesimal proportion, and a trace of cinder-stuff. Science, looking on dispassionately, records merely the facts. If she thinks that five pounds ten shillings was a heavy sum to pay for thirteen pints and a half of water and one pint and a half of spirit, she says nothing: she leaves that to the men and women of sentiment and passionate feeling, buyers and sellers and drinkers all round.

I appeal to the moderate drinker on a higher ground and a nobler motive than self-preservation. I ask him to abstain for the sake of others. As a Christian, what is your influence over the young man drifting to ruin through the drink? You urge him to abstain. If he does as you bid him, he is safe; if he attempts to follow you, he is lost. You cannot say, "Come with us, and we will do you good." You and he must separate here; he cannot and dare not go with you if he would be safe.

We are often accused of abusing the moderate drinker; I have no disposition to abuse or condemn; but in view of the terrible evil we fight, and the knowledge that all this evil must come to an end when the present race of the intemperate shall die out, if there are no more made, and that the drunkards are all drawn from the ranks of moderation, and when death makes gaps in their ranks they are filled by recruits from the army of moderate drinkers,—we must speak out, and implore the moderate drinker to give up his gratification for the sake of others. I have never accused them of wilfully doing harm. I simply ask them to investigate, and to test their position.

I was once entertained by a gentleman as an invited guest. It was a large dinner-party, composed of several magistrates, a member of parliament, one or two ministers of the gospel, and others,—altogether a very intelligent and intellectual company. At the table I noticed that the host became rather uneasy, and looked nervously up and down the board. At last he said, hesitatingly:—

"Gentlemen, I know not but I ought to apologise; not exactly apologise, but explain the absence of wine. It is well known that I present wine, and some of you may have expected wine, or toddy, and may be disappointed when I tell you that I shall provide neither wine nor toddy to-day. I ordered the butler to decant no wine. I do this in honour of Mr. Gough, whom you are invited to meet. We all know his practice, that he is a total abstainer; and though we may not agree with him in all points, yet, out of compliment to him, we will have no wine to-day."

The countenances of several of the guests fell, and a damper seemed to be shut down on the spirits of the company at this announcement that there would be no artificial stimulants to keep up their spirits. I was wofully embarrassed, and felt compelled to say something.

I did not wish to sit there as a block to their enjoyment, or a wet blanket on the sociability of the company, so I said :—

"Sir, I regret that you should have made any change in the customary entertainment of your guests, solely out of compliment to me, or deference to my opinions. I will change no customary arrangement at my own table to suit any man's whims, prejudices, or vagaries. If it is *right* to place wine and toddy on the table, place it there! I would, if I knew it was right to do it. I know it is right to provide water for my guests, and I do it. So, sir, if you know it is right, place the wine before your guests. If it is *wrong*, never place it there under any consideration, even at the demand or request of your guests. If you have the *slightest doubt* as to the right or wrong of the act of presenting wine or toddy at your table, or to your friends, abstain from presenting it till you have settled the doubt."

This is what I ask every moderate drinker to do. I do not abuse, nor do I think any moderate drinker intends to make mischief or to wrong any human being by giving wine; but harm is done. I am no judge of my neighbour; God is the Judge. I only ask, "Can any good arise from the use of intoxicating drinks as a beverage, and may there not be harm?"

A lady told me the following touching story in her experience. She had a son, her pride, her joy; her heart was bound up in her boy—so clean, so sweet and lovely, and withal so manly.

One New Year's morning he came into the breakfast-room, full of life and youthful beauty, and giving her the morning kiss, said :—

"A happy New Year to you, mother, darling!"

After breakfast, he sprang up, saying,—

"Now, mother dear, for the New Year calls! You know I have never before really made any, but I shall make a business of it to-day. Good-bye; again a happy New Year to you!"

He went out; and said she, "I stood in the bay-window, and saw him walking down the street. I was proud of him, my son, eighteen years of age; tall, shapely, clean, sweet. I watched him, my mother's heart yearning to him in tenderest love. After he had turned the corner, I still looked at the spot where I had last seen him. I returned to my household duties, and all day I was thinking of my boy. I heard a hurried or unsteady ring at the door in the evening, and as the servant opened it, I heard some confused noises. I rushed to the hall, and found two young gentlemen, evidently flushed with wine, bearing between them the helpless form of my boy—my boy! I asked them to lift him into the drawing-room, and leave me, thanking them as well as I was able for their trouble. Then I sat down by my boy's side, and lifted his head in my lap; and oh, how I did cry! I thought my heart would break. His lips, that I had kissed in the morning, so pure, so sweet—swollen, dry, and feverish; his hair damp and matted. His clear skin actually seemed coarse; his eyes half-closed, his breath poisoning the air. Oh, so offensive! His clothes disarranged. Yes, there he lay, breathing heavily, utterly unconscious—*helplessly drunk*. My boy! my beautiful boy! What enemy hath done this? Oh, had it been some vile, vindictive enemy who had thus smitten him, had it been some cruel foe of mine that had dealt me this dreadful blow, it would have been a comfort compared with the terrible conviction that this was the work of his friends! He had only been with friends. Friends had sent him home to his mother. Friends had brought him to his mother's door. Oh, if this is the work of my boy's friends, how shall I stand between him and harm? That night of agony I shall never forget. That was his first intoxication, but not his last. His friends laughed at him for being overcome, and presented him with drink,—even ladies invited him,—and now he is far on the road to drunkenness."

This is the result of friendship, so called. Had I a son, I

would pray God more earnestly to save him from such friendship than to shield him from his well-known enemies. For the sake of others, we plead, then, with the moderate drinker, and remind them that no possible good can result from their presentation of wine or strong drink to others; but there may be a possible harm as the consequence. I would rather give the poor drunkard his last glass to allay the terrible thirst that maddens him, than to give him the first glass that lays the foundation of the appetite that leads him to destruction.

CHAPTER XXXIV.

TEMPERANCE AND THE BIBLE—MY VIEWS ON THE SCRIPTURE
QUESTION—INCIDENTS.

Assistance demanded from all Sides—Charity—The Truth our Weapon—Scamp's Tavern—"'The Seven Last Plagues' for Sale here"—Specimen of Liquor-Sellers' Work—The Wine of Scripture and of Commerce—Conflicting Authorities—One of the "Doubtful Disputations"—Dr. Norman Ker's Statement—The Hieroglyphical Argument—Assumed Biblical Commands against Strong Drink—Dr. Samuel H. Cox and J. Fenimore Cooper upon Bible Miracles—Absalom's Hair—What Fish swallowed Jonah—Good Men who endeavour to sanction Drinking—How to answer these Men—Advice to the Reformed Man—Let Arguments alone—The Outcast's Conversion—Many Churches unsafe for the Reformed Drunkard.

ON another page I have already expressed my opinions as to prohibition. I believe that a prohibitory law, based on the public sentiment of antagonism to the drink, will be successfully enforced; and just in proportion as it is upheld by a spasmodic effort, pushed through a legislature without sufficient sentiment to back it, it will be a failure, and in my opinion worse than nothing.

I rejoice in every effort that prohibits, cripples, or lessens in any way the sale of intoxicating liquor. I give full sympathy to the work of the Society for the Suppression of Crime, in its efforts to prevent the dealers from violating existing laws. I welcome every endeavour to break up a single grog-shop, to curtail the hours for selling, if it be but one hour in the day. I say to such a worker: "If you can go no further with us than to reduce the number of licenses where they may be granted by the city or town council, do that; every little helps."

I cry out for assistance from every quarter. Small help is

better than no help; and I will not refuse any aid given from any source to pull down the stronghold of intemperance. While I stand unflinchingly on the platform of total abstinence and absolute prohibition, combining their forces for the entire abandonment of the drinking customs, and the annihilation of the manufacture and sale of alcoholic beverages, I hold out my hand to every worker as far as he can go with me, if it is but a step.

The truth cannot be told without damaging this horrible business. Did the whole people accept the truth, the traffic would cease; the truth would kill it. Even where the truth is accidentally told, it is very damaging. I heard in Connecticut, many years ago, that a man named Stephen Camp kept a tavern, and had procured a new and gaudy sign. There was so much ornamentation about it that room only was left for the initial of the man's first name, and the painter neglected to put the full-stop between the S and the C, so that it read "S Camp's Tavern." The people read it "Scamp's Tavern," and there was so much truth in the statement involuntarily exhibited by the tavern-keeper, that he at once inserted the period. But still the letters ran so close together that the passers-by would read it "Scamp's Tavern," and he was compelled to procure a new sign, large enough to permit him to give the full name, Stephen; and then he was at peace.

A medical gentleman wrote me a letter giving the original of the story, oft repeated, of the "Seven Last Plagues." It has appeared in so many shapes, and with so many differing particulars, that I insert the letter, which is as follows:—

"Dear Sir,— When I heard you last night describing the appropriate signs the rum-sellers ought to hang out, showing the effect of their operations, it occurred to me that I ought to communicate to you a fact which is too good to be lost.

"In Erie there lived, a few years ago, the Rev. Mr. Reed, of the Associate Reformed Church. He published a book on the Revelations, entitled 'The Seven Last Plagues.' This Mr. Reed preached part of his time in Waterford, where one of his elders kept a tavern. So Mr. Reed left several copies of his work for sale with this elder, accompanied with a handbill which contained the title of the book, which was stuck up on the bar, in large letters :—

'"THE SEVEN LAST PLAGUES" FOR SALE HERE.'
"This conspicuous handbill had the effect of arresting the attention of visitors, and you can easily imagine how annoying it soon became to the tavern-keeper, when humorous and fun-loving persons would look up at the bill and utter some sly remark. This so mortified the landlord that he eventually gave up the sale of the poison, and kept a temperance house. Having stopped at the house both before and after the transaction here stated, I know the fact to be as stated."

Were the liquor-sellers compelled to exhibit specimens of their work in the saloon-windows, placing some poor wreck of a man in a conspicuous place, with bloated face, bleared eyes, swollen, cracked, white lips, trembling limbs, noisome breath, offensive to every sense, in his rags and dirt, and label him "Such things as this made out of men here," it would do more to break up this vile business than all the efforts put forth by the most ardent advocate of the temperance reform.

There has been much discussion, and many volumes written, and some strong feelings expressed, and, I think, bitterness engendered, on the wines of Scripture. I pay very little attention to this agitation, as the subject is of no particular moment to me. I am not learned, and know nothing of Hebrew or Greek; and if learned men say that the Bible sanctions the use of alcoholic wine, that the Saviour made and drank intoxicating wine, I can only reply that I do not believe it. But there is no necessity for argument with me, as I do not understand the question, and it is as perfectly immaterial to me what wine the Saviour made and drank, as it is what clothes He wore, or what food He ate; for I am no more bound to drink what He drank than I am to eat what He ate, or to wear the kind of clothing in which He was apparelled.

The question of the wines of Scripture, in my opinion, has nothing whatever to do with the wines of commerce, the ardent spirits, the ale, and other intoxicating drinks we are fighting today. If I believed the Bible condemned total abstinence from alcoholic beverages, I would advocate their disuse no more. If the Bible commanded me to drink alcoholic beverages, I must obey. But I thank God that, with the light He has thrown on the page of His word, and with my conception of the character and mission of Christ on earth, I know, as well as I need to know anything, that there is no condemnation of total abstinence in the Bible to me,—that it is permitted, if not commanded; and if you, with your Hebrew and Greek, and all your learning, can only come to the conclusion of a minister of the gospel who told me that " Christ liked the wine best that had the most alcohol in it," then I thank God I am not an educated man, and know nothing of Hebrew and Greek.

But this is debatable ground. It is an unprofitable discussion; it is one of the "doubtful disputations." While one very learned man insists that it was simply impossible that the ancients could have preserved their grape-juice unfermented, unless they bottled it in air-tight flasks, another equally learned declares not only that it is possible, but proves it by actual experiment. I quote from Dr. Norman Ker:—

"This distinguished divine might as well declare he had demonstrated that no man-child had ever been born in England with a nose on his face. I know that I was born with a nose, because I could see it and feel it: and I know that wine could be preserved unfermented and unintoxicating, because I had it and drank it."

Another very learned man tells us that the "fruit of the vine" used by our Lord was intoxicating red wine. I hope he does not mean the "wine when it is red." Others equally learned deny that. One rabbi will tell you, as one told me, "We use no fermented wine at our Passover. We boil the raisins, and use the liquid juice." Another rabbi declares that they use wine that is fermented; that is, wine that will make men drunk; that some cannot take at all without danger.

Some learned people get angry; and because some others, equally learned, tell us that the red wine was not intoxicating they declare that such men would trample on all that is holy, on Christ Himself, to gain their point and carry out their theories. Some declare that the Bible never commends the use of intoxicating liquors, and some affirm that it countenances and commends them.

The atheist asks, and has asked more than once, "Can a book

be true, or can its inspirer be infallible, when in it liquids which men of science and medical practitioners know to be artificial poisons are explicitly commended and unstintingly approved of?" Let Dr. Norman Ker reply :—

"That believers in the Bible and its Author, who are acquainted with the fact, a fact beyond dispute, that alcohol is a poison, and therefore all alcoholic liquors are poisonous, are absolutely certain that the inspired volume cannot possibly sanction the use of intoxicating beverages."

Then some learned Christian declares that such a defender is as bad as the infidel. And so the discussion waxes warm, and the disputants are claiming each for his own side the victory, reminding you of the battle of "Shirra Muir," of which the old song says :—

> "There's some say that we wan,
> Some say that they wan;
> Some say that nane wan at a', man.
> But one thing I'm sure,
> That at Shirra Muir,
> A battle there was, which I saw, man.
> And we ran and they ran, and they ran and we ran,
> And we ran and they ran awa', man."

Now, amidst all this learning and science and parading of knowledge of the dead languages, where are the poor, illiterate people who desire to do right to take their position? We are bewildered, and sometimes shocked. It is strangely confusing for us, professing no profound learning, to be confronted by so much knowledge! I once received a letter, on one side of the sheet were some passages of Scripture, and on the other some dots and dashes and half-circles, appearing to me as if German text and Old English had gone mad together, and were pulling each other to pieces and scattering the fragments. Then came the question in good sound English, "Are you prepared to deny that this is the correct reading of the quotations I have made ?" I felt more like dropping the paper, and running away, than attempting to come to any decision. It was more like an incantation; it appeared like something " uncanny," as the Scotch say;

and to this day I have never been able to ascertain from the hieroglyphics what the true rendering of the quotations was.

Now, we who are ignorant must go to the learned to ascertain what is correct, and if they do not agree, what shall we do? We are in the position of the voter who could not read, asking a politician to read the declaration of a certain party. You may be sure the politician gave such a version of the document as suited his purposes or preferences. So I give up altogether any interest in the discussion of the Scripture wine question as being to me unprofitable; and amid the smoke and the dust of conflict of opinions, I will look beyond and through it all to the hard fact that intemperance is the curse of the world; and, without judging others for their opinion, will do my best to stay this tide of evil, and work with the means God has put into my hands to lift up the fallen, and build a barrier between the unpolluted lip of the child and the agency that promotes and perpetuates the evil.

I have been met with many quotations other than Paul's advice to Timothy. Here is one sent me as a positive command in the Bible to drink strong drink. Deut. xiv. 26, "Thou shalt bestow that money for whatsoever thy soul lusteth after," for oxen, for sheep, or for wine, or for strong drink, etc.; and Prov. xxxi. 4, "Give strong drink to him that is ready to perish," etc., is often quoted. I was told that a Cameronian in Scotland declared he had a command to drink spirits, "for are we not told to try the spirits?" And so he would try every whiskey-bottle that was presented to him, quoting Scripture at the same time. There is scarcely any absurdity, or even wrong-doing, that some men do not pretend to find a warrant for in Scripture.

I heard a man defend gambling from the passage, "The lot is cast into the lap, but the whole disposing thereof is of the Lord." It is told of another that he refused to believe the Bible, because it was opposed to personal cleanliness; and when asked for evidence, quoted the passage, "He that is filthy, let him be filthy still." It is quite a common thing to hear men of education misquoting Scripture, or repeating some sentence as from the Bible which they have fished up in their reading, or make statements as from the Bible that are not there.

Many years ago, on one of the Hudson River steamboats, Dr. Sam. H. Cox introduced me to James Fenimore Cooper, the very celebrated literary man and author. The conversation turned on temperance, then on the Slavery question, then on Theology, and at last on the Bible and its Divine origin. Doubt was expressed as to the miracles recorded, when Dr. Cox said, "There were miracles recorded in the Bible, but not so many as some people supposed." He said that men would read so carelessly as to imagine a miracle where none was recorded.

"Now," said he, "how did Absalom come by his death?"

The reply was, "He was hung by the hair of his head in the tree, and Joab slew him with darts."

"Where do you get that?"

"In the Bible."

"But the Bible does not say that he was caught by the hair."

"I beg your pardon, but it does."

"I beg *your* pardon, but it does not."

A waiter was called.

"Bring us the Bible."

Dr. Cox, handing it to Mr. Cooper, said, "Find the passage."

The verse containing the incident was found to be: "And Absalom rode upon a mule, and the mule went under the thick boughs of a great oak, and his head caught hold of the oak, and he was taken up," etc. (2 Sam. xviii. 9).

"Now," said the Doctor, "there is not one word about the hair. To be sure we read in another place that he polled his head once a year, because his hair was heavy, and from that, men judge that Absalom on the field of battle rode bareheaded; his long hair floating, so that in riding under the boughs of a tree he was caught by the hair.

"Then," said he, "what fish swallowed Jonah?"

The reply was, "A whale."

"Not so," said the Doctor; and turning to the passage, he read: "'And the Lord had prepared a great fish to swallow Jonah,'" etc. (Jonah i. 17).

"There! the Lord prepared that fish expressly for that purpose. It was not a whale—all naturalists know that a whale could not swallow a man."

This interesting conversation continued for some time, quite a group of interested listeners having gathered round the talkers. Several illustrations were given to show how carelessly many persons read the Bible, and how strangely absurd are some of the quotations.

But I must say I am grieved, and my heart grows sad, at the efforts by good men to sustain the drinking customs by the Bible. Our aim is to lead men to the Word of God, and to the Church of Christ. But when such are told that they are all wrong, that total abstinence is unscriptural,—when the minister who preaches the gospel, to which we commend them, declares that it is fanaticism to abstain, that the Saviour used wine,—it seems to me like striking the knuckles of some poor shipwrecked creature who is clinging to the life-boat.

I will just say to the reformed man : When infidels tell you that Jesus Christ made and drank an article of which the Bible says, "Look not on the wine when it is red," give no reply but this, " I do not believe it." An infidel told me that Jesus made sixty gallons of intoxicating wine for drinking when the whole company was drunk. All I could say was, " I do not believe it." When an infidel tells you that Jesus Christ was guilty of immorality, when He bade His disciples all to drink that which is condemned in the Scriptures as a "mocker," do not believe him. And when, which is far worse in my estimation, a Christian minister or editor, or professor, tells you that Jesus Christ was a drinking man, a moderate drinker of intoxicating wine ; that He drank and commended that which the Bible declares. " biteth like a serpent and stingeth like an adder;" that He gave to others that of which the Bible says, " Woe unto him that giveth his neighbour drink ;" that He made and used, and gave to others, that which is called the " wine of astonishment," the wine through which " the priest and prophet have erred " and " are out of the way, through which they err in vision and stumble in judgment," through which " all tables are full of vomit and filthiness, so that there is no place clean;" that which is called the "poison of dragons," and the "cruel venom of asps;" that Jesus Christ our Saviour made and drank, and gave to others, that which you cannot touch without danger,—tell them you do not believe it.

Do not attempt argument with them, for they will laugh you to scorn for daring to attack them with your limited education, and will overwhelm you with *tirosh, yayin, oinos, gleukos,* and other words you do not understand, and they will bring Oriental travellers, returned missionaries, Jewish rabbis, learned men, to testify against you,—still tell them you do not believe it. There are men on the other side as learned as they are, who deny their position altogether.

Let them bring all the travellers that have ever travelled; all the missionaries that have ever returned; all the Hebrew scholars that have ever lived; all the Jewish rabbis, from the first to the present; and then bring Paul and all the apostles, and all the prophets, priests, and kings, of whom we have any record in the Bible, as evidence,—let them pour out all their learning and knowledge of languages,—answer them not a word but that you do not believe it.

But do this: Carefully and prayerfully study the life of Christ; His mission, His example, His infinite condescension and love, His pity for the fallen, His going about doing good, His sympathetic ministrations. Study Him well, and you cannot believe that He who taught you to pray "Lead us not into temptation," would commend to you that which is the great temptation of your life, against which you fight day by day, and to which, if you yield, you can never see His face, but are banished with adulterers, liars, and all the wicked from His presence for ever. Will you, can you believe that He sets you an example you cannot follow? No! no! no! Then let us "stand up for Jesus;" and notwithstanding all the attempts of any ministers in His name to fix on Him the charge of encouraging wine-bibbing by His example and precept,—let us lovingly, trusting Him and relying on His grace, pursue the path of safety, confidently believing that He approves our efforts to present our "bodies a living sacrifice." This is my advice to any reformed drunkard. Let others attempt to make good this charge against Jesus as a moderate drinker of alcoholic stimulants. Mix not up in what Dr. Fowler calls "undistributed muddle." We will let them fight it out, while we thank Him for the total abstinence that was the means of grace with His blessing by which we have, as we trust, escaped as a bird out of the snare of the fowler. I do not suppose that all the Christian advocates of the intoxicating wine-drinking of our Saviour mean to hinder the poor reformed drunkard from adopting the safe principle, but indirectly it is a hindrance, and a stumbling-block to many.

I pray God that the time may come when the reformed drunkard may find a safe refuge in every church. It is a consolation that Christ often receives those whom His church despises.

When I was in Indiana, at one time, a lady told me that during a revival a poor outcast woman attempted to enter the place of worship, and was rudely pushed back, with a threat of calling the police. She sadly turned her back on the door open for others, but closed to her, and knelt down on the grass in the yard of the church, and told Jesus, when He met her and pardoned her. This lady furthermore told me that she never witnessed such a death-scene as at the bed-side of this poor redeemed outcast; it was glorious,—the exercise of simple faith in Him who received her whom others rejected.

I gladly acknowledge that there are churches, and many of them, who hold out the hand of friendship and cordial sympathy for the reformed drunkard; but there are too many where he can find no safe refuge, where the preaching, the precept, and the example are all against him.

CHAPTER XXXV.

WAR WITH DRINK—TEMPERANCE ORGANIZATIONS—WOMAN'S WORK AND INFLUENCE.

The National Temperance Society—Women's Christian Temperance Union—The Blue and Red Ribbon Armies—American Temperance Society—Growth of the Work—Washingtonian Movement—Growing Unpopularity of Washingtonianism—Favourite Epithets—"We don't want any Religion in the Movement"—Poor Tom Marshall—Danger to Reform Clubs—Sympathy demanded for the Lost—Give the Reformed Man Work—The Temperance Hall a Place of Safety—The Dirt and Discomforts of some so-called Temperance Hotels—Personal Experience—The "Model" and "Central" Coffee Houses of Philadelphia—The Medical Question—Rum by the Keg—Physician giving Poison for Health—Heroism and Fanaticism—"Stand to your Principle."

TIME and space forbid more than an allusion to the various organizations now engaged in the work of enlightening the public mind in reference to the great drink question, in efforts to obtain legislative enactments, and the circulation of temperance literature; the Good Templars, the Sons of Temperance, the Temples of Honour, and kindred associations, all aiming at and working for the same results.

One of the chief of these agencies is the National Temperance Society and Publication House,* whose principal object is the distribution of a sound and reliable temperance literature. The last annual report is a valuable document. In it the managers say that the society has had in its business department the most prosperous year of its existence, and that, " while drinking and drunkenness may have increased in some of our cities, the cause of temperance in the country at large has never made as gratifying advances as during the years just ended, or stood as well before the nation as it does to-day."

* The offices of this Society are at No. 58, Reade Street, New York.

The Women's National Christian Temperance Union was organized in November, 1874. This society was the direct outgrowth of the crusade,—a most wonderful work, which roused the whole people to a consideration of the evils of drunkenness, creating an interest such as the country had never seen since the days of Washingtonianism, forty years ago. It has had a marvellous growth and an amazing success. Mrs. Wittenmyer's Handbook of the Women's National Christian Temperance Union is a most interesting and valuable document. I consider the Union to be the most efficient organization in this country to-day. I believe it has accomplished more permanent good in the short period of its existence than any other for forty years past. These Christian women have worked among children in Juvenile Unions, Bands of Hope, Sunday schools, and day schools. "Much Gospel work has been done outside the churches, in cottage meetings, in halls, and on camp-grounds." "Reform clubs have been organized, and reformatory homes for women established, and in every possible way that Christian women could work the interests of the cause have been pressed all along the line. And through it all continuous prayer has been maintained; for wherever there is a Woman's Temperance Union, there a consecrated band of Christian women meet to pray. Prayer is the vital breath of this society, and the watchword is, 'In God we trust.'"

Springing from and growing out of this grand work of the women, are the reform clubs, and the blue and the red ribbon armies, spreading all over this land, and stretching across the Atlantic. Most of these organizations are now effectually doing good service for the cause of temperance.

We are in the habit of speaking of the "Gospel Temperance Movement" as if it were some new thing. The first effectual effort to stem the tide of intemperance was made by Christian men. I would commend to those who are desirous of knowing the inception and development of the temperance reform, to read the "History of the Temperance Movement," by Rev. J. B. Dunn, D.D., which is embodied in the Centennial Temperance volume, published by the National Society. It is, in my opinion, the most clear, compact, concise, and yet nearly exhaustive history that has ever been written.

The American Temperance Society was formed in 1826. The pledge was, "Total abstinence from ardent spirits." Who were the promoters and members of that association? Christian men, such as Rev. Leonard Woods, D.D., Rev. Justin Edwards, John Tappan, S. V. S. Wilder, Rev. Dr. Hewitt, Rev. William Collier, Rev. E. W. Hooker, and Dr. Lyman Beecher, who preached his six celebrated sermons that year.

In 1829, a day was set apart for fasting and prayer on account of intemperance. The New York State society was organized; the Connecticut State society was formed. The officers of the latter organization were such men as Rev. Jeremiah Day, D.D., President of Yale College, and Rev. Calvin Chapin. And so the cause grew and prospered, steadily increasing in power with men like Dr. Mussey, Dr. Hosack, Dr. Hitchcock, and Professor Wayland. In 1831, there were societies in every State, except Maine, Alabama, Louisiana, Illinois, and Missouri; until, in 1836, at a convention in Saratoga, the total-abstinence pledge from all intoxicating beverages was adopted, and has been the recognized and only pledge for more than forty years.

In 1840, the Washingtonian movement commenced. Dr. Jewett said that at that time nineteen-twentieths of the clergy were total abstainers. Washingtonianism became popular. All other effort seemed to lose its attraction, and truly it was a great work. Men who had been hopeless drunkards reformed and became public teachers. The spirit of the movement was the gospel spirit of charity, kindness, and sympathy for the suffering wrong-doer. The law of love was the Washingtonian law. Soon faithful men who had borne the heat and burden of the day, who had endured persecution for truth's sake, were startled to hear themselves called old fogies, slow men who did not understand the first principles of the reform. Men became leading reformers who were not qualified by experience, or training, or education, to lead, and out of them a class sprung up who became dictatorial, and sometimes insolent. Irreligious men insulted in some instances ministers of religion who had been hard workers for temperance; reformed drunkards sneered at those who had never been intemperate, as if former degradation was the only qualification for leadership.

I was a Washingtonian rescued by the spirit of Washingtonianism, and testify of what I know in saying that more than one minister of the gospel shut the door of his church against some of these men, because he could not sit still and hear in his own pulpit, before his own people and the children of his charge, such loose and sometimes vulgar utterances as were occasionally heard. Any remonstrance was construed at once into opposition to the cause itself, rather than to their method.

All advocacy of law was denounced as opposed to Washingtonianism, and many men who had been prominent not only for their zeal in the temperance cause, but also for their ability and Christian character, were thrown into the background. I do not say that this spirit was universal, but there was enough of it to become an element of weakness which grew into disease, and Washingtonianism as an *ism* passed away; and now I hardly suppose there is a society called by that name in the country, while in the palmy days of the movement every town and village had its society.

My firm belief then and now is that no moral movement can live other than a brief spasmodic existence that would wipe God out of it, and ignore or contend against the Christian element. I have before me two volumes of scraps collected from the temperance papers of 1844—46. This was about the time when some of the societies would have no members but those who had been drunkards; who would permit no minister of the gospel to take any part in their exercises; who occupied the whole of the Sabbath-day in meeting, relating experiences, and singing songs that were occasionally objectionable. I give from these papers a few extracts. After I had returned from my first visit to the western part of New York State, in company with Rev. John Marsh, I gave an account of my tour. The following extracts are from that speech in the Tremont Temple, taken from the *Mercantile Journal* in August 1844:—

"He [Mr. Gough] stated that in some places he visited he was informed by the leading Washingtonians that Washingtonianism, as an *ism*, was dead; that it had done all it could, and the cause was now falling back. The reason assigned for this was, that the people in these places had become disgusted with the many follies dragged before the public in connection with Washingtonianism, theatrical exhibitions, etc.; and what is most important, *infidelity* had attached itself to the car of Washingtonianism, and impeded its progress by endeavouring to drag itself into notice and standing in connection with it.

"To the dismay of thousands, men are found advancing Washingtonianism and infidelity in the same breath, and some presses in our country are devoted to this object. Men of respectability and standing, men of moral feeling, and old temperance men stand aloof from a cause shackled with these evils, and call for a new order of things. They will not give their influence until Washingtonianism has freed itself of these dead weights, and stands forth in its original purity and beauty.

"He [Mr. Gough] said that in every place he visited there was a good feeling existing towards the cause of temperance, but it needed to be brought out and properly directed. . . .

"In one place there had not been a social Washingtonian meeting held for eighteen months. Two of the leading men in the cause endeavoured to raise funds to hire a hall to hold meetings. After canvassing the town, upon comparing notes it was found one had obtained a dollar and forty cents, and the other a dollar and ten cents. What was the cause of this apathy, this backwardness? It was what he had already stated,—the people were disgusted with the many follies and evils which had attached themselves to the movement."

For these utterances I was subjected to an attack, which being the first, wounded me sorely. In October I was thus severely called to account for mixing orthodoxy with my temperance utterances:—

"We beg Mr. Gough to pause, ere he lends his power to any sectarian use in the holy cause of temperance. He is a reformed man, and has ample evidence in his own glorious experience of the all-conquering power of the true Washingtonian principles, and motives innumerable to lay before the poor inebriate in urging his reformation, without going into the future world for them,—motives connected with this life, with the poor sufferer's own temporal well-being and happiness."

Whenever I attempted to appeal to the drunkard on the ground of sin against God, or men's responsibility to God, or in view of future retribution, I was either snubbed or soundly rated for introducing "men's eternal interests, of which I knew nothing," etc. Some of the notices are quite amusing at this late day, but at the time I felt them keenly. I quote from the scraps before me :—

"A religious bigot and ignoramus."
"Perverting the cause to sectarian ends."
"Dwelling on a set of motives which he knows never had an agency in promoting this glorious reform."

These are specimens of the utterances of a portion of the press devoted to the interests of Washingtonianism. I doubt if there are any of these papers in existence now; I know not of one.

Mr. Mitchell, the originator of the movement, was received in 1843 by the people of Boston. I have given a description of that grand demonstration in my Autobiography. I think there has been nothing like it since. He went with me to Salem, and expressed himself very strongly against the introduction of anything religious, and said, "We don't want any religion in the movement."

I heard the Hon. Thomas Marshall, of Kentucky, make a ten minutes' speech in Broadway Tabernacle, at the close of an address of mine, in which he said: "Were this great globe one chrysolite, and I were offered the possession if I would drink one glass of brandy, I would refuse it with scorn; and I want no religion, I want the temperance pledge." With that wonderful voice of his he thundered out: "We want no religion in this movement; let it be purely secular, and keep religion where it belongs." Poor Tom Marshall, with all his self-confidence, fell, and died at Poughkeepsie, in clothes given him by Christian charity.

I know I shall not be—for I cannot be—misunderstood, if I say that in some of our reform clubs I see a tendency to just such a practical repudiation of divine help and assistance. I will make no specifications, except to say that I know some reform clubs that sadly need reforming.

The results of Washingtonianism were grand; I would not depreciate the work; and there were many who laboured faithfully and truly to the end of their lives, like John Hawkins and others. But why should not Washingtonianism be a power in this land now? To be sure, the Blue-Ribbon and Red-Ribbon Armies have sprung up in the country, and are doing immense good. The principle of charity for the intemperate, pity that moves to help, sympathy that offers the hand to lift up, are the same as in the other movement; but when all this charity is Christian, when the pity is Christ-like pity, when the sympathy is Christian sympathy, there is the element of permanence; and I believe that the element of decay is in the irreligious, loose methods adopted by so many workers in the earlier day. The temperance cause is not strictly a religious enterprise; it is a secular movement; but the religious element in it is the measure of its success, and the absence of that element is its decay.

A very important fact not to be ignored is that the drunkard, when he would reform, needs help, human help, human practical sympathy. I have before me a letter, sent by a very dear friend who is engaged in evangelical work, enclosing another letter that he received from a man redeemed from drink after a course of intemperance and degradation. After describing his conversion, the reformed man says:—

"And now, dear brother, you must pardon me if I add a word regarding the duty of Christians toward those whom the Lord has saved from that awful vice. There is a common belief amongst good people that a reformed inebriate has to endure the scoffs and sneers of his former associates, but that he is consoled and strengthened by the rallying around him of Christian people. I have heard *you* say from the platform, in exhorting the inebriate converts to go to work and do something useful, that they would see how the churches would rally around them. Now you must pardon me for saying that all such talk involves a double error: the former associates do *not* scoff, and the churches do *not* rally. And my purpose in writing this letter is to implore you, in behalf of that unfortunate class, to use your great influence with Christian people, wherever you may be, to take those poor castaways by the hand in a sense other than metaphorical.

"What they need is work,—honest, useful work. See that they have it. See that they have a chance, by hard and honest work in any avocation for which they are qualified, to rear again on this fair earth—which belongs, not to Christians, as too many of them seem to think, but to Christ—the edifice of a noble character. I know you think this *is* done; but, believe me, it is not. Magnificent opportunities for worship and for spiritual guidance are indeed afforded, and I thank God for it; but preaching was not the greatest need of the man who fell among thieves: what he most needed was to have his wounds bound up, and be taken to an inn."

A man during the first struggle with his enemy needs a refuge, a place of safety. The poor fellow who came into a temperance club-room very drunk, when asked why he was there, said, "Do not turn me out. I know I am drunk; but I have just signed the pledge, and I came in here for safety." Therefore with all my heart do I approve these refuges for the intemperate men, especially during the first few days of their conflict. I am speaking of those who fight against the terrible craving; for a man who has no appetite to conquer needs no help. I do not mean fashionable boarding-houses, where men can go as to an hospital to be cured of a disease simply, but a home where he may find Christian sympathy, and be led to the only source of refuge,—where appeals are made to his conscience, representing his drunkenness not as a mere peccadillo that he may commit when he will with no moral obliquity, but a sin against his body and soul, and a sin against God.

The coffee-palace movement in England has been productive of great good. I have no sympathy with many places called "temperance houses," where they charge as much for dirt and discomfort as you are required to pay for cleanliness and comfort in any other place; trading on your principles, palming off damaged goods upon you, and swindling in the sacred name of Temperance. I have patronized these houses until, becoming disgusted, and for the sake of my health, I have been compelled to seek entertainment at other houses, or stay in the street. I do not pretend to say that all temperance houses are of this base character, but many are, and have been a disgrace to the name, until among many good people "Temperance House" has been only another name for dirt, discomfort, and overcharging, with incivility. There are first-class houses, kept by earnest and honest men, that are a credit to the cause, and deserve our patronage and recommendation.

These coffee-houses should be made as clean and attractive as any of the gaudy liquor-shops. No man cares to go for refreshments into a dark, dingy, unsavoury place ; and his temperance principles must be very strong to induce him to pass by a place clean, cheery, and bright, for one of those places, simply because there is a sign hung out declaring it to be a temperance saloon or refreshment-room.

I once went into one of these, decoyed by the signboard, and sat down at a table where the cloth looked like a map of the United States, stained with mustard, coffee, and grease, crumbs scattered all over it; the place reminding you of Coleridge's description of Cologne, in which he counted seventy-five distinct smells. I called for a steak, and can hardly describe the sights that met my eyes while that steak was in preparation. First the bread was put on the table,—not a very attractive loaf ; then some butter that had been cut with a dirty knife. The steak, how can that be described ! It reminded you of the man who refused to partake of a similar steak on the ground that it was an infringement of Goodyear's patent for indiarubber. I asked for a cup of tea. It came, reminding you again of the customer who said, " If this is tea, I want coffee ; if it is coffee, I want tea." In the sugar a wet spoon had been so often dipped that it had caked into little drops of discoloured sweetness. The spoon itself was sticky; and the whole affair was so utterly destructive to all healthy appetite, that I left as hungry as I entered.

These coffee-houses may be made very attractive, like the "Model" and "Central" in Philadelphia, established in 1874 by Joshua Bailey, Esq., and feeding four thousand daily. This is a private enterprise, and wholly sustained by Mr. Bailey. The "Model," for completeness in its accommodations, has no superior in the world. A company has been formed in New York, " The New York Coffee-House Company," and one in Brooklyn, organized as the "Sailors' Coffee-House and Reading Room." These and similar establishments, under the right superintendence, may be and will be of great service to the cause of reform.

The medical aspect of the temperance question has been ably

discussed by some of the first physicians of the day, both in this country and on the continent of Europe. So many works have been published on the subject during the last few years, that I will simply say that I never use it as a medicine under any circumstances whatever, and furthermore will employ no doctor who is in the habit of constantly prescribing alcoholic drinks.

Dr. Richardson gives his method of prescription in his address to the medical profession. He says:—

"As a therapeutical agent, I have never excluded alcohol from my practice. But this is what I have done for nine years past; I have, whenever I thought I wanted its assistance, prescribed it purely as a chemical medicinal substance, in its pure form, in precise doses, in definite order of time. As I have prescribed amyl nitrite, or chloroform, or ether, so I have prescribed alcohol.

"By this method I have an absolute experience of the clinical use of alcohol, which, I think I may safely say, does not belong to many other prescribing physicians. There are thousands of physicians who, in the same time, have probably prescribed alcoholic fluids a hundred times to my single time; but if they were to be asked the precise doses they have ordered, the actual purity of the substances they have ordered, they would be quite unable, in most cases, to answer at all. So many ounces of wine, so many ounces of brandy or whiskey, really means nothing at all that is reliable. Therefore an absolute experience of alcohol, and that only, is a novelty."

But I know there are physicians who prescribe it by the keg; that is, the patient is ordered to provide himself with a keg, or so many dozen bottles of ale, and take a glass when he feels a sinking, etc. I am of Dr. Richardson's opinion, that a physician before all other men should be straight and square in his testimony against drunkenness and that which produces it. I quote again from him:—

"A doctor whose example turns the scale ever so little toward intemperance; a doctor who treats this question as a joke; the doctor, moreover, who devotes his energies to his calling of saving life, and who, with forty thousand of his fellow country-folk dying yearly around him from one cause, and who toward that cause exhibits indifference, or carelessness, or apathy,—what pretensions has he to be a healer? Where is his honour, to say no word of his feeling? What if some other great cause of mortality—say, of consumption—were at work, slaying its thousands annually, and that cause were as well known to him as this cause, would he toward that be equally indifferent? Would he hand it about, partake of it himself, give it to his children, laugh at those who are wearying to sweep it away, or tell the afflicted from it that it is a necessity? I am sure he would scorn to do any such thing."

I leave the question to medical and scientific men, only advising my reformed friend never to take it as a medicine. Die rather than run the risk of being ensnared by the deceiver that so nearly destroyed you. There is no physician who will or does prescribe it for me; they know I will not take such a prescription; and when they know you will not take it, they will cease to prescribe it for you.

The principle of total abstinence, taking the word *principle* to mean a rule of life, should be to us a reality, not to be laid down or taken up at the dictates of custom, fashion, habit, or craving, but to be held as a sacred rule to be observed always and at all hazards. Let the opposers call us fanatics. We are in good company. Canon Wilberforce says: "I am a fanatic on this question of drink." Shall we not be willing to suffer for the sake of the interests of the cause to which we owe so much? Let no physician drive or coax us from our position. Let it be for us reformed men an impregnable one.

In a Scotch town last year I was suffering fearfully with neuralgia. It seemed as though fingers of fire were feeling for every nerve in my face, and I could not forbear crying out with the severe pain. A gentleman asked me if I would take a glass of brandy if I knew it would afford relief. When I said no, he told me I was a fanatic. How easy it is to use a term for reproach! Many a man has been frightened from a good work at the cry of fanaticism. They mistake enthusiasm for frenzy. If a man die in defence of his country's flag, even in an unrighteous war, men call him a hero; if a man die for a principle, he is a fanatic. Let me tell those who would sneer at us for our consistency, that it often requires more courage to endure the sneers of companions, the pitying shake of the head from friends, and the expressed contempt of society, than to face the cannon's mouth on the field of battle. Many a man would mount the "imminent deadly breach," rather than face the "slow-moving finger of scorn." So I say to my reformed brethren: Stand to your principle. If you make it the rule of your life to abstain, stand to it, suffer for it, and if need be die for it; and may God help us all that we fall not back into the bondage that so many call freedom, and are deceived thereby.

CHAPTER XXXVI.

STRIKING EXPERIENCES.

Compensations of Old Age—This Young Man—The Old Warrior—Amusing Peculiarities of Public Life—The Liverpool Barber—" 'Enery, sweep up this 'Air "—Great Changes—Reforms—Improvements—Children are Forces—An Important Question—Casket and Jewel—Testimonial presented—Boys' Work Twenty-five Years ago—The Results—Drunkard's Child—" My Little Testament"—Testament sold for Whiskey—" God be merciful ! "—" Evil Habits "—Custom and Habit—No Man lost on a Straight Road—A Good Resolution—Hugh Miller.

OLD age has been described as a "peculiarly wretched state," nothing attractive in its appearance, and in the reality only an evil. Even Shakespeare could not avoid admitting its drawbacks :—

" When thou art old and rich
Thou hast neither heart, affection, limb, nor beauty,
To make thy riches pleasure."

The inconveniences of old age are manifold. Old age cannot be cured, but the necessary consequences may be alleviated. There may be many glorious compensations to those advanced in years. To the young, old age and failing strength appear to be an unmitigated evil. When I was a boy of twelve, or even a man of twenty-one, I looked upon fifty years of life as I now look upon one hundred ; always having a dread of living to be old, associating decrepitude with age. Now, at sixty-three, I suffer no sensible diminution of strength, except in a lessening of the ability for active exertion. I remember the first time I was called an old man. Some years since, I was travelling through Boston to the sea-side, with some of my family, and, while I was looking earnestly at a valise I was not quite sure of, a man who was taking the luggage from the car called out, "Well, old man, what are you looking after?" It sounded queer then, but I am used to it now.

It is quite amusing to look over the earlier notices of my personal appearance; and it seems so short a time since I was spoken of as a young man. "This young man with dark hair;" "This pale, thin young man, looking so attenuated that a tolerably persevering gust of wind would have no difficulty in puffing him to any required part of the compass." Now, I read of "the venerable speaker," "the veteran," "the old warrior," etc. At first I was not pleased at these public reminders of age, or at the constant remarks by persons of no tact: "Ah, age is telling on you!" "You are not as young as you were!" "You are getting old!" "How very gray you are getting!" etc. Though why I should object, is a mystery, for it is my own fault if my gray hairs are not honourable. Yet we do shrink from free remarks about our personal appearance, and especially from personal depreciation.

I remember going from Brooklyn to Flushing, L.I., with a party of friends, many years since. I was to deliver a lecture there. We were somewhat delayed; and when we arrived, the audience had assembled. I sat for a few minutes on the pulpit-stairs waiting for the committee; but none appearing, I went into the desk, and without introduction began my speech. After I had concluded, a man who had looked at me rather curiously from the first moment of my arrival till the end of my discourse, came up to me as I descended the stairs, and holding out his hand, said,—

"Well, you are very much like a singed cat!"

Having never before heard that the expression, "singed cat," was used to denote a person who was better than he looked, I was slightly nettled, and asked one of my friends—who reminded me of the fact the other day—why that man should say I was like a "singed cat," and whether he meant it as an offence.

One of the amusing peculiarities of public life is in the remarks so freely uttered and frequently over-heard.

The last day of my first visit to England I was in Liverpool.

I had spoken the evening before, and was to give my farewell speech that evening. In the course of the day I went into a barber's shop. While the "professor of tonsure," as I saw it announced the other day, was practising on my hair, he began to speak of the plentiful harvest in America. I said,—

"I sail for America to-morrow."

"Ah, indeed, sir! You will have as a fellow-passenger John B. Gough."

"Does he sail to-morrow?"

"Yes; and I have a ticket to hear him to-night."

"Have you ever heard him lecture?"

"No, sir; have you?"

"Yes."

"How do you like him?"

"I do not think much of him."

"Then you are not a teetotaler?"

"Yes, I am."

"I wonder you do not like Mr. Gough."

"I said I did not think much of him, not that I did not like him."

"Ah, that's very much the same thing! What sort of an appearing person is he?"

"A very ordinary-looking person."

"It is plain to see that you do not like him. What might be his size, sir?"

"About my size, I judge."

"Have you heard him more than once?"

"Yes, many times."

"I should hardly think you would go so often to hear him, if you do not like him."

"I never said I did not like him."

"I beg your pardon, sir, but do you know him?"

"Tolerably well."

"Shall you hear him speak this evening?"

"Yes, I expect to do so."

"Did you hear him last evening?"

"Yes."

"I have been quite desirous of hearing him, and I have secured my ticket.—Does your 'air suit you, sir? Shall I put some hoil on it?"

"No, I thank you, it will do very well; and you will have the opportunity of studying your work on the platform, for you have been cutting Mr. Gough's hair."

"Bless my soul, sir! I beg your pardon. I 'ope I 'ave not said anything wrong, or been in hanny way disrespectful."

"Oh no; on the contrary, you have been quite complimentary."

"So you are Mr. Gough. I shall 'ear you to-night.—'Enery, sweep up all this 'air, and take care of it. Good-bye, sir. I am glad I 'ave 'ad the hopportunity and the honour of cutting your 'air."

As I contemplate the past, how much there is to fill the thought and stir the pulses in view of the wonderful progress in all directions, and the great changes that have taken place since my remembrance, and even since my first entry on public life.

In 1842, Louis Philippe was king of the French. In 1848 came the Republic, growing into the Empire. Again, in 1871, after the Commune, came the Republic, routing the Empire. Four great wars have agitated Europe: the Crimean, the Italian, the Franco-German, and the war of Russia with Turkey. In 1857, the great Indian mutiny startled the world. In 1847 occurred the war of the United States with Mexico, and in 1861 commenced the war for the Union.

What great reforms have been inaugurated in the past forty years! In nearly all the civilized portions of the globe, from Japan to christianized Madagascar, from India to our own free country, the battle is going on, and the fight becomes more earnest. Glance rapidly over the world and see. The United States has given freedom to her slaves; Russia has emancipated her millions of serfs. Germany is fighting the double battle in sight of the world, with a keen, relentless, moral despotism on the one hand, and on the other the struggle between the license of materialism and the freedom that walks in steadfast obedience to Divine law. Italy, instead of being a nest of petty states, united only in dense ignorance and abject slavery, now walks among the nations, free to drain her stagnant moral marshes; free to say to all her people, "Rise, for thy light has come." France has made leap after leap for civil and political freedom and equal rights; and though not yet landed on the safe side, still her dissatisfactions are noble, and inspire the world with sympathy toward her struggles. England is bravely grappling with internal problems, and burden after burden is being lifted from the shoulders of her people. Turkey is being pierced with loopholes for light. Egypt tolerates Christian schools. Spain has seen the Inquisition crumble. China's emperor is moving to prevent opium from paralyzing his millions of subjects. Japan asks of the United States teachers of schools after the method of to-day, and takes the Christian Sabbath for her Sabbath;—all this when her ports with one exception were barred against the commerce of the world at the opening of this century. Hear the proclamation of the Queen of Madagascar, where till recently heathenism reigned supreme, with savage cruelties and persecutions to the death of all who dared avow the Christian name:—

" I, Ranovalomajaka, by the grace of God, and the will of my people, Queen of Madagascar, defender of the laws of my kingdom, this is what I say to you, my subjects: God has given me this land and kingdom; and concerning the rum, you and I have agreed it shall not be sold, because it does harm to your persons, to your wives and children; makes foolish the wise, makes more foolish the foolish, and causes people not to fear the laws of the kingdom, and especially makes them guilty before God."

After encouraging the people to trade in good things, the Queen declares:—

"I am not ashamed to make laws in my kingdom which shall do you good; therefore, I tell you if there are people who break my law, I must punish them."

Christian associations now flourish in the Fiji Islands, where cannibalism reigned supreme forty years ago. India and Siam and Persia are saying, through thousands of now Christian voices, "The entrance of Thy words giveth light." And the islands of the sea are flocking to the standard of liberty and Bible light, as doves come to their windows.

In that which tends to personal comfort and national advancement, more has been accomplished, and grander achievements have been realized in this century, than in all the previous lifetime of our race. Since my entrance into public life, the changes have been wonderful. The improvements in the modes of locomotion and communication are amazing. Photography, chloroform, the electric telegraph, sewing-machines, telephones, and many inventions strange and curious at the beginning, now rank among the necessities of our present mode of life.

We are almost bewildered as we look back on the past; and, seeking to penetrate the future, we ask, "What shall it be when the present generation has passed away?" How important it is that those who are to fill our places should feel the responsibility that all this light and development devolves on them! They must reap as they sow, and in the far future will be garnered the harvest of their sowing.

To me a company of children is a most impressive and suggestive sight. The little creatures are forces in the world for good or evil; for none can possibly be neutral in the contest of the ages,—of right against wrong, of truth against falsehood, of Christ against Belial, the kingdom of this world arrayed against the kingdom of our God and of His Christ. With all my heart I rejoice and take courage in view of the fact that a revival of the temperance work among children is taking place. At three important Sunday-school conventions it has been accorded a prominent place, and I have been privileged to speak on these occasions. At the experiment at Framlingham this year, in imitation of the very successful Chautauqua conventions, there was a temperance day. From England, Dr. B. W. Richardson writes, in a letter I lately received from him :—

"Our cause is still making good progress. The young are getting more and more imbued, and they are the propagandists of the true stamp."

Here the question comes to me, What is the most valuable thing that has ever challenged my attention in these thirty-eight years of contact with life? What now seems the most precious occupation for the most choicely endowed men and women of this day and time? Who that takes this thought in mind from any altitude can give any other answer than this, that the children of this land are beyond all comparison the forces that should be first and last considered in all national, patriotic municipal, family, and individual aspirations and plans? All the educational institutions, all legislative enactments, all social customs, every adult example, often the unstudied sentence, touches with beauty or blight this fairest thing in all creation, this most powerful influence, this subtlest and most glorious force, this indestructible life, a little child. Casket and jewel, both so exquisitely formed, having such possibilities of light, fire, attraction, nothing on earth can equal it. And yet this lovely gift to the world is left, in thousands of cases, to be bent and warped and jostled into the ugliest and most dangerous forms, corroded by atmospheres that eat into all its promising outlines, while those who are called by every high motive to reverse all these conditions are using up their lives in scrambling for things which, when obtained, shall bring no satisfaction to themselves nor benefit to others.

It seems to me no occupation can be so important or require such choice qualities as the care and guidance of children, and that it should be reckoned among the most honourable of the professions; and that the brain, mind, and heart of the truest, noblest, and most conscientious toward God and man should be the elected ones to guide into the best possibilities the children. I can desire nothing better for this great country, growing with such startling rapidity, than that a barrier high and strong should be raised between the unpolluted lips of the children and the intoxicating cup; that everywhere the men and women of to-day should raise strong and determined hands against whatever will defile the body, pollute the mind, or harden the heart against God and His truth, of the millions of children in this country. God grant we may none of us forget who it is that has said, "It were better that a millstone were hanged about his neck and he were drowned in the depths of the sea," than that he should be a means of "offence" to "one of these little ones."

We often underrate the capacity of children to work, to be of service in any great movement; and yet what great results have been accomplished by the simple but earnest work and influence of the young! As an instance of what may be done by the hearty and combined efforts of young people, I would relate a very pleasant episode in my last experience in London.

At a meeting held in the Congregational chapel, Victoria Park, May 12th, 1879, a very beautiful and elegantly engrossed and ornamental testimonial was presented to me with the following inscription :—

"THIS TESTIMONIAL
WAS PRESENTED
ON THE 12TH OF MAY, 1879,
TO
MR. JOHN B. GOUGH.
TEMPERANCE ADVOCATE OF AMERICA,

On the occasion of his visiting Bonner's Fields to give an oration at a chapel erected on the very spot where, some twenty years since, a number of youths, inspired by various anecdotes of what good the young may accomplish, told in their hearing by Mr. Gough, in Exeter Hall and elsewhere, were led to hold open-air meetings, which resulted in the formation, at Bonner's Lane, Bethnal Green, of the Twig Folly Christian Temperance Society and Band of Hope, which has produced great good to the neighbourhood, and brought out many earnest labourers for the cause of temperance, who are still at work, not only in the metropolis, but in the country also. As one of the results of your earnest temperance advocacy in London, this may be an interesting and encouraging reminiscence during your future labours, which we hope, under God's blessing, will be continued to be as useful as heretofore. . . . As a grateful acknowledgment of your many services in the cause, the youths above referred to, and the older labourers in the temperance ranks, who helped them in their early efforts, beg you to accept their portraits and signatures."

Fourteen finely-executed photographs surround the inscription, and the whole is most superbly designed and executed.

These gentlemen, when boys, determined to do what they

could for the cause which had interested them, and for a beginning of their effort instituted a series of out-door meetings in Bonner's Fields, obtaining speakers from older societies. This led to the formation of a society which grew rapidly in influence. Branch societies were formed. The parent society now numbers seven hundred members, and their auxiliaries number thousands; and on the spot where they held their first feeble meetings the chapel is erected in which I spoke, when Sir Charles Reed presided and the testimonial was presented. So much for the efforts of boys when determined and encouraged.

The quiet influence of a child has been the means of saving the parent. I remember a little history related to me many years ago by a Christian abstainer. He said he would give me the facts that led to his reform, and the circumstance that arrested him in his career of sin.

Two maiden ladies who lived in the village often noticed a scantily clad girl passing their house with a tin pail. On one occasion one of these ladies accosted her.

" Little girl, what have you got in that pail? "

" Whiskey, ma'am."

" Where do you live? "

" Down in the hollow."

" I'll go home with you."

They soon came to a wretched hovel in the hollow, outside the village. A pale, jaded, worn-out woman met them at the door. Inside was a man, dirty, maudlin, and offensive. The lady addressing the woman, said,—

" Is this your little girl? "

" Yes."

" Does she go to school? "

" No; she has no other clothes than what you see."

" Does she go to Sunday school? "

" Sunday school—in these rags! Oh, no!"

" If I furnish her with suitable clothes, can she go? "

"It is of no use giving her clothes. He would steal them, and sell them for whiskey. Better let the girl alone; there is no hope for her, or for us."

"But she ought to go to school."

An arrangement was entered into whereby the child should call at the lady's house on Sunday morning, be clothed for the school, and after the school was dismissed, call again, and change her garments for home.

The little creature was very teachable, and soon became a favourite with her teacher, who gave her a little Testament, probably the first gift the child had ever received. She was very proud of her Testament, exhibiting it on all occasions with the delighted exclamation,—

"That's my little Testament—my own."

She would take it with her at night, clasping it in her hands till she fell asleep on the wretched rags called a bed. The child was taken ill. The doctor provided by her benefactors declared she would die. Her friends furnished her with what comforts they could, and watched the father, lest he should steal them and sell them for whiskey.

The gentleman then continued the narrative in the first person:—

"One day I went to her bedside. I was mad for drink. I had taken everything I could lay my hands on. I looked round the room. There was nothing left, nothing I could dispose of. Yet I must have drink. I would have sold my child; I would have sold myself, for whiskey. The little creature lay on the bed, with the Testament clasped in her hand, partly dozing. As I sat there she fell asleep, and the book slipped from her fingers, and lay on the coverlid of the bed. Stealthily looking round the room, I stretched out my shaking hand, seized the Testament, and hastily thrust it into my bosom. I soon sneaked out, like a guilty thing, to the grog-shop. All I could get for it was half-a-pint of whiskey. It was a poor little book. I drank the devil's drink almost at a draught, and soon felt relieved from the burning thirst. The stagnant blood in the diseased vessels of my stomach was stimulated by the fiery fluid, and I felt better. What took me back to my child I cannot tell, but I sat again by her side. She still seemed to be sleeping; and I sat there with the horrible craving stayed for the time by the whiskey I had

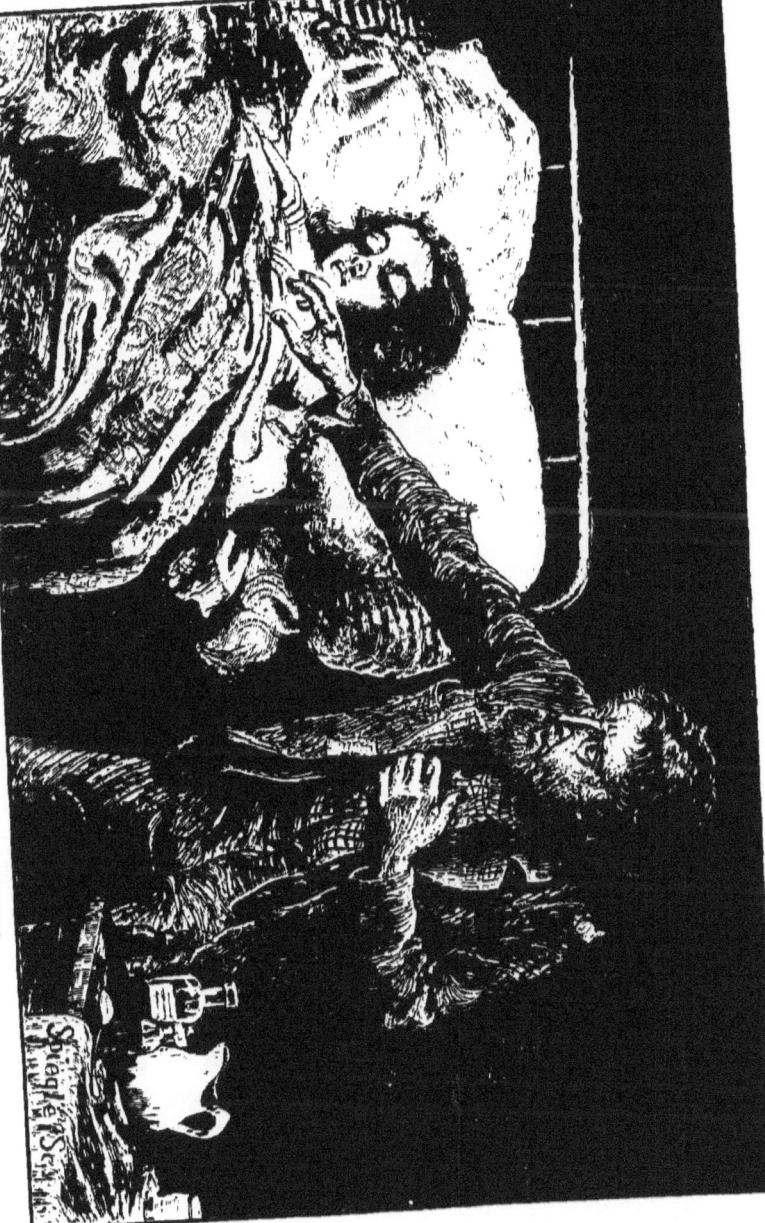

A FATHER STEALING A TESTAMENT FROM HIS DYING CHILD.

drank, when she opened her eyes slowly and saw me. Reaching out her hand to touch mine, she said, 'Papa, listen. I'm going to die, and when I die I shall go to Jesus, for He told little children to come to Him. And I shall go to heaven; for He said that little children were of the kingdom of heaven. I learned that out of my Testament. Papa, suppose when I go to heaven Jesus should ask me what you did with my little Testament. Oh, papa! oh, papa! what shall I tell Him?' It struck me like lightning. I sat a few moments, and then fell down on my knees by the bedside of my child, crying, 'God be merciful to me, a sinner.' That half-pint of whiskey was the last drop of intoxicating liquor that has passed my lips. She died in a few days, with her hand in mine, and her last words to me were, 'Papa, we shall both go to Jesus now.'"

May heaven bless the dear children! We need them as workers, and we must remember that drunkenness would die out with the present race of the intemperate, death alone would remove the evil in thirty years, were there no more drunkards made. There is no necessity for the existence of this curse to the world. But while men and women use intoxicating liquors as a beverage, drunkenness will continue. All past experience testifies to this. Therefore our great hope is in training the children understandingly to abstain from the use of an article which at the best can be but a luxury, and never a necessity as a beverage. I am exceedingly glad that public attention is drawn to these facts, and we have hope for the future.

What I said in the beginning of this book I repeat now: "Man is in a great degree the arbiter of his own destiny." We can make ourselves what we will. Byron said, "I am convinced that men do more harm to themselves than ever the Devil can do to them." To the young I would say, Beware of the formation of evil habits; remember habit is acquired. What we are accustomed to do gives a facility and proneness to do. "How shall ye do good who are accustomed to do evil?" Archbishop Whately says, "Habits are formed not at one stroke, but gradually and insensibly; so that, unless vigilant care be employed, a great change may come over the character without our being conscious of any." Dr. Johnson says, "The diminutive chains of habit are seldom heavy enough to be felt till they are too strong to be broken." Again, Archbishop Whately makes this distinction between custom and habit: "Repeated acts constitute the custom, and habit is the condition of mind or body thence resulting." Thus the custom of drinking produces the habit of craving, and that yielded to, the habit of drunkenness. "By accustoming ourselves to any course of action we acquire an aptness to go on, a facility, a readiness, and often a pleasure in it; our aversion grows weaker, the difficulties lessen, and a new character, in many respects and habits of life not given by nature, may be formed." Acts repeated, like a cable formed by the repetition of twisted threads, soon consolidate into habits that form a second nature. The power of habit to consolidate virtuous character is illustrated in the increasing stability of every good man, the sentiment of whose heart becomes like that of the Psalmist, "I hate vain thoughts, but Thy law do I love;" while its almost invincible power for evil is illustrated in the increasing depravity of sin. "They encourage themselves in an evil matter; they search out iniquities; they accomplish a diligent search." "He hath left off to be wise, and to do good; he deviseth mischief on his bed." If every act tends to the formation of habit, and every habit goes to form character and render it unalterable, who can calculate the interminable consequences attached to every voluntary act!

A friend of mine once said that this motto should be written over the door of every young man's chamber: "No man was ever yet lost on a straight road." As we look back on our own experience, we realize how wide a course of wrong doing and thinking originated in one step from the rough road of duty to the smooth path of inclination. Could we have always been on our guard, what mortifications, regrets, humiliations, and sufferings would have been spared us! Have you by thoughtlessness or recklessness acquired habits that are a hindrance to your prosperity, destructive to your peace, and under the bondage of which you groan? Remember, if you would ever be free, it will be easier to-day to break your fetters than it ever will be again in this world; for habit strengthens with age. It is hard and painful to uproot an old habit; it is harder to unlearn than it is to learn. It is easier to break the single thread than the strong cord. The difficulty is, the thread seems so small you can break it when you will, and with ease. Try it, and you will be surprised at the effort needed. A wire around your little finger, securely fastened to a pillar, holds you as certainly as an iron band with copper rivets. If you are held, it matters not how small or large the agent seems to be; it holds you.

A good resolution faithfully kept has saved many a man. When Hugh Miller was a stone-mason, it is stated that he drank at one time, in company with several of his fellow-workmen, two glasses of whiskey. On reaching home, he took up Bacon's Essays, and found the letters dance before his eyes, and he could not master the sense, when he said, " In that hour I determined that I would never sacrifice my capacity for intellectual enjoyment to a drinking usage, and by the help of God I was able to keep my resolution."

CHAPTER XXXVII.

LAST GLEANINGS.

My First Visit to the Theatre—Booth and Hamblin—"Apostate" and "Review"—The Old Bowery—My Passion for the Stage—Interview with a Manager—Comic Song at the Chatham—Persevering Efforts to be an Actor—The Summit of Ambition—The Old Lion of Boston—Charles Thorne—Charles Eaton—"Roll him in and tap him"—Tinsel and Sham—My Disenchantment—Thanks that my Way was Blocked—Power to Overcome—Coleridge—A Good Impulse—"Art thee crazy, Lad?"—The First Sermon—Paying Debts like a Christian—The Last Race—Retrospection—Contrasts—Lessons learned—Encouragements—Last Words.

MANY of us, in looking back on our experiences of fifty years of life, must recall some instances of merciful interposition, when our own will, purpose, and determination have been set aside by an unseen but powerfully-felt agency, and we, with our will and purpose set, have been compelled to take an entirely opposite course from that we had planned, or have been mysteriously, or I would rather say providentially, hindered from carrying out our determined plans.

When quite a young man, I had an intense desire, almost amounting to a passion, to adopt the theatrical profession. I was fascinated by the theatre, stage-struck, enamoured of all dramatic representation.

I shall never forget the sensation on my first visit to the theatre. It was the Old Bowery. The play was "The Apostate:" Mr. Booth the elder as *Pescara;* Mr. Hamblin, the manager, as *Hemeya;* and Miss Vincent as *Florinda.* The afterpiece was "The Review; or, The Wags of Windsor:" Mr. Booth as *John Lump;* Mr. Hamblin as *Looney McTwolter.* Between the tragedy and the farce, Rice jumped Jim Crow.

I cried and laughed. I was thrilled by the tragedy and convulsed by the farce. It was a new world. How beautiful were the women! how noble were the men! Even *Pescara*, as his eyes flashed with malignant hate, was like a creature above the mere human. The gorgeous dresses, the music and lights dazzled me. I went home to my lodgings fascinated, carried out of myself. How mean and poor was my little bedroom, and what a dreary monotony of life mine was, plodding in a shop to learn a trade! Trade, profession, occupation, business, —all was tame, slow, grovelling, compared with the glorious, the grand, the bewildering pursuit of the actor. Again and again I enjoyed the delicious enchantment, and fully determined that I must be an actor,—I must strut my hour upon the stage. I envied the poor stick who came on to remove the tables and chairs, the poor, despised supe; even the doorkeeper was an object of interest. Yes, I was smitten.

With what awe and reverence would we stage-struck boys watch some celebrated actor in the streets. It was an event worth recording. "I saw Forrest to-day." "I saw Booth to-day." I have even followed them and set my foot on the same stones they had trodden. Remember I was but sixteen years of age. These boys had each their favourite actress, for whom they would fight; ay, and throw down the gauntlet to all comers in her defence. How we would crowd around the stage-door to see some actor or actress pass out or in! Madame Celeste was a great favourite; we were never weary of singing her praises or witnessing her performance. I should hesitate to say how many times I had seen her in "The French Spy."

To some persons all this may appear strange. They cannot conceive the attraction of all the stage paraphernalia and the glamour thrown round certain minds by the glitter and unreality of the stage.

I have been often asked why I did not adopt the stage as a profession. It was not from lack of desire, though I do not pretend that I possessed the ability to become an actor of repute. Why I did not, after all my attempts, I cannot tell, but that I was hindered, blocked in every direction, to my sore vexation.

I will not write here how the desire took full possession of me, and rendered me for a time almost useless. I know it led me to neglect the duty that lay before me. I eagerly devoured any plays that I could lay hold of; learned parts. I could repeat and spout *Jaffier*, in "Venice Preserved." From tragedy to comedy; from farce to melodrama. I even contemplated writing a play. I have carried a tattered play-book surreptitiously to my work-bench, and learned the whole play while at my work, and then would mouth it and tear it to pieces in the most extravagant theatrical style. I joined a dramatic society. I played *Zanga*, in the "Revenge;" the *Doctor*, in the "Duenna;" *Jeremy Diddler*, in the "Raising the Wind;" and some other minor parts; but my resources were so limited I was compelled to give up the dramatic society. Yet all my available funds were expended on theatre tickets.

One day I was determined to make a desperate effort for a footing on the stage; and, getting excused from the shop for a day, I ventured to enter the box-office of the Bowery Theatre and inquire for Mr. Hamblin. I was told that he was on the stage, and that I could see him by applying at the stage-door. So to the stage-door I went, and for the first time I stood behind the scenes. A drearier place I had seldom seen, but my ardour was not damped by the contrast to all the glory I had connected with the stage. When the gentleman appeared, I was fearfully embarrassed, but gathered courage to ask if he wanted an actor. With a smile, he asked me several questions, such as what parts I had studied, what line of business I desired, what I considered myself fit for. I gave such answers as my confusion would allow, and at last blurted out: "I want to be an actor. If you will engage me, I will do anything; black your boots, run your errands, be your servant." He checked me by asking what my business was. I told him, "book-binding;" when he said, "Ah, young man, you had better stick to bookbinding," and turned his back on me. Though rebuffed, I was not discouraged, but determined to persevere.

I then applied to William Sefton, of the Chatham Theatre, for permission to sing a comic song between the pieces. The permission was granted, with a note to the leader of the orchestra to rehearse with me; and under the name of Gilbert, I sang the "Water Party," and actually obtained a generous encore. I remember that night the play was the "Golden Farmer," John Sefton as *Jimmy Twitcher*. The actors were all dressed for their respective parts, and they encouraged me. The stage-manager said I had done very well, but no engagement followed.

Soon after, I left New York, and for awhile I worked in Providence, where I became acquainted with some gentlemen attached to the theatre, lost a good situation through neglect of my duties and a fascination for the stage, and through the influence of a Mr. Barry obtained an engagement at the Lion Theatre, Boston. Surely I am now at the summit of my ambition—a permanent engagement on the staff of artists at a regular theatre. Before, it had been an occasional appearance to fill up a gap at a temporary place of entertainment. Alas! I found the gold to be tinsel. Here I acquired a thorough distaste for all theatrical representations, and all the genius and intellect displayed by the most famous actor has not, and never can, reconcile me to the sham, the tinsel crowns, the pasteboard goblets, the tin armour, the paltry spangles, cotton for velvet, all make-believe, the combats, and the sham blood. Even the nightly disguise became an annoyance; the painting the face, corking the eyebrows, pencilling the wrinkles, the doing up with false whiskers, hair, moustache, the French chalk, the rouge, the burnt cork, to say nothing of the habiliments, rendered the whole thing at the last odious to me; and I never felt meaner, or had less self-respect, than when I was bedizened to do some character. How men of ability and common sense can submit to this caricaturing night after night, passes my poor comprehension.

In that theatre I found some men of education in the higher walks of the profession; but, oh, the disenchantment! The beautiful women were, some of them, coarse and profane; the noble gentlemen often mean, tricky, and sponging. In fact, the unreality of it, the terrible temptation to the lower forms of vice, especially to those of the nervous, excitable temperament, increased by the falsehood and fiction involved in their profession, in seeming to be what they never were or could be, studying virtue to represent it on the stage, while their lives were wholly vicious, repelled me. Mark me well, I do not say this of all actors. I only speak of the special temptations of this special profession.

The Lion Theatre company was selected for a short season. There were some good actors. Charles Thorn was stage-manager. There was Chapman, J. R. Hall, and others I might name; one especially, Charles Eaton, a graduate of one of our principal colleges; genial, warm-hearted, nobody's enemy but his own. I do not believe the elder Booth personated *Iago* more powerfully than Eaton. He was a genius, very ready with his retort, on or off the stage. On one occasion, in the play of "Pizarro," Eaton sustaining that character, one of the attendants rushes in with the cry, "My lord, we have just taken an old *cacique.*" *Pizarro*, who has been worked up by the occurrences of the drama to a fearful pitch of fury, replies, "Drag him before me!" But instead, the supernumerary rushed in and roared out, "My lord, we have just taken an old *cask.*" Eaton, who as *Pizarro* was prepared with the correct reply, looked for a moment amazed: but, startled by a titter among the audience, he shouted out, "Roll him in, and tap him;" and after the roar of applause and laughter had subsided, in which Eaton and all on the stage joined, the play proceeded. Poor Eaton! every one knows what a wreck he became.

In spite of much that was attractive to a young man of my temperament, I felt an unaccountable repugnance to adopting acting as a profession; and so when the theatre closed, in about three weeks after I entered it, I never tried again, being perfectly satisfied with my experience, though it lasted for so short a time. Looking back from my standpoint to-day, I thank God that hindrances were thrown in my way, and that I utterly failed in accomplishing my cherished purpose. It may be I failed for the lack of dramatic genius. However that may be, I am glad that I failed; for, though many have succeeded in resisting the temptation surrounding them in the profession, I know—and the world knows—that many have been wrecked, and I have no conception that I should have escaped; so that I consider the hindrances were merciful.

In my past experience I recall impulses that have come to me mysteriously, and sometimes under strange circumstances. I remember one illustration. When in Worcester, England, twenty-six years ago, I was a guest of a gentleman, a member of Parliament, who resided just opposite the city on the banks of the river, a delightful place, with a lawn, rockwork, and trees artistically planted. I was at that time a smoker, and though I never smoked in a gentleman's house without an invitation, I deemed it necessary to have my smoke after dinner, if by any means I could get it with no annoyance to others. So after dinner I strolled down to the river side, out of sight of the house, took out my cigars and matches, and proceeded to light a cigar. The wind blew out the match. Another was tried, and another. I took off my hat to shield it from the wind. It was of no avail. I got some brimstone down my throat, or something as bad; but the cigar would not ignite. Then I kneeled down close to the rock by the path at the side of the river, and with my hat off endeavoured to secure the object. Now, I never go on my knees but I am reminded of prayer, and the thought came, "If any one should see me, they would probably think that some man had sought that retired spot for private devotion, and that he was saying his prayers; and what am I doing? I am sucking away at a cigar, hoping to obtain fire enough from the match to get a smoke. What would the audience say who heard me last night, should they see me now?" The inconsistency of my practice with my profession struck me so forcibly, that I said, "I'll have no more of it." I rose from my knees, took cigars and matches and threw them into the river, and I never touched a cigar to smoke for eighteen years.

For our encouragement we have some splendid records of the power to overcome when men have yielded to a good impulse, and in God's name and seeking His help have resisted all temptation, and thus have been enabled to fight to the end unflinchingly.

By his own letters and Cottle's reminiscences, it is abundantly proved that for eight or ten years Coleridge, with all his mighty gifts, seemed utterly lost to his friends through intemperance. Wordsworth and Cottle had given him up, and were looking every day to hear of his death. His wife had ceased to hear or to desire to hear any further of or from him, and he probably had not a real friend in the world who had the slightest hopes of ever seeing him reformed. Wordsworth had appointed watchers to be with him night and day. He had violated every pledge, deceived every friend, lost his honour, self-respect, and all confidence in his own power to conquer this all-absorbing vice. When an outcast, without a guinea, he did the wisest and most conscientious thing he had ever done, and which altered the destiny of his whole future life. After some correspondence with a physician, to whom he revealed his situation, he became an inmate of the family of Dr. Gilman, of Highgate. There he lived for thirty years, restored by loving and respectful treatment, and moral and medical care and restraint. He entered the house an humble penitent, the slave of opium. He dwelt there for almost a generation, living and at length dying a Christian; and he earnestly desired that after his death a full statement of his case might be laid before the world.

When a man yields to a good impulse because it is good and right, it will never lead him astray. I met a man who is a living and striking example of this. A brief sketch of his career was published some time since by Rev. John Guttridge, of Manchester, England. He was a sporting man, and was regarded as no ordinary racer. He had been matched and betted on forty-seven times. He was very popular, and he resolved to open a beer-house, which should serve as a place of resort for his associates. There was in him a good deal of natural tenderness, and some conscience; and in my experience I have found among some of the hardest characters a tenderness that was surprising. Jerry McAuley, once a river-thief and a "hard case," now a tender-hearted Christian, the love of Jesus melting the heart once so callous. One day this man noticed a poor woman, with two or three children, whose husband was drinking

LOOKING FOR FATHER.—AN INCIDENT THAT LED TO THE REFORM OF A RUMSELLER.

in his shop, looking anxiously in at the door. The thought of the meanness of selling beer and making money out of the poverty of this family struck him quite forcibly, and the impulse to get out of the miserable business came on him with such power that he said to his wife, "See here, lass, I'll work my fingers to the stumps before I'll keep a box like this; and I'll get out of it." When it was known that he purposed giving up the business, he was advised to advertise and sell it. What was his reply? "Na, na; I give it up because it's bad; and I'll put no man in a bad business for money. If any man goes into this box, he goes in on his own bottom for all me." To a brewer, who offered to put him in a larger and more profitable house, he said, "Na, I would not do it for all the world. I'd die first." At that time he saw no evil in the drink itself, only in its abuse. He therefore secured a house, and took to it several barrels of ale and porter for moderate use. One day he saw a notice in the street of a temperance meeting to be held. He yielded to the impulse, and decided to go. Under the influence of the lecture, which was delivered by Mr. Jabez Inwards, of London, he went home, hastened to the cellar, and turned the tap of every barrel. His wife, being told by one of the children what was going on, rushed into the cellar.

"What are -hee doing, lad?"

"Don't thee see what I be doing?"

"Eh! but wilful waste makes woful want, and thee art wasting the good stuff."

Seeing that she produced no effect by her appeal, she said:—

"Art thee crazy, lad?"

"No, I'm not crazy; I'm coming to my senses."

"But how dost thee think I can care for the children without a drop of ale?"

"Thee must try porridge, for I'll have no more of the stuff in the house."

He soon signed the pledge of total abstinence, and it was to him the dawn of a new life. It was rolling away the stone from the door of the sepulchre. His next good impulse was to go to a place of worship, having never been into one before. The only religious exercise he remembered was part of a prayer by a street preacher. He went of his own accord, with no invitation, to hear the gospel preached for the first time in his life. If I were a preacher, I would prefer an audience of men and women who had never heard the sound of the gospel, than an audience of those who had heard the message for forty years, and been unmoved by it. The first sermon he heard was from the passage in Timothy : " Godliness is profitable unto all things, having the promise of the life that now is, and that which is to come." The preacher was not a learned man, or a refined and eloquent speaker ; but his homely phrases were thoroughly understood, and the effect produced was shown by the remark after the discourse : " If it's true what that chap says, it will just suit me. Only think! good for this life, and good for t'other. All right now, and all right then. Safe here, and safe there. That's just what I want, and I'll have it."

This led to his seeking and finding, and the commencing of a consistent Christian life. His fifteen years' recklessness had left him in debt ; so he did what every Christian should do,—began to pay his debts. He had seven little children, and was owing one hundred and fifty pounds, without a penny to meet his obligations. He went to his principal creditor, to whom he was indebted seventy-five pounds, and engaged to pay five shillings per week, which he did, never missing a week for more than five years. To another creditor, who had never even mentioned the debt to him, he went, three years after he became a Christian, and said:

" I believe I owe thee seven pounds. Now, I've a pig that I've fed instead of feeding the publican, and thou canst have the pig."

" Well, lad," was the reply, " I'll take the pig ; and if there's aught over, I'll pay thee the balance."

The pig was killed, weighed, and the balance of three pounds ten shillings was paid over.

On one occasion an old companion, who did not understand the great change wrought in him, called at his shop to obtain some sporting information, and wished to know who was going to win the race in Hyde Park.

"I do not know anything at all about it."

"Nay, thee canst tell us something about it; thou knowest what they've done afore."

"Nay, lad; I've nobbut another race to run, and then I've done."

"Another race art thee going to run? Another race? Who is it with? Hast thee made another match?"

"Aye; I've made a match with the Devil for eternal life and my own soul, and it will take me all the days of my life to beat him."

His old companion was quite taken aback. A cannon-shot would scarcely have surprised him more than such a reply from one who had been so famous as a sporting character, and so frequently applauded in *Bell's Life*.

When I shook hands with him, last year, he was sixty-four years of age, and had been an earnest worker for temperance and a consistent Christian for twenty-nine years, with a family of six sons and two daughters walking with him in the right road, one of his sons being a successful Christian minister. He occupies a respectable position; has never been forsaken; has been blessed in "basket and store," body and soul, and has been the means of great blessing to others. The beginning of all this was the yielding to a good impulse and giving up what he believed to be wrong. Such a lesson needs no comment.

In the retrospection necessary to the compilation of such a book as this there are multitudes of incidents, passages of experience almost forgotten, that spring up in the memory with a vividness positively startling; and as this work draws to a conclusion, the material seems of larger bulk than at its commencement.

In 1827, when a boy of ten, I was taken by my father to a prayer-meeting held in the lodgings of the celebrated William Wilberforce, in my native village of Sandgate. After the meeting Wilberforce called me to him, I being the only boy there, and laying his hand on my head, gave me his blessing. In 1879, I was a guest of his grandson, Rev. Basil Wilberforce, Canon of Winchester, at the Deanery of St. Mary's, Southampton. In

June, 1829, I left the village of Sandgate, a boy of twelve, on the top of a night-coach, for London, on my way to America. In June, 1879, fifty years after, I visited Sandgate to lay the corner-stone of a memorial coffee-palace, and received a most cordial greeting. As we were entering the village the carriage was stopped, and, in the kindness of their hearts, the people took out the horses and drew us through the main street. On every side were streamers and flags and words of welcome. Between these points, and during the years that intervened, what a varied experience had been mine! And the great lessons learned from it all are, that life is a warfare, a conflict against the power of evil; that life is unsatisfactory unless there has been work done in reference to another and higher state of existence; that there is something to live for above the fleeting, selfish pleasures that so many spend all to obtain, and die miserably poor.

We know that though we may see no results from our whole life's labour, and die without a sign that our work has been approved or successful, yet we must remember that—

"Work done for God, it dieth not."

We may die and be forgotten, but our works shall live after us. The good seed we have been permitted to sow shall result in a harvest that others shall gather. To me the great encouragement is that "He shall subdue all things unto Himself;" "He shall put all things under His feet." Let us not be disheartened, though the evil we seek to remove seems to stand solid and unyielding against all our efforts.

On our rugged and romantic coast we see the mighty bastion of rock withstanding the fury of the waves, and apparently impregnable. Hark to the thunder of the crash, as they dash themselves against these cliffs, and come in full, sweeping charge against these rocks. They fall back, broken, weak, and discomfited. Yet they only give place to fresh levies repeating the assault, and they, like their predecessors, are hurled back defeated. "The war seems endless. Yet by slow degrees the sea gains on its silent enemy; it undermines, it channels, it gnaws caverns, it eats out chasms, it wears away the surface little by little, it grinds into sand, it gashes with scars, and will never rest till it has dragged down its opposing walls into its depths." So, in the great conflict of right and wrong, generation after generation may pass away, apparently defeated, and the wrong appear to gain the mastery and hold it, but victory must come. "If it tarry, wait for it; for it shall surely come." "He shall take to Himself His great name and rule."

And now, as I lay down my pen, in view of all these years of life, I can say, with Montgomery in his sonnet on the "Pilgrim's Progress" :—

> "Yes, I have known and felt and suffered all
> That tempts or thwarts the pilgrim on his way;
> Have proved how bitter 'tis to go astray,
> How hard to climb, how perilous to fall ;
> Now halting, ere I tread the enchanted ground,
> I look behind, before me, and around.
>
> "Back to the Cross, where first my peace was sealed,
> I turn mine eyes : it darts a single ray,
> A clue of light through all 'the narrow way ;'
> Past, present, future are at once revealed.
> Press on, my soul ! what now thy course shall stay ?
> No foe can conquer thee, unless thou yield."

27, PATERNOSTER ROW,
LONDON.

HODDER & STOUGHTON'S
NEW AND RECENT PUBLICATIONS.

HEALTH STUDIES.
By
H. SINCLAIR PATERSON, M.D.
Second Thousand. Crown 8vo, Cloth. Price 2s. 6d.

CONTENTS :—Food and Appetite—Exertion : Muscular and Mental—Worry : its Production and Prevention—Rest and Sleep — Fastness — A Merry Heart — Disease Germs — Rational Principles of Medicine.

STUDIES IN LIFE.
BY THE SAME AUTHOR.
Second Thousand. Crown 8vo, 2s. 6d., Cloth.

CONTENTS :—Nature and the Study of Nature—Life and its Characteristics—The Origin of Life—Varieties of Life—The Records of Life—The Natural History of Life—The Enemies of Life—Results of Life.

"His early studies, and the way in which amidst engrossing pursuits he has kept himself abreast of the rapidly advancing discoveries and speculations in science, enable Dr. Paterson to speak with authority on the subjects treated of in this volume. He states the views held, exhibits their weaknesses and defects, and controverts the positions dogmatically maintained, from the standpoint of a practical acquaintance with biological science."—*British and Foreign Evangelical Review.*

THE HUMAN BODY AND ITS FUNCTIONS.
BY THE SAME AUTHOR.
Second Thousand. Crown 8vo, 2s. 6d., cloth.

CONTENTS :—The Organism—The Tissues—The Preparation of Aliment—The Conveyance of Aliment—Removal of Waste and Noxious Products—The Nervous System—The Special Senses—Evolution and Application of Energy.

"This clear, concise, and absorbingly interesting volume will only lead its readers to a deeper study of the mechanism of the human frame. There is no more valuable, practical—one might almost say Christian— science than this, and we trust this work will find its way into the hands of thousands of young men, and win for this entrancing study a new and devoted band of inquiring students. This will be the author's deserved and truest reward."—*Christian.*

HEROES IN THE STRIFE;
Or, The Temperance Testimonies of Eminent Men.

By

FREDERICK SHERLOCK,

Author of "Temperance and English Literature," etc.

Crown 8vo, cloth. Price 3s. 6d.

CONTENTS:—John Bright, M.P., the Free Trade Orator—John Wesley, the Founder of Methodism—Abraham Lincoln, the Martyred President—Bishop Temple, D.D., the Temperance Teacher—David Livingstone, LL.D., the African Explorer—Charles H. Spurgeon, the Preacher Philanthropist—John Locke, the renowned Philosopher—Cardinal Manning, Founder of the Total Abstinence League of the Cross—W. Lloyd Garrison, the Slave Abolitionist—The Rev. Newman Hall, LL.B., a Temperance Pioneer—Charles Waterton, the South African Traveller—Sir Charles Dilke, Bart., M.P., the *Littérateur* and Statesman—Samuel Johnson, the Christian Moralist—Sir Wm. King Hall, K.C.B., a Naval Champion—Hubert Herkomer, the celebrated Artist—Sir Charles Napier, the Hero of Scinde—Dean Hook, a Model Worker.

ILLUSTRIOUS ABSTAINERS.

BY THE SAME AUTHOR.

Fourth Thousand. Crown 8vo, cloth, 3s. 6d.

CONTENTS:—Sir Garnet Wolseley, K.C.B.—Thomas Burt, M.P.—President Hayes—Sir Henry Thompson—Commodore Goodenough—Dr. Benj. Ward Richardson, F.R.S.—Rev. Canon Farrar—Thomas Edward—Samuel Plimsoll, M.P.—Samuel Morley, M.P.—Rev. Thos. Guthrie—Sir Wilfred Lawson, Bart, M.P.—Sir Henry Havelock, K.C.B.—Father Matthew—John Grubb Richardson—Elihu Burritt—John B. Gough—Rev. Canon Basil Wilberforce, M.A.—Sir Walter C. Trevelyan, Bart.—John Howard.

"A most entertaining and readable little book, in which Temperance principles are temperately treated from the biographical point of view. Mr. Sherlock has given a most effective reply to the common insinuation that it is only weak-minded people who are teetotalers. . . . . We are quite certain that Mr. Sherlock's twenty representative biographies will do great service."—*Daily Telegraph*.

"As the evils of drink are prominently shown by Hesba Stretton, so Mr. Sherlock points triumphantly to the names enrolled in the cause of temperance in 'Illustrious Abstainers,' writing simply and to the point."—*Graphic*.

The FLOWER OF THE GRASSMARKET.

By the Author of "Tim's Troubles," etc.

With five full-page Illustrations.

Second Thousand. Crown 8vo, cloth. Price 5s.

"There is a healthy moral tone of a very high order sustained throughout the work, and an easy grace and diction which make it highly commendable."—*Edinburgh Daily Review*.

"A handsomely got up book. The story is admirably written. The reader never loses his interest in the fortunes of the various characters."—*Sheffield Independent*.

REV. JOSEPH COOK'S
BOSTON MONDAY LECTURES.
AUTHORISED ENGLISH EDITIONS.

HODDER & STOUGHTON having purchased the Stock and Plates of Messrs. D. BRYCE & SON'S Editions, beg to announce the following:—

I.—**Biology**, with Preludes on Current Events.
Crown 8vo., cloth, 3s. 6d.

II.—**Transcendentalism**, with Preludes on Current Events.
Crown 8vo., cloth, 3s. 6d.

III.—**Orthodoxy**, with Preludes on Current Events.
Crown 8vo., cloth, 3s. 6d.

Popular Editions of the above, unabridged, printed in large type, will be issued shortly, in crown 8vo, cloth, **1s. 6d.** *each.*

" Your edition of the BOSTON MONDAY LECTURES is a republication, in all essential particulars, faithful to the American Edition by Houghton, Osgood, & Co. No other British Publisher has the right, which I now give to your firm, to state that the republication of my Lectures is by arrangement with, and under the supervision of, the Author.

" Joseph Cook."

Rev. R. Payne Smith, D.D., Dean of Canterbury.
"The lectures are remarkably eloquent, vigorous, and powerful, and no one could read them without great benefit. They deal with very important questions, and are a valuable contribution towards solving many of the difficulties which at this time trouble many minds."

The late Rev. Alexander Raleigh, D.D., of London.
"The lectures are in every way of a high order. They are profound and yet clear, extremely forcible in some of their parts, yet, I think, always fair, and as full of sympathy with what is properly and purely human as of reverence for what is undoubtedly divine."

Rev. C. H. Spurgeon.
"These are very wonderful lectures. We bless God for raising up such a champion for His truth as Joseph Cook. Few could hunt down Theodore Parker, and all that race of misbelievers, as Mr. Cook has done. He has strong convictions, the courage of his convictions, and force to support his courage. In reasoning, the infidel party have here met their match. We know of no other man one-half so well qualified for the peculiar service of exploding the pretensions of modern science as this great preacher in whom Boston is rejoicing. Some men shrink from this spiritual wild-boar hunting; but Mr. Cook is as happy in it as he is expert. May his arm be strengthened by the Lord of hosts!"

HISTORY OF
THE RISE OF THE HUGUENOTS.

By

HENRY M. BAIRD,

PROFESSOR IN THE UNIVERSITY OF NEW YORK.

In two Vols., Crown 8vo, Cloth, **15s.** *With Maps.*

"He tells his story so well that it cannot fail to interest the reader."—*Saturday Review.*

"Professor Baird has produced a work which for carefulness of investigation and completeness and accuracy of statement, is far in advance of all predecessors. We thank Professor Baird for a book of great historical and moral value, of untiring patience, scrupulous fairness, noble sympathies, and the deepest religious interest."—*British Quarterly Review.*

"A valuable contribution to our historical literature. Mr. Baird writes in a graphic style, he arrives at his conclusions only after sound arguments, and he is one of those historians who, not content with printed authorities, goes to the fountain-head for his information ; his references to MSS. will render his book of great importance to the scholar and future compiler. Mr. Baird, by consulting the archives of England and France, and such publications as have been the result of modern research, has thrown much new light upon the subject, and we may say that he has done for the Huguenots what Motley has done for the Low Countries, and what Froude has done for the Reformation. His work is extremely readable, and deserves to be widely circulated. Nothing can exceed in interest and in picturesque description his accounts of Francis I. and Margaret of Angoulême, of the Civil Wars, and of the terrible massacre of St. Bartholomew."—*Westminster Review.*

"The two volumes testify of so much patient research, such exhaustive investigation, so earnest a desire to be complete and thorough, that one is almost inclined to doubt, upon reflection, whether the history of the Huguenots had ever really been written until now. Let it be added that the style of writing is simple, plain, and lucid ; and that the narrative is put together with due regard for usefulness of form. This usefulness is further promoted by an index, a map, and numerous highly interesting and instructive notes. The whole contents of the two volumes are the history of about half a century, such a half-century as cannot be surpassed even in the history of France for portraits and spectacles calculated to make every one who has eyes to read thrill with admiration, gape with astonishment and incredulity, flush with anger and shame, and tingle with horror and indignation. To take up this work and not read it through must require a strong effort, and such an assertion is no slight commendation."—*Illustrated London News.*

"We may congratulate Professor Baird on the success with which he has handled the story of the Huguenots. His volumes may justly be considered as a standard work."—*Record.*

"Professor Baird has added a new name to that list of gifted American historians, which is already adorned by the names of Motley, Prescott, Bold, and Bancroft. No one has as yet brought so immense a mass of contemporary illustrations to bear upon the subject. The story is told so picturesquely, that the reader will find it difficult to lay down the book."
—*Ecclesiastical Gazette.*

THE SISTERS OF GLENCOE.
Or, Letitia's Choice.
By EVA WYNNE.

Sixteenth Thousand. Crown 8vo, cloth elegant. Price 5s.

"Its life pictures are skilfully drawn, and the most wholesome lessons are enforced with fidelity and power."—*Temperance Record.*

"An admirable story, illustrating in a most effective manner the mischief arising from the use of intoxicating liquors."—*Rock.*

THE FULNESS OF BLESSING;
Or, the Gospel of Christ as Illustrated from the Book of Joshua.
By SARAH F. SMILEY.

Third Edition. Crown 8vo, cloth, price 5s.

"We deem this an esoteric explanation of the book of Joshua of a very high order. If we view it as Miss Smiley has so carefully done, we shall have before us, as is well said, 'a picture the grandest in its proportions, the most lifelike in its groupings, the most striking in its wealth of colouring, and the most skilful in its quiet touches, of any that God has given us in this royal art-gallery of truth.' "—*Record.*

THE CUP OF CONSOLATION; or,
Bright Messages for the Sick Bed from the Two Great Volumes of Nature and Revelation.
BY AN INVALID. With an Introduction by
J. R. MACDUFF, D.D.

The Contents consist simply of a series of texts from Scripture, followed by portions from favourite Authors in prose and verse, which were written from week to week by an invalid for the comfort of a sister invalid at a distance. "She that tarried at home divided the spoil."

Crown 8vo. Cloth limp. Price 3s. 6d.   [*Ready.*

THE TWA MISS DAWSONS.
A New Story.

By the Author of "The Bairns," "Christie Redfern's Troubles," etc.

CONTENTS :—"Auld Miss Jean"—The Brother's Sorrow—A Dreary Day—Saughleas—A New Acquaintance—A Proposal—A Misfortune—Willie Calderwood—An Invitation—Mrs. Calderwood—A Visitor—Northern Seas—A Discovery—Mr. Manners—Mr. Dawson's Will—The "John Seaton"—Home Coming—Another Proposal—George—Marion—A Meeting—Young Mr. Petrie—Danger and Reconciliation—Another Home—Suspense—Safety—At Last !

Crown 8vo, Cloth. Price 5s.   [*Ready.*

CHEAP EDITIONS OF HOOD'S ANECDOTES.

I.

THE WORLD OF ANECDOTE.

An Accumulation of Facts, Incidents, and Illustrations, Historical and Biographical, from Books and Times, Recent and Remote.

BY E. PAXTON HOOD.

SUMMARY OF CONTENTS :—Ways and Means of Doing Good—Romantic Transformation of Human Life—Great Events from Trifles—Dogs, and the Animal World—Crime and Cruelty—Silence and some of its Votaries—Illustrations of Adventure—Ghosts, Dreams, and the Supernatural—Anecdotes of Life and Character—Humour and the Humorous Side of Life—Things Clerical and Pulpit Celebrities—Cooks and Cookery—Varieties of Womanhood—Instances of Human Folly—Lawyers and some of their Words and Ways—Death and Dying.

"Full of wit and wisdom."—*Standard.*

"The humorous, the pathetic, the romantic, the instructive, have all a place."—*Edinburgh Daily Review.*

"The rev. gentleman is not only one of the 'bookiest' men of his day, and one of its most ready writers, but he is one of its best anecdotists. He has the art of being amusing, controlled by a self-respect that keeps him from being frivolous. This book of his is very largely instructive, as well as entertaining, and the research it displays is real and wholesome."—*Leeds Mercury.*

Fourth Thousand. Crown 8vo, 6s. pp. 700.

II.

THE WORLD OF MORAL AND RELIGIOUS ANECDOTE.

SUMMARY OF CONTENTS :—The Noble Army of Martyrs—The Bible—Prayer—Varieties of Usefulness—Heroes of the Church—Christian Eccentricities—Illustrations of Ignorance, Superstition and Folly—Aspects of Heathenism—Incidents in Missionary Work—Conversions—Providence : The Finger of God—Christian Life and Character—Singular Personal Characteristics—Illustrations of Bible Texts and Truths—Preachers and Preaching—Self-Deception—Types of Noble Women—Illustrations of Popish Folly—Kings : Some of their Words and Ways—The Heroic and Noble in Conduct and Character—Temperance and Intemperance—Kindness and Meekness—Fragments of Conversation, Wit, Wisdom, etc.—Presence of Mind—Happy Illustrations and Suggestive Parables—Wonders of God in Creation—Glimpses of The Supernatural—Death-bed Lights.

"A very pleasant book to read ; full of gems from many quarters."—*English Churchman.*

"It is really a very amusing book, which you can hardly open anywhere without feeling a temptation to read on."—*Guardian.*

"The book is both entertaining and useful."—*Post.*

"The book is delightful and amusing, as well as instructive." — *Evangelical Magazine.*

"One of the most charming books in our language."—*Baptist Magazine.*

Fifth Thousand. Crown 8vo, 6s. pp. 776.

OUR DAUGHTERS:
Their Lives Here and Hereafter.
By MRS. G. S. REANEY,
Author of "English Girls, their Place and Power," etc.

CONTENTS :—Introduction : Something that may help—What Constitutes a Happy Christian—Worldly Hindrances in becoming a Christian : the Love of Dress—Flirting—Spiritual Hindrances in becoming a Christian : Doubts—Salvation : What is it?—Constraining Love—Helps and Hints to Young Christians—Thoroughness in Christian Work—The Ministry of Suffering : a few Words to Invalids—The Ministry of Little Things—Recreation—A Good Wife—Christian Work and its Reward.

Crown 8vo, cloth, price 3s. 6d.

THE LIFE OF JOSEPH BARKER.
Written by Himself.
Edited by his Nephew, JOHN THOMAS BARKER.

"A volume of no common interest. It records with an impressive air of truth and sincerity both the outward struggles and the mental history of a man who was in many respects one of the most remarkable of lecturers and preachers of his time. This volume in many respects deserves to take rank with the autobiography of Bunyan, and the quaintly earnest memoirs of the early Quakers."—*Daily News.*

Crown 8vo. Cloth, 7s. 6d. With Steel Portrait.

GOOD THOUGHTS IN BAD TIMES.
And Other Papers.
By THOMAS FULLER, D.D.

Printed on Hand-made Paper. Crown 8vo. Cloth, 6s. With Portrait.

THE LIFE AND WRITINGS OF ST. JOHN.
By the REV. J. M. MACDONALD, D.D.
Edited, with an Introduction, by the
VERY REV. DEAN HOWSON, D.D.
With Maps, and Full-page Illustrations.

"Taking it altogether, it is the most exhaustive and comprehensive review of the life and writings of the evangelist John which the English language contains. It is impossible to speak too highly of this volume, and the publishers deserve our heartiest thanks for introducing it in so substantial and handsome a form to English readers."—*Christian World.*

"The work is quite worthy of a place beside its famed predecessor. 'For exhaustiveness of treatment,' says one competent critic, 'accuracy of detail, and beauty and brilliancy of narrative, it has no rival on the special subject of which it treats.'"—*Family Treasury.*

Popular Edition. Royal 8vo, cloth extra, price 10s. 6d.

THE HEAVENLY WORLD,
Views of the Future Life by Eminent Writers.

CONTENTS.

The Glorious Inheritance: *C. H. Spurgeon.*—Ten Views of Heaven: *Alexander Maclaren, D.D.*—The Intermediate State: *John Foster.*—The Beatific Vision: *Robert Hall, M.A.*—What is Heaven? *Addison, Cowper, etc.*—The Redeemed in the Glorified State: *Isaac Watts, D.D.*—Eternal Rest: *Richard Baxter.*— Heaven and its Associations: *William Jay.*—Nature of the Kingdom of God: *Thomas Chalmers, D.D.* — The Consummation of Happiness: *Matthew Henry.*—The Heavenly State: *Richard Price, D.D.* — The World to Come: *John Bunyan.*—Immortality: *Edward Irving, M.A.*—The Perfect World: *D. Thomas, B.A., J. A. James, R. M. McCheyne, etc.*

Crown 8vo, cloth, price 3s. 6d.

CONSECRATED WOMEN.
By CLAUDIA.

CONTAINING:

Catherine of Siena—Susanna Wesley and Amelia Sieveking—Frau Trüdel—Charlotte Elizabeth Tonna—Margaret Wilson—Matilda Countess Von Der Recke Volmerstein—Christine Alsop—Sarah and Elizabeth A——N—Christian Eddy and Louise Schepler—Fidelia Fiske—Adelaide L. Newton—Lena Huber—Wilhelmina—Isabella Graham—Marie.

Crown 8vo, cloth, price 5s.

THE GENTLE HEART.
A Second Series of "Talking to the Children."

By the Rev.
ALEXANDER MACLEOD, D.D.

CONTENTS.

The Gentle Heart—Some Gentle Deeds—The Gentleness of Christ—On Doing What We Can—Of Not Doing What We Can—Christ's Letters—On Putting the Right Thing First—Giving Pleasure to God—Nicolas Herman—God's Thoughts about Little People—The Patience of Margaret Hope—The Things Which God has Prepared—Christ Reshaping the Soul—The Evil of Forgetting God—Never Too Late to Mend—Men cannot Live by Bread alone.

Crown 8vo, cloth, price 3s. 6d.

New and Recent Publications.

HENDRICKS THE HUNTER;
Or, The Border Farm. A Tale of Zululand.
By
W. H. G. KINGSTON,
Author of "Peter the Whaler," "Clara Maynard," etc., etc.
With Five Full-page Illustrations.

"Affords another proof of Kingston's indefatigable industry, his power of resource, his gift of conception, and his marvellous power of ready writing."—*Edinburgh Daily Review.*

"A most interesting story. The hero is a bold and daring hunter, and his adventures among the Zulus are of a most exciting character."—*City Press.*

Fourth Thousand. Crown 8vo, handsomely bound, 5s.

ALL TRUE:
Records of Peril and Adventure by Sea and Land—Remarkable Escapes and Deliverances—Missionary Enterprises and Travels—Wonders of Nature and Providence—Incidents of Christian History and Biography.
By
DR. MACAULAY.
With Full-Page Illustrations.

"Dr. Macaulay has a peculiar genius for the work he has undertaken in this volume. He is the Editor of 'The Boys' Own Paper,' and the skill he has displayed there has been brought to the preparation of the present volume."—*Congregationalist.*

Fourth Thousand. Crown 8vo, cloth gilt, price 5s.

THE SAINT AND HIS SAVIOUR.
The Progress of the Soul in the Knowledge of Jesus.
By
C. H. SPURGEON.

"This Edition (with portrait of the author) of perhaps the best known and most highly appreciated work of Mr. Spurgeon, is everything that can be desired in the way of paper, type, or finish. The wide circulation of it will lift troubled spirits from prolonged despondency, and throw much and needed light on those dark places and deep secrets of Christian experience which it is so difficult to put into words."—*Evangelical Magazine.*

NEW EDITION. *Crown 8vo, 3s. 6d. With Steel Portrait.*

CHRISTIAN SUNSETS;
Or, The Last Hours of Believers.
By the Rev.
JAMES FLEMING, D.D.,
Author of "Remarkable Conversions."

"Dr. Fleming writes with ease and fluency, and these little sketches of good and eminent people will be pleasant reading. He shows clearly enough that the hour of death is illuminated and gladdened by the conscious presence of Him who has brought life and immortality to light by the Gospel."—*Christian World.*

Cheap Edition. Crown 8vo, price 3s. 6d.

10   Hodder & Stoughton's Recent Publications.

JESUS CHRIST:
His Times, Life, and Work.
By
E. DE PRESSENSE, D.D.
Translated by ANNIE HARWOOD-HOLMDEN.

In issuing a seventh edition of this important work, the Publishers desire to point out the leading features which distinguish it from other Lives of our Lord. More than one-third of the volume is occupied with a full discussion of "Preliminary Questions," including—1. Objections to the Supernatural; 2. Jesus Christ and the Religions of the Past; 3. The Judaism of His Time; 4. The Sources of the Gospel History. Having thus described His relation to ancient and contemporary history, the author proceeds to unfold the life of Jesus, depicting its scenes with a vividness derived from a visit to the Holy Land. The result is a work which has been referred to by Canon Liddon as "a most noble contribution to the cause of truth," and by the *Contemporary Review* as "one of the most valuable additions to Christian literature which the present generation has seen."

Seventh Edition, Unabridged. Crown 8vo, 7s. 6d.

BY THE SAME AUTHOR.

THE EARLY YEARS of CHRISTIANITY:
A Comprehensive History of the First Three Centuries of the Christian Church.

COMPRISING:
I. The Apostolic Age.
II. The Martyrs and Apologists.
III. Heresy and Christian Doctrine.
IV. Life and Practice in the Early Church.

"The four volumes of this work are a splendid addition to our stores of church history.... We so highly appreciate the book that we place it among those which every student should possess. It fires the soul to read the great deeds set forth in such stirring words. A fitting and worthy sequel to Pressensé's Life of Christ."—Rev. C. H. SPURGEON in *Sword and Trowel*.

"The author's keen spiritual insight, his rich eloquence, and his epigrammatic characterisations have given him, among his compeers, perhaps the very foremost place as a Church Historian and Apologist. His work, both in France and England, holds a place of its own, and with a power, completeness, and eloquence, not likely soon to be surpassed."—*British Quarterly Review*.

"The student who cares for a subject, which is becoming one of ever deepening interest, will find his pains amply rewarded, if he gives a close and attentive perusal to M. de Pressensé's pages."—*Spectator*.

New and Cheaper Edition. In Four Vols., price 7s. 6d. each.

M. DE PRESSENSE ON HIS CONTEMPORARIES.
Crown 8vo, 7s. 6d.

CONTEMPORARY PORTRAITS.

"'Contemporary Portraits,' which has been translated with ease and spirit by Mrs. Holmden, is quite above the common, both in the quality of its literary workmanship, and in the subjects which it treats. His comparison of Strauss with Voltaire, and his sketches of such men as Bishop Dupanloup, of Vinet the Academician, are remarkable pieces of psychological analysis."—*Daily News*.

LONDON: HODDER & STOUGHTON, 27, PATERNOSTER ROW.

www.ingramcontent.com/pod-product-compliance
Lightning Source LLC
Chambersburg PA
CBHW032009300426
44117CB00008B/955